W9-DGX-954

MODEL
BUSINESS PLANS
FOR
PRODUCT BUSINESSES

OTHER BOOKS BY DR. WILLIAM A. COHEN

Model Business Plans for Service Businesses (John Wiley & Sons)

Building a Mail Order Business (John Wiley & Sons)

The Entrepreneur and Small Business Problem Solver (John Wiley & Sons)

Developing a Winning Marketing Plan (John Wiley & Sons)

The Entrepreneur and Small Business Marketing Problem Solver (John Wiley & Sons)

The Entrepreneur and Small Business Financial Problem Solver (John Wiley & Sons)

How To Make It Big as a Consultant (AMACOM)

The Paranoid Corporation and 8 Other Ways Your Company May Be Crazy (AMACOM) (with Dr. Nurit Cohen)

Making It! (Prentice-Hall) (with E. Joseph Cossman)

The Art of the Leader (Prentice-Hall)

MODEL BUSINESS PLANS FOR PRODUCT BUSINESSES

William A. Cohen, PhD

John Wiley & Sons, Inc.
New York • Chichester • Brisbane • Toronto • Singapore

Preface

Companies that develop business plans professionally charge up to $50,000 for each plan. I know, because that's the price quoted a few months ago to a friend of mine.

If you want to start your own business, you can save a bundle if you develop your own business plan. And many times, your plan will be a lot better than if someone else developed it. That's because no one knows you, your capabilities, limitations, strengths, weaknesses, desires, interests, and ultimate goals better than you.

However, to create a really outstanding plan, you must first see what a business plan looks like. In fact, you should study several plans before you start composing one. Anything short of outstanding won't do when potential lenders review 1,000 plans or more a month and fund maybe one or two. You have to thoroughly examine more than a few plans to know what is really expected and how to sell your concept to investors.

Some books on entrepreneurial endeavors contain a few business plans. Most contain none. This book contains 9 outstanding business plans for new businesses that sell a product. For businesses that provide a service, 9 more plans are featured in a companion book, *Model Business Plans for Service Businesses*. With this book and its companion, you should be able to find a plan that fits your needs, no matter what your field.

All the plans contain complete financial information for the time and geographic location for which the plan was prepared. Many of these plans aim at millions in sales. No wonder a professional firm would charge so much to develop even one of them!

Let's face facts. You can't go into a serious business today without a business plan. The competition is too tough, and banks and other lenders won't lend you the money.

If you are going into business, you need a business plan:

- To borrow money.
- As a road map to reach your business objectives and goals.
- To make the most efficient use of money and other resources.
- To measure progress and make corrections on your way to success.
- To assist in management control and implementation of your strategy.
- To inform new people you hire of their role and function.
- To assign responsibilities, tasks, and timing to your employees and others.

- To forecast your costs and cash flow on a monthly basis.
- To become aware of problems and opportunities inherent in your business situation.

Why aren't more business plans published? Frankly, the effort to put a single business plan together is considerable. The research required can be difficult if you don't know how to do it. That's one of the reasons that professionally prepared plans are so expensive. When people put that much work into a plan, they don't want to give it away.

There are companies that sell generic business plans for as much as $100 each although such plans can't be as complete as if they were for a specific business. Yet, in this book, you will find 9 model business plans for a variety of businesses.

How did I get so involved in business planning? My early training came as an officer in the military. We were taught how to plan because it is the basis of securing any military objective. The process started with something called "The Estimation of the Situation." In business, we call this a "situation analysis" or "environmental scanning." It serves the same purpose.

When I got into business, I found that organizing for the development of new products and business investments was easy because of my early training. It wasn't a case of so-called marketing warfare. I just had to translate terms and concepts from the battlefield to the boardroom.

Later, when I became a business professor, I was amazed at the inability of business students to produce quality business plans. I vowed to change all that. I started in the classroom. Then, as Director of the Small Business Institute at California State University, Los Angeles, I supervised students and other professors consulting for more than 500 small businesses. Between this work and my work in the classroom, I supervised the preparation of more than 1,000 business plans. I spent 15 years refining my methods of teaching the development of business and marketing plans.

Over the years, my methods proved themselves again and again. In competitions involving many of the best business schools in the country, some of my students won national awards offered by a number of private and governmental organizations.

But, it is even more significant that the students who implemented their own plans frequently got terrific results. One student, Robert Schwartz, put together a plan for a fast-food pizza restaurant. Within a year, he had three outlets and was written up in *Entrepreneur* magazine. He was managing a $48,000 monthly cash flow while still a student. Leon Ashjian, a student from Egypt, made several thousand dollars implementing his plan during my course. Then, he sold it to someone else for another $5,000.

Some time ago, I spoke at the University of Missouri, Kansas City, on how to teach students to develop these plans. Both professors and business leaders were in my audience. During my presentation, I showed some sample plans and described how Leon had sold his plan for $5,000.

A businessman from a firm developing business plans for clients examined my sample plans very carefully. He told me they were the equal of the professional plans his firm produced. "However," he said, "they aren't worth $5,000 each . . . they're worth $25,000 each. I know because that's what we charge."

Since that time, several of my students have elected to become independent consultants after graduation. They make their living developing business plans for others.

My wife and I are continually running into results from my business plan instruction. A few weeks ago, a new restaurant opened in my hometown of Pasadena, California. The restaurant is called "Little Rickey's," and the menu is Cuban and Mexican. We tried it, and the food was delicious. I was surprised to learn that one on my former students, Mary Needham, started Little Rickey's in partnership with her friend, Rachel Perez. And yes, the business plan from my class was the basis for this enterprise that offered such delightful meals.

I especially selected the plans in this book for their variety. The were developed by my students and are used with their permission. You may not find the particular business you are interested in among them, but you are very likely to find one that is close. You will also find somewhat different styles and methods for organizing the plans.

You have in your hands everything you need to develop your own successful business plan. Start off by reviewing the Introduction, which tells you how to go about developing your plan. Then, all you need to do is look through the book for one or more plans for businesses that resemble the one you have in mind. Adapt these plans and the financial and other information to your situation and you are all set. Good luck—I'll be happy to hear about your success!

WILLIAM A. COHEN

Pasadena, California
April 1995

Acknowledgments

Though the responsibility for this book is mine alone, I would like to make the following acknowledgments.

First, the work by those whose plans are contained in this volume. Through their efforts, many can benefit in developing business plans which lead to successful enterprises.

Orca Computer Systems: Wowong Hartono

Baby's Cornucopia: David A. Porter

Sneak Peek—A Student's Guide to University Courses: Tonette Dove, David Grajeda, Anthony B. Lujan, Donna Tom, Huei Ming Tsai, and Caroline Wang

American Baby Food Company: Syed Shehzad Ali

Mudville Greeting Cards: David Yang

Onyx Marketing Group: Anthony Coleman

Mischa's Silverlake Cookies: JulieAnn Peterson

Venchertech Industries, Inc.: Yam Kim Lian, Gunadi Gunadi, Trent Kwan, Duc Hinh, and Louis Cheng

Compact Disc Store Specializing in Used CDs: Kevin M. Krahn

Next, the important contributions in review and editing made by my research assistant, Danielle Benson, as well as those made by Nancy Marcus Land at Publications Development Company of Texas, under the supervision of Mary Daniello at John Wiley & Sons, Inc. Finally, the superb overall development work by my editor at John Wiley & Sons, Ruth Mills.

W.A.C.

Contents

INTRODUCTION   SAVE $50,000 AND SUCCEED WHERE OTHERS FAIL . . . . **xi**

This section explains how to develop an outstanding business plan along with a recommended outline. With it, you will be able to use the sample business plans in the book and adapt them to your own project.

1   BUSINESS PLAN FOR ORCA COMPUTER SYSTEMS . . . . **1·1**

This is a business plan for the assembly and marketing of a new computer. The potential is almost unlimited when you stop to think that similar companies have exploded to over $100 million in less than a year.

2   BUSINESS PLAN FOR BABY'S CORNUCOPIA . . . . **2·1**

Here we have a business plan for a unique newsletter that can be promoted part-time, with additional rental of lists, and so on.

3   BUSINESS PLAN FOR SNEAK PEEK: A STUDENT'S GUIDE TO UNIVERSITY COURSES . . . . **3·1**

Students who have difficulty meeting rising tuition costs will benefit from this. It's a plan for a student's guide to courses and professors, with a revised publication coming out every year. Features include low investment and profit potential in the thousands of dollars.

4   BUSINESS PLAN FOR AMERICAN BABY FOOD COMPANY . . . **4·1**

Babies are literally a growth market . . . if a company can figure out a way to penetrate a market dominated by some very well-entrenched companies. This plan shows how.

5   BUSINESS PLAN FOR MUDVILLE GREETING CARDS . . . . . . **5·1**

Desktop publishing has enabled new opportunities for creative individuals in a number of areas. This business plan shows how to get into this competitive business with a relatively low investment and build a business that can quickly reach a million dollars or more a year.

6   BUSINESS PLAN FOR ONYX MARKETING GROUP . . . . **6·1**

Children's books are a traditional winner. This plan goes one better. Although adaptable to all groups, this plan shows how to niche market by selling to a particular market segment. By satisfying such a market well, you can become the number one company servicing it. Yet, it requires only a $2,000 investment for the first year sales in excess of $100,000.

7   BUSINESS PLAN FOR MISCHA'S SILVERLAKE COOKIES . . . . **7·1**

From Mrs. Field's to Famous Amos, there is a tremendous opportunity for entrepreneurs to score big with homemade cookies. This business plan concentrates first on the regional market and then aims for national expansion.

8   BUSINESS PLAN FOR VENCHERTECH INDUSTRIES, INC. . . . **8·1**

This plan capitalizes on the increased need for latex gloves due to the AIDS crisis and the importation of rubber gloves into the United States. The principles are the same for any import product.

9   BUSINESS PLAN FOR COMPACT DISC STORE SPECIALIZING IN USED CDs . . . . **9·1**

There are lots of CD stores that sell new CDs. But used CDs target a different market. This business plan speaks to this unique product, but the principles are the same in selling used books, magazines, or you name it!

APPENDIX A   SOURCES OF ADDITIONAL MARKET RESEARCH . . . **A·1**

APPENDIX B   FORMS TO HELP YOU DEVELOP THE BUSINESS PLAN . . . . **B·1**

INDEX . . . . **I·1**

Save $50,000 and Succeed Where Others Fail

Developing your own business plan is not difficult . . . once you know how. After you have decided on the business, your task is to learn all you can about it as well as the business climate you will enter. This is what I call doing a situation analysis. As a result of this analysis, you will be able to decide on initial goals and objectives, designate your target market, and obtain other essential information. You will be in a position to develop strategy and tactics to reach your goals and objectives successfully. Flesh this out with tasks to implement your strategy and monitor it with financial data that you assume or calculate, and you're set. That's all there is to it.

In this chapter, I will cover every important element of the business plan. Along the way, I'll tell you where to get the information you'll need. Important elements of the business plan are shown in Exhibit 1. Let's look at each of these in detail.

Exhibit 1   A Business Plan Structure

Executive Summary (Overview of entire plan, including a description of the product or service, the differential advantage, the required investment, and anticipated sales and profits.)

Table of Contents

I. **Introduction** (What is the product or service and why will you be successful with it at this time?)

II. **Situation Analysis**

   1. The General Situation

      A. Demand and demand trends. (What is the forecast demand for the product? Is it growing or declining? Who is the decision maker, the purchase agent? How, when, where, what, and why do they buy?)

      B. Social and cultural factors that may bear on your business.

      C. Demographics in your area of operation.

      D. Economic and business conditions for this product at this time in the geographic area selected.

      E. State of technology for this class of product. Is it high-tech state of the art? Are newer products succeeding older ones frequently (very short life cycle)? How will technology affect this product or service?

(continued)

Exhibit 1   (*Continued*)

    F.   Politics. Will politics (current or otherwise) in any way affect the situation for marketing this product?

    G.   Laws and regulations. (What laws or regulations are applicable here?)

  2. The Situation of Neutral Organizations

    A.   Financial. (How does the availability or nonavailability of funds affect the situation?)

    B.   Government. (Will legislative action or anything else currently going on in federal, state, or local government be likely to affect marketing of this product or service?)

    C.   Media. (What's happening in the media? Does current publicity favor or disfavor this project?)

    D.   Special interests. (Aside from direct competitors, are any influential groups likely to affect your plans?)

  3. Your Competition's Situation

    A.   Describe your main competitors and their products, plans, experience, know-how, suppliers, strategy, and financial, human, and capital resources. (Do they enjoy any favor or disfavor with the customer? If so, why? What marketing channels do competitors use? What are your competitors' strengths and weaknesses?)

  4. Your Situation

    A.   Describe your product, experience, know-how, suppliers, strategy, and financial, human, and capital resources. (Do you enjoy any favor or disfavor with the customer? If so, why? What are your strengths and weaknesses?)

III.   **The Target Market** Describe your target market in detail. (Why is this your target market and not some other?)

IV.   **Problems, Threats, and Opportunities** State or restate every problem and every opportunity. Indicate how you will handle each problem and take advantage of each opportunity.

V.   **Objectives and Goals** Precisely state your objectives and goals in terms of sales volume, market share, return on investment, or other objectives of your plan.

VI.   **Competitive Advantage** State the advantages you have over your competition.

VII.   **Marketing Strategy** Consider alternatives for overall strategy. Fully describe the strategy you are going to adopt and why you are going to adopt it. Note what your main competitors are likely to do when you implement this strategy and what you will do to take advantage of the opportunities created and avoid the threats.

VIII. **Marketing Tactics** State how you will implement the marketing strategies you chose in terms of product, price, promotion, selling, publicity, distribution, and other actions you will take.

IX.   **Schedule and Budget Marketing Actions** What are the actual actions you must take to set your business plan in motion?

X.   **Implementation and Control** Calculate the break-even point for your project. Compute sales projections on a monthly basis for a three-year period. Compute cash flows on a monthly basis for a three-year period. Indicate start-up costs and monthly budget for this period.

XI.   **Summary** Summarize advantages, costs, and profits, and clearly restate the competitive advantage that your plan for this product or service offers over the competition and why your plan will succeed.

XII. **Appendixes** Include all relevant supporting information in your biography and background that support your ultimate success in achieving your goals and objectives in this business.

THE EXECUTIVE SUMMARY

As the name implies, the executive summary is an overview or abstract of your entire business plan, and it is written for an executive audience. The summary is a brief statement describing your business and its potential. It includes what you want to do and states how much money and what other resources you will need. The executive summary is extremely important.

Sure, you write the business plan for your own guidance. However, the executive audience reading it may be almost as important. The executives I'm talking about are venture capitalists, decision makers at banks, the Small Business Administration, or others from whom you may want a loan. As these individuals study your business plan, they will frequently skip around to parts that are of most interest to them. In fact, few business plans will be read by others word for word. Rather, certain sections will be read in detail and other sections, only scanned. Almost everyone, however, will read your executive summary.

So, that section should capture the essence of your plan in a few concise paragraphs. Say what your business is about—your objectives and goals—and provide a bird's-eye view of the strategy you will use to accomplish those objectives and goals. The executive summary shouldn't be longer than two or three pages at most. Many very effective summaries are only one to two paragraphs.

After reading your executive summary, the executives should understand what you want to do, how much it will cost, and what the chances are of success. Of course, you should make clear that your chances are very good. Otherwise, you shouldn't be entering this business in the first place. Readers should also understand the unique advantages you have that will ensure your success.

Although the executive summary comes first, you should write it last. This is because it must capture all the essential points in your business plan and emphasize how you approach starting and building your business. If you write your executive summary first and don't go back to rework it after you complete your plan, you are very likely to miss something important.

TABLE OF CONTENTS

You may wonder why I am discussing something so ordinary as a table of contents. Yet, it is also an important part of your plan. As I said before, most lenders will not read your entire plan in detail. They will look for the executive summary and certain areas they find of particular interest.

Here's what I mean. Financial experts will be very interested in the financial part of your plan. They will want to know how much money you will need and when it will be needed. Others will be more interested in the technical aspects and performance characteristics of your product or service. These technically oriented executives may even skip items that you know are crucial, such as your location or selling methods.

So, not only should every subject area critical to the project be covered in your business plan, you must make it as easy as possible for anyone to find a specific area of interest quickly. The table of contents serves this purpose. If you do not have a table of contents, searching decision makers—after a brief attempt to locate the information—may assume that it is not there. Many borrowers don't get the money they need because someone couldn't find some piece of information the lender considered important. So, don't omit this mundane element of your business plan. It can turn out to be more important than you thought.

THE SITUATION ANALYSIS

The situation analysis is a detailed description of the environment for your entry into business and for the time period covered by your plan. You should include a detailed discussion of the overall situation, the situation of neutral organizations as well as those with which you will compete, and your own. Don't omit anything you consider relevant. Discuss business conditions, technological trends, distribution factors, the law, and all other major situational issues that impact your planned business.

I recommend that you divide this section into four subareas. The first is the general situation. This includes economic and business conditions, cultural or social factors and their impact on what you want to do, the state of technology, and so on. The second section concerns "neutral" organizations whose actions can help you or hurt you. Examples would be consumer advocacy groups and federal regulatory agencies.

In the third subarea, you discuss your competition. Don't tell me you "don't have any competition." This is never true because even though you may not have any direct competitors, there are always alternative ways your prospective customers can spend their money. So there are, at the very least, indirect competitors. For example, you may have the only dry-cleaning establishment in town. But a steam iron used in the home is still indirect competition. You may have developed some breakthrough computer software far in advance of any older program. Well, guess what? Those old obsolete programs are still in competition with you even though the performance of your new program is light years ahead.

You want to find out all you can about the strengths and weaknesses of the competition vying with you for the same market. With only so much business out there in a mature or even declining market, your competition will be a major factor affecting your success.

You can find out all you need to know about the competition by looking at annual reports if they are public companies, talking to suppliers and customers, reading their advertisements and literature, and actually buying from them or using their service.

Finally, you want to analyze your own strengths and weaknesses, just as you did the competition. More than two thousand years ago, the Chinese strategist Sun Tzu noted that he never suffered defeat because he not only knew the strengths and weaknesses of his enemies, but also knew his own.

Where to Get Information for This and Other Sections of Your Business Plan

There are numerous sources for the information you need for your business plan. Most won't cost you a cent. Besides using the following primary sources, you'll want to look at the suggestions for additional research in Appendix A.

Magazine and Newspaper Articles

General magazines have business sections. Many general business magazines such as *Business Week, Entrepreneur, Fortune,* and *INC,* are available at your public library. You will also find *The Wall Street Journal* and other pertinent newspapers. In addition, the library has directories of specialized periodicals. Every industry has publications devoted to its particular products and services. These periodicals may have articles containing information important to your business. These specialized sources can be helpful in other ways. If you are searching for certain information, the editorial staff of an industry magazine, journal, or newsletter may be able to tell you where to get it. Sometimes, the staff may have done studies or surveys of their readership on the very topic you are interested in.

Specialized Books about Your Business

With more than 40,000 books published every year, books are found on every topic imaginable. I have seen books on mail order, consulting, and restaurant businesses, multilevel marketing, silk screen printing, and hundreds of others. In fact, I wrote books on the first two topics (*Building a Mail Order Business,* New York: John Wiley & Sons, 1983, 1985, 1991; and *How to Make It Big as a Consultant,* New York: AMACOM, 1985, 1991). You can also find booklets on a variety of businesses and business topics published by the U.S. Small Business Administration (SBA). Check with your local office of the SBA and ask for a complete list. Some of these may also be available at a U.S. government bookstore if one is in your area. Check in your telephone white pages under "U.S. Government."

Professional and Trade Associations

Just as there are books and magazines for every type of business, there are also professional and trade associations. Frequently these associations have done studies or surveys themselves or can direct you to another source for the information you need. Check your library for directories of national associations. The reference desk librarian will help you. You can also check the phone book under associations to see if it lists one related to your business interests.

Databases

If you have a computer, or maybe even if you don't, you probably already know about databases. There are databases containing information on every topic. Some libraries will do a search for you. If you have a modem and belong to one of the computer services such as CompuServe™ or Prodigy™, you can do your own search.

The Department of Commerce

If you are planning a product or service for export, look under U.S. Government in the white pages of your telephone book and contact the Department of Commerce. You will be amazed by the wealth of information and services available for those who want to export. A "trade specialist" may be willing to come out to see you and provide help as a consultant right away. This won't cost you anything. The department also offers a seminar on the basics of exporting at a nominal cost and can point you in the right direction to get any information about potential markets in various countries, and how to reach them. But to really understand the full ranges of the services currently being offered, check and see if there is an office in your area and visit it in person.

Chambers of Commerce

Almost every city or town has a chamber of commerce with data on the people living, working, and conducting business in that area. If you want to set up shop, it makes sense to investigate who your target market is likely to be, what competitors you may have, and so on.

Embassies and Consulates

If you are fortunate enough to live in or near a large city, chances are there will be foreign consulates nearby. And if you live in or near Washington, DC, you'll be able to reach the embassies themselves. Access to embassies and consulates can be a great help if you want to import products. Every country wants exports to help out its balance of trade. That's why U.S. Department of Commerce is so eager to help you if you want to export American goods. If you are interested in imports, contact a foreign consulate or embassy and ask for the commercial or trade attaché. If you have a particular product in mind, the attaché will probably invite you to the consulate or embassy where you can look at catalogs and prospectuses relevant to your area of interest.

Government Books on Statistics, Industry, and the Economy

One of the best publications I've seen along these lines is the *Statistical Abstract of the United States,* which is published every year. Two other books published annually that will provide background information are *U.S. Industrial Outlook* and *Economic Report of the President.* These books can be obtained at a U.S. government bookstore if you have one in your city. Otherwise, write to the Superintendent of Documents, U.S. Government Printing Office, Washington, DC 20402, and ask for a catalog.

Primary Marketing Research

You are already doing market research by using the sources I've given you. But primary marketing research means you gather the data yourself, instead of looking it up in a book or magazine where someone else has already put it together for you.

There are three main means of marketing research: mail, telephone, and face-to-face. Just as with the business plans, companies exist that will do this for you, and they will charge you a bundle. But there is much you can do for yourself fairly easily. For example, if you wanted to determine the best location for a service station, one factor would be the motor vehicle traffic. You could get this information by simply counting cars going by at similar hours at each potential location. Or, if you wanted to discover whether you could wholesale a particular product, you could obtain one and meet with the appropriate buyer for the type of store that would carry this merchandise. Similarly, if you have a particular service, do a limited mailing to prospective customers and see how many takers you get.

You won't get perfect results by asking people if they would buy a product or service if it were on the market. You should still do this, but keep in mind that many respondents who say yes may still not buy when the product is actually introduced. So, even if the results of interviews and surveys indicate that you have a spectacular winner, be a little conservative in your estimate of potential sales.

THE TARGET MARKET

In this section, you include a complete description of the target market or market segments you are going to service. This should include market characteristics, growth trends, buyer attitudes and habits, geographic location of the market segments, industry pricing, and size of the various market segments in dollars and units.

These decisions and the information for them come from the information sources listed previously. What you must do is study the data to see where the best opportunity is. You can rarely be everything to everybody. You will have a much greater chance of success if you pick a particular niche or market segment to sell to instead of trying to sell your product or service to everybody.

PROBLEMS, THREATS, AND OPPORTUNITIES

Here, you restate some of the results of the situation analysis in a summary of problems, opportunities, and threats. However, it is insufficient simply to state these factors. You must also describe alternative courses of action for overcoming the problems, taking advantage of the opportunities, and avoiding the threats.

Some think that their plan will be more attractive if they omit the problems and threats. Not true. Would-be lenders, such as venture capitalists, may review thousands of business plans every month. They are very knowledgeable about business start-ups and growing businesses. If you omit negative elements, they won't be fooled. They will think you are stupid, dishonest, or both.

It's OK to anticipate problems, threats, or challenges. Every new business idea has such possibilities. What is important is that you think through what you will do about them. How will you avoid the threats? How will you solve the problems? How will you exploit the opportunities? That's what should go in this section. All you need to do is to review what you learned from your situation analysis, and exercise your ingenuity in spotting critical areas, and figuring out what to do about them.

OBJECTIVES AND GOALS

Clearly write out your objectives and goals. An objective might be to become the leading supplier of a certain product or service. That's good. But what exactly will it mean to be "the leading supplier?" To define this means establishing specific goals.

One goal might be attainment of 30 percent market share within the next three years. Goals could pertain to volume of sales, return on investment, or other measurable aims. Be careful that objectives or goals are not mutually exclusive. For example, attaining a very high sales volume could require sacrifice of some profit over the short term. So you might not be able to achieve certain very high levels of sales and profits simultaneously.

Establishing your goals and objectives will probably do more than anything else to make you successful. First, you can't get "there" until you know where "there" is. If you don't describe what success is for you, you won't even know whether your business plan has reached success or not. Your goals and objectives give you a target to shoot at. If you aren't hitting the target, you can make adjustments or midcourse corrections. The nature of business is that you will make mistakes, and since there is no such thing as a "perfect" plan, some of your ideas and concepts will prove faulty and your plans won't work. That's OK as long as you have a clear target that you are heading for. But if you don't know exactly where you are going, you won't know what action to take to get back on course, because there won't be any course to get back on.

COMPETITIVE ADVANTAGE

Now I want to tell you something that you probably already know. You can't succeed unless you have one or more advantages over others in the same business. You can gain competitive advantages through having exclusive rights to sell a product or service, by being faster, by offering higher quality, better value, or lower price, by providing better service, by having a unique means of distributing your products and so forth. Almost anything can be a competitive advantage if it offers a significant benefit to your customers.

Reread the review of yourself and your competitors in the situation analysis. This may help you find a competitive advantage that you overlooked. You should have a clear handle on your competitive advantages, and of course, potential lenders will want to know what they are as well.

MARKETING STRATEGY

Strategies are the actions that you must take to reach your goals and objectives. Mass marketing, which involves selling the same product to everyone, is a marketing strategy (although I seldom recommend it). The opposite strategy is niching, where you dominate a very specific segment of the market and sell your product or provide your services only to that group. Your timing in introducing a new product or service into the market is a strategy. How you differentiate your product or service from those of your competitors is also a strategy. If you position your offering a certain way relative to similar offerings in the market, then that is a strategy, too.

If you decide to sell worldwide, you have a choice of two major strategies. You can sell the same product in the same way in every country. That's called a global marketing strategy. Or you can modify your product so that it's different in every country. You optimize it for the specific country depending on local customs, needs, and buyer behavior.

Whatever you decide, describe your strategies in detail and remind your readers of the competitive advantages and other variables in your situation that make this strategy advisable. Just remember one thing, which is the basis of every strategy: Always strive to concentrate superior resources at the decisive point. Be stronger where it counts. Don't try to be strong everywhere. Concentrating your strength where it counts is the key to success.

MARKETING TACTICS

Tactics are the marketing actions you take to carry out your strategy. A strategy of product differentiation may require product tactics that alter the packaging; pricing tactics that raise or lower the price from standard; promotional tactics that emphasize and promote a previously ignored difference; or distribution tactics that use a faster means of getting the product to the consumer or buyer. If you think about it, you will see how all these tactics differentiate your product from that of your competitors.

SCHEDULES, BUDGET, AND MARKETING ACTIONS

Marketing actions cost effort, time, and money. Money is the most important. You want to know when and how much is required. Sometimes having money when you don't need it is almost as bad as not having it when you do need it. For example, if you borrow $100,000 and don't need it for several months, your timing error could cost you several thousand dollars in interest that you are paying to the lender unnecessarily.

The solution is to use a planning schedule as shown in Exhibit 2. Each task is listed along with its projected time frame and cost. This is usually prepared on a monthly basis. In this way, not only do you know the resources required to implement your plan, but once you have implemented it, you can use the schedule to monitor what you are doing and to make changes as needed to keep within planned budget, on time, and headed toward your objectives and goals.

IMPLEMENTATION AND CONTROL

Once your plan is underway, you'll want to know how you are doing in order to keep on schedule. Your business plan schedule will help you, but you also need other financial information. Because the implementation of your plan requires money, finances and financial data are closely integrated with business planning. Resources are never unlimited, and insufficient funds may make an ideal strategy impossible. You need to adopt a strategy and tactics consistent with your available money, time, and other resources.

Include sales estimates on a monthly basis through the life of the plan, usually about three years. Also include cash flow requirements based on the sales or revenue

Exhibit 2   Project Development Schedule

Months after Project Initiation

Task	1	2	3	4	5	6	7	8	9	10	11	12
Manufacture of units for test manufacturing	$5000											
Initial advertisement in test area	$10,000	$10,000	$10,000									
Shipment of units in test market area	$300	$200										
Analysis of test		$500	$700	$200								
Manufacture of units—1st year				$5,000	$10,000	$10,000	$10,000	$10,000				
Phase I advertising and publicity				$10,000	$30,000	$30,000	$15,000					
Shipment of units					$1,000	$1,000	$1,000	$1,000	$500			
Phase II advertising								$10,000	$10,000	$5,000	$5,000	$5,000

coming in less your costs. You may have already calculated that you should make a huge profit at the end of the year. But, if you have a similarly huge negative cash flow at the halfway point, you may never get to the end of the year to realize that profit.

Certain other calculations and ratios may also be important. One of the easiest to calculate, and most useful, is called "break-even." This is simply the point at which your business has no profits and no losses.

How to Calculate Your Break-Even Point

Here's how to calculate your break-even point. First, what is profit? Profit will be equal to the quantity of your sales less your costs. Now costs are of two basic types. The first type is *fixed costs*. That means you pay the same amount no matter how many units you sell. If you buy a computer for your business, what you pay for that machine won't vary no matter how many or few products you sell.

We refer to the second type of costs as *variable costs*. These costs are directly connected to the sales of your product and vary with each unit. If you have manufacturing costs of $1.00 a unit, your costs vary depending on how many units you sell.

So, profit equals quantity sold times selling price less quantity sold times variable cost and less fixed cost. The break-even point occurs when profits and losses both equal zero. To learn the quantity we must sell to break even, we can move all this information around algebraically and come up with a simple foolproof formula to calculate this required amount:

$$\text{Break-even quantity} = \text{Fixed cost} \div \text{Price} - \text{Variable cost}$$

It's that simple. Let's say you add up all your variable costs and come up with $4.50 per unit. You add up all your fixed costs and come up with $7,700. We'll say your price is $10.

Our equation says that break-even quantity will be $7,700 divided by $10 minus $4.50. That's $7,700 divided by $5.50 or 1,400 units. That means you must sell 1,400 units before you start making any money.

There is a way of calculating all of this graphically without using the formulas. A *break-even chart* has a major advantage over the break-even and profit formulas: It shows pictorially the relationship of fixed variable and total expenses to sales at all volumes of sales. That means that you can calculate profits at any level of sales without using an equation. Here is how to construct a break-even chart.

Step 1. Get some graph paper and label the horizontal line on the bottom *Units Sold*. Label the vertical line at the left of the graph *Dollars (Sales and Expenses)*. Divide each line into equal parts of dollars and units and label it appropriately.

Step 2. Analyze all of your costs for the project and decide whether each is fixed or variable. Decide on the period of sales for your project. Total up your fixed and variable costs.

Step 3. Draw a horizontal line to intersect the proper point on the vertical line to represent fixed costs, as at A in Exhibit 3.

Exhibit 3   A Break-Even Chart

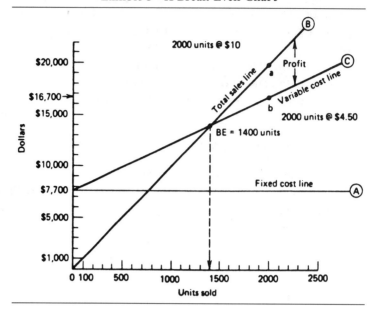

Step 4.   Calculate the dollar value of sales for any unit number. For example, if we sell 2,000 units, how much is this in sales dollars? For red widgets, total sales volume could be 2,000 × $10, or $20,000. Plot this point at 2,000 units and $20,000 on the chart as point a. Put one end of a ruler at the 0 point in the lower left corner of the chart and the other end at the point you just plotted. This is the total sales line B in Exhibit 3.

Step 5.   Calculate the dollar value for variable cost for any unit number. For example, for red widgets, variable cost is $4.50 per unit. At, say, 2,000 units, total variable cost is 2,000 × $4.50, or $9,000. Add $9,000 to the fixed cost (in this case, $7,700) to come up with $16,700. Plot this on the chart (b in Exhibit 3). Lay one end of the ruler at the point where the fixed cost line B intersects the vertical dollar scale and the other at the point you just plotted. Draw a line to form the variable cost line C in Exhibit 3.

Now your break-even chart is complete. The point at which the total sales line and variable cost line intersect is the break-even point, which you read on the horizontal unit scale at the bottom of the chart. In Exhibit 3, break-even is 1,400 units, as we calculated before using our formula.

To calculate profit for any number of units you want, simply subtract the dollar value read at opposite the proper point on the variable cost line C from the dollar value read opposite the proper point on the total sales line B. For example, to calculate the profit if you sell 2,000 red widgets, read right up from 2,000 units on the unit scale to point b on the variable cost line. Read straight across from point b to $16,700 on the vertical dollar scale. Now read straight up from 2,000 units on the unit scale to point a on the total sales line. Read straight across from point a to $20,000 on the vertical dollar scale: $20,000 minus $16,700 equals $3,300 if you sell 2,000 units. Do the same thing for any number of units to calculate profit.

While there are many ways that break-even might be calculated, and you will see several in these business plans, this method, using either the formula or the chart is recommended.

Monitor and Adjust for the Environment . . . It Changes

Simply initiating the plan and hoping for the best isn't enough to ensure success. Because the environment is constantly changing, such a procedure is almost certain to result in failure. Therefore, it is important to specify a means of evaluation and control even before implementing the plan as well as including this process in the plan itself.

What will you do if sales are not at the level you forecast? Will you drop the plan? Modify it? How will you modify it? What if certain tactics in your plan are profitable and others not? What if certain geographic areas are profitable and others not? What will you do about new competitors entering the market or a change in an old competitor's strategy? How will these facts alter your plan? How will you find out these results and determine their effects?

Failing to prepare for evaluation and control is like pointing an automobile at a destination, closing your eyes, pushing the gas pedal, and crossing your fingers. You need feedback to measure the changes in the environment as you proceed. If the road curves, you sure want to know about it. Then, you can and must take action to get back on course to your destination. How you will do this is what I mean by implementation and control.

Now you know everything you need to get started. Start your research into your business, and begin. Refer to the many examples of real business plans that I have provided to see how you can make your business plan the best it can be. In Appendix B, you will find some forms that will help you to think through and complete various sections of the plan.

1

BUSINESS PLAN FOR ORCA COMPUTER SYSTEMS

Developed by
Wowong Hartono

Used with the Permission of the Author

Table of Contents

LIST OF EXHIBITS . . . . **1·4**

EXECUTIVE SUMMARY . . . . **1·5**

1.0 INTRODUCTION . . . . **1·6**

    1.1 Company Description . . . . 1·6
    1.2 Mission Statement . . . . 1·6
    1.3 Major Products . . . . 1·6

2.0 SITUATION ANALYSIS . . . . **1·6**

    2.1 The Situational Environs . . . . 1·6
        2.1.1 Demand and Demand Trends . . . . 1·6
        2.1.2 Social, Cultural, and Demographics Factors . . . . 1·7
        2.1.3 Economic and Political Factors . . . . 1·7
        2.1.4 Product Technology . . . . 1·8
        2.1.5 Laws and Regulations . . . . 1·8
    2.2 The Neutral Environs . . . . 1·8
        2.2.1 Financial Environments . . . . 1·8
        2.2.2 Government Environments . . . . 1·8
        2.2.3 Media Environments . . . . 1·8
        2.2.4 Special Interest Environments . . . . 1·9
    2.3 The Competitor Environs . . . . 1·9
        2.3.1 Educational Sector . . . . 1·9
        2.3.2 Home and Small Business Sectors . . . . 1·9
    2.4 The Company Environs . . . . 1·10
        2.4.1 Product Descriptions . . . . 1·10
        2.4.2 Features of the Firm . . . . 1·12
        2.4.3 Organization . . . . 1·12
        2.4.4 Experience and Resources . . . . 1·12
        2.4.5 Suppliers . . . . 1·14
        2.4.6 Strength and Weaknesses . . . . 1·14

3.0 THE TARGET MARKET . . . . **1·14**

    3.1 Types of Potential Customers . . . . 1·14
    3.2 ORCA's Target Market . . . . 1·15

4.0 PROBLEMS AND OPPORTUNITIES . . . . **1·16**

    4.1 Opportunities . . . . 1·16
        4.1.1 Opportunity to Expand ORCA Business . . . . 1·16

	4.1.2	Market Penetration to Low Competition Sector (Market Differentiation)	1·16
	4.1.3	ORCA's Product Differentiation	1·17
4.2	Problems		1·17
	4.2.1	Competition	1·17
	4.2.2	Consumer Risk	1·17
	4.2.3	Supplier Risk	1·17
	4.2.4	Intracompany Risk	1·17

5.0 OBJECTIVES AND GOALS .... **1·18**

| 5.1 | Objectives and Goals within Four Years | 1·18 |
| 5.2 | Growth and Expansion Plan | 1·18 |

6.0 MARKETING STRATEGY .... **1·18**

6.1	Product Differentiation	1·18
6.2	Market Differentiation	1·19
6.3	Concentric Diversification	1·19

7.0 MARKETING TACTICS .... **1·19**

7.1	Product	1·19
7.2	Price	1·20
7.3	Promotion	1·20
7.4	Distribution	1·20

8.0 IMPLEMENTATION AND CONTROL .... **1·20**

8.1	Breakeven Analysis		1·20
	8.1.1	Breakeven Analysis for ORCA 386SX	1·21
	8.1.2	Breakeven Analysis for ORCA 386	1·21
	8.1.3	Breakeven Analysis for ORCA 486	1·21
	8.1.4	Breakeven Analysis for the Combination of All Products	1·21
8.2	Income Statement (Sales Projections) and Cash Flows		1·21

REFERENCES .... **1·22**

APPENDIX A   LIST OF SUPPLIERS .... **1·38**

APPENDIX B   LIST OF ORCA'S PRODUCT COMPONENTS .... **1·39**

List of Exhibits

Exhibit 1   Computer Industry Output . . . .   1·7
Exhibit 2   ORCA's Organizational Chart . . . .   1·13
Exhibit 3   ORCA's Target Markets: California and Florida . . . .   1·15
Exhibit 4   Marketing Objectives and Goals . . . .   1·18
Exhibit 5   Start-Up and First Year's Cost for Office and Equipment . . . . . .   1·22
Exhibit 6   Financial Statement and Cash Flows, Best Scenario . . . .   1·23
Exhibit 7   Financial Statement and Cash Flows, Moderate Scenario . . . . . .   1·28
Exhibit 8   Financial Statement and Cash Flows, Worst Scenario . . . .   1·33

Executive Summary

Computer industry sales have been growing at a rate of 4% to 6% in the past three years. In fact, the industry has been growing for more than 30 years. There is still a lot of opportunity for new companies to join this technology industry.

ORCA Computer Systems is a newly created computer hardware company located in Los Angeles. The company plans to start its operation in June 1992. It will market several lines of personal computers which include ORCA 386SX, ORCA 386, and ORCA 486. The products will come with a 150-page computer manual and ORCA's custom installation on software.

ORCA's primary objective is to provide reliable and high-quality products at competitive prices and to provide consultation with the customer on his or her needs on the computer and software.

ORCA markets are aimed to faculty members and students at universities in southern California and Florida, and to home and small business users in southern California. As the company grows, it plans to expand its market, introduce new products, and improve quality, performance, and image of the company.

1.0 INTRODUCTION

1.1 Company Description

ORCA Computer Systems is a newly created computer hardware company that intends to incorporate as a Subchapter S Corporation in the state of California. Wowong Hartono, Harry Suhendra, and Woody Lim comprise the three partners of the firm.

1.2 Mission Statement

The firm's mission is to assemble and market personal computer systems that are reliable, good quality, and fully documented. The firm also intends to have good and informative after-sales support.

1.3 Major Products

Initially, the company will market the ORCA line of personal computers. These include ORCA 386SX, ORCA 386, ORCA 486, and ORCA notebook computers. A new addition to ORCA computer systems, ORCA 586, will be introduced to the market approximately June of 1993. The products will be customized according to customer's specifications and needs. This customization includes selections on memory and hard disk capacities, computer cases, monitor types, data drives, add-on boards, coprocessors, printers and preinstalled software.

2.0 SITUATION ANALYSIS

2.1 The Situational Environs

2.1.1 Demand and Demand Trends

Computer industry sales have been growing for more than 30 years. The data show that the overall value of shipments of computer equipment and software increased at a rate of 4% to 6% in the past three years, and as large as 14.9% in the 1987-88 period (see Exhibit 1). This figure includes all seven specific industries: electronic computers, computer storage devices, computer terminals, computer peripheral equipments not elsewhere specified, computer programming services, prepackaged software, and computer integrated systems design.[1]

It is important to recognize that a microcomputer sale involves dealing with individuals at four levels:

Level 1:   Decision makers (executives, high-ranking managers).

Level 2:   Influencers (technically proficient individuals in the organization, highest user level individuals, actual users of the system, outside consultants).

Level 3:   Supervisors of groups which utilize microcomputers.

Level 4:   Actual users of the microcomputers.

Consumers of all levels buy the products based on needs. Top executives see the need of office automation and computerization to achieve faster and better results.

---

[1] U.S. Department of Commerce, International Trade Administration, *U.S. Industrial Outlook 1991*, January 1991, 28-1.

Exhibit 1   Computer Industry Output

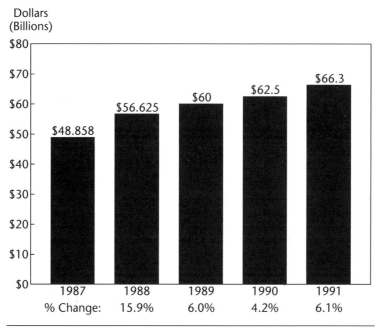

Source: U.S. Department of Commerce, International Trade Administration, *U.S. Industrial Outlook 1991.*

Consultants see the need of a more efficient system in the organizations. Supervisors see the need of computers to help them to achieve the target on time. Finally, the users see the need of computers to do a variety of jobs, such as calculating income statements and payroll, writing business letters, doing homework, and so on.

Another reason consumers want to buy the product is microcomputer's performance and ease of operations. Consumers buy the product if they feel that microcomputer is indeed the necessary solution to the problems and concerns arising out of unsatisfied needs.

Quantity of sales ranges from hundreds of units for level 1 buyers to one unit for level 4 buyers. Most of the upper level consumers purchase the product based on quality, service, and brand preference, regardless of price. On the other hand, the lower level consumers judge their purchases based on price-performance of the computer.

2.1.2 Social, Cultural, and Demographics Factors

ORCA plans to market the products in two geographic regions: southern California and north-central Florida. The target market of ORCA is mostly college students, faculty, and home users. Thus most of ORCA's customers are educated, modern, and in the middle- to upper-class income. They are either computer literate or want to be computer literate.

Computers have been accepted by all social classes and all culturally diverse groups. Demographically, ORCA target market regions consist of diverse ethnic and cultural backgrounds in southern California, to a predominantly white Florida community.

2.1.3 Economic and Political Factors

The current U.S. economic recession will likely come to an end soon and will lead to an economic recovery for the future years. This situation creates a great outlook for U.S. industries in general. During the recession, unprofitable and inefficient firms folded down, and successful and competent firms improved their efficiency and cut down costs. The future of the computer industry will be highly competitive. Yet, with the coming economic recovery, it is a good time for ORCA to enter the market.

2.1.4 Product Technology

The computer industry has been in the growth stage for over 40 years. Unlike many other products, with continuing computer research and development, the computer industry has been able stay in the growth stage almost indefinitely. Currently, the most popular type personal computer in terms of sales is the 80386 microprocessor-based microcomputer, with the lower performance S-based, and the high performance 80486-based following closely. The major piece of the price of a computer lies on its extensive development and research costs. However, computer sales have been increasing at about 6% a year which reduce the fixed cost per computer. The savings in cost is passed on to the consumers who are constantly being offered microcomputers at lower prices and higher performances.

2.1.5 Laws and Regulations

ORCA will retain the services of the legal firm of *Fox and Fox*. Given the relatively small size and complexity of ORCA operations, *Fox and Fox* has estimated service requirements at approximately four hours per month at a quoted fee of $250 per hour. Thus, expenditures for the legal services of *Fox and Fox* will average about $1,000 per month.

The services of *Fox and Fox* will include, but are not limited to, ensuring that ORCA Computer Systems is in compliance with all federal, state, and local government rules, regulations, and ordinances concerning the business transactions (with customers, suppliers, and manufacturers) and employment matters, as well as answering any legal questions that ORCA may have in the course of doing business. However, ORCA will be subject to fees in addition to the above quoted time and money projections for all matters requiring significant and complex legal action.

2.2 The Neutral Environs

2.2.1 Financial Environments

ORCA Computer Systems will be able to provide start-up capital of $100,000 which consists of $40,000 from Wowong Hartono, $30,000 from Harry Suhendra, $15,000 from Woody Lim, and $15,000 from a five-year loan at an annual rate of 8.5%. With the government effort to stimulate economy, there will be plenty of capital resources that ORCA could seek to get the $15,000 business loan.

2.2.2 Government Environments

Current federal government policy to enhance economic recovery by lowering discount rates and encouraging consumers to spend, will favor ORCA's business. With current government actions and future economic recovery, most individuals' disposable income will be likely to increase in the next three years. This means that more people could afford to buy computer products.

2.2.3 Media Environments

There are hundreds of local, regional, and national computer publications in the United States. Computer publications such as computer magazines perhaps are the fastest growing sector of publication today. New nationally published computer periodicals appear almost every six months.

This highly publicized computer industry brings positive impact. More and more people are beginning to learn the benefits and the ease of use of microcomputers. Media exposure increases public knowledge and awareness of computer products.

ORCA computer systems, as with any other competitors, will benefit from such publications. Media environments are expanding consumer bases. Thus, directly or indirectly, the media will help increase ORCA sales.

2.2.4 Special Interest Environments

Current federal budget cuts in the educational sector would result in mixed consequences for ORCA business. These cuts will affect ORCA because the firm's target market is primarily individuals involved in the educational sectors (i.e., students and faculty). All state universities around the United States have suffered from the federal cuts. In order to cope, they reduce the number of classes offered, reduce the services to students, and increase the tuition fees as much as 40%. These actions would reduce the number of faculty members (because there are less classes to teach) and would reduce the buying power of students (because they have to pay more fees).

On the contrary, actions to reduce services to students mean shorter computer lab hours, longer lines to use computer labs, and fewer computer assistants in the lab. This might prompt the students to buy their own computer systems.

2.3   The Competitor Environs

ORCA Computer Systems markets its products in two different targets: educational sectors and home and small business users. The firm is faced with two completely different types of competitors for these two markets.

2.3.1 Educational Sector

Primary competitors of ORCA Computer Systems in the educational sector are IBM and Apple computers. Their strategies in marketing their products include displaying their products in campus bookstores, providing special discount prices for students and faculty, and exhibiting their products in a computer show on campus. To purchase a computer, the consumer usually has to deal with the sales representatives in the bookstore who sometimes know little about the computer. Then, the sales representative fills in the order form and sends it to the company to be processed. The consumer will receive the computer approximately three to four weeks after the order has been placed. Sometimes, the consumer has to pick up the computer from the local IBM or Apple Macintosh dealer.

IBM and Apple corporations, as industry leaders, have been well known by consumers for the quality of their products and their brand names. Currently, both IBM and Apple are differentiating their products from the rest of the competitors in the industry. Apple (Macintosh) has a sole right to use Motorola 68000 series microprocessors. IBM introduced PS/2 system with micro channel architecture that has an IBM patent. This differentiation strategy creates incompatibility problems for the users. For example, the IBM PS/2 owner could not purchase any other brand of computer peripherals (monitors, modems, extra hard drive, and other add-on cards) except IBM brand micro channel architecture. The consumers are faced with limited product selections and very high prices.

2.3.2 Home and Small Business Sectors

In the home and small business sectors, ORCA's primary competitors are small- to medium-sized computer manufacturers that sell their products directly to customers. These include small companies that also participate in the weekly *Computer Show and*

Sale (i.e., Elco, Royal, Comstar) and mail order companies that sell their products by mail (Zeos, Gateway, CompuAdd). These competitors market their products based on low price strategy. The mail order companies advertise heavily (sometimes, more than four full pages) in most computer magazines. Because of large advertising costs, the mail order companies usually price their products higher than small local computer companies (in southern California).

Most of the products that the competitors market have very little differentiation. All are IBM-compatible computers; all have the same options on monitor type and hard drive; and all have little documentation about the products. The competitors assume that the buyers have enough knowledge about the computer and how to configure it. In fact, most buyers only know how to use the software. They do not understand how to configure the computer so that it can be used to the maximum potential.

Most competitors display their products with graphic images in the monitors, and sell their products based on numbers: 386, 486, large hard drive capacity, and competitive price.

2.4   The Company Environs

2.4.1   Product Descriptions

ORCA lines of personal computer consist of ORCA 386SX, ORCA 386, ORCA 486, and ORCA Notebook computers. ORCA products consist of components that are manufactured by different companies. Appendix B displays some of the components that will be used in ORCA products. In general, ORCA microcomputer products consist of the following components:

1. Motherboards with CPU:
   * 80386SX-25MHz, OPTI chip set
   * 80386-33MHz with 64K Cache, OPTI chip set
   * 80386-40MHz with 64K Cache, OPTI chip set
   * 80486-33MHz with 64K/256K Cache, OPTI chip set
2. Video Cards
   * MGP monochrone card
   * Paradise 256K-1C 1024X768 16 colors
   * Paradise 1M-1D 1024X768 256 colors
   * Western Digital WD90C30 1024X 768 32,000 colors
3. Hard Disk Drives
   * Conner IDE   40MB
   * Maxtor IDE   80MB
   * Conner IDE   120MB
   * Conner IDE   200MB
4. Hard Drive Controller
   * Super I/O card (IDE Controller & I/O card: 2 serial ports, 1 parallel port, 1 game port)
5. Computer Cases
   * Slim-size AT case (jet-black, cream)
   * Baby-size Vertical case (jet-black, cream)

- Mid-size Vertical case (jet-black, cream)
- Full-size Vertical case (jet-black, cream)
- Servo case with 12 slots (jet-black, cream)

6. Power Supplies
   - Alfa Power 200 watt power supply (for ORCA 386SX system)
   - Alfa Power 230 watt power supply (for ORCA 386 system)
   - Alfa Power 250 watt power supply (for ORCA 486 system)
   - Alfa Power 400 watt power supply (optional)

7. Monitors
   - REDMS Non-Interlaced 14" 0.28mm VGA
   - REDMS Non-Interlaced 14" 0.28mm 1024-768

8. Keyboards
   - Enhanced click keyboard
   - Enhanced click keyboard with note pad

9. Mouse
   - Microsoft mouse

10. ORCA Notebook computer
    - Clover S-20MHz
    - Clover 80386-25MHz

11. Computer Manuals
    - ORCA 386SX Handbook: Understanding Your Personal Computer
    - ORCA 386 Handbook: Understanding Your Personal Computer
    - ORCA 486 Handbook: Understanding Your Personal Computer

Additional add-ons:

12. Modem - Fax-Modems
    - Zoom 2400 baud modem
    - Zoom 9600 baud modem
    - Zoom 9600/2400 fax-modem

13. Math Co-processors
    - Cyrix 387-33MHz
    - Cyrix 387-40MHz

14. Software
    - Microsoft DOS 5.01
    - Microsoft Windows 3.1
    - Microsoft Word 5.0 DOS/Windows
    - WordPerfect 5.1 DOS/Windows
    - Lotus 123 DOS/Windows
    - Harvard Graphics 4.0
    - Quarterdeck Memory Management 6.01
    - Direct Access 3.52
    - Central Point Anti-Virus

2.4.2 Features of the Firm

The firm will feature the following:

1. Reliable and high quality products at competitive price. Every ORCA system is built with ORCA standard of quality and is fully tested before shipment.

2. Fully documented and easy to read computer manual.

   ORCA Computer System: Understanding Your Personal Computer—a 150-page long manual—will be included in every ORCA system. The manual is divided into three parts:

   a. Understanding Computers (How the computer works, what necessary components are, and what the functions of each component are.)

   b. Enhancements for Your Computer (Tips on how to increase computer performance, tips on additional features that can be added to the computer, and tips for advanced users.)

   c. Troubleshooting Guide (Lets the user fix simple computer problems.)

3. Custom installation on software.

   ORCA will ship the product preinstalled and custom-configured with any popular software packages.

4. One-year warranty on parts and labor.

   ORCA will provide a full one-year warranty on parts and labor for every ORCA product.

5. Full one-year technical support.

   ORCA will provide full technical support for one year. The technical support will be available on Monday through Friday from 10:00A.M. to 5:00P.M.

6. Computer consultation with potential customers.

   ORCA will provide consultation for small businesses in setting up the most suitable system for the company.

2.4.3 Organization

Exhibit 2 illustrates the organizational structure of *ORCA Computer Systems.*

2.4.4 Experience and Resources

All three partners of *ORCA Computer Systems* are advanced users of microcomputers and have had significant experience and know-how in the computer industry. Wowong Hartono has a BS in electrical engineering with emphasis in computer engineering, and will have an MBA in June 1992. He has three years' experience in the computer industry. His professional know-how includes computer assembly, computer consultant, firmware programming, DOS programming, computer security, networking, and software applications.

As a president of *ORCA Computer Systems,* Wowong is charged with the responsibility of coordinating all activities of the partners, and ensuring that the firm remains on course to reach its objectives. The president is the only member of the firm authorized to approve checks issued by *ORCA Computer Systems.* Wowong is also in charge of the finance and marketing of the company. He is responsible for developing and implementing all marketing actions plans to further enhance awareness, image, and demand for ORCA products.

Harry Suhendra has a BS and MS in electrical engineering with emphasis in computer engineering. He has four years' experience in digital hardware and computer industry. Currently, he works as a senior digital engineer in an engineering company.

Exhibit 2   ORCA's Organizational Chart

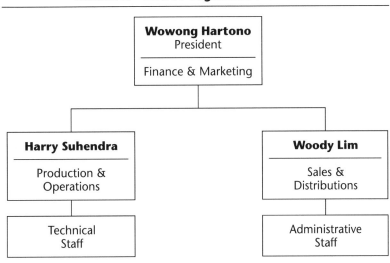

Harry is in charge of ORCA's production and operations. He is assigned the task of developing and monitoring all production and operational activities, including research and development, quality control, and just-in-time operation. He also assists Wowong in sales and marketing in the southern California region.

Woody Lim is currently a senior in computer science at the University of North Florida. He has three years of computer experience as a programmer and computer graphic designer. He will graduate in June 1992 and will be employed by ORCA.

Woody is responsible for ORCA sales and marketing in Florida. He is also assigned the task of identifying and penetrating ORCA's target market in Florida.

Financially, ORCA Computer Systems will provide start-up capital of $100,000 which consists of $40,000 from Wowong Hartono, $30,000 from Harry Suhendra, $15,000 from Woody Lim, and $15,000 from a three-year loan at an annual rate of 8.5%.

ORCA initially will employ four technical staff and a clerk. The technical employees will be trained to be computer assembly technicians by Harry and Wowong. All of the five employees will be paid hourly at $7.00 per hour.

For the first month of operation, the salaried partners have agreed not to draw compensation in order to minimize initial start-up cost. The capital and salary structure for the first six months is set at a modest level to minimize costs during the first critical six months of operations. The salary structure is as follows:

Partners	Capital		Ownership Share	First Six Months Salary
Wowong Hartono	$40,000	(40%)	47%	$3,000/month
Harry Suhendra	30,000	(30%)	35	2,500/month
Woody Lim	15,000	(15%)	18	2,000/month
Bank loan	15,000	(15%)		

ORCA will evaluate the salary structure after six months of operations. If the sales are increasing as expected under the moderate scenario or best scenario, the salaries will be increased by 25% for the next one year, with another 25% increase in 1994. This salary increase, which is based on sales performance, will improve the partners' motivation to increase sales.

2.4.5 Suppliers

Appendix A shows the suppliers' names and addresses. ORCA's suppliers range from small to large multinational companies. Most of the hardware suppliers are located in the Los Angeles area. Close location to the ORCA warehouse is one of the important criteria in selecting ORCA's suppliers. With close location, there will be faster delivery, easier contact, and faster flow of information from suppliers to ORCA.

2.4.6 Strengths and Weaknesses

ORCA's strengths lie on its ability to provide capital and resources. Of the start-up capital, 85% comes from the partners, and only 15% of the capital comes from the bank loan. This capital structure will minimize the interest burden of the company.

Also, the extensive PC knowledge of the three partners is an asset for ORCA. ORCA is expected to have very few technical problems on computer production.

A concern for the company is that the three partners do not have extensive experience in sales and marketing of computer products compared with the competitors. However, the company will be able to penetrate the educational sectors where there are few competitors.

3.0 THE TARGET MARKET

3.1 Types of Potential Customers

The great attraction of the microcomputer business lies in its universality. That is, microcomputers and their accessories can be sold to almost everyone. The utilization of computers by the user is unlimited. Microcomputers fit in everywhere: business, education, science, and entertainment.

There are several types of potential customers who might consider buying ORCA computer products. The first type of possible customer is the computer hobbyist. Since this is a relatively sophisticated individual, his or her main interest lies in the area of features and applications. Unlike the other types of retail customers and all corporate customers, this person has a predetermined set of benefits in mind when he or she starts looking for computer products. The message of the marketing campaign for this type of customer should stress the availability of a wide selection of hardware and software (utility, applications, interfaces, options, peripherals, and add-on boards). Use of buzzwords and technical jargon in marketing the product will be effective marketing strategy for this target market.

The second type of possible customer is a small- to medium-sized business. These customers are likely to buy more than one computer system. They plan to purchase computer systems when they feel that there is a need of using computers. The advertising message for this type of customer should be exclusively needs-oriented. The seller should talk about computer applications and needs such as word processing, account receivables, account payables, payroll, and so on. The strategy is to emphasize ease of operation, service, reliability, and performance.

The third type of possible customer includes individuals who are involved with education. These people include college students and faculty members. College students need to use computers at home for convenience of typing papers and doing homework. By owning a computer, (1) they avoid waiting in line to use computer labs on campus, (2) they can type anytime they want to, and (3) they can learn more about the microcomputer. Faculty members always need the computer at their own office to help their work. Most universities do not provide computers in every faculty office. Some universities do provide a computer lab for faculty use only; however, it is often inconvenient for the faculty member to walk to the computer facility to type his or her work or letters.

The advertising message for this type of customer should also be needs-oriented. The marketer should talk about computer applications such as word processing and spreadsheets for papers and homework. The strategy is to stress ease of operation, service, and reliability. Low price will be one of the appeals for most students and faculty members. Thus, the seller may introduce a special discounted price for students and faculty members.

The final type of customer is an individual who acquires a microcomputer to do some work at home—either job-related or household-related. It also includes parents who want to give offspring a computer to keep their child in tune with the modern trend toward computer literacy. This group is very diverse since it includes executives who may want to do some work at home, housewives who would like to use the computer for home purposes, and children who want to play computer games. The general marketing strategy for this group is to use an informative but nontechnical message on broad and versatile uses of computers.

3.2 ORCA's Target Market

Initially, the company will target educational and home computer users, as well as small businesses. The target area for educational users (students and faculty members) will be concentrated in southern California (Los Angeles area) and Florida. The initial target market in southern California will be faculty members and students of California State University-Fullerton, California State University-Long Beach, California State University-Los

Exhibit 3   ORCA's Target Markets: California and Florida

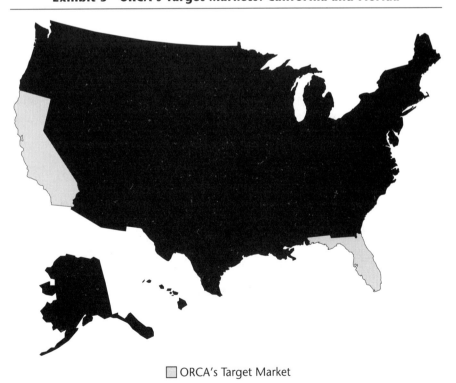

☐ ORCA's Target Market

Angeles, California State University-Northridge, California Polytechnic University-Pomona, Loyola Marimount University, and University of Southern California. The initial target market in Florida will be faculty members and students of University of Florida (Gainesville), University of North Florida (Jacksonville), and University of South Florida (Tampa).

The educational market has been one of the targets of IBM and Apple corporation in marketing their products. However, aside from these two companies, there are very few companies that market their products in this sector. ORCA selects southern California universities because (1) the locations are close to the warehouse, (2) California is the largest market for computer products, (3) few competitors have penetrated educational sectors, and (4) ORCA products are suitable for learning computer applications and educational uses.

There is a great potential of success in marketing ORCA computers in Florida based on several reasons: (1) the Florida market is experiencing rapid growth in computer sales, (2) most competitors in the Florida market are large computer makers which charge high prices to the buyers, and again, (3) ORCA products are suitable for learning and educational uses.

For home and small business targets, the company will market the products in Anaheim, Burbank, Glendale, Northridge, and Costa Mesa. These are the places where people come to see the weekly California Computer Show and Sale. ORCA will exhibit the products in the shows which are attended by an average of 3,500 buyers. People who come to the show are mostly price-wary consumers. This is suitable for ORCA, which markets high-quality products at low prices.

The following are the locations of the show:

1. Anaheim Stadium
   2000 State College Blvd., Anaheim

2. Burbank Hilton Convention Center
   2500 Hollywood Way, Burbank

3. California State University, Northridge, North Campus
   18000 Devonshire Blvd., Northridge

4. Glendale Civic Auditorium
   1401 North Verdugo Road, Glendale

5. Orange County Fairgrounds
   88 Fair Drive, Costa Mesa

4.0 PROBLEMS AND OPPORTUNITIES

4.1 Opportunities

There are several opportunities that ORCA has in the computer business:

4.1.1 Opportunity to Expand ORCA Business

The personal computer industry in the United States has been continuously expanding since the introduction of IBM PC in the 1970s. Currently, industry sales are growing at a rate of 6% a year, and there is still plenty of room for new companies to enter the market and expand their businesses.

4.1.2 Market Penetration to Low Competition Sector (Market Differentiation)

There is little competition in the educational sector where ORCA intends to market the products. IBM and Apple are the only prominent competitors for the company, and they price their products much higher than ORCA's products. Thus, ORCA's low price will be appealing to students and faculty members.

4.1.3   ORCA's Product Differentiation

ORCA will install the software and configure the system according to customer's need. A 150-page computer manual is also included in every ORCA computer. Finally, ORCA products are available in a jet black case, in addition to the regular beige case. This differentiation will set ORCA products apart from the competitors. The 150-page manual will be very appealing to students who want to purchase a personal computer for the first time and want to learn about computers.

4.2   Problems

Every company has its own problems and risks. ORCA business has to be aware of the following potential problems:

4.2.1   Competition

As discussed in Competitor Environs in Chapter 2, competition does exist and there is danger that competitors could fight back by lowering their prices. Because most of the prices of computer components would likely drop in the future, ORCA will be able to lower the price of ORCA products to keep competitive in the future.

4.2.2   Consumer Risk

Consumers may hesitate buying ORCA products because ORCA is a new company in a computer business. However, ORCA will try to eliminate this perception by using product differentiation strategy and having knowledgeable salespeople.

4.2.3   Supplier Risk

Some computer components' prices have dropped as much as 25% in a one-year period.[2] This creates a problem for ORCA. ORCA has to order the components at low enough quantity to take advantage of the price decreases in the future, but also at high enough quantity to benefit from large quantity order discounts. The best strategy is to limit the inventory of components. In other words, just-in-time delivery from the suppliers is an effective strategy to reduce inventory costs and to prevent loss from price reductions in the future.

4.2.4   Intracompany Risk

The firm's partners, although possessing broad business and computer experience, have never worked together and have little experience in starting and operating a business. This inexperience could result in problems which arise from miscalculations, including start-up costs that exceed estimates; sales projections that are not achieved; and greater than expected development and innovation costs to keep pace with competition.

   To reduce this risk, the operations and marketing of *ORCA Computer Systems* will require close and constant monitoring. Forecasts will be scrutinized, updated, and adjusted to reflect actual operational experience. The operations and marketing strategies themselves will also be evaluated and augmented, modified, or abandoned to maintain optimum sales and growth margins.

---

[2] Randy Ross, "Forecast for '92," *Computer Buying World,* January 1992, 62–63.

5.0   OBJECTIVES AND GOALS

5.1   Objectives and Goals within Four Years

The list below indicates ORCA goals and objectives in terms of return on investments (ROI), total monthly sales, total monthly sales in number of units, and liquidity (current ratio). The list represents the achievement targets for ORCA by the end of December of each year.

5.2   Growth and Expansion Plan

ORCA intends to keep up with technological advances in the computer industry. The firm will continuously introduce new products that have a potential market in the future. As the company grows, it will expand its product lines and services. The most prominent prospects for expansion within two years are the introduction of new ORCA 586 computer, ORCA LAN technology, and ORCA consulting services. These future products and services are not included in this business plan. A separate marketing plan for each of these products and services is essential because each of them will have different marketing strategies, tactics, and goals.

6.0   MARKETING STRATEGY

ORCA Computer Systems plans to use several marketing strategies to increase sales growth and market share. The strategies include product differentiation, market differentiation, and concentric diversification.

6.1   Product Differentiation

Most of the competitors' products in the home and small business target sector have similar features and services. The personal computer itself must be based on the high compatibility standards of the IBM personal computer. This high standardization results in limited product variations in terms of product features and performance.

ORCA products enter the market in the second half of the growth stage. During this substage it is important to increase sales to have economies of scale of production. Mass production will bring a drop in the production costs.

ORCA will allocate some portions of its profit for product research and development. The fund will be used to improve the quality and features of the existing products, and to develop new products as explained in Chapter 5.

To differentiate ORCA products from the competitors, ORCA staff will produce a 150-page personal computer manual that will be included in every ORCA product purchase. The manual will include sections on understanding components of the microcomputer, tips on improving computer performance, and a computer troubleshooting guide.

Exhibit 4   Marketing Objectives and Goals

Goals	December 1992	December 1993	December 1994	December 1995
ROI	11%	17%	20%	22%
Total Monthly Sales	$136,000	$340,000	$614,164	$1,177,453
Total Monthly Units	85	221	391	749
Current Ratio	2.15	1.66	3.41	4.04

The troubleshooting guide provides instructions on how to reset the computer back to normal when the user has made some modifications that stalled the computer.

The manual will be attractive to students and novice computer users. It will also reduce the number of calls for technical assistance in case of consumer problems in configuring the computer.

Another differentiation of ORCA is that ORCA will provide preinstalled software and custom configured ORCA computers for every customer. It will reduce the consumers' hassle of having to buy and install the software by themselves. Moreover, the buyers most likely do not know how to configure the software to utilize the optimum computer capability.

The software will be sold at an average of 20% markup, which will increase ORCA's total profit.

6.2   Market Differentiation

The educational sector, one of ORCA's target markets, has not been penetrated by many competitors. As explained in Chapter 3, the educational sector has a lot of market potential for ORCA products.

To market the products, ORCA will employ students of the corresponding universities. The salary will be based on the number of sales (5% bonus from the sales proceeds). The students will be employed as direct marketers to faculty members of the university, and they will visit potential faculty members' offices to introduce ORCA products. In addition to direct marketing, ORCA plans to print flyers and advertisements that can be posted around campuses and in student newspapers.

To reach home and small business customers, ORCA will exhibit its products in the weekly *Computer Show and Sale.* The show is attended by an average of 3,500 prospective buyers on each show (100,000 consumers annually) and is located around southern California.[3]

6.3   Concentric Diversification

As the experience and technological know-how increases in the future, ORCA plans to expand the market by providing a consulting service and local area network (LAN) installation service. LAN is the fastest growing computer networking technology for the future. Most medium-sized businesses have started to use LAN for their computerized information network. LAN technology is a tool for competitive advantages for every business in the future.

ORCA also intends to keep up-to-date on technological advances. ORCA will introduce a new product: ORCA 586 as soon as the microprocessor is introduced by Intel Corp.

7.0   MARKETING TACTICS

7.1   Product

ORCA will build the product according to customer specifications. ORCA's salespeople will also provide suggestions to customers on features and performance level that are needed to accomplish the buyers' objectives. We have allocated seventy-five percent of the research and development fund for improvements in product quality, reliability, styling, and product differentiation. In the long run, the firm will add new models and extra features. The other 25% is allocated for development of new products and services.

---

[3] See Chapter 3 for the locations of the show. See Appendix C for further information about the show.

7.2 Price

ORCA will market its product at low price in order to be competitive in the market. ORCA products will be retailed at 30% markup from cost. However, because ORCA sells its product directly to customers, without any middlemen, ORCA will be able to sell its products at 10% discount below retail price. The discount price will be available for students and faculty members as educational discounts, and to computer shows visitors. This pricing strategy will give a "good deal" perception to prospective buyers.

As discussed in Chapter 4, because of economies of scale and increased competition, the price of computer components has been declining as much as 25% in a one-year span. All of the competitors, including IBM and Apple will most likely lower their sales prices in the future. ORCA will also lower its products' prices in the future, while maintaining a reasonable profit margin at 20% (most competitors maintain about 20% profit margin).

By lowering the price, the microcomputer is getting more affordable; thus it attracts the next layer of price-sensitive consumers.

7.3 Promotion

By having increased profit and more cash in the future, the company plans to increase its advertisement costs to build product awareness and increase sales. Product promotions in the *California Computer Show and Sale* are expected to generate a lot of sales and will be continued.

For the faculty members and students, ORCA will promote the products with a special educational price of 10% off from retail price.

7.4 Distribution

With ORCA's product strategy of building computers and providing custom software installation according to each customer's need and specifications, it is not feasible at this time to provide separate distribution channels. Distribution channels will increase cost and lengthen the time of delivery to customers.

In the future, to increase sales and market share, the company will expand its market segments to include northern California and the other states.

8.0 IMPLEMENTATION AND CONTROL

8.1 Breakeven Analysis

ORCA markets three different products and a number of supporting products (software, add-on boards, etc.). The following lists the sales price and product cost for each of ORCA products:

Product	Product Cost (Var Cost)	One Month Fixed Cost	Sale Price
ORCA 386SX	$ 792.00	$13,774.33	$ 990.00
ORCA 386	1,080.00	13,774.33	1,350.00
ORCA 486	1,279.20	13,774.33	1,599.00

In addition to the products above, sales on software and add-on boards are estimated at about $284 for each computer, with product cost of $227.20.

The basic formula for breakeven calculations is as follows:

$$BreakevenUnits = \frac{FixCost}{SalePrice - VarCost}$$

8.1.1 Breakeven Analysis for ORCA 386SX

For ORCA 386SX, the breakeven calculation is as follows:

Units = {13,774.33/(990 − 792) + (284 − 227.20)}

Units = 54 units per month

This means that the firm must be able to sell a minimum of 54 units of ORCA 386SX, and 0 units of ORCA 386 and ORCA 486.

8.1.2 Breakeven Analysis for ORCA 386

For ORCA 386, the breakeven calculation is as follows:

Units = {13,774.33/(1350 − 1080) + (284 − 227.20)}

Units = 42 units per month

This means that the firm must be able to sell a minimum of 42 units of ORCA 386, and 0 units of ORCA 386SX and ORCA 486.

8.1.3 Breakeven Analysis for ORCA 486

For ORCA 486, the breakeven calculation is as follows:

Units = {13,774.33/(1599 − 1279.20) + (284 − 227.20)}

Units = 37 units per month

This means that the firm must be able to sell a minimum of 37 units of ORCA 486, and 0 units of ORCA 386SX and ORCA 386.

8.1.4 Breakeven Analysis for the Combination of All Products

The firm is expected to sell all of the three products. The estimation of the breakeven units when each of the product is sold at equal quantity is as follows:

$$\frac{13,774.33}{33\%(990 - 792) + 33\%(1350 - 1080) + 33\%(1599 - 1279.20) + (284 - 227.20)} = 44 \text{ units}$$

This means that to reach breakeven point, ORCA must be able to sell a total of 44 units for the three products; that is 14 units for the ORCA 386SX, 15 units for the ORCA 386, and 15 units for the ORCA 486 computer in one month.

8.2 Income Statement (Sales Projections) and Cash Flows

Sales projections and cash flows have been prepared for three scenarios (best, moderate, and worst case). In the best case scenario, all of the company objectives are achieved. As the company expands, almost all of the budget is increased in the long run to accommodate more sales and services.

In the moderate scenario, the sales are expected to have moderate monthly growth. ORCA strategy in one of the target markets may not be quite as effective in attracting the buyers.

In the worst scenario, sales are expected to have a slower growth because of increasing competition in the market. In order to stay in business for the first two years, ORCA will try to minimize operational costs by postponing salary increases, facilities expansion, and new equipment purchases.

Exhibits 5 to 8 show the breakdown of office and equipment costs, monthly sales projections in the income statements, and expected cash flows for the first four years of operation.

REFERENCES

Committee on Science, Space, and Technology, House of Representatives. *Communications and Computers in the 21st Century.* Washington DC: U.S. Government Printing Office, 1987.

Committee on Science, Space, and Technology, House of Representatives. *The Technical Enterprise for Computers, Communications, and Manufacturing in the 21st Century.* Washington DC: U.S. Government Printing Office, 1987.

Dorff, Ralph, L. *Marketing for the Small Manufacturer.* Englewood Cliffs, NJ: Prentice Hall, 1983.

Goldmacher, Irving. *Selling Microcomputers and Software.* New York: McGraw-Hill, 1985.

Kotler, Philip. *Marketing Management.* Englewood Cliffs, NJ: Prentice Hall, 1991.

Luther, William M. *The Marketing Plan: How to Prepare and Implement It.* New York: Amacom, 1982.

Luther, William M. *The Start-Up Business Plan.* New York: Prentice Hall, 1991.

Ross, Randy. "Forecast for '92." *Computer Buying World,* January 1992, 62–63.

Simon, Alan R. *How to Be a Successful Computer Consultant.* New York: McGraw-Hill, 1990.

Stevens, Robert E. *Strategic Marketing Plan Master Guide.* Englewood Cliffs, NJ: Prentice Hall, 1982.

U.S. Department of Commerce, Bureau of the Census. *Current Industrial Reports: Computers and Office and Accounting Machines.* Washington DC: U.S. Government Printing Office, 1989.

U.S. Department of Commerce, International Trade Administration. "Computer Equipment and Software." *U.S. Industrial Outlook 1991,* 28-1–28-12.

Exhibit 5   Start-Up and First Year's Cost for Office and Equipment

Description	Period	Qty	Unit Cost	Start-up Cost	Annual Cost
Security deposit for warehouse lease	start-up	1	$ 1,200	$ 1,200	
Warehouse lease (including utilities, maintenance, janitorial, etc.)	monthly	12	1,000		$12,000
Down payment for truck lease	start-up	1	3,000	3,000	
Transportation (including truck lease, maintenance, fuel, car insurance)	monthly	12	550		6,600
Facilities insurance	annual	1	12,200		12,200
Tools, equipments, storage racks, and assembly tables	start-up	1	4,650	4,650	200
Office furniture, fax, copier, 2 personal computers, laser printer, telephone system, and office accessories	start-up	1	6,240	6,240	
Miscellaneous office supplies	monthly	12	135		1,620
Total Cost				$15,090	$32,620

Exhibit 6   Financial Statement and Cash Flows, Best Scenario

INCOME STATEMENT PROJECTIONS

1992	June	July	August	September	October	November	December
SALES							
ORCA 386SX (Units)	6	11	16	18	19	20	21
ORCA 386 (Units)	12	18	25	28	31	34	37
ORCA 486 (Units)	6	11	16	20	22	24	27
ORCA 386SX	5,940.00	10,890.00	15,840.00	17,820.00	17,955.00	18,852.75	19,795.39
ORCA 386	16,200.00	24,300.00	33,750.00	37,800.00	41,580.00	45,738.00	50,311.80
ORCA 486	9,594.00	17,589.00	25,584.00	31,980.00	35,178.00	38,695.80	42,565.38
Supporting Products	6,816.00	11,360.00	16,188.00	18,744.00	20,362.80	22,130.70	24,061.97
TOTAL SALES	38,550.00	64,139.00	91,362.00	106,344.00	115,075.80	125,417.25	136,734.54
COST OF GOODS SOLD	30,840.00	51,311.20	73,089.60	85,075.20	92,060.64	100,333.80	109,387.63
GROSS MARGIN FROM SALES	7,710.00	12,827.80	18,272.40	21,268.80	23,015.16	25,083.45	27,346.91
OPERATING EXPENSES							
Office and Equipments	15,090.00	2,718.33	2,718.33	2,718.33	2,718.33	2,718.33	2,718.33
Legal Fees	1,000.00	1,000.00	1,000.00	1,000.00	1,000.00	1,000.00	1,000.00
Accounting Fees	163.33	163.33	163.33	163.33	163.33	163.33	163.33
Insurance	866.67	866.67	866.67	866.67	866.67	866.67	866.67
Depreciation	100.00	100.00	100.00	100.00	100.00	100.00	100.00
Advertisement Cost	300.00	250.00	250.00	250.00	250.00	250.00	250.00
Promotions/Comp. Shows	676.00	676.00	676.00	676.00	676.00	676.00	676.00
Staff Salaries	500.00	8,000.00	8,000.00	8,000.00	8,000.00	8,000.00	8,000.00
TOTAL OP. EXPENSES	18,696.00	13,774.33	13,774.33	13,774.33	13,774.33	13,774.33	13,774.33
OPERATING INCOME	(10,986.00)	(946.53)	4,498.07	7,494.47	9,240.83	11,309.12	13,572.58
INTEREST INCOME	410.00	237.96	224.56	227.19	244.05	268.89	299.50
OTHER EXPENSES	233.33	235.86	238.02	240.40	242.80	245.23	247.68
INCOME BEFORE TAXES	(10,809.33)	(944.24)	4,484.61	7,481.26	9,242.08	11,332.78	13,624.39
INCOME TAXES	(2,702.33)	(236.06)	1,121.15	1,870.31	2,310.52	2,833.19	3,406.10
NET INCOME	(8,107.00)	(708.18)	3,363.46	5,610.94	6,931.56	8,499.58	10,218.29

CASH FLOWS PROJECTIONS

	June	July	August	September	October	November	December
BEGINNING CASH	100,000.00	58,038.00	54,770.92	55,412.06	59,524.83	65,583.21	73,048.64
CASH RECEIPTS	19,685.00	51,582.46	77,975.06	99,080.19	110,953.95	120,515.42	131,375.39
CASH PAID OUT							
Accounts Payable	45,420.00	41,075.60	62,200.40	79,082.40	88,567.92	96,197.22	104,860.72
Operating Expenses	18,896.00	13,774.33	13,774.33	13,774.33	13,774.33	13,774.33	13,774.33
Other Expenses	233.33	235.86	238.02	240.40	242.80	245.23	247.88
Income Taxes	(2,702.33)	(236.06)	1,121.15	1,870.31	2,310.52	2,833.19	3,406.10
TOTAL CASH OUT	61,847.00	54,849.53	77,333.90	94,967.44	104,895.57	113,049.98	122,288.83
NET CASH FLOW	(41,962.00)	(3,267.08)	641.16	4,112.74	6,058.38	7,465.44	9,086.57
ENDING CASH	58,038.00	54,770.92	55,412.06	59,524.83	65,583.21	73,048.64	82,135.21

INCOME STATEMENT PROJECTIONS

Exhibit 6 *(Continued)*

1993

	January	February	March	April	May	June	July	August	September	October	November	December
SALES												
ORCA 336SX (Units)	22	23	24	25	27	28	29	31	32	34	36	37
ORCA 386 (Units)	41	45	50	55	60	66	73	80	88	97	101	107
ORCA 406 (Units)	29	32	35	39	42	46	50	55	59	65	71	77
ORCA 366SX	20,765.18	20,652.79	21,885.43	22,769.70	23,906.18	25,103.59	26,358.77	27,676.71	29,060.55	30,513.57	32,039.25	33,641.22
ORCA 386	53,293.24	58,622.56	64,484.82	70,933.30	76,026.61	82,526.17	90,780.99	99,859.08	109,844.99	120,829.49	124,333.55	130,550.23
ORCA 406	45,367.10	49,925.81	54,918.39	59,861.06	61,036.96	66,632.46	72,520.38	79,047.22	86,181.47	93,918.00	100,603.47	109,657.78
Supporting Products	27,646.77	30,063.26	32,746.99	35,563.57	38,813.16	41,849.27	45,567.69	49,556.61	53,866.93	58,612.48	62,320.34	66,283.54
TOTAL SALES	147,112.27	159,264.43	173,835.63	189,117.62	198,585.90	216,113.50	235,247.83	256,139.63	278,953.94	303,871.55	319,296.61	340,132.77
COST OF GOODS SOLD	117,689.82	127,427.54	139,068.51	151,294.10	158,868.72	172,890.80	188,198.26	204,911.70	223,163.15	243,097.24	255,437.29	272,106.21
GROSS MARGIN FROM SALES	29,422.45	31,856.89	34,787.13	37,823.52	39,717.18	43,222.70	47,049.57	51,227.93	55,790.79	60,774.31	63,859.32	68,026.55
OPERATING EXPENSES												
Office and Equipments	2,716.33	2,716.33	2,716.33	2,716.33	2,716.33	2,716.33	2,716.33	2,716.33	2,716.33	2,716.33	2,716.33	2,716.33
Legal Fees	1,000.00	1,000.00	1,000.00	1,000.00	1,000.00	1,000.00	1,000.00	1,000.00	1,000.00	1,000.00	1,000.00	1,000.00
Accounting Fees	183.33	183.33	183.33	183.33	183.33	183.33	183.33	183.33	183.33	183.33	183.33	183.33
Insurance	896.67	896.67	896.67	896.67	896.67	896.67	896.67	896.67	896.67	896.67	896.67	896.67
Depreciation	100.00	100.00	100.00	100.00	100.00	100.00	100.00	100.00	100.00	100.00	100.00	100.00
Advertisement Cost	500.00	500.00	500.00	500.00	500.00	500.00	500.00	500.00	500.00	500.00	500.00	500.00
Promotions/Comp. Shows	876.00	876.00	876.00	876.00	876.00	876.00	876.00	876.00	876.00	876.00	876.00	876.00
Staff Salaries	10,000.00	10,000.00	10,000.00	10,000.00	10,000.00	10,000.00	10,000.00	10,000.00	10,000.00	10,000.00	10,000.00	10,000.00
TOTAL OP. EXPENSES	16,074.33	16,074.33	16,074.33	16,074.33	16,074.33	16,074.33	16,074.33	16,074.33	16,074.33	16,074.33	16,074.33	16,074.33
OPERATING INCOME	13,348.12	15,782.56	18,692.80	21,749.19	23,642.85	27,148.37	30,975.24	35,153.60	39,716.46	44,699.98	47,784.99	51,952.22
INTEREST INCOME	336.75	466.87	509.73	573.50	646.61	733.99	828.80	937.50	1,061.39	1,201.89	1,360.53	1,536.08
OTHER EXPENSES	250.16	252.86	255.19	257.74	260.32	262.92	265.55	268.21	270.89	273.60	276.33	279.10
INCOME BEFORE TAXES	13,434.72	15,996.76	18,947.34	22,064.96	24,031.14	27,619.44	31,538.48	35,822.89	40,506.96	45,628.27	48,869.19	53,209.21
INCOME TAXES	3,356.68	3,996.44	4,736.83	5,516.24	6,007.78	6,904.86	7,884.62	8,955.72	10,126.74	11,407.07	12,217.30	13,302.30
NET INCOME	10,078.04	11,999.32	14,210.50	16,548.72	18,023.35	20,714.58	23,653.86	26,867.17	30,380.22	34,221.20	36,651.89	39,906.90

CASH FLOWS PROJECTIONS

	January	February	March	April	May	June	July	August	September	October	November	December
BEGINNING CASH	82,136.21	91,173.47	101,945.58	114,700.96	129,721.48	146,798.01	165,759.82	187,500.25	212,278.24	240,377.03	272,106.47	307,215.86
CASH RECEIPTS	142,260.16	153,654.22	167,089.76	182,050.13	194,500.37	208,083.89	226,509.46	246,531.23	268,608.18	292,614.63	312,944.61	331,250.77
CASH PAID OUT												
Accounts Payable	113,536.72	122,556.68	133,248.02	145,181.30	155,081.41	165,876.76	180,544.53	196,554.96	214,037.43	233,130.20	249,267.26	263,771.75
Operating Expenses	16,074.33	16,074.33	16,074.33	16,074.33	16,074.33	16,074.33	16,074.33	16,074.33	16,074.33	16,074.33	16,074.33	16,074.33
Other Expenses	250.16	252.86	255.19	257.74	260.32	262.92	265.55	268.21	270.89	273.60	276.33	279.10
Income Taxes	3,356.68	3,996.44	4,736.83	5,516.24	6,007.78	6,904.86	7,884.62	8,955.72	10,126.74	11,407.07	12,217.30	13,302.30
TOTAL CASH OUT	133,221.89	142,882.11	154,314.38	167,029.61	177,423.84	189,121.87	204,769.03	221,853.24	240,509.39	260,885.19	277,835.22	293,427.48
NET CASH FLOW	9,038.26	10,772.10	12,785.38	15,020.52	17,076.53	18,961.82	21,740.43	24,777.99	28,098.79	31,729.44	35,109.39	37,823.29
ENDING CASH	91,173.47	101,945.58	114,700.96	129,721.48	146,798.01	165,759.82	187,500.25	212,278.24	240,377.03	272,106.47	307,215.86	345,039.15

INCOME STATEMENT PROJECTIONS

1994	January	February	March	April	May	June	July	August	September	October	November	December
SALES												
ORCA 386SX (Units)	69	70	71	73	74	76	77	79	80	82	84	85
ORCA 386 (Units)	317	330	343	357	371	386	401	417	434	451	469	488
ORCA 486 (Units)	236	255	273	292	312	334	357	382	409	438	468	501
ORCA 386SX	61,623.09	62,855.55	64,112.66	65,394.91	66,702.81	68,036.87	69,397.60	70,785.56	72,201.27	73,645.29	75,118.20	76,620.56
ORCA 386	398,254.43	403,784.60	411,395.68	418,907.57	435,683.87	453,090.43	471,214.05	490,062.61	509,665.11	530,051.72	551,253.79	573,303.94
ORCA 486	339,187.44	362,930.58	381,622.80	406,229.39	436,805.44	467,381.83	500,098.56	535,105.46	572,562.84	612,842.24	655,527.20	701,414.10
Supporting Products	204,512.80	214,565.93	226,216.84	236,439.24	248,286.86	260,603.84	274,024.55	287,994.12	302,758.39	318,366.17	334,869.43	352,323.49
TOTAL SALES	993,577.85	1,044,156.64	1,062,218.16	1,126,971.12	1,187,461.03	1,249,212.97	1,314,734.76	1,383,947.74	1,457,187.61	1,534,706.42	1,616,768.61	1,703,662.09
COST OF GOODS SOLD	794,862.28	835,325.31	855,774.53	903,176.89	949,968.82	999,450.37	1,051,787.81	1,107,158.19	1,165,750.09	1,227,764.34	1,293,414.89	1,362,929.67
GROSS MARGIN FROM SALES	198,715.57	208,831.33	216,443.63	223,794.22	237,492.21	249,662.59	262,946.95	276,789.55	291,437.52	306,941.08	323,353.72	340,732.42
OPERATING EXPENSES												
Office and Equipments	3,376.33	3,376.33	3,376.33	3,376.33	3,376.33	3,376.33	3,376.33	3,376.33	3,376.33	3,376.33	3,376.33	3,376.33
Legal Fees	1,250.00	1,250.00	1,250.00	1,250.00	1,250.00	1,250.00	1,250.00	1,250.00	1,250.00	1,250.00	1,250.00	1,250.00
Accounting Fees	203.33	183.33	183.33	183.33	183.33	183.33	183.33	183.33	183.33	183.33	183.33	183.33
Insurance	914.50	896.67	896.67	896.67	896.67	896.67	896.67	896.67	896.67	896.67	896.67	896.67
Depreciation	100.00	100.00	100.00	100.00	100.00	100.00	100.00	100.00	100.00	100.00	100.00	100.00
Advertisement Cost	1,500.00	1,500.00	1,500.00	1,500.00	1,500.00	1,500.00	1,500.00	1,500.00	1,500.00	1,500.00	1,500.00	1,500.00
Promotions/Comp. Shows	877.00	676.00	676.00	676.00	676.00	676.00	676.00	676.00	676.00	676.00	676.00	676.00
Staff Salaries	12,000.00	12,000.00	12,000.00	12,000.00	12,000.00	12,000.00	12,000.00	12,000.00	12,000.00	12,000.00	12,000.00	12,000.00
TOTAL OP. EXPENSES	20,221.16	19,982.33	19,982.33	19,982.33	19,982.33	19,982.33	19,982.33	19,982.33	19,982.33	19,982.33	19,982.33	19,982.33
OPERATING INCOME	178,494.41	188,849.00	196,461.30	205,811.89	217,509.88	229,680.26	242,964.62	256,807.22	271,455.19	286,958.75	303,371.39	320,750.09
INTEREST INCOME	6,584.30	7,244.90	7,953.76	8,700.07	10,996.66	11,965.31	12,969.96	14,043.67	15,180.45	16,383.33	17,656.40	19,003.75
OTHER EXPENSES	317.64	320.81	324.02	327.26	330.54	333.84	337.18	340.55	343.96	347.40	350.87	354.38
INCOME BEFORE TAXES	184,761.07	195,773.08	204,091.03	214,184.70	228,176.00	241,501.73	255,597.41	270,510.53	286,291.66	302,994.89	320,676.92	339,399.46
INCOME TAXES	46,190.27	48,943.27	51,022.76	53,546.17	57,044.00	60,375.43	63,899.35	67,627.63	71,572.92	75,748.67	80,169.23	84,849.86
NET INCOME	138,570.81	146,829.81	153,068.29	160,638.52	171,132.00	181,126.30	191,698.06	202,882.90	214,718.74	227,246.02	240,507.69	254,549.59

CASH FLOWS PROJECTIONS

	January	February	March	April	May	June	July	August	September	October	November	December
BEGINNING CASH	1,316,660.56	1,448,976.27	1,560,761.20	1,740,013.33	1,885,978.56	2,061,259.56	2,236,200.67	2,421,356.54	2,617,318.14	2,824,712.92	3,044,207.16	3,276,508.53
CASH RECEIPTS	987,901.56	1,026,112.14	1,071,141.15	1,114,294.70	1,169,212.74	1,230,342.30	1,294,993.83	1,363,365.12	1,435,746.12	1,512,329.65	1,593,393.42	1,679,219.10
CASH PAID OUT												
Accounts Payable	769,053.80	815,093.80	850,549.92	864,476.71	926,672.86	974,709.60	1,025,619.09	1,079,473.00	1,136,454.14	1,196,757.21	1,260,569.61	1,328,172.28
Operating Expenses	20,221.16	19,982.33	19,982.33	19,982.33	19,982.33	19,982.33	19,982.33	19,982.33	19,982.33	19,982.33	19,982.33	19,982.33
Other Expenses	317.64	320.81	324.02	327.26	330.54	333.84	337.18	340.55	343.96	347.40	350.87	354.38
Income Taxes	46,190.27	48,943.27	51,022.76	53,546.17	57,044.00	60,375.43	63,899.35	67,627.63	71,572.92	75,748.67	80,169.23	84,849.86
TOTAL CASH OUT	835,782.87	884,340.21	921,879.03	938,331.48	1,003,929.73	1,055,401.20	1,109,837.95	1,167,423.52	1,228,353.35	1,292,835.61	1,361,092.04	1,433,358.85
NET CASH FLOW	132,118.69	141,771.93	149,262.12	165,963.23	165,283.01	174,941.10	185,155.88	195,961.60	207,394.77	219,494.24	232,301.37	245,860.25
ENDING CASH	1,448,979.27	1,590,761.20	1,740,013.33	1,895,976.55	2,061,259.56	2,236,200.67	2,421,356.54	2,617,318.14	2,824,712.92	3,044,207.16	3,276,508.53	3,522,366.77

Exhibit 6 (Continued)

1 • 25

Exhibit 6 (Continued)

INCOME STATEMENT PROJECTIONS
1995

	January	February	March	April	May	June	July	August	September	October	November	December
SALES												
ORCA 386SX (Units)	196	198	200	202	204	206	208	210	212	214	217	219
ORCA 386 (Units)	2346	2463	2586	2715	2851	2994	3143	3300	3465	3639	3821	4012
ORCA 486 (Units)	3490	3735	3996	4278	4575	4895	5238	5605	5997	6417	6866	7346
ORCA 386SX	166,847.80	168,314.28	169,907.42	171,607.40	173,414.37	175,148.52	176,900.00	178,669.00	180,455.69	182,260.25	184,082.85	185,923.68
ORCA 386	2,636,726.63	2,770,662.97	2,909,196.11	3,054,655.92	3,207,386.72	3,367,756.15	3,536,146.08	3,712,953.38	3,698,801.03	4,093,531.06	4,298,207.64	4,513,118.02
ORCA 486	4,711,789.42	5,041,614.68	5,394,527.71	5,772,144.65	6,176,194.77	6,608,528.40	7,071,125.39	7,566,104.17	8,096,731.46	8,662,432.66	9,266,802.95	9,917,619.16
Supporting Products	2,093,036.48	2,219,189.13	2,353,317.75	2,495,939.54	2,647,605.90	2,808,904.66	2,980,462.55	3,162,947.83	3,357,073.04	3,563,598.01	3,783,333.03	4,017,142.23
TOTAL SALES	9,610,200.33	10,199,781.06	10,827,038.99	11,494,437.51	12,204,603.76	12,960,339.73	13,764,634.00	14,620,674.38	15,531,961.22	16,501,822.01	17,534,426.47	18,633,803.08
COST OF GOODS SOLD	7,665,160.27	8,159,824.84	8,661,631.19	9,195,550.00	9,763,683.01	10,368,271.78	11,011,707.20	11,696,539.49	12,425,488.96	13,201,457.60	14,027,541.17	14,907,042.47
GROSS MARGIN FROM SALES	1,922,040.07	2,039,956.21	2,165,407.80	2,296,887.50	2,440,920.75	2,592,067.95	2,752,926.80	2,924,134.87	3,106,372.24	3,300,364.40	3,506,885.29	3,726,760.62
OPERATING EXPENSES												
Office and Equipments	3,685.20	3,685.20	3,685.20	3,685.20	3,685.20	3,685.20	3,685.20	3,685.20	3,685.20	3,685.20	3,685.20	3,685.20
Legal Fees	1,250.00	1,250.00	1,250.00	1,250.00	1,250.00	1,250.00	1,250.00	1,250.00	1,250.00	1,250.00	1,250.00	1,250.00
Accounting Fees	201.66	201.66	201.66	201.66	201.66	201.66	201.66	201.66	201.66	201.66	201.66	201.66
Insurance	905.64	905.64	905.64	905.64	905.64	905.64	905.64	905.64	905.64	905.64	905.64	905.64
Depreciation	110.00	110.00	110.00	110.00	110.00	110.00	110.00	110.00	110.00	110.00	110.00	110.00
Advertisement Cost	1,500.00	1,500.00	1,500.00	1,500.00	1,500.00	1,500.00	1,500.00	1,500.00	1,500.00	1,500.00	1,500.00	1,500.00
Promotional/Comp. Shows	676.00	676.00	676.00	676.00	676.00	676.00	676.00	676.00	676.00	676.00	676.00	676.00
Staff Salaries	13,800.00	13,800.00	13,800.00	13,800.00	13,800.00	13,800.00	13,800.00	13,800.00	13,800.00	13,800.00	13,800.00	13,800.00
TOTAL OP. EXPENSES	22,128.50	22,128.50	22,128.50	22,128.50	22,128.50	22,128.50	22,128.50	22,128.50	22,128.50	22,128.50	22,128.50	22,128.50
OPERATING INCOME	1,899,911.67	2,017,827.71	2,143,279.30	2,276,759.00	2,418,792.25	2,569,939.45	2,730,798.30	2,902,006.37	3,084,243.74	3,278,235.90	3,484,756.79	3,704,632.12
INTEREST INCOME	128,527.93	135,121.72	144,143.09	153,727.55	163,911.04	174,731.85	186,230.76	198,451.25	211,439.62	225,245.21	239,920.82	255,521.67
OTHER EXPENSES	454.47	459.01	463.60	468.24	472.92	477.65	482.43	487.25	492.12	497.04	502.01	507.03
INCOME BEFORE TAXES	2,025,985.03	2,152,490.41	2,286,958.79	2,430,018.32	2,582,230.37	2,744,193.64	2,916,546.64	3,099,970.37	3,295,191.24	3,502,984.07	3,724,175.39	3,959,646.95
INCOME TAXES	506,496.26	538,122.60	571,739.70	607,504.58	645,557.59	686,048.41	729,136.66	774,992.59	823,797.81	875,746.02	931,043.85	989,911.74
NET INCOME	1,519,488.78	1,614,367.81	1,715,219.09	1,822,513.74	1,936,672.78	2,058,144.23	2,187,409.98	2,324,977.78	2,471,393.43	2,627,238.05	2,793,131.55	2,969,735.21

CASH FLOWS PROJECTIONS

	January	February	March	April	May	June	July	August	September	October	November	December
BEGINNING CASH	21,815,161.08	23,296,847.61	24,852,257.35	26,504,760.85	28,280,524.53	30,128,160.85	32,108,762.33	34,215,732.66	36,455,106.62	38,635,361.36	41,365,623.34	44,055,494.44
CASH RECEIPTS	9,547,717.03	10,040,112.41	10,657,563.11	11,314,465.90	12,013,431.67	12,757,203.59	13,548,717.63	14,391,105.43	15,287,707.41	18,242,066.83	17,258,044.65	18,339,636.64
CASH PAID OUT												
Accounts Payable	7,536,951.26	7,923,992.55	8,410,726.02	8,925,590.80	9,479,616.51	10,065,977.40	10,659,969.49	11,354,123.34	12,081,014.23	12,813,473.29	13,614,499.39	14,467,291.82
Operating Expenses	22,128.50	22,128.50	22,128.50	22,128.50	22,128.50	22,128.50	22,128.50	22,128.50	22,128.50	22,128.50	22,128.50	22,128.50
Other Expenses	454.47	459.01	463.60	468.24	472.92	477.65	482.43	487.25	492.12	497.04	502.01	507.03
Income Taxes	506,496.26	538,122.60	571,739.70	607,504.58	645,557.59	686,048.41	729,136.66	774,992.59	823,797.81	875,746.02	931,043.85	989,911.74
TOTAL CASH OUT	8,066,030.50	8,484,702.67	9,005,059.82	9,556,091.91	10,147,775.52	10,774,631.96	11,441,737.06	12,151,731.69	12,907,432.96	13,711,844.65	14,568,173.75	15,479,839.09
NET CASH FLOW	1,481,686.53	1,555,409.74	1,652,493.30	1,758,773.99	1,865,656.16	1,982,571.64	2,106,990.55	2,239,373.74	2,380,274.74	2,530,241.97	2,689,871.10	2,859,797.55
ENDING CASH	23,296,847.61	24,852,257.35	26,504,750.65	28,260,524.83	30,128,180.69	32,108,732.33	34,215,732.66	36,455,106.62	38,635,361.36	41,365,623.34	44,055,494.44	46,915,291.99

Exhibit 6   (*Continued*)

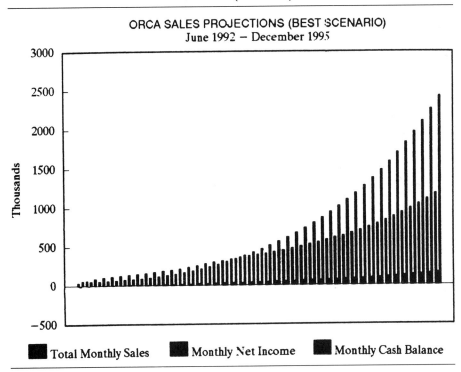

ORCA SALES PROJECTIONS (BEST SCENARIO)
June 1992 – December 1995

Exhibit 7   Financial Statement and Cash Flows, Moderate Scenario

INCOME STATEMENT PROJECTIONS

	1992						
	June	July	August	September	October	November	December
SALES							
ORCA 386SX (Units)	5	9	13	16	17	18	19
ORCA 386 (Units)	10	13	15	19	20	21	22
ORCA 486 (Units)	5	8	11	14	15	15	16
ORCA 386SX	4,950.00	8,910.00	12,870.00	15,840.00	15,960.00	16,758.00	17,595.90
ORCA 386	13,500.00	17,550.00	20,250.00	25,650.00	26,932.50	28,279.13	29,693.08
ORCA 486	7,995.00	12,792.00	17,589.00	22,386.00	23,505.30	24,680.57	25,914.59
Supporting Products	5,680.00	8,520.00	11,076.00	13,916.00	14,611.80	15,342.39	16,109.51
TOTAL SALES	32,125.00	47,772.00	61,785.00	77,792.00	81,009.60	85,060.08	89,313.08
COST OF GOODS SOLD	25,700.00	38,217.60	49,428.00	62,233.60	64,807.68	68,048.06	71,450.47
GROSS MARGIN FROM SALES	6,425.00	9,554.40	12,357.00	15,558.40	16,201.92	17,012.02	17,862.62
OPERATING EXPENSES							
Office and Equipments	15,090.00	2,718.33	2,718.33	2,718.33	2,718.33	2,718.33	2,718.33
Legal Fees	1,000.00	1,000.00	1,000.00	1,000.00	1,000.00	1,000.00	1,000.00
Accounting Fees	163.33	163.33	163.33	163.33	163.33	163.33	163.33
Insurance	866.67	866.67	866.67	866.67	866.67	866.67	866.67
Depreciation	100.00	100.00	100.00	100.00	100.00	100.00	100.00
Advertisement Cost	300.00	250.00	250.00	250.00	250.00	250.00	250.00
Promotions/Comp. Shows	676.00	676.00	676.00	676.00	676.00	676.00	676.00
Staff Salaries	500.00	8,000.00	8,000.00	8,000.00	8,000.00	8,000.00	8,000.00
TOTAL OP. EXPENSES	18,696.00	13,774.33	13,774.33	13,774.33	13,774.33	13,774.33	13,774.33
OPERATING INCOME	(12,271.00)	(4,219.93)	(1,417.33)	1,784.07	2,427.59	3,237.69	4,088.29
INTEREST INCOME	410.00	238.84	217.25	207.08	205.90	211.94	220.13
OTHER EXPENSES	233.33	235.66	238.02	240.40	242.80	245.23	247.68
INCOME BEFORE TAXES	(12,094.33)	(4,216.95)	(1,438.10)	1,750.75	2,390.69	3,204.39	4,060.73
INCOME TAXES	(3,023.58)	(1,054.74)	(359.52)	437.69	597.67	801.10	1,015.18
NET INCOME	(9,070.75)	(3,164.22)	(1,078.57)	1,313.06	1,793.02	2,403.29	3,045.55

CASH FLOWS PROJECTIONS

	1992						
	June	July	August	September	October	November	December
BEGINNING CASH	100,000.00	57,716.75	52,987.84	50,507.96	50,220.33	51,691.58	53,689.83
CASH RECEIPTS	16,472.50	40,185.14	54,995.75	69,995.56	79,606.70	83,246.76	87,406.71
CASH PAID OUT							
Accounts Payable	42,850.00	31,956.80	43,822.80	55,830.80	63,520.64	66,427.87	69,749.27
Operating Expenses	18,696.00	13,774.33	13,774.33	13,774.33	13,774.33	13,774.33	13,774.33
Other Expenses	233.33	235.66	238.02	240.40	242.80	245.23	247.68
Income Taxes	(3,023.58)	(1,054.74)	(359.52)	437.69	597.67	801.10	1,015.18
TOTAL CASH OUT	58,755.75	44,914.05	57,475.62	70,283.22	78,135.45	81,248.53	84,786.46
NET CASH FLOW	(42,283.25)	(4,728.92)	(2,479.87)	(287.64)	1,471.26	1,998.24	2,620.25
ENDING CASH	57,716.75	52,987.84	50,507.96	50,220.33	51,691.58	53,689.83	56,310.07

INCOME STATEMENT PROJECTIONS
1993

	January	February	March	April	May	June	July	August	September	October	November	December
SALES												
ORCA 386SX (Units)	19	20	21	23	24	25	26	27	29	30	32	33
ORCA 386 (Units)	23	24	25	27	28	29	31	32	34	36	38	39
ORCA 486 (Units)	17	18	19	20	21	22	23	24	25	28	28	29
ORCA 386SX	18,476.68	18,356.03	19,276.94	20,239.73	21,251.72	22,314.31	23,430.02	24,601.52	25,831.60	27,123.18	28,479.34	29,903.30
ORCA 386	30,023.00	31,524.15	33,100.36	34,755.38	35,090.57	36,844.06	36,686.25	40,620.56	42,651.59	44,784.17	46,062.91	48,367.05
ORCA 486	26,376.49	27,905.31	29,080.08	30,534.08	29,992.35	31,491.96	33,066.56	34,719.89	36,455.88	38,278.68	39,499.64	41,474.62
Supporting Products	17,867.94	18,781.34	19,699.41	20,684.38	21,718.60	22,804.52	23,944.75	25,141.99	26,399.09	27,719.04	29,104.99	30,560.24
TOTAL SALES	92,743.13	96,336.84	101,155.78	106,213.67	108,062.23	113,454.84	119,127.58	125,083.96	131,336.16	137,905.06	143,166.87	150,325.22
COST OF GOODS SOLD	74,194.50	77,071.07	80,924.62	84,970.85	86,441.78	90,763.87	95,302.06	100,067.17	105,070.53	110,324.05	114,533.50	120,260.17
GROSS MARGIN FROM SALES	18,548.63	19,267.77	20,231.16	21,242.71	21,610.45	22,690.97	23,825.52	25,016.79	26,267.63	27,581.01	28,633.37	30,065.04
OPERATING EXPENSES												
Office and Equipments	2,716.33	2,716.33	2,716.33	2,716.33	2,716.33	2,716.33	2,716.33	2,716.33	2,716.33	2,716.33	2,716.33	2,716.33
Legal Fees	1,000.00	1,000.00	1,000.00	1,000.00	1,000.00	1,000.00	1,000.00	1,000.00	1,000.00	1,000.00	1,000.00	1,000.00
Accounting Fees	183.33	183.33	183.33	183.33	183.33	183.33	183.33	183.33	183.33	183.33	183.33	183.33
Insurance	696.67	696.67	696.67	696.67	696.67	696.67	696.67	696.67	696.67	696.67	696.67	696.67
Depreciation	100.00	100.00	100.00	100.00	100.00	100.00	100.00	100.00	100.00	100.00	100.00	100.00
Advertisement Cost	500.00	500.00	500.00	500.00	500.00	500.00	500.00	500.00	500.00	500.00	500.00	500.00
Promotional/Comp. Shows	676.00	676.00	676.00	676.00	676.00	676.00	676.00	676.00	676.00	676.00	676.00	676.00
Staff Salaries	9,800.00	9,800.00	9,800.00	9,800.00	9,800.00	9,800.00	9,800.00	9,800.00	9,800.00	9,800.00	9,800.00	9,800.00
TOTAL OP. EXPENSES	15,874.33	15,874.33	15,874.33	15,874.33	15,874.33	15,874.33	15,874.33	15,874.33	15,874.33	15,874.33	15,874.33	15,874.33
OPERATING INCOME	2,674.30	3,393.44	4,356.83	5,368.38	5,736.12	6,816.64	7,951.19	9,142.46	10,393.30	11,706.68	12,759.04	14,190.71
INTEREST INCOME	230.87	269.79	300.66	314.96	332.78	363.64	376.84	404.24	436.05	472.52	513.68	559.99
OTHER EXPENSES	250.16	262.66	265.19	267.74	260.32	262.92	265.55	268.21	270.69	273.60	276.33	279.10
INCOME BEFORE TAXES	2,655.01	3,430.57	4,402.49	5,425.60	5,808.57	6,907.35	8,082.48	9,278.49	10,558.47	11,905.61	12,996.60	14,471.61
INCOME TAXES	663.76	857.64	1,100.62	1,356.40	1,452.14	1,726.84	2,015.62	2,319.62	2,639.62	2,976.40	3,249.15	3,617.90
NET INCOME	1,991.25	2,572.92	3,301.87	4,069.20	4,356.43	5,180.52	6,046.86	6,958.87	7,918.86	8,929.21	9,747.45	10,853.71

CASH FLOWS PROJECTIONS

	January	February	March	April	May	June	July	August	September	October	November	December
BEGINNING CASH	84,310.07	87,968.32	80,171.68	82,961.96	86,555.28	70,727.84	76,368.10	80,847.68	87,210.91	94,504.34	102,776.85	111,998.12
CASH RECEIPTS	91,258.96	84,830.77	90,046.17	103,999.83	107,465.67	111,107.17	116,868.05	122,510.01	128,847.11	135,094.13	141,049.85	147,306.04
CASH PAID OUT												
Accounts Payable	72,822.48	76,632.79	76,997.85	82,847.74	85,708.32	88,602.83	93,032.97	97,664.82	102,566.85	107,897.29	112,428.76	117,396.64
Operating Expenses	15,874.33	15,874.33	15,874.33	15,874.33	15,874.33	15,874.33	15,874.33	15,874.33	15,874.33	15,874.33	15,874.33	15,874.33
Other Expenses	250.16	262.66	265.19	267.74	260.32	262.92	265.55	268.21	270.69	273.60	276.33	279.10
Income Taxes	663.76	857.64	1,100.62	1,356.40	1,452.14	1,726.84	2,015.62	2,319.62	2,639.62	2,976.40	3,249.18	3,617.90
TOTAL CASH OUT	89,610.73	92,617.42	96,227.99	100,439.21	103,293.11	106,466.92	111,188.47	116,146.78	121,353.98	126,821.62	131,826.59	137,168.17
NET CASH FLOW	1,648.25	2,213.35	2,820.18	3,863.42	4,172.56	4,640.25	5,479.58	6,363.23	7,293.43	8,272.51	9,221.27	10,137.87
ENDING CASH	87,958.32	90,171.68	82,991.86	86,855.28	70,727.84	75,368.10	80,847.68	87,210.91	94,504.34	102,776.65	111,998.12	122,135.99

Exhibit 7 *(Continued)*

Exhibit 7 (Continued)

INCOME STATEMENT PROJECTIONS

1994

	January	February	March	April	May	June	July	August	September	October	November	December
SALES												
ORCA 386SX (Units)	48	49	50	51	52	53	54	55	56	57	58	59
ORCA 386 (Units)	58	60	63	65	68	70	73	76	79	82	86	89
ORCA 486 (Units)	44	47	50	54	57	61	66	70	75	81	86	92
ORCA 386SX	42,918.49	43,778.86	44,652.40	45,545.44	46,456.35	47,385.48	48,333.19	49,299.85	50,285.85	51,291.57	52,317.40	53,363.75
ORCA 386	70,808.86	73,841.22	75,023.67	76,399.30	79,455.28	82,833.49	86,938.63	89,376.38	92,961.44	98,660.40	100,536.27	104,567.72
ORCA 486	62,444.08	66,815.16	70,237.98	75,164.83	80,415.46	86,044.54	92,067.86	96,512.39	105,406.28	112,788.84	120,681.92	129,129.85
Supporting Products	48,991.33	51,099.00	53,253.70	55,551.69	57,969.64	60,514.64	63,194.23	66,016.41	68,969.73	72,123.25	75,426.64	78,910.16
TOTAL SALES	225,162.76	235,302.24	243,167.94	252,661.07	264,296.73	276,778.15	289,533.90	303,205.04	317,635.28	332,871.16	348,962.23	365,961.29
COST OF GOODS SOLD	180,130.21	188,241.79	194,534.35	202,120.86	211,437.39	221,282.52	231,627.12	242,564.03	254,108.22	266,296.92	279,169.78	292,769.03
GROSS MARGIN FROM SALES	45,032.55	47,060.45	48,633.59	50,530.21	52,859.35	55,315.63	57,906.78	60,641.01	63,527.06	66,574.23	69,792.45	73,192.26
OPERATING EXPENSES												
Office and Equipments	3,376.33	3,376.33	3,376.33	3,376.33	3,376.33	3,376.33	3,376.33	3,376.33	3,376.33	3,376.33	3,376.33	3,376.33
Legal Fees	1,250.00	1,250.00	1,250.00	1,250.00	1,250.00	1,250.00	1,250.00	1,250.00	1,250.00	1,250.00	1,250.00	1,250.00
Accounting Fees	203.33	183.33	183.33	183.33	183.33	183.33	183.33	183.33	183.33	183.33	183.33	183.33
Insurance	914.50	896.67	896.67	896.67	896.67	896.67	896.67	896.67	896.67	896.67	896.67	896.67
Depreciation	100.00	100.00	100.00	100.00	100.00	100.00	100.00	100.00	100.00	100.00	100.00	100.00
Advertisement Cost	1,500.00	1,500.00	1,500.00	1,500.00	1,500.00	1,500.00	1,500.00	1,500.00	1,500.00	1,500.00	1,500.00	1,500.00
Promotional/Comp. Shows	877.00	676.00	676.00	676.00	676.00	676.00	676.00	676.00	676.00	676.00	676.00	676.00
Staff Salaries	11,800.00	11,800.00	11,800.00	11,800.00	11,800.00	11,800.00	11,800.00	11,800.00	11,800.00	11,800.00	11,800.00	11,800.00
TOTAL OP. EXPENSES	19,821.16	19,582.33	19,582.33	19,582.33	19,582.33	19,582.33	19,582.33	19,582.33	19,582.33	19,582.33	19,582.33	19,582.33
OPERATING INCOME	25,211.39	27,478.12	29,051.26	30,947.88	33,277.02	35,733.30	38,324.45	41,058.68	43,944.73	46,991.90	50,210.12	53,609.93
INTEREST INCOME	1,148.48	1,239.35	1,340.63	1,449.71	1,815.74	1,960.27	2,115.73	2,282.74	2,461.93	2,654.01	2,859.69	3,079.76
OTHER EXPENSES	302.22	305.24	308.30	311.38	314.49	317.64	320.81	324.02	327.26	330.54	333.84	337.18
INCOME BEFORE TAXES	26,057.63	28,412.22	30,083.79	32,086.21	34,778.26	37,376.93	40,119.37	43,017.39	46,079.39	49,316.37	52,735.97	56,352.51
INCOME TAXES	6,514.41	7,103.06	7,520.95	8,021.55	8,694.56	9,343.98	10,029.84	10,754.35	11,519.85	12,328.84	13,183.99	14,088.13
NET INCOME	19,543.22	21,309.17	22,562.84	24,064.66	26,083.69	28,032.95	30,089.52	32,263.04	34,559.54	36,988.53	39,551.97	42,244.38

CASH FLOWS PROJECTIONS

	January	February	March	April	May	June	July	August	September	October	November	December
BEGINNING CASH	225,681.00	247,870.30	268,165.52	288,165.52	313,058.14	337,977.27	364,781.08	393,575.02	424,470.95	457,587.47	493,060.42	530,903.28
CASH RECEIPTS	219,491.17	231,471.85	240,575.91	249,369.21	260,269.64	272,397.71	285,171.75	296,652.20	312,882.09	327,907.22	343,776.38	360,541.52
CASH PAID OUT												
Accounts Payable	174,674.17	184,166.00	191,366.07	198,327.60	206,779.12	216,349.95	226,444.82	237,096.58	248,336.13	260,202.57	272,733.35	285,969.41
Operating Expenses	19,821.16	19,582.33	19,582.33	19,582.33	19,582.33	19,582.33	19,582.33	19,582.33	19,582.33	19,582.33	19,582.33	19,582.33
Other Expenses	302.22	305.24	308.30	311.38	314.49	317.64	320.81	324.02	327.26	330.54	333.84	337.18
Income Taxes	6,514.41	7,103.06	7,520.95	8,021.55	8,694.56	9,343.98	10,029.84	10,754.35	11,519.85	12,328.84	13,183.99	14,088.13
TOTAL CASH OUT	201,311.96	211,178.63	218,799.64	226,242.67	236,370.51	245,593.90	256,377.81	267,756.28	279,765.57	292,444.28	305,833.51	319,977.04
NET CASH FLOW	18,179.21	20,295.22	21,776.27	23,116.56	24,919.13	26,803.81	28,793.95	30,896.93	33,116.52	35,462.94	37,942.87	40,564.48
ENDING CASH	247,870.30	268,165.52	288,941.79	313,058.14	337,977.27	364,781.08	393,575.02	424,470.95	457,587.47	493,050.42	530,993.28	571,557.76

Exhibit 7 (Continued)

INCOME STATEMENT PROJECTIONS
1995

	January	February	March	April	May	June	July	August	September	October	November	December
SALES												
ORCA 386SX (Units)	174	176	176	180	181	183	185	187	189	191	193	194
ORCA 386 (Units)	343	360	378	397	417	438	459	482	507	532	558	586
ORCA 486 (Units)	506	545	583	624	668	715	765	818	875	937	1002	1072
ORCA 386SX	148,131.36	149,612.69	151,108.82	152,619.91	154,146.11	155,687.57	157,244.44	158,816.89	160,405.06	162,009.11	163,629.20	165,265.49
ORCA 386	365,725.39	405,011.66	426,262.24	446,525.36	468,851.63	492,294.21	516,908.92	542,754.36	569,892.08	598,386.68	628,306.02	659,721.32
ORCA 486	697,763.16	735,906.58	767,420.04	842,639.45	901,517.21	964,623.41	1,032,147.05	1,104,397.34	1,181,705.16	1,264,424.52	1,352,934.24	1,447,639.63
Supporting Products	366,227.92	375,155.03	395,253.85	416,596.94	439,285.67	463,346.52	488,930.44	516,115.25	545,005.04	575,710.62	608,350.92	643,051.58
TOTAL SALES	1,577,847.95	1,665,686.94	1,739,044.95	1,855,281.66	1,963,780.81	2,075,951.70	2,195,230.85	2,322,083.84	2,457,007.34	2,600,531.13	2,753,220.38	2,915,678.03
COST OF GOODS SOLD	1,262,276.28	1,332,549.57	1,407,235.96	1,486,625.32	1,571,024.65	1,660,761.36	1,756,184.68	1,857,667.08	1,965,605.87	2,080,424.90	2,202,576.30	2,332,542.42
GROSS MARGIN FROM SALES	315,569.67	333,137.39	351,808.99	371,656.33	392,756.16	415,190.34	439,046.17	464,416.77	491,401.47	520,106.23	550,644.08	583,135.61
OPERATING EXPENSES												
Office and Equipments	3,665.20	3,665.20	3,665.20	3,665.20	3,665.20	3,665.20	3,665.20	3,665.20	3,665.20	3,665.20	3,665.20	3,665.20
Legal Fees	1,250.00	1,250.00	1,250.00	1,250.00	1,250.00	1,250.00	1,250.00	1,250.00	1,250.00	1,250.00	1,250.00	1,250.00
Accounting Fees	201.66	201.66	201.66	201.66	201.66	201.66	201.66	201.66	201.66	201.66	201.66	201.66
Insurance	905.64	905.64	905.64	905.64	905.64	905.64	905.64	905.64	905.64	905.64	905.64	905.64
Depreciation	110.00	110.00	110.00	110.00	110.00	110.00	110.00	110.00	110.00	110.00	110.00	110.00
Advertisement Cost	1,500.00	1,500.00	1,500.00	1,500.00	1,500.00	1,500.00	1,500.00	1,500.00	1,500.00	1,500.00	1,500.00	1,500.00
Promotions/Comp. Shows	676.00	676.00	676.00	676.00	676.00	676.00	676.00	676.00	676.00	676.00	676.00	676.00
Staff Salaries	14,500.00	14,500.00	14,500.00	14,500.00	14,500.00	14,500.00	14,500.00	14,500.00	14,500.00	14,500.00	14,500.00	14,500.00
TOTAL OP. EXPENSES	22,828.50	22,828.50	22,828.50	22,828.50	22,828.50	22,828.50	22,828.50	22,828.50	22,828.50	22,828.50	22,828.50	22,828.50
OPERATING INCOME	292,741.07	310,308.89	328,980.49	348,827.83	369,927.66	392,361.84	416,217.67	441,588.27	468,572.97	497,277.73	527,815.58	560,307.11
INTEREST INCOME	22,741.36	24,061.24	25,482.90	26,968.66	28,543.77	30,213.87	31,984.94	33,863.34	35,856.66	37,969.73	40,212.65	42,592.83
OTHER EXPENSES	454.47	469.01	463.60	466.24	472.92	477.86	482.43	487.26	492.12	497.04	502.01	507.03
INCOME BEFORE TAXES	315,027.96	333,931.12	353,999.79	376,328.24	397,998.51	422,098.06	447,720.18	474,964.36	503,936.71	534,750.41	567,526.21	602,392.90
INCOME TAXES	78,757.00	83,482.78	88,499.95	93,832.06	99,499.63	105,524.52	111,930.05	118,741.09	125,984.18	133,687.60	141,881.55	150,598.23
NET INCOME	236,270.96	250,448.34	264,499.84	281,496.18	298,498.88	316,473.54	334,790.14	354,223.27	377,952.53	401,062.81	425,644.66	451,794.66

CASH FLOWS PROJECTIONS

	January	February	March	April	May	June	July	August	September	October	November	December
BEGINNING CASH	3,820,927.20	4,161,938.32	4,393,802.75	4,840,766.79	4,921,339.30	5,209,286.27	5,514,644.72	5,838,506.95	6,182,044.92	6,546,506.10	6,933,215.53	7,343,561.26
CASH RECEIPTS	1,574,269.91	1,845,848.65	1,737,848.86	1,835,631.95	1,939,675.00	2,050,080.13	2,167,576.22	2,292,520.69	2,425,401.45	2,566,736.97	2,717,066.40	2,877,042.03
CASH PAID OUT												
Accounts Payable	1,241,236.83	1,297,413.93	1,360,692.77	1,399,930.64	1,526,824.99	1,615,893.01	1,706,473.02	1,806,925.86	1,911,636.47	2,023,015.39	2,141,500.80	2,267,559.36
Operating Expenses	22,828.50	22,828.50	22,828.50	22,828.50	22,828.50	22,828.50	22,828.50	22,828.50	22,828.50	22,828.50	22,828.50	22,828.50
Other Expenses	454.47	469.01	463.60	466.24	472.92	477.86	482.43	487.25	492.12	497.04	502.01	507.03
Income Taxes	78,767.00	83,482.78	86,499.95	93,832.06	99,499.63	105,524.52	111,930.05	118,741.09	125,984.18	133,687.60	141,881.55	150,598.23
TOTAL CASH OUT	1,343,278.79	1,404,184.22	1,461,684.82	1,564,059.44	1,651,826.03	1,744,723.67	1,843,713.99	1,948,982.72	2,060,941.27	2,180,028.04	2,306,712.87	2,441,493.12
NET CASH FLOW	231,011.12	241,664.43	276,164.04	271,572.51	287,848.97	305,356.46	323,862.22	343,537.97	364,460.18	386,710.43	410,376.73	435,548.91
ENDING CASH	4,161,938.32	4,393,802.75	4,849,788.79	4,921,339.30	5,209,286.27	5,514,644.72	5,838,506.95	6,182,044.92	6,546,506.10	6,933,215.53	7,343,561.26	7,779,140.17

Exhibit 7   (Continued)

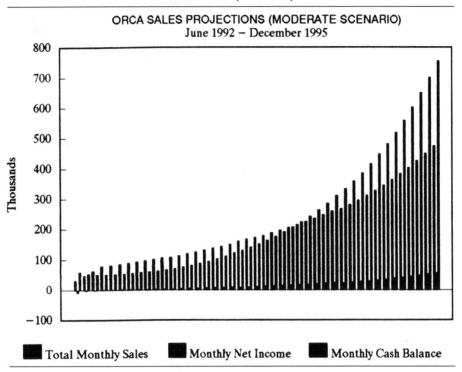

ORCA SALES PROJECTIONS (MODERATE SCENARIO)
June 1992 – December 1995

Exhibit 8   Financial Statement and Cash Flows, Worst Scenario

INCOME STATEMENT PROJECTIONS

	1992 June	July	August	September	October	November	December
SALES							
ORCA 386SX (Units)	4	6	8	11	11	12	12
ORCA 386 (Units)	7	9	10	13	13	14	14
ORCA 486 (Units)	4	6	7	10	10	11	11
ORCA 386SX	3,960.00	5,940.00	7,920.00	10,890.00	10,763.50	11,086.41	11,419.00
ORCA 386	9,450.00	12,150.00	13,500.00	17,550.00	18,076.50	18,818.79	19,177.36
ORCA 486	6,396.00	9,594.00	11,193.00	15,990.00	16,469.70	16,963.79	17,472.70
Supporting Products	4,260.00	5,964.00	7,100.00	9,656.00	9,945.68	10,244.05	10,551.37
TOTAL SALES	24,066.00	33,648.00	39,713.00	54,066.00	55,255.38	56,913.04	58,620.43
COST OF GOODS SOLD	19,252.80	26,918.40	31,770.40	43,268.80	44,204.30	45,530.43	46,896.35
GROSS MARGIN FROM SALES	4,813.20	6,729.60	7,942.60	10,817.20	11,051.08	11,382.61	11,724.09
OPERATING EXPENSES							
Office and Equipments	15,090.00	2,718.33	2,718.33	2,718.33	2,718.33	2,718.33	2,718.33
Legal Fees	1,000.00	1,000.00	1,000.00	1,000.00	1,000.00	1,000.00	1,000.00
Accounting Fees	163.33	163.33	163.33	163.33	163.33	163.33	163.33
Insurance	866.67	866.67	866.67	866.67	866.67	866.67	866.67
Depreciation	100.00	100.00	100.00	100.00	100.00	100.00	100.00
Advertisement Cost	300.00	250.00	250.00	250.00	250.00	250.00	250.00
Promotions/Comp. Shows	676.00	676.00	676.00	676.00	676.00	676.00	676.00
Staff Salaries	500.00	8,000.00	8,000.00	8,000.00	8,000.00	8,000.00	8,000.00
TOTAL OP. EXPENSES	18,696.00	13,774.33	13,774.33	13,774.33	13,774.33	13,774.33	13,774.33
OPERATING INCOME	(13,882.80)	(7,044.73)	(5,831.73)	(2,957.13)	(2,723.25)	(2,391.72)	(2,050.24)
INTEREST INCOME	410.00	234.99	209.39	168.60	173.74	164.88	158.39
OTHER EXPENSES	233.33	235.66	238.02	240.40	242.80	245.23	247.68
INCOME BEFORE TAXES	(13,706.13)	(7,045.41)	(5,860.36)	(3,008.64)	(2,792.32)	(2,472.28)	(2,141.53)
INCOME TAXES	(3,426.53)	(1,761.35)	(1,465.09)	(752.16)	(698.08)	(618.07)	(535.38)
NET INCOME	(10,279.60)	(5,284.06)	(4,395.27)	(2,256.48)	(2,094.24)	(1,854.21)	(1,606.15)

CASH FLOWS PROJECTIONS

	1992 June	July	August	September	October	November	December
BEGINNING CASH	100,000.00	57,313.80	51,071.55	48,069.78	42,376.00	40,164.82	38,144.85
CASH RECEIPTS	12,443.00	29,091.99	36,889.89	47,088.39	54,844.43	56,248.89	57,923.13
CASH PAID OUT							
Accounts Payable	39,626.40	23,085.80	29,344.40	37,519.60	43,736.55	44,867.37	46,213.39
Operating Expenses	18,696.00	13,774.33	13,774.33	13,774.33	13,774.33	13,774.33	13,774.33
Other Expenses	233.33	235.66	238.02	240.40	242.80	245.23	247.68
Income Taxes	(3,426.53)	(1,761.35)	(1,465.09)	(752.16)	(698.08)	(618.07)	(535.38)
TOTAL CASH OUT	55,129.20	35,334.24	41,891.66	50,782.17	57,055.61	58,268.86	59,700.02
NET CASH FLOW	(42,686.20)	(6,242.26)	(5,001.77)	(3,693.78)	(2,211.18)	(2,019.97)	(1,776.89)
ENDING CASH	57,313.80	51,071.55	46,069.78	42,376.00	40,164.82	38,144.85	36,367.96

1 • 33

Exhibit 8 *(Continued)*

INCOME STATEMENT PROJECTIONS

1993	January	February	March	April	May	June	July	August	September	October	November	December
SALES												
ORCA 386SX (Units)	12	13	13	14	14	14	15	15	16	16	17	17
ORCA 386 (Units)	15	15	16	16	16	17	17	18	19	19	20	20
ORCA 486 (Units)	11	12	12	12	13	13	13	14	14	15	15	16
ORCA 386SX	11,761.57	11,464.06	11,807.98	12,162.22	12,527.09	12,902.90	13,289.99	13,688.69	14,099.35	14,522.33	14,958.00	15,406.74
ORCA 386	19,021.10	19,591.73	20,179.48	20,784.87	20,585.01	21,202.56	21,838.64	22,493.80	23,168.61	23,863.67	24,087.99	24,810.63
ORCA 486	17,445.39	17,968.75	18,507.81	19,063.04	18,368.17	18,919.21	19,486.79	20,071.39	20,673.53	21,293.74	21,554.40	22,201.04
Supporting Products	10,867.91	11,193.95	11,529.77	11,875.66	12,231.93	12,598.89	12,976.86	13,366.16	13,767.15	14,180.16	14,605.57	15,043.73
TOTAL SALES	59,095.97	60,218.49	62,025.05	63,885.80	63,712.20	65,623.57	67,592.27	69,620.04	71,708.64	73,859.90	75,205.96	77,462.14
COST OF GOODS SOLD	47,276.77	48,174.79	49,620.04	51,108.64	50,969.76	52,498.85	54,073.82	55,896.03	57,366.92	59,087.92	60,164.77	61,969.71
GROSS MARGIN FROM SALES	11,819.19	12,043.70	12,405.01	12,777.16	12,742.44	13,124.71	13,518.45	13,924.01	14,341.73	14,771.98	15,041.19	15,492.43
OPERATING EXPENSES												
Office and Equipments	2,718.33	2,718.33	2,718.33	2,718.33	2,718.33	2,718.33	2,718.33	2,718.33	2,718.33	2,718.33	2,718.33	2,718.33
Legal Fees	1,000.00	1,000.00	1,000.00	1,000.00	1,000.00	1,000.00	1,000.00	1,000.00	1,000.00	1,000.00	1,000.00	1,000.00
Accounting Fees	183.33	183.33	183.33	183.33	183.33	183.33	183.33	183.33	183.33	183.33	183.33	183.33
Insurance	896.67	896.67	896.67	896.67	896.67	896.67	896.67	896.67	896.67	896.67	896.67	896.67
Depreciation	100.00	100.00	100.00	100.00	100.00	100.00	100.00	100.00	100.00	100.00	100.00	100.00
Advertisement Cost	500.00	500.00	500.00	500.00	500.00	500.00	500.00	500.00	500.00	500.00	500.00	500.00
Promotions/Comp. Shows	676.00	676.00	676.00	676.00	676.00	676.00	676.00	676.00	676.00	676.00	676.00	676.00
Staff Salaries	8,500.00	8,500.00	8,500.00	8,500.00	8,500.00	8,500.00	8,500.00	8,500.00	8,500.00	8,500.00	8,500.00	8,500.00
TOTAL OP. EXPENSES	14,574.33	14,574.33	14,574.33	14,574.33	14,574.33	14,574.33	14,574.33	14,574.33	14,574.33	14,574.33	14,574.33	14,574.33
OPERATING INCOME	(2,755.14)	(2,530.63)	(2,169.32)	(1,797.17)	(1,831.89)	(1,449.62)	(1,055.88)	(650.32)	(232.60)	197.85	466.86	918.10
INTEREST INCOME	149.11	170.69	180.53	151.14	143.07	136.85	128.96	123.52	119.53	117.04	116.12	116.60
OTHER EXPENSES	250.16	252.86	255.19	267.74	260.32	262.92	265.55	268.21	270.89	273.60	276.33	279.10
INCOME BEFORE TAXES	(2,856.19)	(2,612.40)	(2,243.98)	(1,903.77)	(1,949.14)	(1,575.69)	(1,192.45)	(795.00)	(383.96)	41.10	306.65	755.60
INCOME TAXES	(714.05)	(653.10)	(565.99)	(475.94)	(487.28)	(394.17)	(298.11)	(198.75)	(95.99)	10.27	76.66	188.90
NET INCOME	(2,142.14)	(1,959.30)	(1,677.98)	(1,427.83)	(1,461.85)	(1,182.52)	(894.33)	(596.25)	(287.97)	30.82	229.99	566.70

CASH FLOWS PROJECTIONS

	January	February	March	April	May	June	July	August	September	October	November	December
BEGINNING CASH	36,367.96	34,178.26	32,106.71	30,228.07	28,614.16	27,169.67	25,796.02	24,704.81	23,905.78	23,408.95	23,224.65	23,320.03
CASH RECEIPTS	59,007.31	59,828.12	61,282.30	63,106.56	63,942.07	64,803.73	66,736.90	68,729.68	70,783.87	72,901.32	74,849.06	76,450.65
CASH PAID OUT												
Accounts Payable	47,086.56	47,725.78	48,897.42	50,364.34	51,039.20	51,734.31	53,286.34	54,884.93	56,531.47	58,227.42	59,826.35	61,067.24
Operating Expenses	14,574.33	14,574.33	14,574.33	14,574.33	14,574.33	14,574.33	14,574.33	14,574.33	14,574.33	14,574.33	14,574.33	14,574.33
Other Expenses	250.16	252.66	255.19	257.74	260.32	262.92	265.55	268.21	270.89	273.60	276.33	279.10
Income Taxes	(714.05)	(653.10)	(565.99)	(475.94)	(487.28)	(394.17)	(298.11)	(198.75)	(95.99)	10.27	76.66	188.90
TOTAL CASH OUT	61,197.00	61,899.68	63,160.94	64,720.47	65,386.56	66,177.39	67,828.11	69,528.71	71,280.70	73,085.62	74,553.67	76,109.57
NET CASH FLOW	(2,189.70)	(2,071.56)	(1,878.64)	(1,613.90)	(1,444.49)	(1,373.65)	(1,091.21)	(799.03)	(496.83)	(184.30)	95.38	341.08
ENDING CASH	34,178.26	32,106.71	30,228.07	28,614.16	27,169.67	25,796.02	24,704.81	23,905.78	23,408.95	23,224.65	23,320.03	23,661.11

Exhibit 8 (Continued)

INCOME STATEMENT PROJECTIONS
1994

	January	February	March	April	May	June	July	August	September	October	November	December
SALES												
ORCA 386SX (Units)	25	25	26	26	27	28	28	29	29	30	30	31
ORCA 386 (Units)	30	31	32	34	35	37	38	40	41	43	44	46
ORCA 486 (Units)	23	24	26	27	28	30	31	33	34	36	38	40
ORCA 386SX	22,405.65	22,853.77	23,310.84	23,777.06	24,252.60	24,737.65	25,232.40	25,737.05	28,251.79	26,776.83	27,312.37	27,858.61
ORCA 386	36,768.99	38,280.55	38,978.91	39,693.52	41,281.28	42,932.51	44,649.81	46,435.81	48,293.24	50,224.97	52,233.97	54,323.33
ORCA 486	33,236.04	34,897.84	35,999.88	36,999.86	39,689.86	41,674.36	43,758.07	45,945.98	48,243.28	50,655.44	53,188.21	55,847.62
Supporting Products	22,231.02	23,044.93	23,891.89	24,773.31	25,890.70	26,845.61	27,639.68	28,674.61	29,752.19	30,874.28	32,042.83	33,259.87
TOTAL SALES	114,661.69	119,057.09	122,181.52	126,043.76	130,914.42	135,990.13	141,279.97	146,793.44	152,540.50	158,531.52	164,777.37	171,289.44
COST OF GOODS SOLD	91,729.36	95,245.67	97,745.21	100,835.01	104,731.54	108,792.10	113,023.98	117,434.76	122,032.40	126,825.21	131,821.90	137,031.55
GROSS MARGIN FROM SALES	22,932.34	23,811.42	24,436.30	25,208.75	26,182.88	27,198.03	28,255.99	29,358.69	30,508.10	31,706.30	32,955.47	34,257.89
OPERATING EXPENSES												
Office and Equipments	3,076.33	3,076.33	3,076.33	3,076.33	3,076.33	3,076.33	3,076.33	3,076.33	3,076.33	3,076.33	3,076.33	3,076.33
Legal Fees	1,250.00	1,250.00	1,250.00	1,250.00	1,250.00	1,250.00	1,250.00	1,250.00	1,250.00	1,250.00	1,250.00	1,250.00
Accounting Fees	203.33	203.33	203.33	203.33	203.33	203.33	203.33	203.33	203.33	203.33	203.33	203.33
Insurance	914.50	914.50	914.50	914.50	914.50	914.50	914.50	914.50	914.50	914.50	914.50	914.50
Depreciation	100.00	100.00	100.00	100.00	100.00	100.00	100.00	100.00	100.00	100.00	100.00	100.00
Advertisement Cost	1,500.00	1,500.00	1,500.00	1,500.00	1,500.00	1,500.00	1,500.00	1,500.00	1,500.00	1,500.00	1,500.00	1,500.00
Promotions/Comp. Shows	877.00	877.00	877.00	877.00	877.00	877.00	877.00	877.00	877.00	877.00	877.00	877.00
Staff Salaries	9,400.00	9,400.00	9,400.00	9,400.00	9,400.00	9,400.00	9,400.00	9,400.00	9,400.00	9,400.00	9,400.00	9,400.00
TOTAL OP. EXPENSES	17,321.16	17,321.16	17,321.16	17,321.16	17,321.16	17,321.16	17,321.16	17,321.16	17,321.16	17,321.16	17,321.16	17,321.16
OPERATING INCOME	5,611.18	6,490.26	7,115.14	7,887.59	8,861.72	9,876.87	10,934.83	12,037.53	13,186.94	14,385.14	15,634.31	16,936.73
INTEREST INCOME	306.85	325.74	347.90	373.11	465.08	501.39	542.14	587.53	637.77	693.08	753.68	819.82
OTHER EXPENSES	317.64	320.81	324.02	327.26	330.54	333.84	337.18	340.55	343.96	347.40	350.87	354.38
INCOME BEFORE TAXES	5,600.39	6,495.19	7,139.02	7,933.44	8,996.27	10,044.41	11,139.79	12,284.51	13,480.75	14,730.82	16,037.12	17,402.17
INCOME TAXES	1,400.10	1,623.80	1,784.76	1,983.36	2,249.07	2,511.10	2,784.95	3,071.13	3,370.19	3,682.71	4,009.28	4,350.54
NET INCOME	4,200.29	4,871.39	5,354.27	5,950.08	6,747.20	7,533.31	8,354.84	9,213.38	10,110.56	11,048.12	12,027.84	13,051.63

CASH FLOWS PROJECTIONS

	January	February	March	April	May	June	July	August	September	October	November	December
BEGINNING CASH	61,370.40	65,148.77	69,580.62	74,622.44	80,186.30	86,446.44	93,472.18	101,298.04	109,960.07	119,495.93	129,944.94	141,348.20
CASH RECEIPTS	112,858.94	117,185.13	120,967.20	124,485.75	128,944.17	133,953.67	139,177.19	144,624.24	150,304.74	156,229.08	162,408.12	168,853.22
CASH PAID OUT												
Accounts Payable	90,041.67	93,487.51	96,495.44	99,290.11	102,763.27	106,761.82	110,908.04	115,229.37	119,733.58	124,428.80	129,323.56	134,426.72
Operating Expenses	17,321.16	17,321.16	17,321.16	17,321.16	17,321.16	17,321.16	17,321.16	17,321.16	17,321.16	17,321.16	17,321.16	17,321.16
Other Expenses	317.64	320.81	324.02	327.26	330.54	333.84	337.18	340.55	343.96	347.40	350.87	354.38
Income Taxes	1,400.10	1,623.80	1,784.76	1,983.36	2,249.07	2,511.10	2,784.95	3,071.13	3,370.19	3,682.71	4,009.28	4,350.54
TOTAL CASH OUT	109,080.57	112,753.28	115,925.38	118,921.89	122,664.04	126,927.93	131,351.33	135,962.20	140,768.88	145,780.07	151,004.87	156,452.80
NET CASH FLOW	3,778.37	4,431.85	5,041.82	5,563.86	6,260.14	7,025.74	7,825.86	8,662.03	9,535.86	10,449.02	11,403.26	12,400.42
ENDING CASH	65,148.77	69,580.62	74,622.44	80,186.30	86,446.44	93,472.18	101,298.04	109,960.07	119,495.93	129,944.94	141,348.20	153,748.62

Exhibit 8 *(Continued)*

INCOME STATEMENT PROJECTIONS

1995	January	February	March	April	May	June	July	August	September	October	November	December
SALES												
ORCA 386SX (Units)	57	58	59	61	62	63	64	66	67	68	70	71
ORCA 386 (Units)	110	114	119	123	128	134	139	144	150	156	162	169
ORCA 486 (Units)	107	113	118	124	130	137	144	151	158	166	175	183
ORCA 386SX	48,581.14	49,552.76	50,543.81	51,554.69	52,585.78	53,637.50	54,710.25	55,804.45	56,920.54	58,058.95	59,220.13	60,404.54
ORCA 386	123,476.59	128,414.82	133,561.20	136,893.25	144,448.98	150,226.94	156,236.02	162,485.46	168,984.88	175,744.27	182,774.04	190,085.00
ORCA 486	144,783.15	152,022.30	159,623.42	167,604.59	175,984.82	184,784.06	194,023.26	203,724.43	213,910.65	224,606.18	235,836.49	247,628.31
Supporting Products	77,860.63	80,955.00	84,181.88	87,547.20	91,057.17	94,718.28	98,537.32	102,521.39	106,677.91	111,014.67	115,539.79	120,261.78
TOTAL SALES	394,700.50	410,944.67	427,900.31	445,599.73	464,076.75	483,366.78	503,506.85	524,535.72	546,493.98	569,424.08	593,370.46	618,379.64
COST OF GOODS SOLD	315,760.40	328,755.74	342,320.25	356,479.78	371,261.40	386,693.42	402,805.48	419,828.58	437,195.18	455,539.26	474,696.36	494,703.71
GROSS MARGIN FROM SALES	78,940.10	82,188.93	85,580.06	89,119.95	92,815.35	96,673.36	100,701.37	104,907.14	109,298.80	113,884.82	118,674.09	123,675.93
OPERATING EXPENSES												
Office and Equipments	3,367.50	3,367.50	3,367.50	3,367.50	3,367.50	3,367.50	3,367.50	3,367.50	3,367.50	3,367.50	3,367.50	3,367.50
Legal Fees	1,250.00	1,250.00	1,250.00	1,250.00	1,250.00	1,250.00	1,250.00	1,250.00	1,250.00	1,250.00	1,250.00	1,250.00
Accounting Fees	201.66	201.66	201.66	201.66	201.66	201.66	201.66	201.66	201.66	201.66	201.66	201.66
Insurance	905.64	905.64	905.64	905.64	905.64	905.64	905.64	905.64	905.64	905.64	905.64	905.64
Depreciation	110.00	110.00	110.00	110.00	110.00	110.00	110.00	110.00	110.00	110.00	110.00	110.00
Advertisement Cost	1,500.00	1,500.00	1,500.00	1,500.00	1,500.00	1,500.00	1,500.00	1,500.00	1,500.00	1,500.00	1,500.00	1,500.00
Promotions/Comp. Shows	676.00	676.00	676.00	676.00	676.00	676.00	676.00	676.00	676.00	676.00	676.00	676.00
Staff Salaries	11,700.00	11,700.00	11,700.00	11,700.00	11,700.00	11,700.00	11,700.00	11,700.00	11,700.00	11,700.00	11,700.00	11,700.00
TOTAL OP. EXPENSES	19,710.80	19,710.80	19,710.80	19,710.80	19,710.80	19,710.80	19,710.80	19,710.80	19,710.80	19,710.80	19,710.80	19,710.80
OPERATING INCOME	59,229.30	62,478.14	65,869.26	69,409.15	73,104.55	76,962.56	80,990.57	85,196.35	89,588.00	94,174.02	98,963.29	103,965.13
INTEREST INCOME	4,896.38	5,171.94	5,454.80	5,753.20	6,067.86	6,399.48	6,748.84	7,116.73	7,503.98	7,911.45	8,340.06	8,790.76
OTHER EXPENSES	454.47	459.01	463.60	468.24	472.92	477.65	482.43	487.25	492.12	497.04	502.01	507.03
INCOME BEFORE TAXES	63,671.21	67,191.06	70,860.46	74,694.11	78,699.49	82,884.39	87,256.99	91,825.83	96,599.85	101,588.42	106,801.34	112,248.85
INCOME TAXES	15,917.80	16,797.77	17,715.11	18,673.53	19,674.87	20,721.10	21,814.25	22,956.46	24,149.96	25,397.11	26,700.33	28,062.21
NET INCOME	47,753.41	50,393.30	53,145.34	56,020.58	59,024.62	62,163.29	65,442.74	68,869.37	72,449.89	76,191.32	80,101.00	84,186.64

CASH FLOWS PROJECTIONS

	January	February	March	April	May	June	July	August	September	October	November	December
BEGINNING CASH	844,203.25	891,713.24	940,482.11	991,931.89	1,046,182.54	1,103,359.45	1,163,593.74	1,227,022.47	1,293,788.96	1,364,043.02	1,437,941.32	1,515,647.69
CASH RECEIPTS	398,379.77	407,994.53	424,877.29	442,503.23	460,906.10	480,121.25	500,185.66	521,138.02	543,018.83	565,870.48	589,737.33	614,665.80
CASH PAID OUT												
Accounts Payable	314,786.71	322,258.07	335,537.99	349,400.02	363,870.59	378,977.41	394,749.45	411,217.03	428,411.88	446,367.22	465,117.81	484,700.04
Operating Expenses	19,710.80	19,710.80	19,710.80	19,710.80	19,710.80	19,710.80	19,710.80	19,710.80	19,710.80	19,710.80	19,710.80	19,710.80
Other Expenses	454.47	459.01	463.60	468.24	472.92	477.65	482.43	487.25	492.12	497.04	502.01	507.03
Income Taxes	15,917.80	16,797.77	17,715.11	18,673.53	19,674.87	20,721.10	21,814.25	22,956.46	24,149.96	25,397.11	26,700.33	28,062.21
TOTAL CASH OUT	350,869.78	369,225.65	373,427.51	388,252.58	403,729.19	419,886.96	436,756.92	454,371.54	472,764.77	491,972.17	512,030.96	532,980.08
NET CASH FLOW	47,509.99	48,768.88	51,449.78	54,250.64	57,176.91	60,234.29	63,428.73	66,766.48	70,254.06	73,898.31	77,706.36	81,685.72
ENDING CASH	891,713.24	940,482.11	991,931.89	1,046,182.54	1,103,359.45	1,163,593.74	1,227,022.47	1,293,788.96	1,364,043.02	1,437,941.32	1,515,647.69	1,597,333.41

Exhibit 8   (*Continued*)

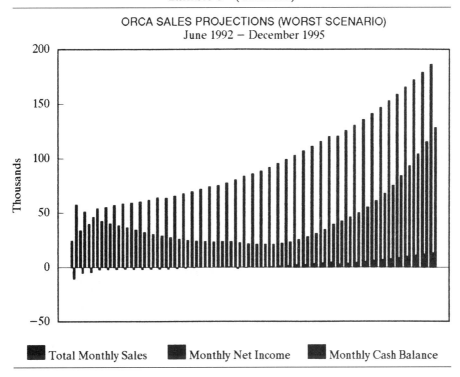

ORCA SALES PROJECTIONS (WORST SCENARIO)
June 1992 – December 1995

APPENDIX A

List of Suppliers

Alfa Power Inc.	20311 Valley Blvd. Suite L Walnut, CA 91789 Tel. (714) 594-7171, Fax (714) 595-4863
Central Point	15220 N.W. Greenbrier Pkwy., #200 Beaverton, OR 97006 (503) 690-8088
Clover Business Systems, Corp.	15046 E. Nelson Ave. Suite 8 City of Industry, CA 91747 Tel. (818) 333-8699, Fax (818) 333-1499
Computer Peripherals, Inc.	667 Rancho Conejo Blvd. Newbury Park, CA 91320 Tel. (805) 499-5751, Fax (805) 498-8848
Fifth Generation Systems	10049 N. Reiger Rd. Baton Rouge, LA 70809 (504) 291-7221
Lotus Development Corp.	55 Cambridge Pkwy. Cambridge, MA 02142 (617) 577-8500
Microsoft Corp.	One Microsoft Way Redmond, WA 98052 (206) 882-8080
Quarterdeck Office Systems	150 Pico Blvd. Santa Monica, CA 90405 (213) 392-9851
WordPerfect Corp.	1555 N. Technology Way Orem, UT 84057 (801) 222-4050

APPENDIX B

List of ORCA's Product Components

** EFFECTIVE : 01/05/1992 **
** PRICE SUBJECT TO CHANGE WITHOUT NOTICE **
** ALL CLOVER SYSTEMS AND BAREBONE SYSTEMS ARE FCC CLASS B APPROVED **

CLOVER COMPLETE SYSTEM:

ITEM CODE	286/12	286/20	386SX/16	386/25	386/33	486/33
MEMORY:	2MB	2MB	2MB	2MB	4MB	4MB
PRICE :	$410	$425	$510	$675	$799	$1,189

EVERY SYSTEMS ARE STANDARD INCLUDING : CASE W/POWER SUPPLY
MOTHERBOARD W/CPU
TEAC 1.2MB FLOPPY
TEAC 1.44 MB FLOPPY
AT I/O CARD (2S, 1P, 1G) PORT
IDE CONTROLLER CARD (2H, 2F)
101 ENHANCED CLICK KEYBOARD
MS DOS 5.0 AND WINDOW 3.0/MOUSE

OPTION: HARD DRIVE	OPTION : MONITOR
CONNER 40MB.... $ 195.00	SVGA MONITOR 1024X768
MAXTOR 80MB.... $ 299.00	W/SVGA CARD ....$ 350.00
CONNER 120MB... $ 369.00	MGP MONITOR
CONNER 200MB .. $ 599.00	W/MGP CARD ....$ 89.00

CLOVER BAREBONE SYSTEM:

ITEM CODE	DESCRIPTION	1..9pc.	10..50pc.	50 up
SYS286-12F	80286-12 BOARD W/CPU DESKTOP CASE W/200W POWER SUPPLY	$ 149	$ 144	$ 14(
SYS286-16F	80286-16 BOARD W/CPU DESKTOP CASE W/200W POWER SUPPLY	$ 169	$ 166	$ 16:
SYS386-SX16F	80386-16SX BOARD W/CPU DESKTOP CASE W/200W POWER SUPPLY	$ 249	$ 239	$ 23·
SYS386-33F	80386-33DX BOARD W/OUT CPU DESKTOP CASE W/200W POWER SUPPLY	$ 269	$ 267	$ 26
SYS386-33F	80386-33DX BOARD W/OUT CPU MED TOWER CASE W/200W POWER SUPPLY	$ 279	$ 277	$ 27
SYS486-33F	80486-33DX BOARD W/OUT CPU FULL TOWER CASE W/230W POWER SUPPLY	$ 409	$ 405	$ 39

CLOVER NOTEBOOK:

NB-324	80386-20SX :	$ 1,680	$ 1599	CAL
	2MB TO 5MB, 40MB HARD DRIVE, ONLY 7LBS !!!!			
	FEATURES : Internal 2400b modem & 9600b fax option. 1 serial, 1 parallel, and 1 scanner port. 40mb / 80mb hard drive option. Docking station option.			

CLOVER CASES: MANUFACTURE DIRECT, MINI TOWER SPECIALIST.	10..50pc	50 up	
CS-01W : CHOICE OF VERTICAL OR HORIZONTAL DESIGN RESPECTIVELY			
MINI TOWER CASE, DIGITAL	$ 27.00	$ 26.50	$ 26.00
CS-02W : CHOICE OF VERTICAL OR HORIZONTAL DESIGN RESPECTIVELY			
MINI TOWER CASE	$ 25.50	$ 24.50	$ 23.50
CS-01PW: CHOICE OF VERTICAL OR HORIZONTAL DESIGN RESPECTIVELY			
MINI TOWER CASE, DIGITAL, 200W POWER SUPPLY	$ 52.00	$ 51.50	$ 50.50
CS-02PW: CHOICE OF VERTICAL OR HORIZONTAL DESIGN RESPECTIVELY			
MINI TOWER CASE, 200W POWER SUPPLY	$ 50.00	$ 49.50	$ 48.50
CS-360P: FIVE DISK DRIVERS-3 x 5 1/4" FDD/HDD, 1 x 3 1/2" FDD, 1 x 3 1/2"HDD			
DESKTOP CASE, 200W POWER SUPPLY	$ 55.00	$ 53.00	$ 52.00
CS-861P: 6 x 5 1/4" DRIVE & 1 x HIDDEN FULL HEIGHT HDD			
FULL SIZE CASE, 250W POWER SUPPLY	$105.00	$ 95.00	$ 92.00

MOTHER BOARD :

	10..50pc	50 up	
MB-21A, 286/20MHZ, UP TO 4MB W/CPU/BABY/DIP	$ 72.00	$ 69.00	$ 67.00
MB-25A, 286/25MHZ, UP TO 4MB W/CPU/BABY/DIP	$ 101.00	$ 98.00	$ 95.00
MB-31A, 386/16SX, OPTI CHIP SET, W/CPU	$ 155.00	$145.50	$140.00
MB-32A, 386/25SX, OPTI CHIP SET W/CPU	$ 175.00	$168.00	$161.00
MB-32S, 386/25MHZ, OPTI CHIP SET W/o CPU	$ 110.00	$105.00	$ 98.00
MB-33P, 386/33MHZ, 64K CACHE, OPTI CHIP SET	$ 155.00	$142.50	$138.00
MB-34A, 386/40MHZ, 64K CACHE, OPTI CHIP SET	$ 170.00	$168.00	$155.00
MB-42A, 486/20SX, OPTI CHIP SET, W/o CPU	$ 120.00	$110.00	$108.00
MB-43H, 486/33MHZ, 64/256K CACHE,			
OPTI CHIP SET, 64K C.	$ 175.00	$160.00	$155.00

VIDEO CARD :

MGP-01A MGP CARD	$10.50	$10.00	$ 9.90
VGA-02P ~ PARADISE 256K-1C 1024X768 16 Colors	$49.50	$48.50	$47.50
VGA-12P ~ PARADISE 1MB-1D 1024X768 256 Colors	$82.00	$78.00	$77.00
VGA-11P TRIDENT SVGA 1MB 1024X768	$78.00	$76.00	CALL

HARD DRIVE CONTROLLER IDE AND I/O CARD :

HDC-01 2 HARD DRIVE & 2 FLOPPY CONTROLLER	$12.50	$ 11.50	CALL
HDC-02 MULTI I/O (IDE CONTROLLER & I/O CARD)	$22.50	$ 21.50	$ 19.50
I/O-01A I/O CARD, 2S, 1P, 1G	$10.50	$ 9.50	CALL

HARD DRIVE :

HD-C3044 CONNER 40MB / 25ms / 8K / 1"H	$175.00	CALL	CALL
HD-C30104 CONNER 120MB / 19ms / 64K / 1"H	$345.00	CALL	CALL
HD-3204 CONNER 200MB / 16ms / 64K / 3.5"	$595.00	CALL	CALL

MONITOR :

MON-1401 REMDS NON-INTERLACED 14" 0.28mm VGA	$295.00	$ 275.00	CALL
MON-1402 REDMS NON-INTERLACED 14" 0.28mm 1024X768	$355.00	$ 345.00	CALL

2

BUSINESS PLAN FOR BABY'S CORNUCOPIA

Developed by

David A. Porter

Used with the Permission of the Author

EXECUTIVE SUMMARY

Baby's Cornucopia is a report and newsletter which is targeted to expectant, new, and not-so-new parents to show them how to save money on a variety of goods and services for their children. Primary research was conducted in the form of a structured marketing questionnaire. The questionnaire was designed to measure the respondents' preferences as well as demographic data. Analysis of the results contributed to the establishment of appropriate marketing mix strategies. The major findings include (1) over 59 percent of the respondents stated they are either excited or enthusiastic about the product, (2) the most accepted price range for a one-time report is between $5.00 and $5.50; the most accepted price range for the annual newsletter subscription is between $11.00 and $12.00, (3) in regards to distribution, over 60 percent of respondents stated they expect the product to be made available by mail, and (4) as far as advertising is concerned, 59 percent of those surveyed said they envision the product to be advertised in doctors' offices.

Baby's Cornucopia is presently in the introductory stage of its life cycle; therefore, the current objectives for Baby's Cornucopia are to increase awareness and stimulate demand for the product. The pricing and distribution strategies detailed in this report follow close in line with the above-stated questionnaire results. A two-part strategy is recommended for effective promotion of Baby's Cornucopia. While in the introductory stage, a viable, affordable sales promotion technique, in the form of an informational bookmark, should be placed in doctors' offices, daycare centers, and other similar facilities. Once Baby's Cornucopia matures as a product, other strategies recommended include making use of printed media including newspapers and magazines and a direct mail campaign geared towards households with children. The latter strategies will become more feasible as Baby's Cornucopia develops financial stability.

Baby's Cornucopia is a distinctive compilation of information regarding goods and services for children. With no competitors and a sizable market in which to penetrate, the potential for Baby's Cornucopia is unlimited.

TABLE OF CONTENTS

I. **COMPANY PROFILE** . . . . **2 · 5**

    A. Owner Biography . . . . 2 · 5

    B. Mission Statement . . . . 2 · 5

II. **SITUATION ANALYSIS** . . . . **2 · 5**

    A. Product Profile . . . . 2 · 5

    B. Report . . . . 2 · 6

    C. Newsletter . . . . 2 · 6

    D. Strengths . . . . 2 · 6

    E. Weaknesses . . . . 2 · 6

    F. Problems . . . . 2 · 6

    G. Opportunities . . . . 2 · 7

III. **TARGET MARKET** . . . . **2 · 7**

IV. **BUSINESS ENVIRON** . . . . **2 · 7**

    A. Social Environ . . . . 2 · 8

    B. Legal Environ . . . . 2 · 8

    C. Competitive Environ . . . . 2 · 8

    D. Technological Environ . . . . 2 · 8

V. **MARKETING RESEARCH** . . . . **2 · 9**

VI. **MARKETING TACTICS** . . . . **2 · 10**

    A. Product Strategy . . . . 2 · 10

       a. Product Life Cycle . . . . 2 · 10

       b. New Products . . . . 2 · 11

    B. Pricing Strategy . . . . 2 · 11

    C. Distribution Strategy . . . . 2 · 11

    D. Promotion Strategy . . . . 2 · 11

VII. **PROMOTION MIX** . . . . **2 · 12**

    A. Introductory Stage Promotional Mix . . . . . 2 · 12

       a. Sales Promotion . . . . 2 · 12

       b. Public Relations . . . . 2 · 12

B. Growth Stage Promotional Mix . . . . 2 · 13
   a. *Advertising* . . . . 2 · 13
   b. *Sales Promotion* . . . . 2 · 13
   c. *Public Relations* . . . . 2 · 13

VIII. IMPLEMENTATION AND CONTROL . . . . **2 · 13**

IX. SUMMARY . . . . **2 · 14**

APPENDIX I: FINANCIAL STATEMENTS . . . . **2 · 15**

APPENDIX II: PROTOTYPE OF ONE-TIME REPORT . . . . **2 · 18**

APPENDIX III: COPY OF QUESTIONNAIRE . . . . **2 · 27**

APPENDIX IV: TABLES AND GRAPHS OF SURVEY RESULTS . . . . . **2 · 28**

APPENDIX V: PROTOTYPE OF BOOKMARK (SALES PROMOTION) . . **2 · 37**

I. COMPANY PROFILE

Baby's Cornucopia was founded by Antonieta Kashimbiri, a sole proprietor, in early 1993. Ms. Kashimbiri came up with the idea of a report and newsletter for expectant, new, and not-so-new parents when her son was born. She took the time and effort to find out about special offerings and promotions by certain companies which targeted the baby/toddler market segment. She founded the company with one goal in mind: to give expectant, new, and not-so-new parents the benefit of her experience as a parent pertaining to discounts and free goods or services which they can obtain from manufacturers and other sources.

Ms. Kashimbiri's feelings toward this report are that "it is the gift that keeps on giving for expectant, new, and not-so-new parents." She is still in the development stage and plans to get her business off the ground within the next few months. She will be conducting her business out of her residence located at 3653 7th Avenue, Los Angeles, CA 90018.

A. Owner Biography

Antonieta Edwards Kashimbiri, born and raised in the Republic of Panama, holds a B.S. degree in Computer Science from Loma Linda University and a M.S. degree in Computer Science from West Coast University. Ms. Kashimbiri is bilingual in Spanish and English. She immigrated to the United States in 1970 and settled in California in 1976. She is married and has a two-year-old son. Ms. Kashimbiri enjoys reading, shopping, and sewing.

B. Mission Statement

The mission of Baby's Cornucopia is to provide benefit and value to all parents and/or parents-to-be in Los Angeles County through distribution of the report and/or newsletter. Baby's Cornucopia is born of experience and is shared with the hope that all users will benefit as much as the author did from the many gifts waiting to be bestowed.

II. SITUATION ANALYSIS

A. Product Profile

Baby's Cornucopia is a report and newsletter which is targeted to expectant, new, and not-so-new parents. The report and newsletter will show parents how to save money on a variety of goods and services for their children (e.g., disposable diapers, baby formula, videos, toys, clothing, clubs, and associations). Ms. Kashimbiri has spent much time researching the subject matter. She likes collecting information and was able to obtain many things for herself and child by following up on leads. In talking with others, she found that the average parent does not know of these abundant resources and has, therefore, not used them. She would like to share her knowledge with others. She gets her information from a gamut of sources: reading magazines, newspapers, trade journals, and other specialty publications which cater to the expectant and new parent. She updates her information frequently and is continually compiling new information which may be useful to future parents. She verifies her sources every six months to ensure that the information she is providing is as accurate and up-to-date as possible.

The advantage to customers is that they are able to save a substantial amount of money because they do not have to pay retail for these services or products and are alerted to organizations that can assist them with information of a specific nature that new parents usually need, but only become aware of after the fact. The newsletter and/or report contains addresses and phone numbers, and, where pertinent, any additional data needed to be able to take advantage of the service.

B.   Report

The report (refer to Appendix II to see a prototype of the report) will be approximately sixteen pages long and will contain money-saving tips and coupons. This report will retail for approximately $5.50 and it is anticipated that half of those purchasing the report will become annual subscribers of the newsletter. The report will be printed once containing ongoing (more than one year) information, offers and discounts, with current and updated information in the form of a four-page newsletter printed bimonthly.

C.   Newsletter

The bimonthly newsletter's annual subscription will cost approximately $12.00 and will contain current and updated information including savings and promotions that will last as little as two months and as long as the manufacturers' dictate. It will also contain tips to make parenting easier. Obtaining this information would be a very time-consuming task for the average parent—that is why this is also an ideal gift. This newsletter will be approximately four pages in length.

D.   Strengths

- Baby's Cornucopia has no current competitors.
- Target market expanded due to increase in national birth rate.
- Founder has a strong motivation and energy to help fellow parents.
- Due to current hardships, parents are seeking ways to save money, which is one of the main objectives of Baby's Cornucopia.
- This business plan gives Baby's Cornucopia a plan of action.

E.   Weaknesses

- Lack of appropriate funding.
- Poor economic environment for new business ventures.
- The sole proprietor's inexperience in the business field.

F.   Problems

Setting realistic and dependable forecasts of future demand and sales is never an easy task. This task is more difficult in recessionary times. Baby's Cornucopia intends to operate in southern California, chiefly Los Angeles. At present, this region of the country is mired in a deep recession, with economic indicator measurements trailing those for the remainder of the United States.

Another obstacle for Baby's Cornucopia to overcome is lack of needed information. In an ideal world, the planner would have close at hand all pertinent information required on industry and market trends, technological advances, and the intentions of present and future competitors. The realities are far from this ideal however. Baby's Cornucopia neither has the financing or ability to research the entire baby-care industry. It has chosen instead to concentrate on a certain niche, namely, the transference of available child-care information to expectant, new, and not-so-new parents.

G. Opportunities

Several opportunities exist in which Baby's Cornucopia can overcome the above mentioned problems and weaknesses. To help overcome the lack of ideal information about the external environment, as well as consumer opinions regarding costs and product opinions in today's uncertain regional economy, a marketing survey was developed to get more concrete knowledge about local consumer preferences and attitudes about the product. The reliable sample ensures that the information obtained from the survey is representative of this target market.

By developing this business plan, Baby's Cornucopia will be able to apply for funding from the Coalition of Women in Economic Development (CWED). These funds, if obtained, will be used to implement the marketing strategies that the plan discusses. Other funds could also be applied for and obtained through the Small Business Administration and local banking authorities. Ms. Kashimbiri has an extremely focused vision and is eagerly awaiting funding to begin operations.

As the product advances out of the introductory stage, product modifications as well as new product additions can be devised. Because Baby's Cornucopia is entering a market niche with no current competitors, future competition would have the burden playing catch-up as well as starting their own learning curve.

III. TARGET MARKET

Of the qualified available market—the set of consumers who have interest, income, access, and qualifications for the particular market offer—Baby's Cornucopia intends to serve those located in the greater Los Angeles area. The target market potential customer is expectant, new, and not-so-new parents (with toddlers up to three years of age), their friends and relatives.

This target market affirmation can be broken down into a primary market and a secondary market. The primary market consists of the actual parents or parents-to-be. The secondary market consists of the grandparents, other relatives, and friends of the parents who would like to offer this product as a gift: perfect for baby showers, Mother's Day, or even bridal showers.

IV. BUSINESS ENVIRON

The business environ consists of the actors and forces that affect the company's ability to develop and maintain successful transactions and relationships with its target market. Of special concern to Baby's Cornucopia are the marketing environ realm of social, legal, competitive, and technological forces. To achieve success, these "uncontrollable" elements must be monitored and responded to.

A. Social Environ

The social environ is made up of forces that affect society's basic values, perceptions, preferences, and behaviors depending on current social trends. Although not matching the enormous number of births in the baby-boom period, the United States is currently experiencing an increase in births over the slow-down decade of the 1970s and early 1980s. This translates to a broad market for a report and newsletter such as Baby's Cornucopia. With the downturn in the economy and the move toward conservation and recycling, people are striving to economize all of their resources. Retailers are increasing their offers of refunds and coupons. The baby supply industry offers an abundance of opportunities for those who use their services to save not only on their products, but also on related products.

One of the main trends seen in the United States is a geographic shift in population. There has been a movement to the sunbelt states, particularly the West. The southern California region is expected to increase in population by roughly 30 percent in the next decade. This serves to expand the present target market of Baby's Cornucopia.

B. Legal Environ

The legal environ is made up of laws, government agencies, and pressure groups that influence and limit various organizations and individuals in society. The Coalition for Women's Economic Development (CWED) is a nonprofit organization that assists low-income individuals in starting or expanding their microbusinesses. A microbusiness is smaller than a "small business," usually home-based, with low start-up and operating costs, employing 1 to 10 individuals on average. CWED considers start-up as businesses operating less than 6 months and existing businesses as operating 6 months or longer. The requirements to participate in CWED include the following: attending a CWED Saturday orientation meeting and completion of an application. Loans are offered to those who have low income according to HUD guidelines for Los Angeles county and for those who live in Los Angeles county or are willing to attend training and borrowers' meetings in Los Angeles county.

The legal environ serves to protect Baby's Cornucopia from infringement by competitors, through federal copyright laws. A copyright is the exclusive legal right to reproduce, publish, and sell the matter and form of a literary, musical, or artistic work.

C. Competitive Environ

The norm for a company is that it faces a wide range of competitors. These competitors should be identified and monitored in order to sustain customer loyalty. The business concept states that to be successful the company must satisfy the needs and wants of consumers better than their competitors do. Companies must gain a strategic advantage by strongly positioning their offerings against competitor's offerings in the minds of consumers. Oddly enough, Ms. Kashimbiri has found a niche in the market that is currently untapped, which places her in the unique situation of holding a monopoly in the market. The one thing she must monitor is the onset of future competitors once the economies of scale of the industry are recognized.

D. Technological Environ

The most dramatic force shaping people's destiny is technology. The technological environ consists of forces that affect new technology creating new product and market opportunities.

Therefore, the marketer should observe trends in technology. In the case of Baby's Cornucopia, the advent of computer technology has made desktop publishing possible for Ms. Kashimbiri to perform at home. A publication-quality document can be created using the home computer. One benefit of this technology for Baby's Cornucopia is cost. The low cost of obtaining such equipment and software is a plus for the financially limited company. This is especially important for Ms. Kashimbiri since she is also a homemaker in the process of raising a young child.

V. MARKETING RESEARCH

Primary research was conducted in the form of a structured marketing questionnaire (refer to Appendix III to view copy of questionnaire utilized). The initial survey was designed to elicit responses pertaining to the marketing mix (i.e., product, price, place of distribution, and promotion) as well as obtaining demographic data on the sample. A consumer survey was distributed to 196 respondents, chosen at random at various locations where expectant, new, and not-so-new parents would be likely to congregate. The following is an analysis of survey (refer to Appendix IV for tables and graphical analysis of questionnaire results) findings.

The first question of the questionnaire was to probe whether or not a potential market segment exists for the product. A majority of the respondents (59%), when asked the question, "What is your immediate reaction to the idea of a newsletter of this type?" stated that they were either excited or enthusiastic about the prospect of the project. Based upon the survey results, a potential market segment exists for this type of product.

The second question was designed to measure the respondents' feeling toward purchase of the product in the form of the question "What best expresses your feeling about buying this product if it was available right now?" An overwhelming percentage of those surveyed (90%) would at least think about purchasing the product. This correlates with the first question in that a potential market segment exists for the product.

The next two questions focused on the price that customers were willing to pay for the one-time report as well as an annual subscription to the newsletter. In regards to the one-time report, two-thirds of those surveyed targeted the $5.00–$5.50 range as the cost they were willing to pay for the product. As for the annual subscription price for the bimonthly newsletter, over 65 percent of those surveyed chose the $11.00–$12.00 range as the cost they were willing to pay. Based on these strong price preferences, strong attention should be paid to these results when actual product pricing strategy is enacted.

Another question was geared toward gauging consumer opinion about expected distribution channels. Over 60 percent of those surveyed responded that they would expect the product to be made available by mail. Alternative channels of distribution available for choice included newsstands, family planning centers, and doctors' offices.

The next question was designed to measure promotional aspects of the product. When asked "Where would you expect to see this product advertised?" 59 percent of the respondents said that they expected the product to be advertised in doctors' offices. Based on this result and the results regarding distribution, the appropriate strategy for the product would be to advertise the product in doctors' offices, but distribute the product via mail.

The remainder of the questions in the questionnaire were designed to obtain demographic data on the sample. Over 90 percent of the respondents were female. Due to the nature of the product, this result was expected. In addition, the majority (62%) of the respondents were in the 19–30-year-old age range, with the 26–30 subrange being most prevalent. These findings are not surprising given the trends of increased working mothers and delayed child-rearing.

Another demographic area examined was that of respondent occupation. Twenty-three percent of the respondents reported that they were in the "professional" category. The "homemaker," "office worker," and "other" categories followed the professional category with 18 percent each.

As regards education, 38 percent of the respondents have graduated from college, while 26 percent have at least two years of college education. With respondent family income, almost 25 percent of the respondents stated that their total family income was over $50,000. The next most prevalent income range was $25,001–$35,000. These findings are not too surprising in that they correlate with the trend of increased working mothers (leading to an increase of two or more income families) as well as the value of higher education with respect to salary.

The final two questions of the questionnaire dealt with household make-up. When asked how many adults were in the respondents' households, 70 percent said their household consisted of two adults, followed by 17 percent of respondents who said their household contained only one adult. Nine percent of respondents said there were three adults in the household. A 1983 report showed that only 9 percent of all households in the United States were made up of only one adult. This survey depicts the slowly rising number of single working parents in today's society.

When asked the number of children under the age of three in the household, 38 percent of the respondents said there was one child in the household and 34 percent replied there were no children in the household. Twenty-eight percent of households stated they have two or more children in the household. The high number of households with only one or no children is a growing trend of smaller family sizes, compared with previous decades.

VI.   MARKETING TACTICS

Once the particular consumer group, the target audience, is identified and analyzed, the rest of the marketing mix for the product can be defined. Although there are thousands of marketing variables involved with a particular product, marketing decision making can be divided into four strategies: (1) product, (2) pricing, (3) distribution (place), and (4) promotion; commonly known as the "4 P's of Marketing."

A.   Product Strategy

Product strategy comprises product decisions about package design, branding, trademarks, warranties, guarantees, product life cycles, and the development of new products. This concept involves more than just the physical product, it also considers the satisfaction of all consumer needs in relation to the product.

a.   Product Life Cycle

Focusing on the product life cycle, products pass through a series of stages. Successful products pass through four stages—introduction, growth, maturity, and decline—before their death. Baby's Cornucopia is just entering the introductory stage of its life cycle. The objective for Baby's Cornucopia at this point is to increase awareness and to stimulate demand for the product. In this phase, the public must become acquainted with the merits of Baby's Cornucopia, not only before a purchase will be considered, but even before it's accepted as a worthy project.

Losses are quite common during the introductory stage of a product's life cycle, due to promotional expenses and product development expenditures before sales of the product actually take place. As earlier discussed within the business environ, the United States is experiencing a current rise in birth rates along with being mired in a recessionary slump economically. These forces combined create a substantial economic opportunity for a product of this variety. The introductory stage of Baby's Cornucopia is laying the groundwork for future profits. Ms. Kashimbiri can expect to recover her costs and begin earning a profit as Baby's Cornucopia moves into its second stage of the product life cycle-growth.

b. New Products

Once the initial product has been established and is successfully growing, the product's concept can then be branched out into other products to capitalize on its success, as well as to ward off new imitative competitors. Subscriptions to Baby's Cornucopia will yield a database of customers, which can be targeted for future products within the same product-type. In addition, the mailing lists can be sold to outside marketers for a profit.

B. Pricing Strategy

Pricing is one of the most difficult areas of a marketing decision. It not only encompasses setting a profitable, yet justifiable price to the product, it also must evaluate the image that a particular price will send to the target audience. Baby's Cornucopia is entering a market with few, if any, competitors. This has given Ms. Kashimbiri considerable freedom in pricing the product. Based on the consumer survey, the ideal price range for the one-time report is $5.00–$5.50. The price range dictated by the majority of respondents for the bimonthly newsletter annual subscription is $11.00–$12.00. As demand schedules become more apparent, Baby's Cornucopia can alter its price in order to capture the customer's marginal utility. In addition, Ms. Kashimbiri can concentrate on nonprice factors for the product such as product features, service, and promotion.

C. Distribution Strategy

Distribution strategy (place) deals with the physical distribution of the product. How does the product get from the producer to the consumer? Distribution channels are the steps goods follow in getting from the producer to the consumer. Organizations often spend most of their resources on the three P's in marketing (product, price, and promotion) and ignore the fourth P, place. Place is a generic term for matching the customers' needs with the firm's products. Several factors are considered when the business plans distribution: route types, physical distribution, and customer service policy. Overall, distribution encompasses more than delivering a product; it represents a vital part of business. Skillful distribution planning may even stimulate demand.

Survey results revealed that a majority of the consumers would find distribution by mail to be most effective. Ms. Kashimbiri needs to first rent a post office box for receipt of subscription orders and other related correspondence. The second step she must take is in regards to bulk mailing of her one-time reports and bimonthly newsletters. This would require an initial $40 investment for the right to bulk mail with each piece of correspondence costing an additional $.18. All communication between producer and consumer, including customer service, will be conducted by mail. Customer service would entail customer feedback, suggestions, comments, questions, and any ideas for future product enhancement.

D. Promotion Strategy

Promotion is used to communicate with individuals directly or indirectly by persuading the target market to accept a firm's products or services. To maximize benefits from the promotional efforts, the business must coordinate planning, implementation, and control of communication. These strategies involve personal selling, advertising, and sales promotional tools. The various aspects of a promotional strategy must be blended together in order for a product to be communicated effectively to the marketplace.

Baby's Cornucopia's promotional campaign is created around the two first product life cycle stages. There will be an initial strategy implemented for the introductory stage of Baby's Cornucopia, and depending upon the time it enters into the growth stage, a second promotional strategy will be put into effect.

The overall objective is to build a customer base, but due to limited funds, promotional activity is constrained. Hence, the first strategy is very price sensitive and will only involve promotion that is cost effective for Baby's Cornucopia during its young life. This will involve a simplistic marketing approach directed towards the local target audience for Ms. Kashimbiri. The second strategy will take into account a growing customer base, increasing revenue, higher efficiency due to publication experience, and hence an expanded marketing approach will then be implemented to propel Baby's Cornucopia into a truly profitable future.

Details of the specific promotional elements utilized to implement the above strategies will be discussed in the promotion mix section below.

VII. PROMOTION MIX

Promotion, the fourth variable in the marketing mix, can be defined as the function of informing, persuading, and influencing the consumer's purchase decision. In an organization of any type, the goals and objectives of its promotional strategy must be set in accordance with the overall organizational objectives. Based on these goals, the various elements of the strategy—advertising, personal selling, sales promotion, and public relations—are formulated in such a way to achieve the optimal promotional blend.

As touched upon earlier, Baby's Cornucopia's marketing efforts involve two promotional strategies: (1) introductory stage and (2) growth stage. Both strategies require the use of different elements of the marketing mix, which will be outlined in the following discussion.

A.   Introductory Stage Promotional Mix

The introductory stage promotional mix will make use of two elements, one which falls under the category of sales promotion and the other public relations.

a.   Sales Promotion

Methods of sales promotion include those marketing activities, other than personal selling, advertising, and publicity, that stimulate consumer purchasing.

For Baby's Cornucopia, a viable, affordable sales promotion technique will be in the form of placing an informational bookmark in doctors' offices, day-care centers, church parish houses, family planning clinics, Lamaze coaching classes, hospital reception areas and other areas where children or expectant mothers congregate. The purpose of this bookmark is to stimulate awareness which will, in turn, increase demand and generate sales of the report.

Sales of the report will be the driving force behind the subscription to the newsletter by readers who are interested in continuing their exposure to the gamut of available goods and services.

b.   Public Relations

Public relations is defined as a firm's communications and relationships with its various publics, including customers, employees, stockholders, suppliers, the government, and the society in which it operates. Public relations can be particularly effective in building awareness and product knowledge, for both new and established products. It can make a memorable impact on public awareness at a fraction of the cost of advertising.

One of Ms. Kashimbiri's first steps in terms of launching Baby's Cornucopia into the marketplace is to build publicity for the new product. Being a firm entering a brand-new market, publicity will enable Baby's Cornucopia to create an awareness of its product(s) to the public. Community newspapers are an ideal vehicle in which to promote Baby's Cornucopia. Press releases and portions of the prototype should be sent to local newspapers and radio stations. Although the message that is sent to the target market is out of the control of the owner, any publicity generated is well worth the effort.

B. Growth Stage Promotional Mix

The growth stage promotional mix strategy for Baby's Cornucopia involves three elements—advertising, sales promotion techniques, and public relations.

a. Advertising

Advertising can be defined as paid, nonpersonal communication through various media by business firms, nonprofit organizations, and individuals who are in some way identified in the advertising message and who hope to inform or persuade members of a particular audience. It involves the mass media—newspapers, television, radio, magazines, billboards, and so on.

Ms. Kashimbiri should consider placing ads in publications, such as *Parents Magazine*, *L.A. Parent*, and even the yellow pages. It will be necessary for her to establish a business phone to help stimulate demand, as well as handle direct customer service.

b. Sales Promotion

Once Baby's Cornucopia begins to make a profit and rise into its growth stage, Ms. Kashimbiri should consider obtaining a one-time mailing list from an established mail order house. This list will specifically target the parents of babies and toddlers; however, this can be costly and does not give Baby's Cornucopia a fixed customer database. Higher gross profit during the growth stage will justify such an expense.

c. Public Relations

One of Ms. Kashimbiri's first steps in terms of maintaining Baby's Cornucopia in the public eye is to continue to build credibility through community acceptance. Being a unique firm, publicity will be necessary to support this niche market. Once her business has been established and a client base built, she will be able to utilize more sophisticated means of promotion. Press releases aimed towards media specials, such as television news segments devoted to parenting and radio talk-show formats discussing child rearing are suitable avenues for the promotion of Baby's Cornucopia in the growth stage.

VIII. IMPLEMENTATION AND CONTROL

The success of Baby's Cornucopia will depend on control measures developed and analyzed periodically by Ms. Kashimbiri. The initial outpouring of promotional materials such as the bookmarks and direct contact with expectant, new, and not-so-new parents will result in an influx of orders and feedback. After a one-month period from the date of completion of initial distribution, the numbers of new orders will be compared to the costs of promotion. Has the recent sales activity eroded the negative profits favorably? If so, then a second, stronger wave of introductory stage promotion and sales activities should take place. The recommended marketing mix of elements shall remain the same. Feedback other than sales must also be taken into account at this time. What changes have been requested by a majority of respondents?

Finally, a full-scale review of the Baby's Cornucopia business shall take place four months from date of initial distribution of promotional materials. The financial viability of the company must be analyzed. If a favorable profit situation is arising, then, and only then, shall Ms. Kashimbiri expand into aggressive growth stage marketing strategies as outlined in the marketing plan.

IX. SUMMARY

By defining its target market, identifying strengths and weaknesses as well as problems and opportunities, paying close attention to the marketing environ, and adopting the above-mentioned two-part strategy detailed for the promotion mix during the introductory stage and the growth stage, Baby's Cornucopia has a promising future. Adhering to the controls set forth in this plan will aid Ms. Kashimbiri with decisions related to the future of the company. By implementing this business plan, Ms. Kashimbiri is apt to see Baby's Cornucopia into the maturity stage of its life cycle. This business plan was devised to accommodate the dynamic business environ of the 1990s.

APPENDIX I

Financial Statements

Forecasted Owner's Equity Statement
End Year: 1

Cash balance—beginning of year	$ 0
Cash receipts—end of year (Based on estimated sales of 1000 one-time reports and 500 prorated annual subscriptions for the remainder of yr: $1,000 × $5.50 + 500 × $8.00 = $9,500)	9,500
Total Receipts	$ 9,500
Direct material	
Paper	$ 100
Postage	560
Computer hardware supplies	100
Accountant's fee	200
Manufacturing overhead (printers' costs)	2,100
Total Expenses	$(3,060)
Excess Cash	$ 6,440
Financing: (borrowing $3,000 from CWED)	
Repayments	$ 1,500
Interest (15% APR)	225
Total Financing Costs	$(1,725)
Cash Balance—Year End	$ 4,715

Forecasted Owner's Equity Statement
End Year: 2

Cash balance—beginning of year	$ 4,715
Cash receipts—end of year (Based on estimated sales of 1200 one-time reports and 600 prorated annual subscriptions for the remainder of the yr: $1,200 × $5.50 + 600 × $8.00 = $11,400)	11,400
Total Receipts	$16,115
Direct material	
Paper	$ 105
Postage	590
Computer hardware supplies	130
Accountant's fee	250
Manufacturing overhead (printers' costs)	2,200
Total Expenses	$ (3,275)
Excess Cash	$12,840
Financing: (borrowing $3,000 from CWED)	
Repayments	$ 1,500
Interest (15% APR)	225
Total Financing Costs	$(1,725)
Cash Balance—Year End	$ 8,125

Forecasted Owner's Equity Statement
End Year: 3

Cash balance—beginning of year	$ 8,125
Cash receipts—end of year (Based on estimated sales of 1300 one-time reports and 700 prorated annual subscriptions for the remainder of the yr: $1,300 × $5.50 + 700 × $8.00 = $12,750)	12,750
Total Receipts	$20,875
Direct material	
Paper	$ 130
Postage	640
Computer hardware supplies	163
Accountant's fee	275
Manufacturing overhead (printers' costs)	2,327
Total Expenses	$ (3,535)
Excess Cash	$17,340
Financing: (CWED loan paid off)	
Total Financing Costs	$ 0
Cash Balance—Year End	$17,340

Break-Even Analysis for Baby's Cornucopia

One-Time Report:

Report price:	$5.50
Variable cost per report:	$1.50
Fixed cost:	$1,500

$\$5.50r = \$1.50r + \$1,500$

$\$4.00r = \$1,500$

$$r = 375 \text{ one-time reports/yr.}$$

Annual Subscription:

Price for 4 bi-monthly issues:	$8.00
Variable cost for Newsletter:	$1.50 for 4 issues
Fixed cost:	$700

$\$8.00s = \$1.50s + \$700$

$\$6.50s = \$700$

$$s = 108 \text{ annual subscriptions}$$

Balance Sheet
Year 1

Assets	
Current Assets: Cash	$4,715
Capital and equipment:	
386 DX desktop PC + HP LaserJet printer (used)	1,200
Postage fee for bulk mailing	40
Copyright license	25
Software/supplies	400
Total Assets	**$6,380**
Liabilities	
CWED loan	$3,000
Retained earnings	3,380
Total liabilities	**$6,380**

APPENDIX II

Prototype of One-Time Report

INTRODUCTION

Hi, and welcome to Baby's Cornucopia—the gift that keeps on giving. It is my hope that you will find this information very helpful as you begin to navigate uncharted waters. There is a lot to learn and there are many opinions; however, the final decision is YOURS (Isn't that nice?). There are many who are willing to share their resources with you—free or at a minimal cost.

- The objective of Baby's Cornucopia is to introduce to you some of these sources (along the way you will find others); the tip the iceberg; and to share with you inexpensive ways of enhancing your parenting experience.
- One of the best sources of resources is your doctor's office. Cultivate a relationship with those who work there. It is a golden opportunity. You will find that you are always remembered when something new that is of interest comes in. Anyway, just ask—generally people like to be helpful.

Sincerely

Antonieta Kashimbiri
Editor

MAGAZINES

There are many on the market, and there are many that are free. The following is a list of parenting magazines that you can obtain free or at minimal cost. Some may be obtained only at your doctor's/pediatrician's/obstetrician's office. Others will come to your home and some you will have to seek.

Free Subscription

Please send the following information.

> Your full name
> Address including zip code and apartment number where applicable
> Baby's birth date—mo/day/yr
> Sex of child

American Baby   A national magazine that offers a free six-month subscription to expectant and new parents. Good timing of your free subscription will also bring you "First Time Parents" and "Childbirth," which are only one time publications for expectant parents. A call will enroll you.

> P.O. Box 53093
> Boulder, CO 80322-3093
> 1-800-678-1208

Baby Care   A quarterly magazine distributed by the makers of Pampers. It contains articles on child-care and developmental issues from birth to 24 months.

> P.O. Box 10166
> Des Moines, IA 50347-0166
> 1-800-543-0480

Baby Talk   A monthly magazine published by Parenting Unlimited. It is available free of charge in the children's department of your local Sears or through Dy-Dee Diapers services. Articles on child and parent health with questions and answers and more.

Family Times   A quarterly publication that aims to provide resources that are designed to enhance personal relationships and family skills, based on Christian principles.

> c/o Parent Scene/Family Matters
> P.O. Box 7000
> Cleveland, TN 37320

Free at Doctors' Offices

Healthy Kids   A magazine for parents from the American Academy of Pediatrics. A series of magazines the first from age 0–3.

Ser Padres   The Spanish edition of *Parents Magazine*. It contains articles on all aspects of child-care, child development, and family matters.

L.A. Parent   A monthly magazine that will keep you abreast of the activities for you and your child in the L.A. County area. They list paid and free services, Mommy and Me, and other activities for the parents and children. The magazine has extensive articles as well as a calendar section. It is available at most locations where children related activities go on.

443 E. Irving Dr.
P.O. Box 3204
Burbank, CA 91504
818-846-0400

Paid Subscription

The Exceptional Parent   A magazine for parents of children with disabilities. It offers information on education, social skills, health-care . . . etc. It also includes a resource directory.

P.O. Box 3000
Dept. ED
Denville, NJ 07834-9919
617-730-5800
Annual subscription—$16.00
Sample issue—free

The Single Parent   The magazine of the organization for parents without partners. It blends practical advice with real life experiences.

Parents Without Partners, Inc.
8807 Colesville Rd.,
Silver Springs, MD 20910
1-800-638-8073
Annual subscription—$15.00
Sample issue—$1.00

REFUNDS/REBATES/COUPONS

These manufacturers frequently have refunds, rebates, premiums, and/or coupons. Here is a great source of savings. You buy for less because you use coupons, then you get money back for using the product. You are able to purchase a desired item at a discounted price using your proof of purchase. This is how I get the best for less.

1. Buy newspaper on the day that coupons come out and on the day that sales are announced.
2. Purchase items only when on sale (unless there is a need) and use coupons for extra savings.
3. Shop where double coupon value is given and purchase as many as money and store policy will allow.
4. Ask anyone willing to save their coupons in designated categories (baby and other related items).

In addition to the newspaper, your grocer is the next best source of information on refunds . . . etc. Ask where they display this information and look there every time you go in. To be prepared to take advantage of these offers when they occur, it is important that you do the following:

1. Save your cash register receipts for all purchases.
2. Save the packaging on all purchases—or if you prefer only proofs of purchases properly marked so that they can be identified by you.
3. Save the packaging from gift items—or proof of purchase.
4. Photocopy your cash register receipt when you have more than one purchase that qualifies for a rebate and send the photocopy. You can also take advantage of the other offers when you send in the photocopy.

Pampers/Luvs   In addition to their Baby Care Magazine, they have a quarterly rebate for proofs of purchases. Their qualifiers are the points on their packages.

> 1-800-543-0480
> Procter & Gamble
> Cincinnati, OH 45202

Earth's Best   Maker of organically grown baby food. They publish a newsletter and will send you coupons and special offers. You may call the following number to be put on their mailing list.

> 1-800-442-4221
> P.O. Box 887
> Middlebury, VT 05753

Kodak   Their proof of purchase will bring you premiums at least on a quarterly basis. We have received an Olympic Commemorative Watch, stuffed animals, and Disney books with tapes. You may call if you have questions on anything related to Kodak.

> 1-800-242-2424
> Eastman Kodak Co.
> Rochester, NY 14650

Betty Crocker   For points plus cash you can receive gifts for yourself as well as your children including classic baby gifts such as Oneida's 6-piece silver-plated growth set. Dinnerware and flatware as well as toys are available at substantial discounts. Request a catalog by calling or writing.

> General Mills Inc.
> 13400 15th Ave N.
> P.O. Box 1118
> Minneapolis, MN 55440-1118
> 1-800-328-8360

Huggies Pullups   It has a quarterly rebate for their proof of purchase points as well as catalog from which you can purchase products (e.g., toys or clothing) for cash plus proof of purchase.

Occasionally, they offer other great savings such as toilet training books and videos. They will also send you coupons in the mail or proof of purchase for points.

> 1-800-544-1847
> Kimberly Clark Corporation
> Dept. HULB-30
> P.O. Box 2020
> Neenah, WI 54957-2020

Gerber They have a gold mine of offerings waiting for you from feeding spoons with name and birth date engraved to food and baby items. These can be obtained for proof of purchase and cash. Keep proof of purchase from all baby care items and foods (full wrappers from bottles and proofs from boxes).

> 1-800-4-GERBER
> Gerber Products Co.
> Fremont, MI 49413

Fuji Film They have a vast range of offerings for a wide audience from Olympic commemorative pins to stuffed toys. They always give the options of receiving an item free of charge for proof of purchase only or proof of purchase and cash.

Beech Nut

> 1-800-523-6633

Carnation Formula

> 1-800-782-7766

Johnson & Johnson

> 1-800-526-3967

OTHER MONEY SAVING TIPS

Most new parents learn the hard way and costly way. The following steps should be followed.

1. Keep an updated inventory of what is in stock (not in use).
2. Look for trends or sale cycles and use them to your advantage.
3. Do not buy more than three (3) items of one (1) type in a given size. Your child will outgrow it before it wears out.
4. Consider exchanging gifts at the place of purchase for other items you really need, i.e., larger sizes, different colors . . . etc.
5. Go to discount stores.
6. Stock up on things like socks and underwear when there is a good price.
7. Consign with a resale shop your items which do not have much wear, but are small.
8. Shop at a resale shop for great prices.
9. Share with others. It is amazing how much you receive.
10. Before buying your baby's furniture, determine your budget and cost. Then look for your local newspaper for deal from other parents.

11. Take a picture of yourself pregnant. It makes a great starter for your child's album to show the child what you looked like before and after the pregnancy.

12. Buy a camera that imprints the date of the event on your pictures. It will save you guesswork at a later date and give you a nice album. Vivitar has one for about $50.00.

13. If you plan to breast feed and will need a pump, check with your insurance carrier before you rent one. Ask:

   ■ What is their policy?

   ■ What are the exceptions?

   ■ Whose name should the prescription be in?

   ■ Do you need preapproval?

   ■ When should they be notified?

ORGANIZATIONS

There are those of you who join because you share something in common and there are those that exist only to share information to make you a wiser consumer. They are both there to help you, should you have a need.

The Danny Foundation   It exists to educate the public about crib dangers.

> 3160-F Danville Blvd.
> P.O. Box 680
> Alamo, CA 94507
> 1-800-83-DANNY

La Leche League   Everything you want to know about breast feeding is discussed in this group. They offer encouragement to new breast-feeding mothers, meetings, and a bimonthly newsletter of shared experiences in child rearing.

> 9616 Minneapolis Ave.
> P.O. Box 1209
> Frankling Park, IL 60131-8209
> 1-800-LA-LECHE
> 708-455-7730

National Organization of Circumcision Information Resource Center   A nonprofit organization that provides expectant parents with information on circumcision. They offer pamphlets on the pros and cons of the procedure. Send a self-addressed business size envelope with $0.52 postage.

> P.O. Box 2512
> San Anselmo, CA 94979

The Sudden Infant Death Syndrome Alliance (SIDS)   An alliance of several national and local organizations that fund research into the cause of Sudden Infant Death Syndrome. They will mail you a free brochure of facts about SIDS and can put parents in touch with a nationwide network of support groups or with local organizations that offer information by telephone.

> 330 N. Charles St.
> Suite 203
> Baltimore, MD 21201
> 301-837-8300

National Highway Traffic Safety Administration (NHTSA)   When you begin to shop for a car seat, give them a call. It will make you a wiser shopper.

> 1-800-424-9393

Depression After Delivery   A self-help mutual aid support group for women who are experiencing postpartum depression or psychosis. It has a periodic newsletter. A letter or phone call will bring a list of names of women in your area who have experienced postpartum illness and who are willing to listen and help.

> P.O. Box 1282
> Morrisville, PA 19067
> 215-295-3994

Adoptive Families of America Inc.   A national support organization for adoptive and prospective adoptive families that can direct members to local support groups and adoptive agencies.

> 3333 Highway 100 N.
> Minneapolis, MN 55422
> 612-535-4827
> Membership—$24.00 annually

Parent Care Inc.   An organization dedicated to offer information, referrals, and other services to families, parent support groups, and professionals concerned with infants who require intensive or special care at birth. They publish a quarterly newsletter (news briefs) with articles by lay, professionals, and references to other support groups. Other services are literature reviews and videos. They also sponsor a yearly conference.

> 9041 Colgate St.
> Indianapolis, IN 46268

Intensive Caring Unlimited   A bimonthly newsletter for parents and professional caretakers of children with medical and developmental problems, grieving parents, and those experiencing high-risk pregnancies.

> 87 Haycroft Ave.
> Springhouse, PA 19477
> 215-233-4723
> Membership—$8.00
> Sample issue—free

One and Only   International organization for parents of only children.

> P.O. Box 35351
> Station E
> Vancouver, BC Canada V6M462

Fatherhood Project   A national research demonstration and dissemination project, designed to encourage wider options for male involvement in child bearing. The project offers information on fatherhood related topics and referrals to resources for and about fathers.

c/o Bank Street College of Education
610 W. 112th St.
New York, NY 10025
212-663-7200

National Organization of Mothers of Twins Clubs   This group includes father, grandparents, adoptive, as well as foster parents. Also, parents of triplets, quadruplets, and quintuplets are members of this club.

12404 Princess Jeanne N.E.
Albuquerque, NM 87112-4640
505-275-0955
Membership—$10.00 annually which includes a newsletter

Working Mothers Network   A national organization of working mothers that offers seminars and workshops. The group also includes a gift buying service, a quarterly newsletter, "exchange" with advice on work, home, and child rearing, money matters, and an annual resource guide.

1529 Spruce Street
Philadelphia, PA 19102
1-800-648-8455
215-875-1178
Membership—$15.00 annually

Parents Anonymous   A network of self-help support groups of parents who feel isolated, overwhelmed, or afraid of the way they find themselves dealing with their children. There are local and national groups with weekly meetings.

6733 S. Sepulveda Blvd.
Suite 270
L.A. CA 90045
1-800-421-0353
213-410-9732

VIDEOS

Before you go out to buy a video, please consider the following two offerings. They are available free of charge from your doctor or you may call the manufacturer requesting a copy. When you consider the cost of videos, this is a bargain.

Breast Feeding Your Baby: A Special Starter Kit from Mead Johnson   It is a 3-part video that contains segments on breast feeding, bottle feeding, and formula use. The package also includes coupons for Enfamil as well as a booklet entitled "Nursing the First Two Months."

Mead Johnson Nutritionals
Evansville, IN 47721
1-800-442-2902

Baby Care Basics (Ross Laboratories)   It is a 37-minutes video covering daily care, immunization, and safety. Each topic is given 10 + minutes. Suggested retail price is $29.95.

Ross Laboratories
Columbus, OH 43216
1-800-637-6772

CLUBS

Manufacturers hope that they will be chosen to provide your child's formula at the time you decide to use one. To keep you aware of their product, they are willing to cultivate your friendship by means of clubs. They will keep you informed of issues relevant to child-care and give you premiums to woo you. This does not make you obligated; however, it does make you an informed consumer. You may choose to join one or all, and see your mailbox become a source of pleasant surprises.

My Baby's Health Club (Mead Johnson the maker of Enfamil, Pro Sobec, Nutramigen Infant formulas)   A free membership in this club for new parents and babies will bring you health, nutrition, and safety information during the first year. You will also receive valuable coupons and gifts including Beatrix Potter items. The tale "Meet Peter Rabbit" by Beatrix Potter is your first gift.

Mead Johnson Nutritionals
c/o Curtis Distribution Center
P.O. Box 20066
Evansville, IN 47708-9962
1-800-442-2902

Welcome Addition Club (Ross Laboratories maker of Similac and Isomil)   Receive a free Rosco Teddy Bear as your first gift. This is followed by Mom and baby care tips and money savings checks good for their formulas. Gifts, special offers, and just for dad items are also included.

Ross Laboratories
P.O. Box 2971
Shawnee Mission, KS 66201-9121
1-800-BABYLINE

SMA "Family Way Programs"   It will keep you updated with prenatal literature and their newsletter during your pregnancy. It will also send you complimentary gifts and samples of their formula. To enroll you must ask your obstetrician for a card. If your doctor is unaware of the program, you can call and give your doctor's name and address and the company will contact the doctor to determine eligibility.

Triaminic Parent Club   A quarterly publication on child health and safety. It contains coupons for Triaminic products and a variety of safety products at reduced prices. It also has free information for parents columns as well as answers to parents concerns.

Triaminic Parent Club
3816 Grandview Ave.
Gurnee, IL 60031

APPENDIX III

Copy of Questionnaire

MARKETING SURVEY

A report/newsletter will show expectant , new, and not-so-new parents of small children how to save money on a variety of goods and services for their children (e.g., disposable diapers from Huggies, Pampers, Luvs; baby formulas from Similac, Gerber, or Carnation; toys...etc). Your help in answering this survey is greatly appreciated and the results from this survey will help the publishers tremendously.

1) What is your immediate reaction to this idea?
   ☐ excited   ☐ enthusiastic ☐ OK   ☐ poor

2) What best expresses your feeling about buying this product if it is available right now?
   ☐ gotta have it!   ☐ will buy it ☐ think about it   ☐ will not buy it

3) How much would you pay for a one-time report filled with money saving tips and coupons worth up to $200?
   ☐ $5.00 - $5.50   ☐ $5.51 - $6.00   ☐ $6.01 - $6.50   ☐ $6.51 - $7.00

4) How much would you pay for an annual newsletter subscription (6 issues per year, one every two months) which will provide you with information on savings on baby products throughout the year?
   ☐ $11.00 - $12.00 ☐ $12.01 - $13.00   ☐ $13.01 - $14.00   ☐ $14.01 - $15.00

5) Where would you expect to find this product sold?
   ☐ by mail   ☐ doctor's office   ☐ newsstand   ☐ family planning office

6) Where would you expect to see this product advertised?
   ☐ doctor's office   ☐ flyers   ☐ newspaper inserts   ☐ by mail

7) Are there suggestions you would care to make that you think might improve the product?

   _____

   _____

8) Demographic data:
   a) ☐ female   ☐ male
   b) In what category does your age fall?
      ☐ below 18   ☐ 19 - 25   ☐ 26 - 30   ☐ 31 -35   ☐ 36 - 40
   c) Occupation:
      ☐ factory worker   ☐ professional   ☐ self employed   ☐ student
      ☐ homemaker   ☐ office worker   ☐ other
   d) Formal education (check the highest completed):
      ☐ high school ☐ technical school   ☐ junior college   ☐ university   ☐ post graduate
   e) Please state your total family income:
      ☐ below $10,000   ☐ $10,001 - $15,000   ☐ $15,001 - $20,000   ☐ $20,001 - $25,000
      ☐ $25,001 - $35,000 ☐ $35,001 - $50,000 ☐ over $50,000
   f) Number of adults in household:
      ☐ 1   ☐ 2   ☐ 3   ☐ 4   ☐ 5 or more
   g) Number of children in household at or under the age of 3:
      ☐ 0   ☐ 1   ☐ 2   ☐ 3 or more

APPENDIX IV

Tables and Graphs of Survey Results

Table 1   Immediate Reaction to Baby's Cornucopia

Choices	Number of Responses	Percent of Total
Excited	56	29
Enthusiastic	58	30
OK	74	37
Poor	8	4

Table 2   Respondents' Feeling about Buying the Product

Choices	Number of Responses	Percent of Total
Gotta have it!	28	4
Will buy it	82	42
Think about it	67	34
Will not buy it	19	10

Table 3   Cost Willing to Pay for One-Time Report

Choices	Number of Responses	Percent of Total
$5.00–$5.50	129	66
$5.51–$6.00	30	15
$6.01–$6.50	13	7
$6.51–$7.00	24	12

Table 4   Cost Willing to Pay for Annual Subscription

Choices	Number of Responses	Percent of Total
$11.00–$12.00	119	61
$12.01–$13.00	48	24
$13.01–$14.00	7	4
$14.01–$15.00	22	11

Table 5   Expected Distribution Channels

Choices	Number of Responses	Percent of Total
By mail	119	61
Doctor's office	20	10
Newsstand	26	13
Family Planning Ctr	31	16

Table 6   Expected Advertising Channels

Choices	Number of Responses	Percent of Total
Doctor's office	118	59
Flyers	11	6
Newspaper inserts	15	8
By mail	52	27

Table 7-A   Gender of Respondents

Choices	Number of Responses	Percent of Total
Female	176	90
Male	20	10

Table 7-B   Age of Respondents

Choices	Number of Responses	Percent of Total
18 and under	5	3
19–25	55	28
26–30	67	34
31–35	42	21
36 and over	27	14

Table 7-C   Occupation of Respondents

Choices	Number of Responses	Percent of Total
Factory worker	3	2
Homemaker	36	18
Professional	46	23
Office worker	35	18
Self-Employed	26	13
Student	15	8
Other	35	18

Table 7-D   Respondents' Education (Highest Completed)

Choices	Number of Responses	Percent of Total
High School	46	23
Technical School	5	3
Junior College	51	26
University	75	38
Post-graduate	19	10

Table 7-E   Respondents' Total Family Income

Choices	Number of Responses	Percent of Total
Below $10,000	13	7
$10,001–$15,000	16	8
$15,001–$20,000	19	10
$20,001–$25,000	34	17
$25,000–$35,000	40	20
$35,001–$50,000	28	14
Over $50,000	46	24

Table 7-F   Number of Adults in Respondents' Households

Choices	Number of Responses	Percent of Total
1	34	17
2	139	70
3	17	9
4	2	1
5 or more	4	3

**Table 7-G   Number of Children
under Age 3 in Respondents' Households**

Choices	Number of Responses	Percent of Total
0	67	34
1	75	38
2	31	16
3 or more	23	12

Figure 1   Immediate Reaction to Baby's Cornucopia

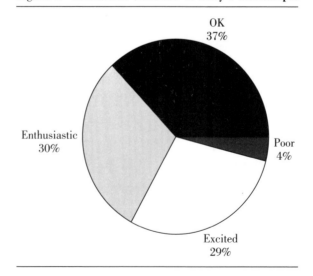

Figure 2   Respondents' Purchase Feeling

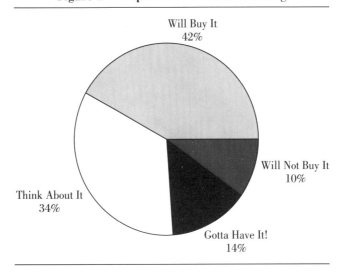

**Figure 3   Cost Willing to Pay for
One-Time Report**

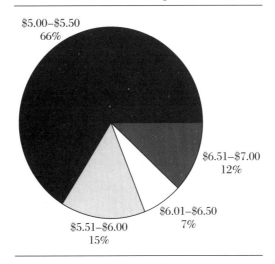

Figure 4   Expected Cost for Annual Subscription

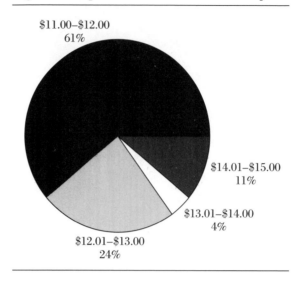

Figure 5   Expected Distribution Channels

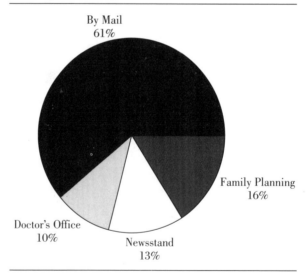

Figure 6   Expected Advertising Channels

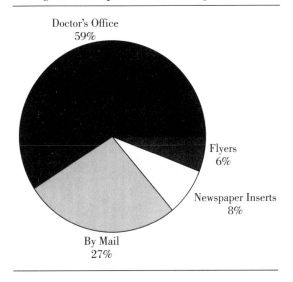

Figure 7-A   Gender of Respondents

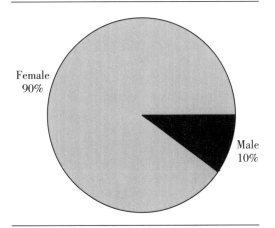

Figure 7-B   Age of Respondents

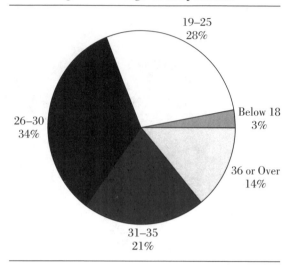

Figure 7-C   Occupation of Respondents

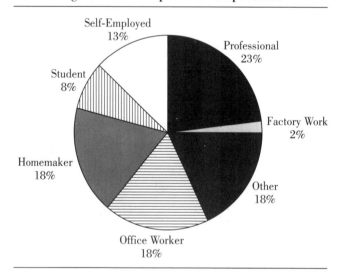

Figure 7-D   Respondents' Education (Completed)

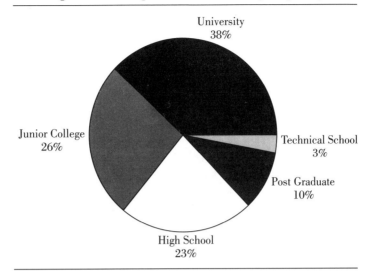

Figure 7-E   Respondents' Total Family Income

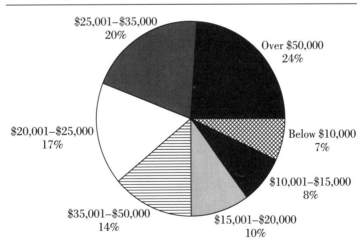

Figure 7-F   Number of Adults in Respondents' Households

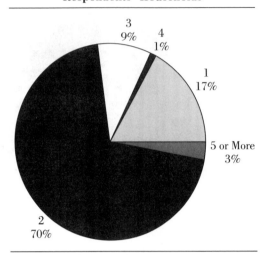

Figure 7-G   Number of Children under the Age of 3 in Respondents' Household

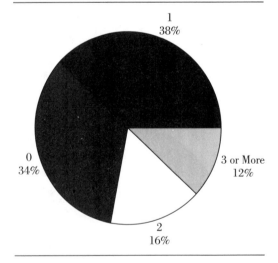

APPENDIX V

Prototype of Bookmark (Sales Promotion)

Save
on
baby
Money

Baby's Cornucopia
"the Gift that keeps on
Giving . . ."

will show you

- How to get free magazines and videos
- How to save money on all your baby's purchases
- Who will send you money and how to qualify
- How your baby can begin getting free stuff before he/she is born
- Who is willing to give you services and information

Save
on
baby
Money

Baby's Cornucopia
"the Gift that keeps on
Giving . . ."

will show you

- How to get free magazines and videos
- How to save money on all your baby's purchases
- Who will send you money and how to qualify
- How your baby can begin getting free stuff before he/she is born
- Who is willing to give you services and information

Save
on
baby
Money

Baby's Cornucopia
"the Gift that keeps on
Giving . . ."

will show you

- How to get free magazines and videos
- How to save money on all your baby's purchases
- Who will send you money and how to qualify
- How your baby can begin getting free stuff before he/she is born
- Who is willing to give you services and information

3

BUSINESS PLAN FOR SNEAK PEEK

A Student's Guide to University Courses

Developed by

Tonette Dove, David Grajeda, Anthony B. Lujan, Donna Tom, Huei Ming Tsai, and Caroline Wang

Used with the Permission of the Authors

Executive Summary

This business plan was developed to study the economic feasibility of distributing a campus publication. *Sneak Peek: A Student's Guide* serves as a detailed brochure for students about courses offered at the California State University at Los Angeles (CSULA) campus. Preliminary research indicates there exists a strong demand for this product and a stable target market. As of Fall 1989 the student population of CSULA was 20,804 and has remained fairly constant at the 20,000–21,000 range for the past four years (see Appendix A). Primary research data have established that 70% of the target market would be willing to purchase this product at a price range of under $10.00. Of this market, 50% will be captured the first year (i.e., 35% of the total market) and sales are expected to increase by at least 50% per year thereafter. Further appeal is that the brochure has very low overhead, minimal competition, and benefits both students and the quality of CSULA's education.

This venture would require an initial capital investment of $18,000 (6 shares at $3,000 each). This initial capital investment will be paid back the first year. Furthermore, a first-year return on investment of 44% is expected. The sales projection for the initial year is $128,055.53. Of the first year's revenue, 12.8% will be from local business advertising sales. Throughout the five-year projection, sales are projected to grow tremendously.

Table of Contents

INTRODUCTION . . . . 3 · 4

SITUATION ANALYSIS . . . . 3 · 4

PROBLEMS AND
OPPORTUNITIES . . . . 3 · 7

FINANCIAL ANALYSIS . . . . 3 · 8

OPERATIONAL ASPECTS . . . . . . 3 · 8

MARKETING STRATEGY . . . . 3 · 9

IMPLEMENTATION SCHEDULE . . . 3 · 12

FINANCIAL DATA . . . . 3 · 12

CONCLUSION . . . . 3 · 13

BIBLIOGRAPHY . . . . 3 · 13

REFERENCES . . . . 3 · 13

APPENDIX A: CSULA TARGET
POPULATION STATISTICS
(FACT SHEET) . . . . 3 · 14

APPENDIX B: GUIDE TO
CLASSES AND INSTRUCTORS
OF CSULA SURVEY . . . . 3 · 17

APPENDIX C: STATISTICAL
ANALYSIS OF CSULA
COURSE/INSTRUCTOR
GUIDE SURVEY . . . . 3 · 18

APPENDIX D: SAMPLE FORMAT
OF COURSE/INSTRUCTOR
INFORMATION . . . . 3 · 19

APPENDIX E: SAMPLE FORMAT
OF LOCAL BUSINESS
ADVERTISING . . . . 3 · 20

APPENDIX F: SAMPLE FORMAT
OF INVITATION TO BE A
STUDENT RESPONDENT . . . . . . 3 · 21

APPENDIX G: SAMPLE FORMAT
OF INVITATION TO ADVERTISE
IN RECYCLER . . . . 3 · 22

APPENDIX H: SAMPLE FORMAT
OF RECYCLER SECTION FOR
USED BOOKS ADVERTISING . . . . 3 · 23

APPENDIX I: SAMPLE FORMAT
OF STUDENT TELEPHONE
SURVEY . . . . 3 · 24

APPENDIX J: SAMPLE FORMAT
OF INVITATION TO PLACE
ADVANCE ORDER . . . . 3 · 25

APPENDIX K: CSULA *UNIVERSITY
TIMES* ADVERTISING RATES . . . . 3 · 26

APPENDIX L: FINANCIAL DATA . . 3 · 27

INTRODUCTION

The objective of this business plan is to study the feasibility of publishing a student's inside guide to courses and instructors at CSULA. Based upon a preliminary survey of 450 currently enrolled CSULA students, an 88% favorable response rate for this product and a 70% buy rate from students who desired to purchase this product were established. This survey represents a cross section of all students currently attending CSULA. Surveys were purposely done at random times during the day and evening throughout campus. This gave a representative mix of undergraduate and graduate students as well as dormitory and commuter students (see Appendix C).

Demand for the product will be strong because CSULA has a high percentage of commuter students (97%) with limited access to word-of-mouth recommendations on class and instructor information. Primary research data on 450 randomly selected CSULA students indicates only 62% had access to word-of-mouth recommendations from friends for classes they were planning to take the next quarter. This information gap is further compounded by the fact that many CSULA students have less time for social interactions than traditional college students. Many CSULA students are trying to balance full-time jobs and family responsibilities in conjunction with school demands (see Appendix A). This guidebook will provide a reasonable alternative to traditional word-of-mouth recommendations college students of the past utilized when they had the time and opportunity to develop a social network with fellow dorm residents and classmates.

Promotion and advertising of this publication will be directed along CSULA's mass communication channels (CSULA *University Times* ads, *Quarterly Schedule of Classes* ads, campus fliers, and advertising/sales booths during New Student Orientation Days). Students will be offered discount coupons for the publication or free advertising of their used books on a selected basis. This will be a means of generating increased awareness and interest in the guidebook.

Printing and advertising costs will constitute the major expense. To maintain production costs at a minimum and keep the final product at a reasonable price to cost-conscious students, the guidebook will be limited to 160 pages for the initial printing. The guidebook will consist of six sections:

1. Information on courses and instructors.
2. Business advertising space (encourage free or discount coupon offers).
3. Invitation for students to participate in the next publication as a respondent.
4. Invitation to advertise in the recycler section for free.
5. Recycler section (will need to limit this section since it is being used as a promotion technique, i.e., loss leader).
6. Invitation to place an advance order.

One of the methods that will be employed to offset publishing costs will be to entice local businesses (fast food, laundry, printing or photocopying establishments, bookstores, apartment managers, or other student-oriented services) to advertise in the guidebook for a fee. This additional advertising revenue will make it feasible to keep the price charged for the publication under $10.00. This should aid greatly in overcoming student price resistance.

Based upon the results of a random survey of 450 CSULA students, sales and market share projections will be forecasted for the initial year. This will be followed by a complete analysis of capital expenses, promotion and distribution costs, start-up costs, and a quarter-to-quarter cash flow projection for a five-year period.

SITUATION ANALYSIS

In this section, various factors that affect the marketability of the product will be discussed. Customer profile, relevant social and cultural factors, prevailing economic and business conditions, legal and political aspects, and other environmental factors impacting the product will be examined.

Customer Profile

Sneak Peek's target market is comprised of CSULA's student body. Of the total quarterly

20,000 plus enrollment, the specific target marketing will be directed toward the freshman, sophomore, and junior class levels. It is this 45.2% of total students who enroll in the general and lower division courses that have been selected for the student guide's first edition. Totaling 12,407 as of Fall 1989, this undergraduate segment population will be the primary focus, but not to the exclusion of the 54.8% senior class and graduate level. It is believed the intended target market will actively seek this product. Sneak Peek enhances the opportunity to effectively choose classes which otherwise would require informational networking that may not be easily accessible.

Location Profile

Realistically, the two most visible and therefore most ideal sites to sell the product would be the University Square Bookstore and the Student Book Mart located at 1689 N. Eastern Avenue. These two locations have established themselves as CSULA student oriented outlets and generate tremendous student traffic. Secondary methods of generating sales would be to employ direct marketing techniques to solicit sales through advertising in the CSULA quarterly *Schedule of Classes,* the CSULA *University Times,* and fliers' distribution throughout campus. Another ideal site location would be to set up a booth during new student orientation days and pass out sales information on the guidebook.

The fact that this venture does not require a permanent store front as a prerequisite to doing business is a definite advantage. By avoiding this major fixed overhead expense, this business can be initiated on a shoestring budget.

Sales Projections

The average student at CSULA spends approximately $40 to $50 on textbooks per course. The guidebook will be priced at under $10.00.

In most student's eyes, this would be perceived as a bargain. Insights obtained from the publication are valuable if it allows one to avoid the ordeal of registration's drop and add. Also, there is the added "hook" of the recycler section to aid in increasing sales. Students will

have the opportunity to contact other students and purchase used books at a savings. Thus, all or a significant portion of the cost of the guidebook can be recouped. Another positive selling feature of the guidebook is the discount or free coupons offered by local merchants in the Business Advertising section.

Based on the CSULA student survey, a conservative sales rate of 35% of the 20,804 total student population is anticipated. This represents 50% of the students who said they would buy based upon a selling price of less than $10.00. Therefore, the first-year sales projection on guidebooks is approximately $111,602.00 based upon an introductory direct mail price of $5.00 and a wholesale price of $4.00 for the publication. The calculation used was a 70% buy response × 50% sales rate × total CSULA student population × selling price of guidebook × 4 issues per year (with the added stipulation that direct mailing will account for 20% of total sales for the first year). Sales are targeted to increase by 50% per year since 88% of the respondents saw a need for the publication, but only 70% said they would actually buy. Through word-of-mouth customer recommendations and additional product features, the remaining market population will be captured within a three-year period.

Additional revenue will be attained through advertising sales to local businesses: $175 per quarter, $330 for two quarters, $435 for three quarters, and $540 for four quarters for a ¼ page advertisement in the guidebook. This represents 50% less than rates charged by the CSULA *Schedule of Classes* publication. Revenues generated from this source will add a minimum of $10,000 to $15,000 in yearly profits using a conservative target of twenty advertisers per issue. Therefore, total sales projections for the first year from sales of guidebooks and sales of advertising space is $128,055.53.

Additionally, if the option to charge $2.00 per used book ad is utilized in the Recycler Section, profits will once again increase.

Competition

As with any business, competition is always a critical factor. Currently, CSULA does not have a publication similar to the guidebook available

15. Additional payments are due June 15, September 15, and January 15. At the time of each payment, adjustments to the estimate will be made. Other than the risk of a libel suit and payment of taxes, there are no other basic regulations at the federal level that must be complied with.

At the state level, according to Jamie Green of the State Board of Equalization, quarterly periodicals are not subject to state taxes. Therefore, the price charged on the guidebook is the price that must be charged to retail customers. State sales tax will not be collected at the wholesale or the retail level. By registering Sneak Peek at the office of the State Board of Equalization, a resale number can be obtained through which sales can be made to vendors. At the state level, no business license is required. This type of licensing is done only at the municipal level.

Obtaining a normal business license to fulfill city-level requirements involves filing and paying license fees at the county clerk's office. There are two licenses that are required: The Consumer Retail Sales License (CRS) and the Wholesale Sale License (WSL). The CRS has an initial cost of $100.78, and the WSL has a first-time cost of $107.50. Every January, thereafter, the CRS requires a payment of $1.25 per $1,000.00 worth of units sold. Likewise, every subsequent January, the WSL requires a payment of $1.25 per $1,000.00 worth of units sold. Once these two licenses are obtained, it is legal to operate this business in the city.

However, this does not mean Sneak Peek automatically receives the approval of the California State University at Los Angeles. According to Ruth Goldway, Director of Public Affairs-CSULA, the first step to getting the school to approve this project is through Office of Student Life, Student Union 425. Vera Perez, Office of Student Life, stated that printing the guidebook could be approved by the university. However, final approval must be obtained from Central Reservations, Student Union 410. Any item that is circulated throughout the University must have a University stamp of approval.

Once "Sneak Peek" has this stamp, total freedom is allowed in marketing it to students. Setting up a table in front of the Student Union would cost $25.00 per day and promote high visibility of the product. On the other hand, selling this guidebook through the University Book Store would require the approval of Catherine Rembol, CSULA University Square Bookstore Manager. Per Ms. Rembol, the retail cost to students for each guidebook would be the product's wholesale price plus a 25% markup.

PROBLEMS AND OPPORTUNITIES

A primary survey of 450 CSULA students yielded encouraging statistics. Seldom does a company have the opportunity to market a new product to a target group where 88% of the market believes there is a need for that product, 63% of the target market is willing to participate in the production of that product, and 70% of the market is also willing to buy the finished product when it becomes available (see Appendix C, Table 2). It was of interest to note that 97% of the freshman class (the best indicator of future sales) believes there is a need for this product and 76% were willing to buy the guide if it was priced at less than $10.00. Once again, this reinforces the belief that even with access to word-of-mouth recommendations (52% for freshmen), students are still eager to find out more about classes and instructors, especially from a reasonably priced source.

It is expected that the demand for this product will continue to grow until the full market share of 70% is attained and then remain constant because customers will be encouraged to repeat buy each quarter. Some students may choose to photocopy sections of the guide rather than purchase it, but this will be a relatively low number due to the low price ($5.00) of the product. To encourage repeat buyers, the courses selected for the guide will vary slightly each quarter to correspond to courses offered by the university. Additionally, emphasis will be placed on obtaining business advertisers who will offer discount coupons on goods and services in their advertisements through the guidebook. Finally, the possible savings on purchasing used books through the guide's Recycler Section will spur sales and encourage repeat buyers.

Perhaps the primary obstacle to the success of this venture will be compiling the required data quickly enough to update the publication every quarter. This requires being totally dependent upon the input of students responding to invitations to be part of the student panel. Therefore, the incentives offered (discount coupon or free advertising space) must be compelling enough to entice students to participate. Based on the students' survey, 63% of the respondents said they were willing to participate for these incentives. Of this group, 60% preferred receiving the discount coupon, 25% the free advertising, and 15% had no preference (see Appendix C, Table 3). It is anticipated that one person using the telephone to collect all required information should be able to update the publication each quarter.

Due to the quarterly publication of the product, inventory levels must be monitored very carefully. With experience, the ability to accurately judge demand for the product will be gained. Strict inventory control will increase profits by reducing the amount of outdated merchandise created by the quarterly turnover of this product. To address this problem, the "Just-In-Time" method of inventory control will be utilized.

FINANCIAL ANALYSIS

In order to determine start-up and operational costs, the following financial analysis was compiled.

Initial Investment

The initial investment for the proposed business is for capital equipment (typewriter, telephone, answering machine) and miscellaneous expenses (stationery, phone line, optional P.O. Box). This business is designed to run out of one's home. As stated earlier, the major expense will be printing costs and postage costs for the respondents.

First-Year Operations

From the target sales of $111,602 for the first year, the net income of $38,320 is derived after deducting cost of sales and all other operating expenses (See Appendix N, Table 2, Projected Profit and Loss Statement—Year 1). This represents a return of 30% on sales and 44% on investment. A positive cash flow of $33,450 is projected at the end of the first year of which

$30,000 is available for distribution to the partners ($5,000 per partner). The break-even analysis for the first year is based on a total fixed cost of $6,934.28.

Five-Year Projection

In the five-year projection, sales are estimated to grow at 50% for year 2, 75% for year 3, 40% for year 4, 25% for year 5. This growth objective is realistic based upon the strategy of sales of not only the guidebook but of increasing sales from local business advertising and student used books advertising in subsequent years.

OPERATIONAL ASPECTS

This section will describe the actual product to be published and the process utilized to gather and coordinate course/instructor information from fellow students.

Product

The publication shall consist of six sections:

1. Course/Instructor Information.
2. Local Business Advertising.
3. Invitation to Be a Student Respondent.
4. Invitation to Advertise in Recycler Section for Free.
5. Recycler Section.
6. Invitation to Place an Advance Order.

The largest section of the guidebook (70–90 pages) will be the information on course requirements and instructors. The criteria for segmenting courses was based on identifying those courses needed by students to fulfill their undergraduate degree requirements. General Education courses form the foundation for every undergraduate student. Selecting these courses will result in the greatest demand for this guidebook and promote active sales. For the first edition of the guidebook, General Education courses which attract the most enrollment will be selected. Essentially, courses offering more than two choices of instructors will be included in the guidebook. This translates into surveying approximately

128 classes for course requirements and instructor information to be published in the first edition of the guidebook.

Future issues will utilize the same basic strategy as above. Each quarter, courses will be analyzed and those with the most enrollment selected for publication. Future expansion and marketing strategy would call for plans to produce a separate guidebook for graduate students and select majors with high enrollment. For example, analyzing the core requirements of Business and Economic majors would yield a marketable product as would examining Child Development and Nursing coursework (see Appendix A).

Once the courses for inclusion into the publication are selected, responses from students who wish to participate in the publication (Appendix F) will be culled to select those who are currently taking the courses to be evaluated. These students will be contacted by phone and the appropriate information collected (see Appendix I). A minimum of three to five students will be polled for each course in order to gain a representative overview of students' opinions on course and instructor requirements (see Appendixes D and I). This information will be compiled, collated, and organized for final publication. By updating course requirements each quarter, any recent changes in course requirements will be noted. This action does not obviate the necessity of including a disclaimer stating in effect that up-to-date information on courses and instructors has been compiled but there is no guarantee that future courses taught by this instructor will follow the described format. Although course requirements may vary slightly from quarter to quarter, the information presented on instructors' teaching and grading methods is still applicable and will be of value to customers.

The final product is envisioned to be approximately 160 pages and will be printed by ART'S Press, 4727 E. Olympic Blvd., Los Angeles, CA 90020, (213) 262-0431. The guidebook will consist of 40 pages of 11×17 inch standard stock white paper saddle-stitched down the middle (160 total pages of $8 \frac{1}{2} \times 11$ inch paper printed on both sides) with a goldenrod cover of slightly heavier stock paper and done in one-color print. Total printing time for 2,000 copies is seven days, plus an additional

seven days to typeset the first edition. Total printing costs for the first batch of 2,000 copies is $2,500 including typesetting. Additional runs of 2,000 copies will take 7 days printing time and cost $1,900 per batch as quoted by Paul Go, owner of ART'S Press.

The just-in-time method of inventory control will be utilized and the appropriate number of copies reordered when available stock drops below 500 copies. Since this publication is updated quarterly, outdated merchandise from overestimating demand is a concern. It is anticipated that after the first two quarters of publication, data on product demand will become accurate.

MARKETING STRATEGY

Basically, the guidebook will consist of the six sections mentioned previously. Each section will play a distinct role in the marketing of the product.

Product Strategy

Overall product strategy is to develop a product that is of universal appeal to CSULA students. A guidebook on course and instructor information seems the most logical product to market to students. To separate this publication from the CSULA General Catalogue, which also gives course information, the guidebook shall include information on grading methods and student insights. Also, a more free-flowing, entertaining style of writing will be employed to make the publication enjoyable to read. Therefore, initial product strategy was threefold:

1. Offer course information from a student's perspective with student tips on how to do well.
2. Keep the price of the publication low to fit students' tight budget.
3. Offer free services or discounts on merchandise to create the feeling that the buyer was getting his money's worth.

To accomplish these objectives, six sections to the guidebook were devised.

Section 1: Course/Instructor Information (70 to 90 Pages)

This section will contain a brief description of course content to lend substance and credibility to the product. This description will be kept short so as to not cover the same information presented in the CSULA General Catalogue. Students' insights on how to prepare for tests and helpful hints will be included. Student comments on instructors will be carefully reviewed to ascertain if they are appropriate for inclusion in the guidebook. There is no wish to threaten or antagonize instructors by becoming too personal or subjective in instructor evaluations. Each course will receive a ½-page write-up in the guidebook.

Section 2: Local Business Advertising (10 to 20 Pages Maximum)

This section was designed as a means of offering free or discount goods to students from local merchants while serving as an important source of revenue for the guidebook through paid advertising fees. Local merchants will be strongly encouraged to offer student discounts when placing their advertisements.

Section 3: Invitation to Be a Student Respondent (2 Pages)

This will save the cost of advertising in other publications to recruit student participants (see Appendix F). A copy of the student Participant Questionnaire (see Appendix I) will be included in the guidebook so interested students will know what information will be needed in evaluating courses for the guidebook. The invitation shall include a postcard-size prepaid reply card for interested students to mail in to the guidebook's P.O. Box.

Section 4: Invitation to Advertise in the Recycler Section for Free (1 Page)

This free offer will be used to generate student interest in the publication. Promotion will emphasize *Free Used Book Advertising* to attract students to read further sales text introducing the guidebook and how to obtain the free advertising. It is anticipated that students advertising used books through the guidebook will also buy a copy to see their name in print.

After all, everyone appreciates a brief moment in the limelight.

Section 5: Recycler Section (40 to 50 Pages)

This section contains brief ads for used books (see Appendix H). Students will call each other based on information contained in the ad. The staff of the guidebook will not be involved with these used book sales. Depending on student response, there are plans to turn the Recycler into a third avenue of income in the future through sale of Used Book advertising.

Section 6: Order Form for Advance Book Sale (1 Page)

This form will allow students to order the next issue of the guidebook in advance (see Appendix J). By selling at a retail price ($5.00/copy) instead of a wholesale price ($4.00/copy), an additional $1.00/copy of sales revenue is obtained at the expense of $.35/copy in mailing costs. More importantly, advance sales will help in maintaining adequate inventory levels. It is projected that direct mail sales will constitute 20% of total sales the first year and increase slightly each year as students become familiar with the content and quality of the product.

Price Strategy

Marketing strategy dictates setting the price of this publication below $10.00 per copy. In fact, the price for the first edition is only $5.00 by direct mail (postage and handling included), or $5.00 through the University Square Bookstore or the Student Book Mart. This will allow the publication to be perceived as a bargain. It offers students a range of desirable features as well as the opportunity to recoup their investment through the Recycler Section and merchant discount coupons. This low price will lend an initial price advantage over future competitors and hopefully discourage them from entering the market. It will also make it easier to repeat sell the publication each quarter to the same clientele.

As a means of keeping production costs low and therefore product price low, local businesses will be actively solicited to advertise in the publication and offer free services or goods. Advertisement in Sneak Peek can be done on a quarterly or yearly basis for a fee far less than conventional advertising rates. The CSULA *Schedule of Classes* is published quarterly and charges for a ¼ page ad: $350 for one quarter, $660 for 2 quarters, $870 for 3 quarters, and $1,080 for 4 quarters. Businesses in the CSULA local area will be approached to solicit advertisements at rate 50% less than those charged by the publishers of the CSULA quarterly *Schedule of Classes*. This additional revenue will be used to keep the price charged for the guidebook low. It is anticipated that 10 to 20 business ads will be placed in the guidebook each quarter the first year. Business advertising revenue is targeted to increase by 50% each year.

Promotion Strategy

The promotion for this product will concentrate on mass advertising through campus publications and activities. Direct mail solicitation through the CSULA *Schedule of Classes,* the CSULA *University Times,* and flier distribution throughout campus will be utilized. Also, information and sales booths will be set up on campus during New Student Orientation days.

Advertising costs for the above-mentioned publications are as follows: CSULA *University Times* has a flat fee of $337.00 per year for an advertisement that is placed in the classified section of the campus newspaper in a two-column, three-inch-deep, boxed enclosure. It will run for thirty consecutive issues. The *University Times* is printed three days a week, Monday, Wednesday, and Thursday with a circulation of 8,000 copies each quarter; 6,000 copies are printed each Monday and Thursday and 12,000 copies are printed for Registration, Welcome Back, and Special issues. The *University Times* has a daily readership over 23,500 of which 20,000 are students, 1,500 are faculty, and 2,000 are campus employees. The *University Times* is distributed free on campus from circulation boxes located at high traffic points and also at the student housing complexes.

The CSULA *Schedule of Classes* is issued on a quarterly basis. The advertising fee for a ¼ page ad depends upon the frequency: $350 for one quarter, $660 for two quarters, $870 for three quarters, $1,080 for four quarters. The University Square Bookstore orders 23,000 to 25,000 *Schedule of Classes* per quarter according to Katherine Rembold, General Manager of the University Square Bookstore.

Posters will also be utilized on campus to inform potential customers of this publication. The posters will be placed in high traffic points, such as the Student Union, the cafeterias, in and around the Library, kiosks, and housing complexes. The size of the poster mentioned will be 11 × 17 inches.

Flier distribution promoting the features of the publication and how to obtain a copy will be hand placed on windshields of cars during the period of class registration. The size of the fliers mentioned will be 8½ × 11 inches.

Distribution Strategy

This product will be available for in-person sales through the University Square Bookstore and the Student Book Mart. Rates these establishments charge for their services are as follows: The University Square Bookstore will mark up the wholesale price charged them by 25% to obtain the retail price. The Student Book Mart will discount the retail selling price of the University Square Bookstore by 10%–15% to obtain their selling price.

Alternatively, the publication can be purchased at the booth set up during New Student Orientation Days provided this does not conflict with sales at the University Square Bookstore. Permission to operate a booth outside the Student Union can be obtained through the Student Union management.

Another source for obtaining the publication will be through the direct mail ads run in the *Schedule of Classes* and the *University Times*. Purchases can be made by calling the listed telephone number to request an order form or by sending in an order form and a check to a P.O. Box or dropping it off at a campus mailbox. Approval from the University as a legitimate business is required before a campus mailbox can be obtained from the Associated Student Office, Student Union 424. One of the incentives for students to use direct mail purchase is the opportunity to order the publication in advance to obtain the guidebook before it is released through the bookstores. Advance sales give students first opportunity at the used books offered. In terms of product distribution, advance sales are beneficial in maintaining adequate product inventory levels. It decreases demand peaks and reduces unplanned shortages due to insufficient supply.

Statistics will be followed for each of the above-mentioned distribution methods to determine which avenues generate the most sales. Future advertising budget and distribution efforts will be concentrated on the most effective mediums.

IMPLEMENTATION SCHEDULE

The advertising period of Sneak Peek will extend throughout CSULA's school year. Advertising will be heavy beginning the fifth week of Spring 1990. This is Sneak Peek's introduction period. Promotion continues through Summer quarter with emphasis on the third through eighth week coinciding with student registration. Special emphasis will be placed on promotion for New Student Orientation and the Fall 1990 Quarter.

Immediate

Collecting data will begin the first week of the Spring 1990 quarter. Class schedule data will be continuously accumulated throughout the school year. Information such as the instructors' curriculum data and students' input will be gathered until the second week of the Fall 1990 quarter.

Spring 1990 Quarter

During this period, Sneak Peek's advertising and promotion begin as follows:

University Times Ads	Submit ad for year-round circulation.
Fliers and Posters	Print-up and distribute.
	Announce arriving campus product.
Schedule of Classes Ad	Submit ad to directory of classes for each upcoming quarter scheduled publication.

In this quarter, students will be invited to participate in a survey in exchange for free advertising of a used book or for a $2.00 discount coupon off the purchase price of the publication.

Summer 1990 Quarter

All scheduled objectives, except product distribution, implemented. Advertising, data collection, editing, and promotion will continue through the span of this quarter. Accumulated data is edited and revised. Organization of collected information is prepared for the Fall 1990 quarter's second week.

Fall 1990 Quarter

Advertising, promotion, printing, and distribution are the main emphasis on this scheduled section. By the end of week one, all required editing will be completed and the finished draft sent to the printers. The final product made available by the fourth week. This is the optimum time for release of this publication since it coincides with peak demand for the product.

Distribution (direct mailing and bookstore circulation) will begin the fifth week. This will correspond with CSULA's winter 1991 Schedule of Classes and Winter registration period. Promotional activities will be carried through as indicated under the Promotion heading of the Implementation Schedule (Appendix K).

FINANCIAL DATA

The initial investment is a relative low amount of $3,000 for each person with a total of $18,000. The reason for this low initial investment is the low cost of expenses. For example, a retail outlet is not needed, personnel are limited, and the distribution is solely through the bookstores or through mail order. These advantages greatly reduce costs. The initial fiscal year will start from Fall 1990. The financial data used is in a conservative form so all projections of expenses and costs will not be less than actual cost. Also, the expected sales will not be less than the actual sales. Sales of $128,055.53 are expected for the first year from both guidebook and advertising sales.

Total sales will grow by 50% for year 2, 75% for year 3, 40% for year 4, and 25% for year 5. A total sales of $588,255.07 are expected by year 5. The best selling season is Fall quarter (see Appendix N: Profit and Loss Statement). The seasonal factors used were Fall 1.35, Winter 1.1, Spring 0.9, and Summer 0.65. These factors are based on the enrollment of students each quarter on campus. For example, the Fall quarter is the highest selling quarter because it has the largest enrollment, and Summer will be our lowest quarter in sales because it has the smallest enrollment. Sneak Peek is so profitable that the return on investment is 44%, which is 10% more than the normal industry. This is due to high demand for this item by the students. Each investor will receive a $5,000 return on investment for the first year. This will increase by 15% for year 2, 50% for year 3, 75% for year 4, 50% for year 5. The distribution for each investor will increase five-fold by the end of year 5.

CONCLUSION

In conclusion, this business plan has clearly outlined why this product will be successful. High student demand for this product (88%), as exhibited by willingness of students to participate in the production of the guidebook (63%) and in their desire to purchase the finished product (70%), has conclusively been established. Thus, the first caveat of marketing has been accomplished, namely, "Produce or obtain a product that sells itself." Another positive feature is the variety of ways this publication generates revenue: through direct mail sales, wholesale sales, business advertising sales, and student advertising sales. Besides being highly profitable with a 44% first-year return on investment and first-year

sales of $128,055.53, required initial start-up capital is minimal ($18,000) due to low overhead and very low product costs. This coupled with the flexibility of being able to quickly adapt the publication to respond to student needs or to branch off into more specialized guidebooks for specific degree majors ensures both the present and future viability of this product.

BIBLIOGRAPHY

Cohen, William, *Building a Mail Order Business,* John Wiley & Sons, New York, 1982.

Cohen, William and Nurit, J. *Top Executive Performance,* John Wiley & Sons, New York, 1984.

Office of Public Affairs and Analytical Studies, *Facts #2: Fall 1989 Enrollment Information,* California State University at Los Angeles, January 1990, p. 2.

Office of Public Affairs and Analytical Studies, *Facts #1: Fall 1988 Enrollment Information,* California State University at Los Angeles, January 1989, p. 2.

Office of Public Affairs and Analytical Studies, *Facts Sheet: Fall 1987,* Enrollment Information, California State University at Los Angeles, January 1988, p. 1.

REFERENCES

Ruth Goldway—Public Affairs Director (213) 343-3050.

Katherine F. Rembold—General Manager of University Square Bookstore (213) 343-2500.

Terrance Timmins, J.D.—Coordinator, Legal Information CSULA (213) 343-3110 or (213) 343-3414.

State Board of Equalization

County Clerk's Office

APPENDIX A

California State University, Los Angeles Target Population Statistics

Apportioned by class level, part-time, and full-time status
Years 1987, 1988, and 1989

	Fall 1987		Fall 1988		Fall 1989	
Total	21,189	100.00%	21,150	100.00%	20,804	100.00%
Freshmen	2,903	13.70	3,363	15.90	3,375	16.20
Sophomores	2,373	11.20	1,967	9.30	2,144	10.30
Juniors	4,047	19.10	3,997	18.90	3,888	18.60
Seniors	5,827	27.50	5,901	27.90	5,976	28.70
Grad-PB	6,039	29.50	5,922	28.00	5,421	26.00
Part-time	10,806	51.00%	10,617	50.00%	10,358	49.00%
Full-time	10,383	49.00	10,300	49.00	10,446	50.00
Comprehensive exams			233	1.00		

Fall 1989 Population Statistics

Commuter students	20,217	97.18%
Campus residents	587	2.82

Notes:

Office of Public Affairs and Analytical Studies, *Facts Sheet: Fall 1987 Enrollment Information,* California State University, Los Angeles, January 1988, page 1.

Office of Public Affairs and Analytical Studies, *Facts #2: Fall 1988 Enrollment Information,* California State University, Los Angeles, January 1989, page 2.

Office of Public Affairs and Analytical Studies, *Facts #3: Fall 1989 Enrollment Information,* California State University, Los Angeles, January 1989, page 2.

February 1990

FOR
INFORMATION
REGARDING
CONTENT PLEASE
CALL (213) 343-2730

PREPARED BY THE OFFICES OF PUBLIC AFFAIRS AND ANALYTICAL STUDIES

The Offices of Analytical Studies and Public Affairs have developed this fact sheet to provide the campus community with pertinent information about the University. Data are presented for Fall Quarter 1989, since the fall term is generally considered representative of the academic year.

Additional fact sheets will be released as needed to keep the campus community informed about institutional issues.

- Cal State L.A. enrolled 20,804 students in Fall 1989 (excluding students registered for comprehensive examinations only).
- The full-time equivalent student (FTES) figure was 13,943.

Enrollment by Class Level

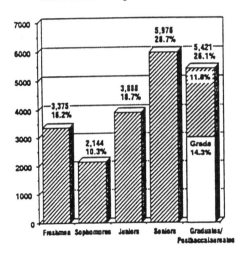

Total Enrollment..............................20,804

Enrollment by Gender

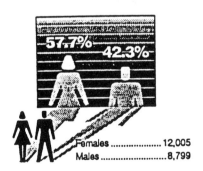

Females 12,005
Males 8,799

Enrollment by Class Load

Full time (12 or more units) 10,446   50.2%
Part time (7-11 units) 4,654   22.4%
Part time (1-6 units) 5,704   27.4%

- Cal State L.A.'s student population is comprised of approximately equal proportions of part-time and full-time students. Many are employed on a full-time basis.
- The average unit load is 10.05.

Enrollment by Ethnic Group*

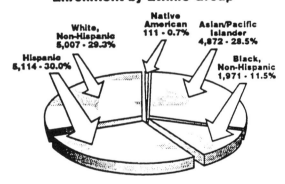

White, Non-Hispanic 5,007 - 29.3%

Native American 111 - 0.7%

Asian/Pacific Islander 4,872 - 28.5%

Hispanic 5,114 - 30.0%

Black, Non-Hispanic 1,971 - 11.5%

* Ethnic data are voluntarily reported; only U.S. citizens and resident aliens identifying an ethnic group are included.

- The average age of undergraduates is 25; that of graduates and postbaccalaureates is 35. The weighted average for the combined groups is 28.

Enrollment by School

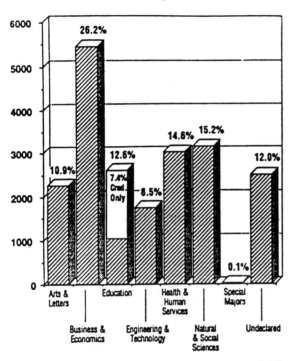

Enrollment by Citizenship Status

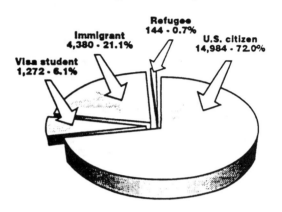

Visa student
1,272 - 6.1%

Immigrant
4,380 - 21.1%

Refugee
144 - 0.7%

U.S. citizen
14,984 - 72.0%

Arts & Letters	2,258
Business & Economics	5,450
Education	2,619
degree objective	968
credential/certificate/professional growth	1,651
Engineering & Technology	1,758
Health & Human Services	3,031
Natural & Social Sciences	3,158
Special Major	12
Undeclared	2,493

1988-89 Degrees Granted

Bachelor's 1,785
Master's 648
PhD 3

Total Awarded 2,436

Largest Enrolled Undergraduate Programs

BS Business Administration–Accounting option	1,236
BS Business Administration–Option undecided	1,041
BA Child Development	851
BS Engineering–Electrical option	728
BA Psychology	557

Highest Undergraduate Degrees Granted

BS Business Administration–Accounting option	17*
BA Child Development	134
BS Engineering–Electrical option	117
BS Business Administration–Finance option	1C2
BS Business Administration–Marketing option	99

Largest Enrolled Graduate Programs

MA Educational Administration	269
MBA Business Administration	256
MA & MS Psychology	178
MA Special Education	124
MS Nursing	107

Highest Graduate Degrees Granted

MA Educational Administration	126
MBA Business Administration	67
MA Education–Secondary Teaching option	30
MA Education–Elementary Teaching option	28
MA Special Education	28
MS Electrical Engineering	26

Note: Percents not summing to 100% are due to rounding.

APPENDIX B

Guide to Classes and Instructors of CSULA Survey

1. MALE _____ FEMALE _____

2. FRESHMAN _____ SOPHOMORE _____ JUNIOR _____ SENIOR _____

   GRADUATE STUDENT _____ INSTRUCTOR _____

3. DO YOU THINK THERE IS A NEED FOR A STUDENT GUIDE TO CLASSES AND INSTRUC-TORS OF CSULA?

   YES _____ NO _____

4. DO YOU THINK STUDENTS HAVE A RIGHT TO KNOW EACH INSTRUCTOR'S COURSE RE-QUIREMENTS AND GRADING PERSONALITY HABITS BEFORE SIGNING UP FOR HIS OR HER COURSE?

   YES _____ NO _____

5. DO YOU HAVE ACCESS TO WORD-OF-MOUTH RECOMMENDATIONS FROM FRIENDS FOR THE CLASSES YOU INTEND TO TAKE NEXT QUARTER?

   YES _____ NO _____

6. WOULD YOU BE WILLING TO PARTICIPATE ANONYMOUSLY AS ONE OF THE STUDENTS WE POLLED TO GAIN INFORMATION ON COURSES AND INSTRUCTORS IN EXCHANGE FOR A $2.00 DISCOUNT COUPON ON OUR PUBLICATION OR AN OPPORTUNITY FOR FREE ADVERTISING OF A USED BOOK YOU WISH TO SELL?

   YES _____ NO _____

   I PREFER: DISCOUNT COUPON _____ FREE ADVERTISING _____

7. WOULD YOU BE WILLING TO PAY LESS THAN $10.00/COPY FOR THIS PUBLICATION?

   YES _____ NO _____

THANK YOU FOR YOUR PARTICIPATION IN THIS SURVEY!!!!!!!

APPENDIX C

Statistical Analysis of CSULA
Course/Instructor Guide Survey

Table 1   CSULA Student Sample Population Breakdown by Class Levels

	Freshman	Sophomore	Junior	Senior	Grad.	Total
No. of Students	64	92	119	132	40	450
% of Total	14	21	27	29	9	100

Table 2   Percentage of "Yes" Response to Survey Questions

	Freshman	Sophomore	Junior	Senior	Grad.	Total
Need for guide	97	85	86	92	79	88
Right to know	96	83	88	91	83	88
Access to word of mouth recommendations	52	65	60	73	40	62
Willingness to participate	67	71	60	59	43	63
Will buy guide	76	76	73	66	54	70

Note: Also polled 1 instructor who voted yes on Need for Guide and Right of Students to know course and instructor information before signing up for a class.

Table 3   Analysis of Incentive Offering for Student Participation (in %)

	Freshman	Sophomore	Junior	Senior	Grad.	Total
Willingness to participate	67	71	60	59	43	63
Discount coupon	58	72	56	54	47	60
Free ad	33	20	20	29	29	25
Either	9	8	24	17	24	15

APPENDIX D

Sample Format of
Course/Instructor Information

COURSE NUMBER/SECTION:

INSTRUCTOR:

COURSE REQUIREMENTS: Tests   (Number of Tests)
                                             (Comprehensive or Non-Comprehensive Final Exam)
                                           (Multiple choice, Essay, True/False Format)
                                           (Covers Lectures only, Textbook only, or both)

                       Papers

                       Projects

                       Presentations

                       (What percentage do each of the above contribute to the final grade?)

COURSE INFORMATION: (Obtained from students who have taken this course previously)

1. Plan to spend _____ hours outside of school studying for this course each week.

2. On a scale of 1 to 5, to what degree does this class give you practical knowledge you could apply immediately to improve your job or personal life? (Use Not at all = 1 . . . A great deal = 5)

   This course received a _____ rating.

3. Students felt that this class (_____ did _____ did not _____ not sure) offer them more than they originally expected when they enrolled for the class.

4. Students (_____ would _____ would not) recommend this course to their friends.

5. Students felt it (_____ was _____ was not) necessary to do well in prerequisite requirements to handle the class load of this course.

6. Students gave this class an average difficulty rating of _____ (using a scale of 1 to 5 with Easy = 1, Average = 3, Extremely difficult = 5)

ADDITIONAL STUDENT COMMENTS: _____

_____

_____

APPENDIX E

Sample Format of Local Business Advertising

C·H·O·I·C·E·S

Located next to Eagles' Landing
Choices has an all-you-can-eat buffet and salad bar with courteous waiters to serve you. So why not keep those lunch dates on campus and let us serve you in a quiet relaxing atmosphere.
Mon. - Fri. 11:30 a.m. - 1:45 p.m.   (Fri. soup & salad bar only)

PJ's

Located next to King Hall,
for those people who have to eat
on the run. We have a nice selection
of grab-and-go-items

Mon. - Thurs. 7:30 a.m. - 8:00 p.m.

THE PUB

Second Floor Student Union
J.Newbauer's has a large menu to choose from including a variety of hot sandwiches, Itza-pizza, beer and wine.

45" GIANT screen TV

Mon. - Thurs. 11:00 a.m. - 8:30 p.m.
So come by and check us out

Pumperknikles deli FIRST FLOOR STUDENT UNION

Pumperknikles offers a wide variety of fresh sandwiches and salads.
Fast friendly courteous service. Custom line of non-dairy frozen yogurt.
Mon. - Thurs.   10:30 a.m. - 8:00 p.m.
Fri. & Sat.   10:00 am - 1:30 p.m.

Eagles' Landing
offers a large
selection
of food
for all tastes
including Mexican cuisine, deli, Itza-pizza, grille, and a large selection of hot entrees. Try our garden fresh salad bar.

Mon. - Thurs.   7:00 a.m. 6:30 p.m.
Friday   7:00 a.m. - 1:30 p.m.

EAGLE EXPRESS

Our modular food service trailer located in Lot C
Beverages, Sandwiches, Snacks, and other grab & go items
Open Mon. - Thurs. 9:00 a.m. - 8:30 p.m.

THE SPOT

Our Convenience Store Located in Housing Phase I

From self-serve drinks and snacks to microwavable dinners. Also, most of your household items to stock up the apartment.
Open Sun. - Fri. 5:00 p.m. - 10:00 p.m.

APPENDIX F

Sample Format of Invitation to Be a Student Respondent

JOIN THE CROWD ! ! !

Be a participant in our next issue. Fill in the application below and we'll send you a $2.00 discount coupon good for our next issue if you're selected to be a student participant.

NAME: _____

PHONE: (   ) _____   Best time to call me is ____AM ____12–6PM ____PM

CLASSES I'M TAKING FALL QUARTER 1990:

COURSE NO.   SECTION   INSTRUCTOR   TIME

_____

_____

_____

_____

_____

MAIL TO: SNEAK PEEK
             P.O. BOX 109
             MONTEREY PARK, CA 91754

APPENDIX G

Sample Format of Invitation to Advertise in Recycler

DO YOU HAVE A USED BOOK YOU'D LIKE TO SELL? ? ?

Put an ad in our recycler section. IT'S FREE! ! !

Hurry though, we only have a limited number of ads we can run.

NAME OF BOOK: _____

COURSE/INSTRUCTOR: _____

YOUR FIRST NAME: _____

PHONE NUMBER: _____

BEST TIME FOR BUYER TO CALL YOU IS: ___AM ___AFTERNOONS ___PM

SELLING PRICE: _____ (OPTIONAL)

MAIL TO: SNEAK PEEK
             P.O. BOX 109
             MONTEREY PARK, CA 91754

APPENDIX H

Sample Format of Recycler Section for Used Books Advertising

USED BOOKS FOR SALE . . . BUY NOW! ! ! !

Principles of Accounting
Accounting 200A
Prof. M. Davidson
$18.00
Contact: Tim
(818) 388-9276
Leave a message on machine

Fundamentals of Astronomy
ASTR 151
Prof. R. Carpenter
$22.00
Contact: Jonathan Riley
(213) 728-3535
Call anytime between 2PM and 5PM

Basic Spanish
SPAN 100A
Prof. G. McCurdy
$20.00
Contact: Juli McNamara
(213) 555-3667
Call between 3:30PM and 4:30PM

Extemporaneous Speaking
SPCH 150
Prof. Robert Powell
$26.00
Contact: Ann Markell
(818) 377-8799
Call between 10AM and 12NOON

Modern Man
ANTH 250
Prof. E. Oring
$27.00
Contact: Reanna
(213) 377-5988
Leave message on machine

Principles of Biology
BIOL 101
Prof. Wayne P. Alley
$32.00
Contact: Anthony
(213) 666-5667
Leave Message

Principles of Biology
BIOL 101
Prof. Wayne P. Alley
$32.00
Contact: Donna
(818)322-2633
Call between 10AM and 2PM

The World of Plants
BIOL 155
Prof. B. Capon
$34.00
Contact: Caroline
(213) 585-2356
Leave message on machine

APPENDIX I

Sample Format of Student Telephone Survey

(Instructions: Please call in all information to our telephone answering machine operating 24 hours a day. Start at the top of the page with your Name, ID Number, Phone, and Address. Then proceed to the questions and give your responses in order using complete sentences (example: Say "Question 1: I spend 5 to 10 hours outside of school studying per week," etc.). You must call in your responses before the following date _____. We will send you your $2.00 discount coupon to your address as soon as your telephone survey is received. Thank you for your participation in this survey.

NAME: _____   PHONE: _____

ADDRESS: _____   ZIP CODE: _____

STUDENT RESPONDENT NUMBER: _____ (Stamped in right upper corner of this form)

(Students, please be completely honest in answering all questions. Remember, other students will be relying on your answers for the selection of their classes. Furthermore, feel free to make additional comments at the end of this questionnaire.)

1. How many hours outside of school did you have to study per week?

   _____ 0–5 _____ 6–10 _____ 11–20 _____ more than 20 hrs.

2. To what degree did your class give you knowledge you could apply immediately to improve your job or personal life?

   On a scale of 1 to 5, I would rate this class a _____.
   (Use: Not at all = 1, Average = 3, and Helped a great deal = 5)

3. Do you feel that the class offered more than you originally expected?

   _____ Yes _____ No _____ Not Sure.

4. Would you recommend this course to your friends? _____ Yes _____ No

5. Does doing well in the prerequisites for this course come in handy for handling the class load?

   _____ Yes _____ No

6. How do you rate the difficulty of this course on a scale of 1 to 5?

   (Use: Easy = 1, Average = 3, and Extremely Difficult = 5)

   I would rate this course a _____.

Any additional comments concerning course or instructors are welcome. If you have suggestions on questions to ask in future issues please let us know. This publication is for your benefit so let us help you get the information you need to pick your classes!

APPENDIX J

Sample Format of Invitation to Place Advance Order

(to be run in the *University Times* 4 weeks prior to release of our guide)

ORDER YOUR NEXT ISSUE OF SNEAK PEEK IN ADVANCE!

Be the first to buy your books through our Recycler Section.

Give yourself the time to plan your classes next quarter.

Get the inside scoop on courses and instructors with Sneak Peek as your guide.

SEND A CHECK OR MONEY ORDER FOR $5.00 (Includes taxes and postage, and handling charge) to:

> SNEAK PEEK
> P.O. BOX 109
> MONTEREY PARK, CA 91754

(If you have a discount coupon, take $2.00 off above price and mail in check and coupon.)

Yes, I'd like to order the Winter Quarter of Sneak Peek now.

Send to: NAME _____

ADDRESS _____

_____ ZIP CODE _____

APPENDIX K

CSULA *University Times* Advertising Rates

	Spring Quarter 1 2 3 4 5 6 7 8 9 10 11	Summer Quarter 1 2 3 4 5 6 7 8 9 10 11	Fall Quarter 1 2 3 4 5 6 7 8 9 10 11

Advertising
- Posters
- *University Times* Ads
- Fliers

Collect Data
- Class Schedule Information
- Student Questionnaires

Editing
- Writing
- Review Questionnaires
- Instructor's Opinion Review

Promotion
- Student Union Table Setup
- New Student Orientation
- Flier Distribution

Printing
- Fliers and Posters
- Guidebooks

Distribution
- University Bookstore
- Student Bookmart
- Direct Mailing

APPENDIX L

Financial Data

Table 1 Sneak Peek: Breakeven Analysis

Fixed Cost per Year	Amount
Post office box	$ 28.00
Business license	101.78
Wholesale license	107.50
Ad on university times	337.00
Ad on schedule of classes	1,080.00
Bulk rate postage permit	60.00
Bulk rate postage fee	60.00
Postage paid address permit	60.00
Copyright on publication	40.00
Answering machine	60.00
Telephone	30.00
Telephone/utilities	840.00
Typewriter	130.00
Legal/accounting	2,080.00
Insurance	1,500.00
Orientation booth	200.00
Fliers	140.00
Posters	80.00
Total	$6,934.28

Variable Cost per Year	Amount
Wholesale licensee	$ 116.48
Business licensee	36.40
Postage for response	14,414.40
Transportation cost	291.20
Postage for mail orders	2,038.40
Printing cost	36,400.00
Total	$ 1.83
$P = (U \times p) - (U \times V) - F$	$10,317.50
$U = F/(p - V)$	2,926

Note:

P = profits
p = price
U = breakeven quantities
V = variable costs per unit
F = fixed costs

A BREAKEVEN CHART

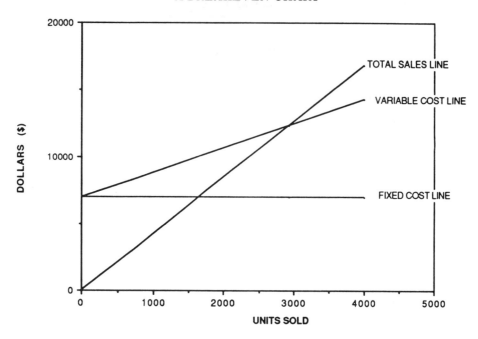

Table 2   Sneak Peek: Five-Year Projected Profit and Loss Statement

| | Quarters after Starting Business | | | | |
	1 Fall	2 Winter	3 Spring	4 Summer	Year 1
Sales	$29,192.80	$28,100.80	$27,227.20	$27,081.60	$111,602.40
Advertising sales	2,025.00	3,037.50	4,556.25	6,834.38	16,453.13
Cost of sales	12,481.56	10,170.16	8,321.04	6,009.64	36,982.40
Gross Profit	$18,736.24	$20,968.14	$23,462.41	$27,906.34	$91,073.13
Operating Expenses					
Advertising	$ 619.99	$ 505.18	$ 413.33	$ 298.51	$ 1,837.00
Postage	5,552.82	4,524.52	3,701.88	2,673.58	16,452.80
Payroll	6,952.50	5,665.00	4,635.00	3,347.50	20,600.00
Office supplies	624.36	622.77	635.67	678.32	2,561.11
Permit and fee	70.20	57.20	46.80	33.80	208.00
Legal and accounting	520.00	520.00	520.00	520.00	2,080.00
Telephone/utilities	200.00	170.00	170.00	170.00	710.00
Licenses and taxes	103.67	94.11	86.47	76.91	361.16
Copyright	10.00	10.00	10.00	10.00	40.00
Insurance	375.00	375.00	375.00	375.00	1,500.00
Other administrative and selling expenses	1,560.89	1,556.92	1,589.17	1,695.80	6,402.78
Total Operating Expenses	$16,589.42	$14,100.69	$12,183.31	$ 9,879.42	$ 52,752.85
Profit	$ 2,146.82	$ 6,867.45	$11,279.10	$18,026.91	$ 38,320.28

Table 2 (*Continued*)

	Quarters after Starting Business				
	5 Fall	6 Winter	7 Spring	8 Summer	Year 2
Sales	$43,789.20	$42,151.20	$40,840.80	$40,622.40	$167,403.60
Advertising sales	3,037.50	4,556.25	6,834.38	10,251.56	24,679.69
Cost of sales	18,722.34	15,255.24	12,481.56	9,014.46	55,473.60
Gross Profit	$29,104.36	$31,452.21	$35,193.62	$41,859.50	$136,609.69
Operating Expenses					
Advertising	$ 929.98	$ 757.76	$ 619.99	$ 447.77	$ 2,755.50
Postage	8,329.23	6,786.78	5,552.82	4,010.37	24,679.20
Payroll	10,428.75	8,497.50	6,952.50	5,021.25	30,900.00
Office supplies	936.53	934.15	953.50	1,017.48	3,841.67
Permit and fee	105.30	85.80	70.20	50.70	312.00
Legal and accounting	780.00	780.00	780.00	780.00	3,120.00
Telephone/utilities	300.00	255.00	255.00	255.00	1,065.00
Licenses and taxes	155.50	141.17	129.70	115.37	541.74
Copyright	15.00	15.00	15.00	15.00	60.00
Insurance	562.50	562.50	562.50	562.50	2,250.00
Other administrative and selling expenses	2,341.34	2,335.37	2,383.76	2,543.70	9,604.15
Total Operating Expenses	$24,884.13	$21,151.03	$18,274.97	$14,819.14	$ 79,129.27
Profit	$ 3,220.23	$10,301.18	$16,918.64	$27,040.37	$ 57,480.42

	Quarters after Starting Business				
	8 Fall	10 Winter	11 Spring	12 Summer	Year 3
Sales	$76,631.10	$73,764.60	$71,471.40	$71,089.20	$292,956.30
Advertising sales	5,315.63	7,973.44	11,960.16	17,940.23	43,189.45
Cost of sales	32,764.10	26,696.67	21,842.73	15,775.31	97,078.80
Gross Profit	$49,182.63	$55,041.37	$61,588.83	$73,254.13	$239,066.95
Operating Expenses					
Advertising	$ 1,627.47	$ 1,326.08	$ 1,084.98	$ 783.60	$ 4,822.13
Postage	14,576.15	11,876.87	9,717.44	7,018.15	43,188.60
Payroll	18,250.31	14,870.63	12,166.88	8,787.19	54,075.00
Office supplies	1,638.93	1,634.76	1,668.63	1,780.59	6,722.92
Permit and fee	184.28	150.15	122.85	88.73	546.00
Legal and accounting	1,365.00	1,365.00	1,365.00	1,365.00	5,460.00
Telephone/utilities	525.00	446.25	446.25	446.25	1,863.75
Licenses and taxes	272.13	247.04	226.98	201.90	948.05
Copyright	26.25	26.25	26.25	26.25	105.00
Insurance	984.38	984.38	984.38	984.38	3,937.50
Other administrative and selling expenses	4,097.34	4,086.90	4,171.58	4,451.47	16,807.29
Total Operating Expenses	$43,547.23	$37,014.31	$31,981.20	$25,933.49	$138,476.22
Profit	$ 5,635.40	$18,027.06	$29,607.63	$47,320.64	$100,590.73

Table 2   (*Continued*)

	Quarters after Starting Business				
	13 Fall	14 Winter	15 Spring	16 Summer	Year 4
Sales	$107,283.54	$103,270.44	$100,059.96	$ 99,524.88	$410,133.32
Advertising sales	7,441.88	11,162.81	16,744.22	25,116.33	60,465.23
Cost of sales	45,869.73	37,375.34	30,579.82	22,085.43	135,910.32
Gross Profit	$ 68,355.68	$ 77,057.91	$ 86,224.36	$102,555.78	$334,693.78
Operating Expenses					
Advertising	$ 2,278.45	$ 1,856.52	$ 1,518.97	$ 1,097.03	$ 6,750.98
Postage	15,304.96	12,470.71	10,203.31	7,369.05	45,348.03
Payroll	25,550.44	20,818.88	17,033.63	12,302.06	75,705.00
Office supplies	2,294.51	2,288.67	2,336.08	2,492.82	9,412.08
Permit and fee	257.99	210.21	171.99	124.22	764.40
Legal and accounting	1,911.00	1,911.00	1,911.00	1,911.00	7,644.00
Telephone/utilities	735.00	624.75	624.75	624.75	2,609.25
Licenses and taxes	380.98	345.86	317.77	282.66	1,327.26
Copyright	36.75	36.75	36.75	36.75	147.00
Insurance	1,378.13	1,378.13	1,378.13	1,378.13	5,512.50
Other administrative and selling expenses	5,736.27	5,721.66	5,840.21	6,232.06	23,580.20
Total Operating Expenses	$ 55,864.47	$ 47,663.13	$ 41,372.58	$ 33,850.53	$178,750.70
Profit	$ 12,991.22	$ 29,394.79	$ 44,851.78	$ 68,705.25	$155,943.03

	Quarters after Starting Business				
	17 Fall	18 Winter	19 Spring	20 Summer	Year 5
Sales	$134,104.43	$129,088.05	$125,074.95	$124,406.10	$512,673.53
Advertising sales	9,302.34	13,953.52	20,930.27	31,395.41	75,581.54
Cost of sales	57,337.17	46,719.17	38,224.78	27,606.78	169,887.90
Gross Profit	$ 86,069.60	$ 96,322.33	$107,790.45	$128,194.73	$418,367.17
Operating Expenses					
Advertising	$ 2,848.07	$ 2,320.65	$ 1,898.71	$ 1,371.29	$ 8,438.72
Postage	12,435.28	10,132.45	8,290.19	5,987.36	36,845.27
Payroll	31,838.05	26,023.59	21,292.03	15,377.58	94,631.25
Office supplies	2,868.14	2,860.83	2,920.10	3,116.03	11,765.10
Permit and fee	322.48	262.76	214.99	155.27	955.50
Legal and accounting	2,388.75	2,388.75	2,388.75	2,388.75	9,555.00
Telephone/utilities	918.75	780.94	780.94	780.94	3,261.56
Licenses and taxes	476.22	432.33	397.21	353.32	1,639.08
Copyright	45.94	45.94	45.94	45.94	183.75
Insurance	1,722.66	1,722.66	1,722.66	1,722.66	6,890.63
Other administrative and selling expenses	7,170.34	7,152.08	7,300.28	7,790.08	29,412.75
Total Operating Expenses	$ 63,134.66	$ 54,122.97	$ 47,251.78	$ 39,089.20	$203,598.61
Profit	$ 22,934.94	$ 42,199.42	$ 60,528.87	$ 89,105.52	$214,768.56

Table 3   Sneak Peek: Five-Year Cash Flow Projections

	Year 1	Year 2	Year 3	Year 4	Year 5
Cash Balance (Beginning of Year)	$ 8,775.14	$ 3,451.40	$ 5,966.90	$ 18,992.08	$ 34,231.84
Receipts					
Sales	111,602.40	167,403.60	292,956.30	410,138.82	512,673.53
Ad sales	16,453.13	24,679.69	43,189.45	60,465.23	75,581.54
Total Cash Available	$120,377.54	$170,855.00	$298,923.20	$429,130.90	$546,905.37
Disbursements					
Printing cost	$ 36,982.40	$ 55,473.00	$ 97,078.80	$135,910.32	$169,887.90
Payroll cost	20,600.00	30,900.00	54,075.00	75,705.00	94,631.25
Advertising cost	1,837.00	2,755.00	4,822.13	6,750.00	8,438.72
License and taxes	361.16	541.74	948.05	1,327.26	1,659.08
Postage	16,452.80	24,679.20	43,188.60	45,348.03	36,845.27
Insurance	1,500.00	2,250.00	3,937.50	5,512.50	6,890.63
Legal/accounting	2,080.00	3,120.00	5,460.00	7,644.00	9,555.00
Telephone/utilities	710.00	1,065.00	1,863.75	2,609.25	3,261.56
Office supplies	2,561.11	3,841.67	6,722.92	9,412.08	11,765.10
Other administrative expense	3,841.67	5,762.49	10,084.38	14,118.12	17,647.65
Total Disbursements	$ 86,926.14	$130,388.10	$228,181.12	$304,336.56	$360,582.16
Cash before distribution	$ 33,451.40	$ 40,466.90	$ 70,742.08	$124,794.34	$186,323.21
Distribution	30,000.00	34,500.00	51,750.00	90,562.50	135,843.75
Cash Balance (End of Year)	$ 3,451.40	$ 5,966.90	$ 18,992.08	$ 34,231.84	$ 50,479.46

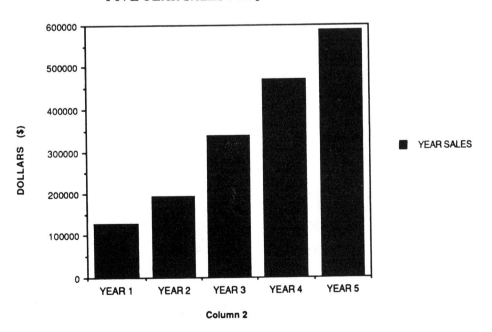

FIVE-YEAR SALES PROJECTION

FIVE-YEAR PROJECTED PROFIT

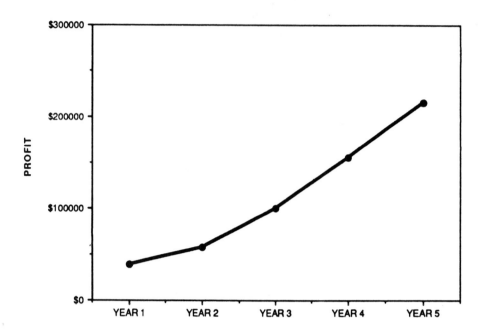

Table 4   Sneak Peek: Initial Investment Cost $18,000.00

Initial Investment		
Less:		
Answering machine	$ 60.00	
Phone	30.00	
Typewriter	130.00	
Copyright	10.00	
Telephone and utilities	70.00	
Post office box	28.00	
Postage permit	120.00	
Office supplies	270.00	
License	208.28	
Legal/Accounting	520.00	
Insurance	375.00	
		$ 1,821.28
Preopening expenses		16,178.72
Postage for response	3,603.60	
Postage paid permit	60.00	
Advertising	619.99	
Printing cost	2,500.00	
Promotions	619.99	
		7,403.58
Cash Balance—Beginning of Operations		$ 8,775.14

Table 5   Sneak Peek: Balance Sheet (Pro Forma)

	Year 1	Year 2	Year 3	Year 4	Year 5
Assets					
Current assets					
Cash	$ 3,451.40	$ 5,966.90	$ 18,992.08	$ 34,231.84	$ 50,479.46
Inventory	2,500.00	3,750.00	6,562.50	9,187.50	11,484.38
Account receivables	22,422.40	50,450.40	103,002.90	127,921.41	192,337.45
Fixed assets					
Furniture/fixture	3,000.00	4,500.00	7,875.00	7,875.00	7,875.00
Telephone	30.00	60.00	90.00	120.00	120.00
Typewriter	130.00	260.00	520.00	520.00	520.00
Answering machine	60.00	60.00	60.00	60.00	
Office supplies	138.76	208.14	364.24	509.93	637.42
Less: Accumulated					
depreciation	(335.88)	(844.69)	(1,735.61)	(2,644.11)	(4,576.21)
Other assets					
Copyright	40.00	40.00	40.00	40.00	40.00
Total Assets	$31,436.68	$64,450.75	$135,771.10	$177,821.58	$258,917.49
Liabilities and Capital					
Liabilities					
Accounts payable	$ 5,116.40	$15,150.05	$ 37,629.67	$ 14,299.62	$ 16,470.73
Capital					
Capital—beginning	18,000.00	26,320.28	49,300.70	98,141.43	163,521.96
Add: Earnings	38,320.28	57,480.42	100,590.73	155,943.03	214,768.55
Less: Distributions	(30,000.00)	(34,500.00)	(51,750.00)	(90,562.50)	(135,843.75)
Capital—ending	26,320.28	49,300.70	98,141.43	163,521.96	242,446.76
Total Liabilities and Capital	$31,436.68	$64,450.75	$135,771.10	$177,821.58	$258,917.49

FIVE – YEAR PROJECTED DISTRIBUTION

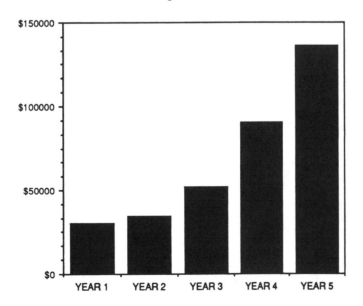

4

BUSINESS PLAN FOR AMERICAN BABY FOOD COMPANY

Developed by
Syed Shehzad Ali

Used with the Permission of the Author

Los Angeles, California. Dr. Horton has worked with children in hospital-based and private practices.

Together, the principals have spent the past two years developing, refining, and testing ABFC's products. ABFC product line will satisfy the market demand for healthy and nutritious children's food. The maximum amount of nutrients will be retained in the food, providing children with more nutritional benefit than most products presently on the market. The menu items chosen will reflect the tastes most preferred by children. A broad product line will also provide a diverse and nutritionally balanced meal plan.

FINANCIAL SUMMARY

Based on the detailed financial projections prepared by American Baby Food Company, it is estimated that $1,050,000 of equity investment is required to start The Company's operations. The funds will be used to finance initial business activities, research and development, and provide working capital during the first two years of operation.

The following is a summary of American Baby Food Company's projected financial information:

	Year 1	Year 2	Year 3
Sales	$1,824,000	$2,280,000	$3,979,500
Gross Margin	50%	50%	50%
Net Income after Tax	(570,000)	(456,000)	22,500
Net Income after Tax/Sales	—	—	0.57%
Return/Equity	0%	0%	10.56%
Return/Assets	0%	0%	2.52%

Table of Contents

I. **INTRODUCTION** . . . . **4·5**
    A. Child Foods . . . . 4·5
    B. The Company's Services . . . . 4·7

II. **SITUATION ANALYSIS** . . . . **4·7**
    A. Traditional Children's Food Industry . . . . 4·7
    B. Health Food Trade . . . . 4·7

III. **TARGET MARKETS** . . . . **4·8**
    A. Health Food Consumers . . . . 4·8
    B. Child-Care Centers . . . . 4·8

IV. **PROBLEMS AND OPPORTUNITIES** . . . . **4·9**
    A. Traditional Children's Food Industry . . . . 4·9
    B. Health Food Industry . . . . 4·10
    C. Differential Competitive Advantage . . . . 4·10

V. **BUSINESS OBJECTIVES AND GOALS** . . . . **4·11**

VI. **MARKETING STRATEGY AND TACTICS** . . . . **4·11**
    A. Public Relations . . . . 4·11
    B. Price . . . . 4·11
    C. Advertising . . . . 4·12
    D. Sales Promotion . . . . 4·12
    E. Packaging and Point-of-Sale Material . . . . 4·12
    F. Distribution . . . . 4·12

VII. **IMPLEMENTATION AND CONTROL** . . . . **4·12**
    A. Sales Projection . . . . 4·13
    B. Projected Income Statements . . . . 4·14
    C. Projected Cash Flows . . . . 4·16
    D. Projected Balance Sheets . . . . 4·18
    E. Projected Break-Even Analysis . . . . 4·20
    F. Projected Annual Financial Ratios . . . . 4·20

VIII. **SUMMARY** . . . . **4·21**

ENDNOTES . . . . **4·21**

BIBLIOGRAPHY . . . . **4·21**

APPENDIX A. COMPETITIVE ANALYSIS . . . . **4·22**

APPENDIX B. PRODUCT LINE PROFIT ANALYSIS . . . . . . **4·23**

I. INTRODUCTION

ABFC is developing a complete line of health food products for children, using minimal processing techniques. All products contain wholesome ingredients, such as herbs and naturally derived vitamins, minerals, and other supplements. Products contain no chemicals or additives.

Eating ABFC's products in the context of the holistic dietary program The Company has designed will reduce, if not eliminate, the need for supplemental vitamins.

While other companies claim to sell healthy and nutritious baby foods, their cooking processes extract many of the product's natural nutrients. The Company's unique process leaves these nutrients in the products, resulting in a product superior in quality to those of major children's food companies. The products have been developed over a two-year period, utilizing research data from a clinical, nutritionally oriented pediatric practice.

The ABFC product line is designed to provide a broad range of children's natural food products. Initially, The Company plans to introduce selected items, and will slowly increase the selection in each of its two major product groups. ABFC plans to develop and market a complete product line of main courses, side dishes, and desserts, as it believes the market potential for these is significant. The following are some of the key products The Company plans to sell.

A. Child Foods

ABFC has developed lines of foods for children ages 6 to 12 months and 1 to 3 years. These food products are designed to retain the maximum nutritional value of the ingredients while remaining free of artificial nutrients, chemical additives, preservatives, coloring agents, flavor enhancers, iodized salt, and refined sugar. Such additives cause hyperactivity in children, and are suspected to be related to dyslexia, a learning disability.

Additionally, ABFC's baby food products have been thoroughly tested by an independent organization. In all tests, ABFC products were at least as well taken by children as Gerber's and Beech-Nut's. In some cases, children actually preferred ABFC's natural formula to those of the well-known competitors.

In the 6- to 12-month group, traditional baby foods will be offered in 4½ ounce jars. A variety of items will be offered in the following categories: main dishes, meats, vegetables, desserts, fruits, and biscuits. All items will be free from artificial ingredients and will be cooked using a proprietary process that ensures they will not lose their nutrients. A few products will be introduced initially in each category, and new products will be introduced as development funds become available and successful testing is completed.

For children ages 1 to 3 years, a frozen, 100% natural complete and balanced line of foods will be included in the ABFC product line. These foods will be packaged in plastic bags that are to be heated in boiling water, making them convenient to prepare yet wholesome. ABFC will also introduce a line of sandwich meats that are prepared through a patented process and contain no chemical additives or fillers. A line of naturally sweetened snack foods specially formulated for this age group will be available in popular shapes and sizes. Desserts and fruits will be the same formulations as for the 6- to 12-month group, with a greater emphasis on mixed fruits.

The following is the anticipated product listing. Most items will be available immediately; those that have asterisks beside them will be introduced during the first year after funding.

American Baby Food Company Product Listing 6 to 12 Months

Dinners

Chicken and mixed vegetables	*Veal and mixed vegetables
Beef and mixed vegetables	*Beef, noodles, and vegetables
Turkey and mixed vegetables	*Macaroni, tomato, and beef

Meats

Chicken	*Veal
Beef	*Lamb
Turkey	

Vegetables

Peas	Mixed vegetables
Carrots	*Spinach
Squash	*Beets
Green beans	*Sweet potatoes

Desserts

Tapioca pudding with rice	Banana pudding
Tapioca pudding with fruit	Chocolate pudding

Fruits

Applesauce	Mixed fruits
Bananas	*Cherries
Apricots	*Peaches
Apples	*Pears

Biscuits and Cookies

Teething biscuits	Molasses cookies

American Baby Food Company Product Listing 1 to 3 Years

Prepared Foods, Main Dishes

Spaghetti in meat sauce	*Lasagna
*Lamb stew	

Prepared Foods, Side Dishes

Same vegetables as in 6- to 12-month group

Sandwich Meats/Lunch Items

Bologna	*Salami
Peanut butter	*Turkey roll

Desserts

Same as in 6- to 12-month group

Fruits

Same as in 6- to 12-month group

Biscuits and Cookies

Molasses cookies

B. The Company's Services

In addition to its baby food products, ABFC plans to offer both professional and consumer education programs that will serve to promote the ABFC holistic concept, increase consumer awareness of chemical additives in food and the health needs of children, and expose parents to The Company products.

Glen Horton, MD, pediatrician, has published articles and has appeared on radio and television talk shows concerning holistic pediatric medicine and disease prevention and will continue to do so. These efforts will educate consumers and child-care professionals regarding the holistic approach to children's health, and expose them to ABFC's products and services.

John Kemp will offer seminars to educate parents and child care professionals on how to improve children's health through better nutrition. Mr. Kemp will emphasize how ABFC's products, along with other available health foods, can be combined to provide children with a diet that meets all of their daily nutritional needs without the addition of synthetic nutrients.

II. SITUATION ANALYSIS

The packaging of children's food is under the jurisdiction of the Food and Drug Administration. The Company is required to follow FDA standards for canning and packaging. Also, all labels and ingredient lists must be registered with each state.

ABFC can expect to face competition from two areas:

A. Traditional Children's Food Industry

The children's food industry is highly competitive with a small number of very powerful suppliers. Three children's food manufacturers presently supply nearly 87% of the total industry.[2]

The largest of these companies operates with an advertising budget in excess of $20 million. In view of these companies' dominance of the market, ABFC has developed an initial approach to marketing that will focus on outlets other than mass merchandisers.

As with mass-market food products for adults, there has been a noticeable trend towards food products for children that make nutritional or quasi-nutritional claims. This trend is helpful to ABFC in that it increases consumer awareness of the importance of nutrition. However, these products are not competing with ABFC's products because they are primarily sold in the children's food sections of standard supermarkets. ABFC believes the nutritional value and quality of these traditional manufacturers' items will be viewed as inferior as consumers become aware of health food products.

B. Health Food Trade

More direct competition is to be found in the health food trade. Competition here is of three types: broad-line companies that market some child-related products; those that sell a few selected children's items such as cereals; and local companies that supply children's foods in a limited geographic area.

Some of the local companies that supply children's foods in a limited geographic area are starting to expand their product lines and planning for national distribution of their products. ABFC believes it is well equipped to compete in this market because of its extensive market and product research to date and expertise of its principals.

It can be expected that some competitors will react to ABFC's entrance into the children's health food market. The traditional children's food industry participants have already reacted to what they perceive as changes in the marketplace. They have altered their marketing approach to emphasize that their products are natural with no artificial additives or sweeteners.

Because of this, and the fact that ABFC will not display its products alongside the traditional products (only in the health food sections of supermarkets and in health food stores), ABFC expects some adverse reaction by these companies to its nationwide introduction in the future. ABFC's advertising and promotion campaign will clearly differentiate its "holistic" products from those of its competitors.

ABFC expects the most direct competition to come from other manufacturers of health foods, who will finally recognize the potential market for children's health foods. ABFC's head start in the development and test marketing of its products will give it an advantage over the later entrants.

Appendix A includes a summary of all the companies ABFC considers its major competitors and a few important characteristics of each.

III. TARGET MARKETS

As previously mentioned, ABFC intends to approach the marketplace primarily through health food outlets and natural food centers in major supermarket chain stores. The two major target markets that The Company plans to approach through these outlets are:

- Parents who are concerned about their children's health and demand higher quality and more nutritionally balanced products.
- Operators of child-care centers who provide meals to children.

A. Health Food Consumers

ABFC intends to focus its initial marketing efforts to health food consumers who have children. Approximately 15% of all households (13.8 million) have children under three years of age.[3] The health food consumer will primarily purchase ABFC's products at health food outlets.

In addition to traditional health food stores, ABFC plans to direct its efforts in marketing to the health food consumer through major supermarket chains. Health food distributors with established relationships with supermarkets can be used to guarantee access to supermarket shelf space. The ability to sell its products in the natural food centers of major supermarket chains will greatly increase the exposure of ABFC's products to interested consumers, which will have a positive impact on sales.

Geographically, ABFC plans to direct its initial marketing efforts towards consumers in major metropolitan areas on the West Coast. In the past, these areas have been the most receptive to trends in the health food industry and ABFC believes initial acceptance by consumers in these areas will facilitate the acceptance of ABFC products throughout the nation.

B. Child-Care Centers

During the past few years, the number of child-care centers has increased due to an increase in the number of working mothers. At present, there are approximately 30,000 child-care centers throughout the nation, with an estimated enrollment of 200,000 children.[4] These child-care centers purchase baby food individually or as a group, usually in large volume, directly from distributors. They can be made aware of ABFC's products through various organizations and trade publications. The emphasis on health in child-care centers is an attraction for potential customers. This segment is expected to represent about 20 percent of ABFC's sales by the second year of operation.

The distributors who service institutions with other health care products will be approached to handle the distribution of ABFC's products to child-care centers.

IV. PROBLEMS AND OPPORTUNITIES

ABFC intends to direct its efforts to the sale of its products through health food retail outlets and natural food centers located within most major supermarkets.

ABFC will initially direct its efforts on the West Coast area. The West Coast area has a high concentration of adult health food consumers who ABFC has found, through market research and analysis, to be most receptive to health concepts for children.

ABFC intends to increase the number of markets during the first three years if resources are available and if such an increase would be profitable to the shareholders. To understand more about the market ABFC's products will address, we must actually evaluate two separate and distinct industries:

1. Traditional children's food industry.
2. Health food industry.

The traditional children's food industry must be analyzed to understand the growth trends and market characteristics of the children's care industry in general. The health food industry must also be evaluated since ABFC intends to market its products through retail distribution outlets currently associated primarily with the sale of adult health foods and other natural products.

A. Traditional Children's Food Industry

Despite a 3% fall in the number of births in 1991, sales of baby food increased by approximately 5%, due primarily to an increased emphasis on wholesomeness and convenience.[5] A growing number of working mothers are concerned with convenience, while all parents are more concerned with wholesomeness.

Some of the baby food companies are introducing new products that try to fill the gap during the transition period from baby food to adult food—ages 1 through 3 years. These products have met with limited success.

Currently, baby food market accounts for $590 million in supermarket sales (excluding formula).[6] The following is the breakdown:

Type of Food	Sales	Percent of Total Sales (%)
Dinners	$114,460,000	19.40
Meats	92,630,000	15.70
Vegetables	94,990,000	16.10
Desserts	70,800,000	12.00
Biscuits and cookies	8,260,000	1.40
Cereals	70,800,000	12.00
Juices	116,820,000	19.80
All other foods	21,240,000	3.60
Total	$590,000,000	100.00

Due to the highly competitive nature of the traditional children's food industry, ABFC has determined that the most effective way to market its products initially is through health food outlets, including single outlet health food stores and health food chains. Natural food centers located in major supermarket chain stores will be approached as The Company becomes confident of being able to service them properly. Industry experts say that the continued growth of health food centers in supermarket chains will greatly increase the total sales volume of all health foods. ABFC intends to take advantage of this growth by aggressively selling through these outlets.

ABFC's products capitalize on the trend toward wholesomeness with its unique cooking process, and on the trend toward convenience with its "boil-in" bags. The Company's foods for the 1- to 3-year age group help fill the perceived gap between baby food and adult food, with products free from potentially harmful chemicals and additives.

B. Health Food Industry

It is estimated that the sales of children's health food is only 0.50 percent of total health food sales. In 1990, when total health food industry sales were estimated at $3.6 billion, children's health food sales were only approximately $18 million.[7]

ABFC has obtained estimates from numerous health food distributors that this market will grow substantially as more companies enter it and more consumers become aware of the benefits of health-related products for children and the possible dangers of traditional children's food products.

Over the past 5 years, the health food industry has grown at a 25 percent annual rate as more people have come to recognize that a direct relationship exists among diet, physical exercise, and health.[8] The medical profession, consumer groups, and government agencies have all supported this concept, and the mass media have reported it widely.

At present, the health food industry comprises about 8,000 retail stores, plus numerous supermarket health food sections. In 1990, the retail sales were approximately $3.6 billion, with $3 billion from individual stores and $600 million from large health food chains and supermarket health food sections.[9]

Industry experts predict a continued high rate of growth. Currently, only 9 percent of adults shop even occasionally in health food stores, and only 0.50 percent shop there regularly. Yet, over 35 percent of adults express a strong interest in eating more nutritional foods.[10] Parents who hold these attitudes can also be expected to want their children to eat healthier foods.

The problem has been a lack of product exposure. This is being corrected by the rapid entry of supermarkets into the field and the development of health food chain stores.

It is very important for ABFC's products to gain wide acceptance in health food stores in order to establish their credibility as high-quality food items with the supermarket shoppers and distributors of health food products.

The primary sources of supply for health food stores are health food distributors, who carry 9,000 to 12,000 items and often supply stores over a multistate area. ABFC's research has determined that 19 such distributors hold between 80 and 90 percent of the retail sales volume.

C. Differential Competitive Advantage

ABFC will be the only company in the industry that offers a complete children health food product line and a comprehensive education program aimed at increasing awareness of the holistic concept, thereby increasing the sales of its products.

ABFC's entire marketing effort will be in the area of health food for children, and its product sales will benefit from the broad-based appeal generated through the numerous retail outlets ABFC intends to utilize. This focus will distinguish ABFC from other competing health food companies who offer a broad line of adult-oriented products to which they have added a narrow line of children's products. The Company will distinguish itself from the major baby food makers by positioning itself as a maker of superior quality health food products.

V. BUSINESS OBJECTIVES AND GOALS

ABFC is a company founded on the belief that children can grow up healthier and live longer if they are fed a natural, nutritionally balanced diet starting earlier in life. ABFC's goal is to increase awareness of this link between diet and health.

The Company expects to be operating in two of the 15 U.S. markets within three years. The Company projects to have sales of $3,979,500 by the end of year three and $4,974,375 by the end of year four (detailed projections for year four are not provided in this business plan).

ABFC expects to have a positive cash flow (without short-term borrowing) in the last quarter of year three. By the end of year four, The Company anticipates operating at a 50 percent gross profit margin; a 9.6 percent of sales after-tax profit with a return on equity of 48.9 percent.

VI. MARKETING STRATEGY AND TACTICS

Initially, The Company plans to limit its sales efforts to the following areas:

- Through health food distributors to health food stores.
- Through health food distributors and other specialty food distributors to supermarkets and other mass merchandisers active in health food retailing.

By aggressively merchandising a comprehensive line that meets the highest health and nutritional standards, ABFC intends to dominate the chosen distribution channels.

The specific details of the business programs and strategies will be developed during the first three months of The Company's operations. The following summary outlines the market programs and specific implementation strategies planned:

A. Public Relations

ABFC's principals plan to continue the public relations efforts in which they are presently involved. These efforts will be formalized further so that the ABFC story can be appropriately developed and positioned in the media to generate significant ongoing coverage.

The programs will include the uniqueness of the concept, the health-promoting qualities of the products, and the experience of the technical and professional staff. The goal will be to increase awareness of the relationship between diet and health.

B. Price

ABFC plans to position its products as slightly higher priced health care items due to its complete line and services. It is estimated that this will place ABFC products 5 to 10 percent above the suggested retail price of the products of the major baby food producers.

C. Advertising

Materials will be developed that promote the uniqueness and quality of ABFC products. ABFC expects that the majority of its advertising will take the form of print advertisements in industry publications.

D. Sales Promotion

ABFC plans to distribute discount coupons to children's health food consumers and bulk purchase discount coupons to child-care centers. Other appropriate incentive programs will be developed that will gain and keep the attention of the trade as well as the consumer.

E. Packaging and Point-of-Sale Material

Packaging that promotes the message of health and superior quality will be developed. It will be designed to educate the consumer about the holistic concept, to create consumer awareness of the point of sale and clearly define the specific products in ABFC's line. Materials will be created, designed, and executed for use in retail outlets and will include shelf talkers, posters, and display units. Also, The Company plans to offer literature about the products and the holistic approach to child health.

F. Distribution

ABFC is familiar with the distribution route of both the health food and children's food industries.

Health food stores, co-ops, and health food chains are supplied through traditional health food distributors. Natural food sections of supermarkets are supplied either in the same way or by food brokers. Child-care centers are supplied directly by distributors.

The health food industry on the West Coast is very efficient at the wholesale level because only 6 distributors give a manufacturer access to approximately 70 to 80 percent of retail sales volume.

The 6 distributors, their locations, and ownership affiliations, are as follows:

Distributor	Location	Group
Northwest Health Food	Seattle, WA	Well-Balanced Foods
Weisberg Foods	Portland, OR	Independent
Porter Distribution	San Francisco, CA	Friendly Foods
Serlen & Sivin	Los Angeles, CA	Independent
Nature's Best	Los Angeles, CA	Independent
Foods for Health	Phoenix, AZ	Independent

VII. IMPLEMENTATION AND CONTROL

Based on the detailed analysis of ABFC's projected financial results presented in this section, The Company projects a need for $1,050,000 in equity investment.

These funds will be used to finance the initial business efforts, to complete the development and testing of other products, and to provide sufficient working capital for The Company as it begins operations.

The breakdown of the use of funds is as follows:

	Dollars	%
Initial marketing campaign	$ 544,500	51.86
Product development & testing	187,500	17.86
Working capital	318,000	30.28
Total	$1,050,000	100.00

A. Sales Projection

Sales were projected using assumptions on the number of stores, the number of orders monthly, and the average order size (see Appendix B). Sales are expected to grow by approximately 25 percent annually. Presented on pages 4·13–4·14 are the sales projections on a monthly basis for a period of three years.

American Baby Food Company Sales Projection Year 1

Month	6–12 Months Group	1–3 Years Group	Total
January	$ 56,280	$ 078,680	$ 134,960
February	57,375	80,254	137,629
March	58,523	81,859	140,382
April	61,030	83,744	144,774
May	62,224	85,414	147,638
June	63,442	87,117	150,559
July	64,684	88,854	153,538
August	65,952	90,628	156,580
September	67,244	92,435	159,679
October	68,562	94,279	162,841
November	69,906	96,159	166,065
December	71,278	98,077	169,355
Total	$766,500	$1,057,500	$1,824,000

American Baby Food Company Sales Projection Year 2

Month	6–12 Months Group	1–3 Years Group	Total
January	$ 71,320	$ 98,554	$ 169,874
February	72,774	100,521	173,295
March	74,257	102,526	176,783
April	75,770	104,572	180,342
May	77,313	106,659	183,972
June	78,887	108,788	187,675
July	80,492	110,960	191,452
August	82,130	113,175	195,305
September	83,800	115,434	199,234
October	85,503	117,738	203,241
November	87,241	120,088	207,329
December	89,013	122,485	211,498
Total	$958,500	$1,321,500	$2,280,000

American Baby Food Company Sales Projection Year 3

Month	6–12 Months Group	1–3 Years Group	Total
January	$ 96,733	$ 136,772	$ 233,505
February	102,815	145,196	248,011
March	109,263	154,125	263,388
April	116,098	163,590	279,688
May	123,342	173,624	296,966
June	131,022	184,259	315,281
July	139,162	195,532	334,694
August	147,790	207,482	355,272
September	156,936	220,147	377,083
October	166,631	233,574	400,205
November	176,908	247,806	424,714
December	187,800	262,893	450,693
Total	$1,654,500	$2,325,000	$3,979,500

B. Projected Income Statements

ABFC's projected quarterly income statements for three years are presented on pages 4·14–4·15.

AMERICAN BABY FOOD COMPANY
PROJECTED INCOME STATEMENT
YEAR 1

	QUARTER 1		QUARTER 2		QUARTER 3		QUARTER 4		TOTAL YEAR 1	
	DOLLARS	%	DOLLARS	%	DOLLARS	%	DOLLARS	%	DOLLARS	%
Net Sales:										
Ages 6-12 Months	$172,178	42	$186,696	42	$197,880	42	$209,746	42	$766,500	42
Ages 1-3 Years	240,793	58	256,275	58	271,917	58	288,515	58	1,057,500	58
Total Sales	$412,971	100	$442,971	100	$469,797	100	$498,261	100	$1,824,000	100
Cost of Sales:										
Ages 6-12 Months	84,367	20	91,481	21	96,961	21	102,190	21	375,000	21
Ages 1-3 Years	120,397	29	128,138	29	135,959	29	155,508	31	540,000	30
Total Cost of Sales	$204,764	50	$219,619	50	$232,920	50	$257,698	52	$915,000	50
Gross Margin	208,207	50	223,352	50	236,877	50	240,563	48	909,000	50
Operating Expenses:										
R & D	70,205	17	75,305	17	75,168	16	74,822	15	295,500	16
Sales & Marketing	140,410	34	159,470	36	164,429	35	158,191	32	622,500	34
General & Admin.	123,891	30	132,891	30	140,939	30	151,278	30	549,000	30
Total Operating Exp.	$334,507	81	$367,666	83	$380,536	81	$384,291	77	$1,467,000	80
Interest Income	750	0	750	0	750	0	750	0	3,000	0
Interest Expense	3,453	1	3,642	1	3,845	1	4,060	1	15,000	1
Net Income(Loss) Before Taxes	(129,003)	(31)	(147,206)	(33)	(146,754)	(31)	(147,038)	(30)	(570,000)	(31)
Tax Expense	0	0	0	0	0	0	0	0	0	0
Net Income(Loss) After Taxes	($129,003)	(31)	($147,206)	(33)	($146,754)	(31)	($147,038)	(30)	($570,000)	(31)

AMERICAN BABY FOOD COMPANY
PROJECTED INCOME STATEMENT
YEAR 2

	QUARTER 1		QUARTER 2		QUARTER 3		QUARTER 4		TOTAL YEAR 2	
	DOLLARS	%	DOLLARS	%	DOLLARS	%	DOLLARS	%	DOLLARS	%
Net Sales:										
Ages 6–12 Months	$218,351	42	$231,970	42	$246,422	42	$261,757	42	$958,500	42
Ages 1–3 Years	301,601	58	320,019	58	339,569	58	360,311	58	1,321,500	58
Total Sales	$519,952	100	$551,989	100	$585,991	100	$622,068	100	$2,280,000	100
Cost of Sales:										
Ages 6–12 Months	106,992	21	113,665	21	120,747	21	128,096	21	469,500	21
Ages 1–3 Years	150,801	29	160,010	29	169,785	29	180,906	29	661,500	29
Total Cost of Sales	$257,792	50	$273,675	50	$290,531	50	$309,002	50	$1,131,000	50
Gross Margin	262,160	50	278,314	50	295,460	50	313,066	50	1,149,000	50
Operating Expenses:										
R & D	77,993	15	77,278	14	82,039	14	88,190	14	325,500	14
Sales & Marketing	150,786	29	137,997	25	134,778	23	125,439	20	549,000	24
General & Admin.	166,385	32	176,636	32	187,517	32	196,962	32	727,500	32
Total Operating Exp.	$395,164	76	$391,912	71	$404,334	69	$410,590	66	$1,602,000	70
Interest Income	1,875	0	1,875	0	1,875	0	1,875	0	7,500	0
Interest Expense	4,966	1	4,211	1	793	0	529	0	10,500	0
Net Income(Loss) Before Taxes	(136,095)	(26)	(115,934)	(21)	(107,792)	(18)	(96,178)	(15)	(456,000)	(20)
Tax Expense	0	0	0	0	0	0	0	0	0	0
Net Income(Loss) After Taxes	($136,095)	(26)	($115,934)	(21)	($107,792)	(18)	($96,178)	(15)	($456,000)	(20)

AMERICAN BABY FOOD COMPANY
PROJECTED INCOME STATEMENT
YEAR 3

	QUARTER 1		QUARTER 2		QUARTER 3		QUARTER 4		TOTAL YEAR 3	
	DOLLARS	%	DOLLARS	%	DOLLARS	%	DOLLARS	%	DOLLARS	%
Net Sales:										
Ages 6–12 Months	$308,811	41	$370,462	42	$443,888	42	$531,339	42	$1,654,500	42
Ages 1–3 Years	436,093	59	521,473	58	623,161	58	744,273	58	2,325,000	58
Total Sales	$744,904	100	$891,935	100	$1,067,049	100	$1,275,612	100	$3,979,500	100
Cost of Sales:										
Ages 6–12 Months	154,406	21	185,231	21	221,944	21	264,920	21	826,500	21
Ages 1–3 Years	218,047	29	260,737	29	311,581	29	372,136	29	1,162,500	29
Total Cost of Sales	$372,452	50	$445,968	50	$533,525	50	$637,056	50	$1,989,000	50
Gross Margin	372,452	50	445,967	50	533,525	50	638,556	50	1,990,500	50
Operating Expenses:										
R & D	74,490	10	89,194	10	106,705	10	131,611	10	402,000	10
Sales & Marketing	126,634	17	142,710	16	170,728	16	204,929	16	645,000	16
General & Admin.	193,675	26	214,064	24	234,751	22	247,010	19	889,500	22
Total Operating Exp.	$394,799	53	$445,968	50	$512,184	48	$583,550	46	$1,936,500	49
Interest Income	375	0	375	0	375	0	375	0	1,500	0
Interest Expense	15,118	2	11,545	1	6,337	1	0	0	33,000	1
Net Income(Loss) Before Taxes	(37,090)	(5)	(11,171)	(1)	15,379	1	55,381	4	22,500	1
Tax Expense	0	0	0	0	0	0	0	0	0	0
Net Income(Loss) After Taxes	($37,090)	(5)	($11,171)	(1)	$15,379	1	$55,381	4	$22,500	1

Cost of Sales

Cost of sales is estimated to be approximately 50 percent of sales. The salaries of the pre-mix operations staff have been included in cost of sales. The terms of all sales are assumed to be 45 days. Payments to the manufacturer that will produce ABFC products on a subcontractor basis comprise 85 percent of cost of sales. The remaining 15 percent is for raw material and direct labor for the purchase and preparation of premix that ABFC will provide to the subcontractor.

Research and Development Expenses

R&D expenses include salaries of $90,000 annually and, beginning in year three, additional salaries of $36,200. Benefits for all ABFC employees are estimated at 20 percent of their annual salaries. All salaries are assumed to increase at 10 percent per year. Expenses of $187,500 related to the further testing of new products will be incurred and expensed in year one. These expenses are expected to increase at 10.25 percent per year.

Sales and Marketing Expenses

The breakdown for sales and marketing expenses is as follows:

	Year 1	Year 2	Year 3
Promotional products	$135,000	$114,750	$122,000
Test-market maintenance	27,000	23,760	27,750
Packaging design	82,500	72,600	85,470
Market planning	112,500	99,000	116,500
Advertising & other promotions	188,000	160,790	204,470
National sales manager	61,000	67,100	73,810
Other miscellaneous	16,500	11,000	15,000
Total	$622,500	$549,000	$645,000

General and Administrative Expenses

The breakdown for general and administrative expenses is as follows:

	Year 1	Year 2	Year 3
Salaries & benefits	$201,600	$340,800	$430,800
Accounting & legal	64,000	64,000	76,800
Rent	152,000	159,600	207,600
Telephone	12,250	14,750	16,500
Utilities	14,500	16,500	21,500
Travel	33,500	42,000	54,950
Other	71,150	89,850	81,350
Total	$549,000	$727,500	$889,500

C.   Projected Cash Flows

ABFC's projected monthly cash flows for three years are presented on pages 4·17–4·18. A minimum cash balance of $22,500 at the end of each year (12th month) is assumed for the purpose of these projections.

AMERICAN BABY FOOD COMPANY
CASH FLOW PROJECTION
YEAR 1

	MONTH 1	MONTH 2	MONTH 3	MONTH 4	MONTH 5	MONTH 6	MONTH 7	MONTH 8	MONTH 9	MONTH 10	MONTH 11	MONTH 12
Beg. Cash Bal.	$22,500	$20,869	$19,557	$18,416	$17,484	$16,793	$16,385	$16,303	$16,588	$17,465	$18,621	$20,286
Cash Receipts:												
Collections	108,388	111,720	114,965	118,306	121,748	125,294	128,945	132,707	136,761	140,571	144,681	148,914
Interest	250	250	250	250	250	250	250	250	250	250	250	250
LT debt	0	0	0	0	0	0	0	0	0	0	0	0
Eq. Financing	56,250	56,250	56,250	56,250	56,250	56,250	56,250	56,250	56,250	56,250	56,250	56,250
Total Receipts	$164,888	$168,220	$171,465	$174,806	$178,248	$181,794	$185,445	$189,207	$193,261	$197,071	$201,181	$205,414
Disbursements:												
Direct Labor	3,499	3,567	3,632	3,697	3,764	3,832	3,901	3,972	4,044	4,118	4,193	4,281
Raw Material	53,547	54,517	55,505	56,513	57,542	58,591	59,661	60,752	61,866	63,002	64,160	65,344
Mfg. Overhead	6,330	6,440	6,557	6,676	6,798	6,922	7,048	7,178	7,309	7,443	7,580	7,719
Capital Exp.	2,374	2,415	2,459	2,503	2,549	2,596	2,643	2,692	2,741	2,791	2,843	2,894
LT Debt	0	0	0	0	0	0	0	0	0	0	0	0
Interest Exp.	1,131	1,151	1,171	1,191	1,214	1,237	1,258	1,282	1,305	1,329	1,353	1,378
Operating Exp.	99,299	101,097	102,930	104,800	106,708	108,653	110,638	112,662	114,727	116,833	118,981	121,172
Total Disbursement	$166,180	$169,187	$172,254	$175,380	$178,575	$181,831	$185,149	$188,538	$191,992	$195,516	$199,110	$202,788
Net Cash Flow	(1,292)	(967)	(789)	(574)	(327)	(37)	296	669	1,269	1,555	2,071	2,626
Cash Before Loans	21,208	19,902	18,768	17,842	17,157	16,756	16,681	16,972	17,857	19,020	20,692	22,912
ST Borrowing	7,230	7,361	7,494	7,630	7,770	7,911	8,055	8,203	8,353	8,506	8,663	8,824
ST Repayment	7,569	7,706	7,846	7,988	8,134	8,282	8,433	8,587	8,745	8,905	9,069	9,236
Ending Cash Bal.	$20,869	$19,557	$18,416	$17,484	$16,793	$16,385	$16,303	$16,588	$17,465	$18,621	$20,286	$22,500

AMERICAN BABY FOOD COMPANY
CASH FLOW PROJECTION
YEAR 2

	MONTH 1	MONTH 2	MONTH 3	MONTH 4	MONTH 5	MONTH 6	MONTH 7	MONTH 8	MONTH 9	MONTH 10	MONTH 11	MONTH 12
Beg. Cash Bal.	$22,500	$7,976	$1,107	$1,087	$756	$643	$448	$1,368	$2,434	$5,424	$10,453	$16,267
Cash Receipts:												
Collections	161,628	166,596	171,435	176,417	181,550	186,838	192,282	197,892	203,937	209,619	215,747	222,060
Interest	625	625	625	625	625	625	625	625	625	625	625	625
LT debt	0	0	0	0	0	0	0	0	0	0	0	0
Eq. Financing	31,250	31,250	31,250	31,250	31,250	31,250	31,250	31,250	31,250	31,250	31,250	31,250
Total Receipts	$193,503	$198,471	$203,310	$208,292	$213,425	$218,713	$224,157	$229,767	$235,812	$241,494	$247,622	$253,935
Disbursements:												
Direct Labor	4,402	4,488	4,569	4,651	4,735	4,821	4,908	4,997	5,088	5,181	5,275	5,386
Raw Material	74,559	75,910	77,285	78,689	80,122	81,582	83,072	84,591	86,143	87,724	89,337	90,985
Mfg. Overhead	8,817	8,970	9,133	9,299	9,469	9,641	9,817	9,998	10,180	10,367	10,558	10,751
Capital Exp.	2,749	2,607	2,461	2,426	2,292	1,860	1,598	1,423	1,080	1,140	1,353	1,511
LT Debt	0	0	0	0	0	0	0	0	0	0	0	0
Interest Exp.	791	1,754	2,421	1,962	1,384	865	584	126	83	218	176	135
Operating Exp.	121,792	122,889	123,026	124,207	124,432	125,700	127,015	128,375	130,783	133,239	136,243	139,798
Total Disbursement	$213,110	$216,618	$218,896	$221,233	$222,433	$224,470	$226,994	$229,510	$233,357	$237,869	$242,942	$248,567
Net Cash Flow	(19,607)	(18,146)	(15,586)	(12,941)	(9,009)	(5,757)	(2,837)	257	2,456	3,624	4,680	5,368
Cash Before Loans	2,893	(10,170)	(14,479)	(11,855)	(8,253)	(5,115)	(2,389)	1,624	4,890	9,049	15,133	21,635
ST Borrowing	6,665	14,786	20,409	16,534	11,663	7,293	4,926	1,062	700	1,841	1,486	1,135
ST Repayment	1,582	3,509	4,843	3,923	2,767	1,731	1,169	252	166	437	353	269
Ending Cash Bal.	$7,976	$1,107	$1,087	$756	$643	$448	$1,368	$2,434	$5,424	$10,453	$16,267	$22,500

AMERICAN BABY FOOD COMPANY
CASH FLOW PROJECTION
YEAR 3

	MONTH 1	MONTH 2	MONTH 3	MONTH 4	MONTH 5	MONTH 6	MONTH 7	MONTH 8	MONTH 9	MONTH 10	MONTH 11	MONTH 12
Beg. Cash Bal.	$22,500	$10,087	$10,392	$10,993	$11,219	$11,447	$8,919	$8,060	$9,834	$13,224	$12,554	$15,597
Cash Receipts:												
Collections	264,819	272,960	280,888	289,051	297,461	306,124	315,045	324,236	334,141	343,450	353,492	363,834
Interest	125	125	125	125	125	125	125	125	125	125	125	125
LT debt	0	0	0	0	0	0	0	0	0	0	0	0
Eq. Financing	0	0	0	0	0	0	0	0	0	0	0	0
Total Receipts	$264,944	$273,085	$281,013	$289,176	$297,586	$306,249	$315,170	$324,361	$334,266	$343,575	$353,617	$363,959
Disbursements:												
Direct Labor	7,675	7,824	7,967	8,110	8,257	8,406	8,557	8,713	8,871	9,033	9,198	9,391
Raw Material	125,621	127,896	130,214	132,579	134,993	137,454	139,964	142,524	145,137	147,802	150,519	153,296
Mfg. Overhead	14,808	15,065	15,339	15,617	15,902	16,193	16,487	16,791	17,098	17,411	17,732	18,057
Capital Exp.	3,052	3,105	3,162	3,218	3,277	3,338	3,398	3,461	3,524	3,588	3,655	3,721
LT Debt	0	0	0	0	0	0	0	0	0	0	0	0
Interest Exp.	3,643	6,004	5,471	4,746	4,080	2,719	2,383	2,241	1,713	0	0	0
Operating Exp.	141,436	143,997	146,608	149,271	151,989	154,759	157,587	160,470	163,411	166,411	169,470	172,591
Total Disbursement	$296,235	$303,892	$308,760	$313,541	$318,498	$322,869	$328,376	$334,199	$339,754	$344,246	$350,574	$357,056
Net Cash Flow	(31,292)	(30,807)	(27,747)	(24,365)	(20,912)	(16,619)	(13,207)	(9,838)	(5,488)	(671)	3,043	6,903
Cash Before Loans	(8,792)	(20,720)	(17,356)	(13,372)	(9,693)	(5,172)	(4,288)	(1,778)	4,345	12,554	15,597	22,500
ST Borrowing	18,878	31,112	28,349	24,591	21,140	14,091	12,348	11,612	8,879	0	0	0
ST Repayment	0	0	0	0	0	0	0	0	0	0	0	0
Ending Cash Bal.	$10,087	$10,392	$10,993	$11,219	$11,447	$8,919	$8,060	$9,834	$13,224	$12,554	$15,597	$22,500

Cash Receipts

Collections are assumed to be made in 45 days. Equity financing of $1,050,000 is assumed to be raised by issuance of additional shares of common stock. To simplify the projections, $675,000 out of the total equity financing of $1,050,000 will be raised based on straight line during the first 12 months. The remaining $375,000 will be raised equally throughout the second year of operation.

Cash Disbursements

Projected direct labor relates entirely to production of the premix and product quality testing, since production is carried out by a subcontractor. Raw material and manufacturing overhead include costs for premix and payments to the subcontractor. Direct labor costs are assumed to be paid as incurred; all other expenses are assumed to be paid within 30 days.

Capital expenditures include purchase of office equipment, microcomputers, and various computer softwares.

Short-Term Borrowing and Repayment

Short-term financing is assumed to be based on a revolving credit line with a maximum limit of $300,000. Funds will be borrowed monthly to cover cash shortfalls. Short-term debt is repaid as funds become available.

D.   Projected Balance Sheets

ABFC's projected annual balance sheets for the first three years of operation are presented on page 4·19.

AMERICAN BABY FOOD COMPANY
PROJECTED BALANCE SHEET
YEARS 1 THROUGH 3

MONTH	OPENING BALANCE	YEAR 1	YEAR 2	YEAR 3
ASSETS:				
Cash	$22,500	$22,500	$22,500	$22,500
Accounts Receivable	0	291,000	285,000	519,000
Inventory	0	18,000	55,500	108,000
Fixed Assets	0	31,500	54,000	94,500
Accumulated Depreciation	0	(3,000)	(10,500)	(24,000)
Deferred Start–Up Costs	244,500	220,000	195,500	171,150
TOTAL ASSETS	$267,000	$580,000	$602,000	$891,150
LIABILITIES:				
Accounts Payable	$0	$212,500	$248,000	$343,650
Short–Term Debt	25,500	21,000	88,500	259,500
Taxes Payable	0	0	0	0
Long–Term Debt	75,000	75,000	75,000	75,000
TOTAL LIABILITIES	$100,500	$308,500	$411,500	$678,150
OWNERS EQUITY:				
Capital Stock	$166,500	$841,500	$1,216,500	$1,216,500
Retained Earnings	0	(570,000)	(1,026,000)	(1,003,500)
TOTAL OWNERS EQUITY	$166,500	$271,500	$190,500	$213,000
TOTAL LIABILITIES & OE	$267,000	$580,000	$602,000	$891,150

Assets

Cash includes short-term investments. A minimum cash balance is assumed to be maintained through borrowing of short-term funds as necessary.

Accounts receivable are projected assuming a 45-day receivable period.

Inventory is projected based on an analysis of inventory turns in the health food industry and projected market expansion.

Fixed assets include the capital expenditures such as purchase of office equipment, microcomputers, and computer softwares. Fixed assets are depreciated on a straight-line basis over five years.

Liabilities

Accounts payable include all trade payable and nonincome tax accrued expenses. On average, these expenses are paid in 30 days.

Short-term debt is projected to finance cash shortfalls. Projected short-term debt is based on a revolving credit line that is repaid as funds become available.

Long-term debt is entirely comprised of a $75,000 loan received prior to this proposed financing.

Owners Equity

Projected equity is comprised of initial equity of investment by the principals of $166,500 and $1,050,000 in additional equity financing projected in years one and two.

Retained earnings includes income and losses beginning in year one. All prior costs are included in deferred start-up costs and amortized over 10 years.

E.   Projected Break-Even Analysis

Years 1 & 2

Fixed costs = $1,011,000.

Variable costs as a percentage of sales = 0.759868421

The following is break-even analysis for ABFC:

$$\text{Break-even sales} = \frac{\text{Fixed costs}}{\text{Contribution margin}}$$

Where contribution margin = 1 − (variable costs as a percentage of sales)

$$\text{Break-even sales} = \frac{\$1,011,000}{1 - 0.759868421}$$

$$\text{Break-even sales} = \frac{\$1,011,000}{0.240131579}$$

Break-even sales = $4,210,192

Year 3

It is projected that as ABFC enters into a new market in the third year of operation, its variable costs as a percentage of sales will decrease. As a result, ABFC will need less sales to break even than before.

Fixed cost = $1,011,000

Variable costs as a percentage of sales = .740670939

$$\text{Break-even sales} = \frac{\$1,011,000}{1 - 0.740670939}$$

$$\text{Break-even sales} = \frac{\$1,011,000}{0.259329061}$$

Break-even sales = $3,898,522

F.   Projected Annual Financial Ratios

The following are projected annual financial ratios for ABFC:

	Year 1	Year 2	Year 3
Inventory turns	68	36	25
Days receivables	45	45	45
Days payable	30	30	30
Gross profit/sales	49.84%	50.39%	50.02%
Net income/sales	0%	0%	0.57%
Return on equity	0%	0%	10.56%
Return on assets	0%	0%	2.52%
Return on investment	0%	0%	1.85%
Current ratio	1.42	1.08	1.08

VIII. SUMMARY

There are several advantages for ABFC to enter into children's health food business, as follows:

- The United States is entering a mini baby boom that will increase the potential market base for ABFC's products. This increase, combined with an expected future annual growth rate of 25 percent will increase the demand for ABFC's products.
- ABFC is uniquely positioned to take advantage of the children's health food market opportunity due to the managerial and field expertise of its founders, and its products' distinct benefits.
- The continued growth of health food centers in supermarket chains will greatly increase the total sales volume of all health foods.

According to ABFC's projected financial results, ABFC will incur some losses in the first two years of operation. In the third year, ABFC will start showing profits, and it is expected that its profits will grow in the future years.

ABFC will be the only company in the industry that offers a complete children health food product line. ABFC's entire marketing efforts will be in the area of health food for children; this focus will distinguish ABFC from other competing health food companies that offer a broad line of adult-oriented products to which they have added a narrow line of children's products. Also, The Company will distinguish itself from the major baby food makers by positioning itself as a maker of superior quality health food products.

ENDNOTES

1. Simmons Market Research Bureau, Inc., *1990 Study of Media & Market,* Summer 1990, P-29.
2. Ibid., Summer 1990, P-29.
3. *The Survey of Buying Power: Demographics,* USA 1991.
4. U.S. Department of Commerce, *Statistical Abstract of the United States, 1990,* Bureau of the Census, Ed. 110.
5. Ibid., Ed. 110.
6. M. Wold, "Baby Foods [Supermarket Sales]," *Progressive Grocer* vol. 70, p. 65–6, July 1991.
7. Simmons, op. cit., Summer 1990, P-29.
8. "Healthy Foods to Dominate Next Decade," *Marketing News* vol. 21, p. 7, June 1987.
9. Simmons, op. cit., Summer 1990, P-29.
10. Ibid., Summer 1990, P-29.

BIBLIOGRAPHY

1990 Study of Media & Marketing, Simmons Market Research Bureau, Inc., Summer 1990, P-29.

"Baby Foods & Needs [Consumption Survey]," *Progressive Grocer,* vol. 66, p. 101–2, September 1987.

"Healthy Foods to Dominate Next Decade," *Marketing News,* vol. 21, p. 7, June 1987.

Statistical Abstract of the United States, 1990, U.S. Dept. of Commerce, Bureau of the Census, Ed. 110.

The Survey of Buying Power: Demographics, USA 1991.

Wold, M. "Baby Foods [Supermarket Sales]," *Progressive Grocer,* vol. 70, p. 65–6, July 1991.

APPENDIX A

Competitive Analysis

COMPANY	PRODUCT BENEFITS	ADVERTISING/PROMOTION	SALES/DISTRIBUTION	PRODUCTS
Health Valley	No additives, preservatives No chemicals, insecticides, etc. Palatibility	Advertises in HF magazines Good display of products Good Packaging Good handout information	Ships direct Some HF distributors	Cereal
Familia	No additives, preservatives No chemicals, insecticides, etc. Industry leader	National health journals and radio Provides nutritional hotline Good Packaging Booth at trade shows	Uses own sales force Uses HF distributors	Cereal
Gerber	No salt or preservatives Different foods for different stages of development	Advertises in national magazines	Uses own sales force Uses supermarket distributors	Variety of meats, vegetables, fruits, desserts, juices, cereals
Beech–Nut	No salt or preservatives Different foods for different stages of development	Advertises in national magazines	Uses own sales force Uses supermarket distributors	Variety of meats, vegetables, fruits, desserts, juices, cereals
Heinz	No salt or preservatives Different foods for different stages of development	Advertises in national magazines	Uses own sales force Uses supermarket distributors	Variety of meats, vegetables, fruits, desserts, juices, cereals

APPENDIX B

Product Line Profit Analysis

Market—1

AGES 6 – 12 MONTHS								
PRODUCT	NUMBER OF CASES ORDERED	QUANTITY PER CASE	PRICE PER CASE	REVENUE PER ORDER	COST PER ORDER DOLLARS	%	PROFIT PER ORDER DOLLARS	%
Dinners	5	36/4.5 oz.	$21.60	$108.00	$58.35	54%	$49.65	46%
Meats	6	36/4.5 oz.	16.20	97.20	49.50	51%	47.70	49%
Vegetables	6	36/4.5 oz.	16.20	97.20	48.60	50%	48.60	50%
Desserts	5	36/4.5 oz.	16.20	81.00	40.50	50%	40.50	50%
Fruits	6	36/4.5 oz.	16.20	97.20	49.50	51%	47.70	49%
Biscuits, Cookies	4	12/10 oz.	19.80	79.20	42.00	53%	37.20	47%
Total				$559.80	$288.45	52%	$271.35	48%

AGES 1 – 3 YEARS								
PRODUCT	NUMBER OF CASES ORDERED	QUANTITY PER CASE	PRICE PER CASE	REVENUE PER ORDER	COST PER ORDER DOLLARS	%	PROFIT PER ORDER DOLLARS	%
Dinners	4	36/4.5 oz.	$21.60	$86.40	$46.65	54%	$39.75	46%
Meats	4	36/4.5 oz.	16.20	64.80	33.00	51%	31.80	49%
Vegetables	4	36/4.5 oz.	16.20	64.80	32.40	50%	32.40	50%
Desserts	6	36/4.5 oz.	16.20	97.20	48.60	50%	48.60	50%
Fruits	3.5	36/4.5 oz.	16.20	56.70	28.95	51%	27.75	49%
Biscuits, Cookies	3	12/10 oz.	19.80	59.40	31.50	53%	27.90	47%
Prepared Foods	4	42/ 6 oz.	56.70	226.80	122.40	54%	104.40	46%
Sandwich Meats	6	24/12 oz.	21.60	129.60	67.35	52%	62.25	48%
Total				$785.70	$410.85	52%	$374.85	48%

Market—2

AGES 6 – 12 MONTHS								
PRODUCT	NUMBER OF CASES ORDERED	QUANTITY PER CASE	PRICE PER CASE	REVENUE PER ORDER	COST PER ORDER DOLLARS	%	PROFIT PER ORDER DOLLARS	%
Dinners	4	36/4.5 oz.	$21.60	$86.40	$46.65	54%	$39.75	46%
Meats	6	36/4.5 oz.	16.20	97.20	49.50	51%	47.70	49%
Vegetables	5.4	36/4.5 oz.	16.20	87.45	43.80	50%	43.65	50%
Desserts	5	36/4.5 oz.	16.20	81.00	40.50	50%	40.50	50%
Fruits	6	36/4.5 oz.	16.20	97.20	49.50	51%	47.70	49%
Biscuits, Cookies	4	12/10 oz.	19.80	79.20	42.00	53%	37.20	47%
Total				$528.45	$271.95	51%	$256.50	49%

AGES 1 – 3 YEARS								
PRODUCT	NUMBER OF CASES ORDERED	QUANTITY PER CASE	PRICE PER CASE	REVENUE PER ORDER	COST PER ORDER DOLLARS	%	PROFIT PER ORDER DOLLARS	%
Dinners	3	36/4.5 oz.	$21.60	$64.80	$34.95	54%	$29.85	46%
Meats	3	36/4.5 oz.	16.20	48.60	24.75	51%	23.85	49%
Vegetables	3	36/4.5 oz.	16.20	48.60	24.30	50%	24.30	50%
Desserts	5	36/4.5 oz.	16.20	81.00	40.50	50%	40.50	50%
Fruits	2	36/4.5 oz.	16.20	32.40	16.50	51%	15.90	49%
Biscuits, Cookies	4	12/10 oz.	19.80	79.20	42.00	53%	37.20	47%
Prepared Foods	4	42/ 6 oz.	56.70	226.80	122.40	54%	104.40	46%
Sandwich Meats	6	24/12 oz.	21.60	129.60	67.35	52%	62.25	48%
Total				$711.00	$372.75	52%	$338.25	48%

5

BUSINESS PLAN FOR MUDVILLE GREETING CARDS

Developed by
David Yang

Used with the Permission of the Author

EXECUTIVE SUMMARY

With sports events drawing over a half billion fans and billions of dollars being spent on sports perennially, the United States was proclaimed a "sports-crazy" nation by *U.S. News and World Report.** The magazine also reports that over 100 million Americans participate in sports and other fitness activities.

Although it is apparent that there are many sports fans and athletes in the United States, there are very few greeting cards designed to give to them. In a research study conducted by visiting retail stores, it was found that less than one out of every one thousand greeting cards have a sports theme. Virtually every card found that had a sports theme was a "cute" card for giving to elementary school or preschool children.

Mudville will produce an entire line of sports greeting cards suitable for giving to sports fans and athletes of all ages. The line of cards will feature baseball, football, basketball, hockey, golf, tennis, aerobics, weight lifting, bowling, skiing, running, volleyball, boxing, and auto racing. Some cards will be made to excite, some to inform, and some to humor. There will also be cards picturing famous athletes in action.

There are very strong competitors in the greeting cards industry, such as Hallmark, which has annual sales of over $2.7 billion. However, newcomers to the industry have had success entering with "alternative" design greeting cards, a very fast growing segment of the industry. Sports cards will be Mudville's niche in the alternative card market.

Mudville will also distinguish itself from the competitors by selling at nontraditional card outlets. Mudville cards will be sold at sporting good stores, sports apparel stores, sports accessory stores, sports novelty stores, trading card stores, and fitness facilities, as well as at traditional locations.

To sell retailers, Mudville's management team will attend national trade shows and visit Southern California retail stores or their corporate offices. Manufacturer's representatives will be contracted to sell to retailers outside of Southern California.

The end users of Mudville cards will be anyone who has a friend or relative who is a sports fan or athlete. Mudville will promote to the end users with posters in retail stores and with advertisements on shopping carts.

Mudville, an "S" corporation, will be entirely owned by David Yang, who will serve as the president. David Yang has a B.S. in business entrepreneurship from the University of Southern California, and he is highly knowledgeable in sports from over 20 years of participation. David's sisters, Jenny and Sophia, will hold vice president positions. For their services they will be vested with phantom stock.

To start the venture, an investment of $80,000 will be required. Mudville is projected to reach break-even one and a half years after start-up. Three years after start-up, Mudville is projected to yield approximately $500,000 in profits. David Yang will be entitled to 40 percent of the profits, and Jenny and Sophia Yang will each get 30 percent.

For the $80,000 investment, David Yang will ask his father, Charles Yang, for a loan. The entire loan will be paid back before the end of the second year of the venture. In addition to paying back the money, David will promise to provide employment for his two sisters and to support a luxurious retirement for his parents.

* Maloney, Lawrence. "Sports-Crazy Americans," *U.S. News and World Report*, August 13, 1984.

TABLE OF CONTENTS

EXECUTIVE SUMMARY . . . . 5 · 2

CONCEPT . . . . 5 · 4

MANAGEMENT AND ORGANIZATION . . . . 5 · 4

PRODUCT . . . . 5 · 5

PRODUCTION PLAN . . . . 5 · 7

COMPETITION . . . . 5 · 8

PRICING . . . . 5 · 11

MARKETING PLAN . . . . 5 · 13

FINANCIAL PLAN . . . . 5 · 17

OPERATING AND CONTROL SYSTEM . . . . 5 · 21

SCHEDULE . . . . 5 · 21

GROWTH PLAN . . . . 5 · 22

CONTINGENCY PLAN . . . . 5 · 23

THE DEAL . . . . 5 · 24

BIBLIOGRAPHY . . . . 5 · 25

CONCEPT

- *Distinct Function of Product*   Mudville greeting cards will be designed for giving to sports fans and athletes of all levels.

- *Proprietary Aspects*   Mudville will reserve copyrights on all pictures, drawings, and inscriptions printed onto Mudville cards.

- *Innovative Technology*   Currently, there are few sports-related greeting cards in the market and none that are as appealing as the cards Mudville will produce.

- *Position in the Industry*   Mudville will be both producer and wholesale distributor of greeting cards.

- *Intended Customers*   Mudville cards are intended to be purchased by friends and relatives of sports fans and athletes.

- *Customer Benefits*   Customers will gain the satisfaction of expressing their feelings to the recipients of the cards and/or gain the satisfaction of instilling positive feelings in the recipients.

- *Market Penetration Method*   Mudville cards will be sold through various retail stores such as greeting card stores, athletic apparel stores, athletic accessory stores, sports novelty stores, sporting goods stores, trading card stores, drug stores, grocery markets, and department stores.

- *Who Will Make the Product*   Mudville cards will be designed in-house, using photographs and drawings purchased from independent photographers and artists. Printing of the cards will be subcontracted out, as will the production of the envelopes.

MANAGEMENT AND ORGANIZATION

Management Team

Mudville will be completely owned and managed by the Yang family. David Yang, the founder of Mudville, will serve as president and his two sisters, Jenny and Sophia, will occupy vice president positions. The need for additional management personnel will not arise until the second or third year of operation.

Officer duties will be defined very loosely. Although areas of responsibility will be assigned, each officer will be involved in all aspects of the company. For all important decisions, the vice presidents will make recommendations, but the president will have unchallengeable power.

As president of Mudville, David Yang will oversee all activities and will also be primarily responsible for finance and production. David earned a bachelor's degree in business entrepreneurship from the University of Southern California and is presently working towards a MBA at Cal State L.A. His vast knowledge in sports comes from twenty years of being an avid "all" sports fan. He played baseball in high school and now participates in recreational tennis, golf, softball, basketball, bowling, and skiing.

Jenny Yang will have the title of vice president of sales and marketing. She has a B.A. in history from Barnard College. Her experiences in athletics include lettering three years in high school softball and basketball. One of her favorite activities is attending Dodger games.

The other vice president, Sophia Yang, will be in charge of personnel and shipping. She earned a B.S. in business administration from Cal State Northridge, and is currently an assistant manager of Powerhouse Gym.

Mudville, to be set up as an "S" corporation, will be entirely owned by David Yang. Jenny and Sophia Yang will each be given 30 shares of phantom stock, with each share entitling the bearer to one percent of Mudville profits. In the event that Jenny or Sophia wishes to disassociate themselves with the company, David will purchase their shares at a price he feels is fair.

Compensation

The management team will receive no compensation other than dividends of profit. The time and amount of the dividend payments will be determined by David Yang.

There are no contracts between the vice presidents and the company. The relationships are based on trust between family members.

Advisory Board

Among those providing guidance to Mudville are Wayne Wilson, founder and president of L'Image Graphics; Dave Craven, regional operations manager of Hallmark; Jack Steel, sales and marketing director of Quality Greeting Cards Distributing Company; and Lauren Frederick, assistant manager of Card America in Plaza Pasadena.

Wayne Wilson
President
L'Image Graphics
8040 Robertson Boulevard
Culver City, CA 90232
(310) 837-4588

Jack Steel
Sales and Marketing Director
Quality Greeting Cards Dist. Co.
930 Monterey Pass Road
Monterey Park, CA 91754
(818) 264-3365

Dave Craven
Regional Operations Manager
Hallmark Marketing Corporation
4685 Mac Arthur Court, Suite 200
Newport Beach, CA 92660
(714) 476-2406

Lauren Frederick
Assistant Branch Manager
Card America
287 The Plaza Pasadena
Pasadena, CA 91106
(818) 449-7790

PRODUCT

Purpose of the Product

Mudville cards makes available greeting cards to give to sports fans and athletes that will be appreciated for more than just the friendly gesture. The card itself may instill in the recipient feelings of excitement, nostalgia, identification, inspiration, or humor.

Unique Features

Mudville cards are unique in that the sports theme cards currently in the market do not have a pure sports flavor. Unlike Mudville cards, most of the sports theme cards currently in the market are not designed to deliver "extra" satisfaction to sports fans and athletes. The pictures Mudville selects to be featured on its cards will all be "art gallery" quality.

Stage of Development

Mudville cards are still in the idea stage. Photographs and drawings of the type Mudville seeks have been clipped out of magazines. Photographers and artists will soon be sought to provide the actual pictures to be imprinted on the cards.

Shelf Life

The shelf life of the cards can vary greatly among the different cards. The major determining factor is the amount of time the sports celebrity pictured on a particular card remains popular. Another factor is that if a potential customer knows or suspects that the recipient has already been given a particular card, they will refrain from buying that card. The estimated shelf life of Mudville cards range from one to four years.

Production

Because Mudville wants its card designs to be high quality, production of the cards will be labor intensive. Most of the cards will be designed by the president of Mudville, David Yang. The pictures used in the cards will be purchased from outside sources. Printing of the cards will be subcontracted out.

Future Research and Development

Mudville's management team will continually stay alert to new developments in the industry by exploring retail stores, attending trade shows, and reading trade magazines. The management team will also continually search for pictures and ideas to use on Mudville cards.

Trademark, Patents, Copyrights, Licenses, and Royalties

The name Mudville is a trademark that cannot be used by any other company in a similar field. Mudville will not obtain official copyrights for its cards; however, the copyright symbol will be printed on the back of the cards. According to Wayne Wilson of L'Image Graphics, once a card bearing a company's name is placed in the market, that company automatically reserves a copyright that can stand up in court.

Royalties will be paid to the photographers and artists whose pictures are used on the cards. The amount of the royalty paid for each piece of work will be separately negotiated and will be based on the complexity and quality of the picture. Royalties can be a percentage of profits, a fixed fee, or both.

Royalties will also be paid to sports celebrities pictured on the cards. The amount is negotiable, but Mudville will target 10 percent of gross revenues generated by the particular item.

When a team logo is used, royalties also have to be paid to the league. That amount is also negotiable but is usually close to 15 percent of revenues.

Spinoffs

Mudville will keep an open mind to producing other gift items such as wrapping paper, calendars, mugs, stickers, figurines, and t-shirts.

PRODUCTION PLAN

In-house Production

It is foreseen that 90 percent of Mudville cards will be designed in-house. All photographs and drawings for the cards will be purchased from outside sources. The printing will be subcontracted out. The envelopes for the cards will be purchased from outside sources.

Subcontractors

Listed below are printers who are able to print greeting cards for Mudville. The prices and terms demanded by the various printers are essentially the same. The price to print a batch of 2000 to 5000 of 5 × 6.5 greeting cards is approximately 15 cents each, more or less depending on the complexity. A 50 percent deposit is required at the time of order, and the remaining payment is due at the time of pick up. Printing usually takes two to three weeks.

Tempo Printing and Graphics
1125 S. Central Avenue
Glendale, CA 91208
(818) 246-8133

California Master Printers
600 W. Foothill Boulevard
Glendora, CA 91016
(818) 963-5991

Sinclair Printing Co.
4005 Whiteside Avenue
Los Angeles, CA 90026
(213) 264-4808

Raw Material Supplies

Envelopes suitable for Mudville cards can be purchased from many different locations. The cost for high-quality color envelopes is approximately one cent each for large quantities. Listed below are the potential suppliers Mudville may purchase from.

Advance Envelope Mfg. Co.
1025 S. Fremont Avenue
Alhambra, CA 91803
(818) 283-9101

Transo Envelope Co.
6501 San Fernando Road
Glendale, CA 91202
(213) 245-8433

Facility

Designing of the cards will be done at the Yang's residential house located in Pasadena. Computers and drawing tables for designing are already owned. The house will also serve as an administrative base during the first year of operation, and in the second year, an office will be rented.

Inventory Storage

Because greeting cards do not take up much space, a room at the Yang's residence will be used for storage. When an office is rented, it would also be used for storage.

Quality Control System

Mudville cards will be inspected on a regular basis by the management team to assure quality. However, there will be no formal system.

COMPETITION

Direct Competitors

Presently, no greeting card company targets friends and relatives of sports fans and athletes. Those people who Mudville will target currently settle for non-sports-related cards. It is very likely that the cards they currently purchase are cards made by Hallmark, American Greetings, Gibson, or a subsidiary of one of those three biggest companies in the industry.

Hallmark, the industry leader, owns 43 percent of the market share in the retail card market.[1] Hallmark, a privately held corporation, has been in the card business for over 80 years. Currently, the company employs 22,000 people world-wide and has annual sales of about $2.7 billion. Hallmark produces 11 million greeting cards every working day in its five plants. Hallmark's personnel include a 700-person creative staff, which produces more than 18,000 card designs annually. Hallmark advertises on television extensively, thus virtually every American is familiar with their products. Hallmark was once known as a slow-moving company, but that is no longer true. According to Dave Craven, a regional operations manager of Hallmark, their Shoebox line of cards found its way into the market just three months after its conception. Hallmark cards can be purchased from over 36,000 retail outlets across America. Those outlets include Hallmark specialty store franchises which exclusively carry Hallmark cards.

The second greatest number of market shares is held by American Greetings. After researching the industry by visiting various Southern California retail stores, Mudville's management team has concluded that American Greetings holds approximately 30 percent of market share. American Greetings products are carried by popular retail stores such as Sears, Thrifties, and Hughs Market. Carlton, a subsidiary of American Greetings, markets its cards through specialty stores.

Also by visiting stores, Mudville's management team estimates that Gibson owns 10 percent of market shares. Gibson products are carried by Fedco, a popular membership store chain in Southern California.

---

[1] Weiner, Steve. "Do They Speak Spanish in Kansas City?" *Forbes*, January 25, 1988.

Although there are hundreds of small card companies, the industry is essentially an oligopoly. However, the smaller card companies have been successful marketing alternative cards, that is cards with less conservative designs than traditional cards. Because alternative cards are increasing in popularity at a very rapid rate, the card industry's Big Three have been aggressively fighting for shares in that market. Wayne Wilson of L'Image Graphics estimates that the Big Three currently splits 60 percent of the alternative cards market and the remaining 40 percent goes to smaller companies. Mudville cards would fit into the category of alternative cards.

Mudville will compete with the industry by marketing sports theme greeting cards. None of the Big Three nor the smaller companies produces a wide variety of sports cards. Furthermore, the sports cards on the market do not have the appeal of Mudville cards. Searching through Lin's Stationers, a Hallmark specialty store in Pasadena, only three sports cards were found. Two of the cards were "cute" in appearance intended for giving to very young children; the other card featured only drawings on sports equipment and is specifically for giving to one's grandson. Searching through a Thrifties drug store, which carries American Greetings, only two sports cards were found, both intended for giving to very young children. Fedco carried a Gibson card picturing Michael Jordan playing basketball. That card is along the line of what Mudville will produce; however, the Gibson card is slightly less appealing. Besides that one card, Gibson markets no other card of that type. There were two other Gibson sports cards but those were the "cute" type. Mudville will market a long line of cards featuring action or still pictures that would be appealing to sports fans and athletes of all ages.

Another way Mudville will differentiate itself from the competitor is by distributing its cards through nontraditional locations. Mudville cards will be sold at sporting goods stores, sports apparel stores, sports accessory stores, sports novelty stores, trading card stores, and fitness facilities, as well as in traditional locations. Utilizing nontraditional locations alleviates the difficulties of competing for shelf-space at traditional locations. The large companies try very hard to coerce retail stores into carrying their lines exclusively. It is unlikely that the large card companies would attempt to tap the nontraditional locations because it may require major restructuring of their companies' systems. Considering that the potential volume is relatively low at nontraditional locations, it would not be worth their efforts.

The competition in the card industry is very fierce, and the large companies are known to take extremely aggressive action to gain or regain market shares. Usually when a card company introduces a new design that experiences success in the market, the large companies immediately copy it. In a *Forbes* article about Hallmark, Steve Wiener wrote, "Roses are red, violets are blue, take my growth markets and I'll copy you."[2] That was a line referring to Hallmark copying Blue Mountain Arts cards. Hallmark was banned by the court from selling cards that resembled Blue Mountain Arts cards. Hallmark settled a case out of court for marketing their Shoebox line, which are strikingly similar to Recycled Paper Products cards. If Mudville cards prove to be highly profitable, Hallmark and other companies are expected to introduce their own line of sports cards similar to Mudville's.

Mudville's strategy to compete against the competition is to reach the marketplace first and tie up the channels of distribution. Mudville will produce top quality cards so that other companies cannot push in by marketing better quality cards. Mudville will attempt to establish good relationships with dealers by providing fair prices, timely deliveries, and courteous and prompt service.

---

[2] Weiner, Steve. "Do They Speak Spanish in Kansas City?" *Forbes*, January 25, 1988.

Hallmark and the other large card companies are also very aggressive in fighting for distribution outlets. Hallmark, for instance is known to intimidate dealers by threatening to pull Hallmark cards from the stores that carry other brands of cards. In other cases, dealers were offered money to replace competitive cards with Hallmark cards.[3] If traditional card outlets turn away Mudville cards, then Mudville will concentrate its efforts in selling through nonconventional outlets.

Indirect Competitors

Mudville indirectly competes with sports trading card companies. Potential Mudville customers may choose to substitute sports greeting cards with sports trading cards. On the other hand, some customers may purchase Mudville sports greeting cards to add to their sports memorabilia collection. The trading card companies which Mudville may compete against include Topps, Upper Deck, Donruss, Bowman, Score, and Fleer. The trading card companies, however, specialize in major sports, such as football, baseball, basketball, and hockey. Mudville cards will also feature recreational sports.

Emerging Competitors

If Mudville cards are successful, it is possible that trading card companies would begin producing sports greeting cards. Since they already have pictures of athletes and have developed relationships with athletes and league offices, trading card companies could easily copy Mudville products.

Customer Viewpoint

During conversations with a few friends, David Yang asked his friends to discuss their decision process in buying greeting cards. The conclusion drawn from the conversations was that people are more concerned with buying a card that fits a recipient's personality than they are with selecting a particular brand. However, because they want to give a card that has a quality appearance, they tend to first think of Hallmark, which many people associate with quality. Hallmark's motto, "when you care enough to send the very best," is frequently heard on television.

Other important factors in the customer's decision process are convenience and selection. The customers choose locations which are not too far out of their way and locations with a wide selection to increase their chances of buying the most fitting card.

When it comes to purchasing a card for a sports fan or athlete, the people spoken to suggested that they would choose Mudville cards over Hallmark or other brands of cards since Mudville cards are far more fitting than all other cards available. They would even travel a slightly longer distance to purchase the more fitting cards.

Lauren Frederick, the assistant manager of Card America in Plaza Pasadena, said that customers frequently asked for cards featuring popular athletes. The store, which carried primarily the Carlton line of American Greetings cards, was unable to satisfy those customers' demands.

[3] Weiner, Steve. "Do They Speak Spanish in Kansas City?" *Forbes*, January 25, 1988.

Nature of Competition

The key to success in the alternative card industry lies in creativity. A company must be able to produce a card that is both unique and appealing to an adequately sized group of people.

Because of the extremely specialized nature of each line of cards, the industry accommodates many different companies. Newcomers with a good, fresh idea have historically entered the industry with relative ease. However, as mentioned before, new companies which experience great amounts of success have had their line of cards copied by larger companies. Another problem small companies face is the pressure placed on dealers by large companies to carry their lines exclusively.

PRICING

Price Sheet

Mudville takes orders by phone, mail, or in person. Full payment must be made prior to delivery. Quantity discounts are not offered.

	Mudville's Prices			
	Wholesale	*Retail*	*Mark-Up*	*%*
Standard	$0.85	$1.75	$0.90	51%
Celebrity	0.95	1.95	1.00	51

Competitive Price Strategy

Listed below are prices of competitors' cards. Most card companies carry many different styles of cards and thus offer many different prices. To insure a relevancy, competing cards which most resemble Mudville cards in size, material, and complexity were selected for price comparison.

	Competitors' Prices			
	Wholesale*	*Retail*	*Mark-Up*	*%*
Ambassador	$0.70	$1.75	$1.05	60%
Carlton	0.70	1.75	1.05	60
Gibson	0.70	1.75	1.00	60
Blue Mountain	0.75	1.75	1.00	57
American Greetings	0.60	1.50	0.90	60
Hallmark	0.60	1.50	0.90	60
L'Image	0.75	1.50	0.75	50
Recycled Paper Products	0.50	1.25	0.75	60

*Estimations by Jack Steel of Quality Greeting Cards Distributing Co.

According to Jack Steel, director of marketing and sales at Quality Greeting Cards Distributing Company, the wholesale cost of greeting cards charged by most manufacturers is 40 percent of retail price. L'Image Graphics charges 50 percent of retail. Wayne Wilson, the president of L'Image, maintains that L'Image cards is able to obtain a higher percentage because of the lack of competition in their niche, which is cards for African Americans.

Because of the lack of competition in the sports cards niche, Mudville will adopt a whole-sale pricing strategy similar to L'Image Graphics. Mudville's wholesale prices will be slightly below 50 percent of retail. However, as shown in the price sheets, retailers can earn about the same dollar amount per Mudville card sold as they would with most other cards. Mudville's wholesale prices may be adjusted if a competitor with similar products appears and offers retailers a better deal.

Jack Steel suggested that quantity discounts are not customary in the card industry. Mudville has no plans to offer quantity discounts unless it is instrumental to securing a deal with a large retail chain.

Because selling greeting cards is an unprecedented activity at many of Mudville's proposed retail outlets, it may be necessary to eliminate some risk in order to convince the retailers to carry Mudville products. During Mudville's first six months of operation, a money-back guarantee will be offered to retailers. Before the predetermined deadline, any unsold cards may be returned to Mudville for a full refund.

Mudville's suggested retail prices, as shown on the price sheet, are on the high end compared to other cards of similar size, material, and complexity. However, the number of other cards selling at $1.75 is in abundance, and Mudville's standard cards would not likely be viewed as high priced by customers. At $1.95, Mudville's celebrity cards are priced above all other cards in its class, but there are many other cards, usually ones larger in size, that are priced the same or higher.

Due to the lack of quality substitute sports cards, Mudville's target market is not expected to be highly price sensitive. Furthermore, most stores that will carry Mudville cards do not carry other brands of greeting cards. Most customers who make their selections with particular celebrities in mind are not anticipated to be reluctant to pay twenty cents over the price of a Mudville standard card for a Mudville celebrity card.

Gross Margin on Products

Mudville Standard Cards

Price per card		$0.85
Printing and material	$0.15	
Envelopes	0.01	
Art and design*	0.05	
Direct costs		0.21
Gross margin		$0.64

Mudville Celebrity Cards

Price per card		$0.95
Printing and material	$0.15	
Envelopes	0.01	
Art and design*	0.05	
Celebrity royalties	0.10	
Direct costs		0.31
Gross margin		$0.64

*Price of art is estimated at $500 and is allocated among 10,000 cards. Actual figures will vary according to the amount paid for each individual picture and the volume printed. Because the designing will be performed by David Yang, no designing cost is allocated.

MARKETING PLAN

Industry Profile

According to Dave Craven of Hallmark, in 1992 Americans will spend over 4 billion dollars on greeting cards, of which approximately 30 percent are alternative greeting cards. After visiting several retail stores, Mudville's management team concludes that less than one of every one thousand cards in the market features a sports theme. America is a "sports-crazy" country,[4] yet there are few greeting cards designed for giving to sports fans and athletes. Americans spend over $27 billion a year on sporting goods[5] and many more dollars on attending sports events and purchasing sports memorabilia. Below is a chart showing the number of Americans who participated in particular sports in 1985. The numbers are estimated to be significantly higher for 1991, and are presumed to be increasing every year.

Americans Who Participated in Sports during 1985

Basketball	42 million	Football	32 million
Softball	28 million	Baseball	26 million
Golf	21 million	Tennis	27 million
Weight lift	36 million	Aerobics	39 million
Fishing	63 million	Bowling	40 million
Jogging	33 million	Volleyball	36 million

Source: U.S. News and World Report, August 11, 1986.

There is a significant seasonal factor in the card industry, with a large percentage of cards being sold for Christmas, but at the same time the industry never faces slumps because of the year-round occurrences of birthdays. Sales are also strong during the Valentine's Day period. There is a growing popularity in nonoccasion cards. In 1990, nonoccasion cards accounted for 14 percent of all greeting cards sold, and unit sales of nonoccasion cards are growing at an estimated 10 percent a year.[6] Fitting into the nonoccasion category, a majority of Mudville's cards will not mention an occasion and allow the customer to fill in the purpose of the card. Mudville will also market greeting cards specifically for birthdays and for Christmas.

Baseball, basketball, football, and hockey are seasonal sports, but there is always at least one sport season in progress. Interest in a particular sport may still linger even if that sport is not in season. Mudville will carry cards from the four major sports in addition to year-round activities such as golf, tennis, aerobics, and weight training. Mudville cards are expected to experience relatively steady sales year-round.

Customer Profile

Dave Craven maintains that 80 percent of all greeting cards are sold to women. Because men generally appreciate sports more than women do, the percentage of Mudville cards sold to women is not expected to be consistent with the norm. Mudville predicts that approximately 60 percent of its customers will be women and 40 percent men. Many customers are likely to be parents buying a card for a son over 7 years old. People of all income levels buy greeting cards, with the frequency of purchase increasing with income levels. Customers are a lot more likely to

---

[4] Maloney, Lawrence. "Sports-Crazy Americans," *U.S. News and World Report,* August 13, 1984.
[5] Weisman, Adam. "The Business of Staying Fit," *U.S. News and World Report,* August 11, 1986.
[6] Levine, Joshua. "Love Means Never Having to Say Anything," *Forbes,* April 1, 1991.

be raised in the United States than new immigrants, who usually do not fully appreciate American sports. Customers are likely to reside in cities with professional sports franchises. Customers of Mudville celebrity cards will most likely live in the city in which the featured celebrity plays sports. The one thing virtually all customers will have in common is that they are a friend or relative of a sports fan or athlete. It is also possible that a customer himself is a sports fan or athlete wanting to express his passions. The customer may also be a sports memorabilia collector wanting to add Mudville cards to his collection.

Mudville cards are designed to be given to fans and participants of all levels of baseball, basketball, football, hockey, golf, tennis, and physical fitness. Other activities Mudville cards may feature include skateboarding, softball, skiing, bowling, fishing, and auto racing. Over 90 percent of the recipients will likely be male, and approximately 65 percent of recipients are likely to be under 18 years of age.

Customer Benefits

Mudville cards offer customers the satisfaction of giving cards that recipients, who are sports fans or athletes, will value more than other brand of card that they could have received. Most cards currently in the market have little or no intrinsic value. Cards are usually appreciated only because of its representation of the giver's thoughtfulness. On the other hand, Mudville cards also provide recipients with excitement, knowledge, or humor.

Mudville cards can also be beneficial for parents who want to encourage their children to participate in sports. Giving Mudville cards to children communicates to them that their athletic pursuits are supported. Mudville celebrity cards could help steer children to adopt athletic role models.

Customer Needs

The greeting cards industry is often referred to as the "social expression" industry. Mudville cards fill the needs of customers who want to express their sports-related thoughts.

By making Mudville cards available at sports miscellany stores, customers can save time by not having to go to separate places to buy a sports gift item and to buy a card.

Market Niche

Mudville will produce a line of greeting cards that features sports themes. No other greeting card company aggressively targets people with sports fans and or athletes on their gift list. There are a few cards in the market with sports themes; however, those cards are not as exciting as Mudville cards. Furthermore, most sports greeting cards currently in the market are designed for very young boys. Mudville will market cards appropriate for giving to males and females of virtually every age.

Target Market

Potential customers of Mudville cards are likely to visit sporting goods stores, sports apparel stores, sports novelty stores, sports trading card stores, physical fitness facilities, greeting card specialty stores, grocery markets, department stores, and drug stores. Those retail outlets are, therefore, Mudville's target market. Many people visit sports miscellany stores to buy gifts for sports fans and athletes. The sports miscellany stores are considered Mudville's prime targets not only because of the presence of many potential customers, but also because of the absence of competitors. Currently, no sports stores carry greeting cards, but Mudville will attempt to be the first to have cards sold in those stores. Because it is not likely for sports stores to carry an excessive number of cards, it would be difficult for competing card companies to target that market after Mudville has tied it up.

Market Penetration Method

Mudville cards will be sold to Southern California retail outlets primarily by Mudville's management team, who will personally engage the outlets or the corporate offices and will display the cards at trade shows. Mudville will also utilize manufacturer's representatives to penetrate markets outside of Southern California. According to Wayne Wilson of L'Image, the standard commission for manufacturer's representatives is 20 percent of gross revenues generated by their efforts.

Advertising and Promotions

To familiarize retailers with Mudville cards, color catalogs with Mudville's current product lines will be periodically mailed to retailers and handed out at trade shows. The catalogs will include pictures of cards, ordering codes of each card, price sheet, order form, and Mudville's phone number. In addition, Mudville will place quarter-page advertisements in *Greetings Magazine* and *Sporting Goods Business* every month during the first year of operation and every other month during the second year.

To promote Mudville cards to the end users, 5″ × 7″ signs will be placed near or on retailer's cash registers. In addition, advertisements will be displayed on grocery market shopping carts. The advertisements on the shopping carts will mainly target women, who are the predominant purchasers of greeting cards. Men are more likely than women to recognize the benefits of Mudville cards without the help of advertisements.

Estimated Advertising and Promotions Cost for First Year	
Shopping cart ads	$10,000
Catalogs (6,000)	3,000
Sporting goods business ads (12)	1,800
Greetings magazine ads (12)	1,500
Trade shows (3)	1,500
5″ × 7″ signs (3,000)	500
Miscellaneous	2,000

Customer Reactions

Retailers

David Yang, president of Mudville, visited retail stores that are potential carriers of Mudville cards and asked employees if they felt there would be a demand for sports greeting cards and if there is a chance their stores would carry the cards:

- *M. G., Manager, Oshman's Sporting Goods, Plaza Pasadena*   M. G. said that he is not sure whether or not greeting cards would sell well in a sporting goods store except during Christmas. He said that "pick-up" items, items under two dollars placed near the cash register, sell extremely well during Christmas, and Mudville cards could fall into that category. Oshman's corporate office decides what the store carries, but Mark thinks they would be interested in carrying Mudville cards at least during Christmas.

- *F. S., Manager, Fan Club (athletic shoes and apparel), Plaza Pasadena*   F. S., manager of the athletic shoes and apparel store, thinks there is at least a moderate demand for sports greeting cards. He says that he has a few friends that he would give Mudville cards. Because the owners of Fan Club have never considered carrying any items besides shoes and apparel, F. G. does not think they would adopt Mudville cards; however, he also said that "you never know."

- *T. V., Manager, Fan Fair (sports apparel), Plaza Pasadena*   T. V. thinks that Mudville cards will sell well in his store because a large percentage of their customers go there to buy gifts for someone else. He is unsure if his store's corporate office would want to carry greeting cards, but he suggested that sports novelty stores would be very interested in carrying Mudville cards.

- *L. F., Assistant Manager, Card America, Plaza Pasadena*   L. F. believes that sports greeting cards would definitely sell well at her store. She indicated that she always has people asking her if the store carried greeting cards featuring professional athletes. The store carries predominantly Carlton Cards, which offers only two sports-related cards and offers none that feature professional athletes. The store also carries five brands of alternative greeting cards but none featuring sports. L. F. believes that there is a good chance their corporate offices would want to carry Mudville Cards in their stores.

- *R. R., Manager, All Star Sports (sports trading cards)*   R. R. thinks that Mudville cards have great potential if done right. He said that if the cards are designed and printed in very high quality, people may want to buy the cards to collect. His store would be interested in carrying Mudville cards which feature sports celebrities if the cards are produced in collectible quality.

End Users

David Yang spoke to eight of his friends about Mudville cards; all of them indicated they know someone who would appreciate receiving Mudville cards. Below are responses of a few of those people:

- *M. V., Housewife, age 26*   M. V. said that if Mudville cards were available her husband would want her to buy one for their son because he wants their son to grow up to be a baseball player. M. V. also said that her husband would appreciate receiving a card featuring the Raiders to add to his collection of Raiders shirts, jacket, hat, slippers, and drinking glasses.

- *J. V., Acoustical Ceiling Contractor, age 26*   J. V. said that if sports greeting cards were available there would be no question he would always choose it over other cards for his son. He would also buy it for many of his friends during Christmas. For his father, who is an avid golfer, he would buy one featuring golf.

- *D. H., Exercise Equipment Sales Representative, age 24*   D. H. suggested that he would send out Mudville cards featuring physical fitness themes for both personal and business purposes. D. H. said he would also buy a Mudville card for his wife, who regularly lifts weights and takes aerobics classes.

Comparison with Competition

Mudville produces a large variety of sports cards for giving to sports fans and athletes of all ages and genders, while other companies produce only a few cards featuring sports, mostly for young boys.

Mudville differs in choice of distribution outlets with other card companies. Mudville cards will be carried by sporting goods stores, sports apparel stores, sports novelty stores, and sports trading card stores, in addition to traditional locations such as greeting card specialty stores, grocery stores, department stores, and drug stores.

Trade Shows

The 1992 trade shows planned for Mudville cards to be shown are the Greater Los Angeles All Sports Show at the Los Angeles Convention Center from July 13 to 16, the Stationery and Gift Show at the San Diego Convention and Performing Arts Center on August 28, and the Annual Labor Day Sports Card Show at the Anaheim Convention Center on September 7.

The trade shows are opportunities for selling Mudville products to retailers and for meeting manufacturer's representatives willing to help sell Mudville products. Only having to display one rack of greeting cards, Mudville's trade show booths will be relatively small in size and fees and other costs should be minimal.

FINANCIAL PLAN

Assumptions

The projected sales figures in the financial statements are based on the assumption that Mudville will achieve a level of success similar to that of L'Image Graphics, a greeting cards company that started up in 1984. L'Image was built by the efforts of two inexperienced entrepreneurs, Wayne Wilson and Taylor Barnes.

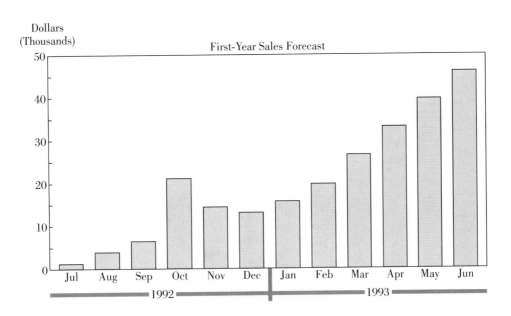

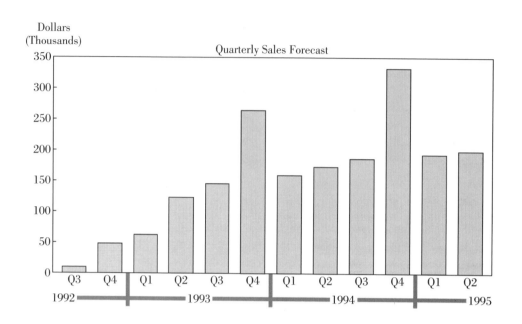

Dollars (Thousands)

Quarterly Sales Forecast

MUDVILLE
FIRST YEAR SALES & CASH FLOW PROJECTION

Description	Premise	Start-up	1992 July	August	September	October	November	December	1993 January	February	March	April	May	June	Totals
Units Sold															Units Sold
Standard		0	1,000	3,000	5,000	16,000	11,000	10,000	12,000	15,000	20,000	25,000	30,000	35,000	183,000
Celebrity		0	500	1,500	2,500	8,000	5,500	5,000	6,000	7,500	10,000	12,500	15,000	17,500	91,500
CASH IN															
Standard $0.85/card		0	850	2,550	4,250	13,600	9,350	8,500	10,200	12,750	17,000	21,250	25,500	29,750	155,550
Celebrity $0.95/card		0	475	1,425	2,375	7,600	5,225	4,750	5,700	7,125	9,500	11,875	14,250	16,625	86,925
Investment		80,000	0	0	0	0	0	0	0	0	0	0	0	0	80,000
Total Cash In		80,000	1,325	3,975	6,625	21,200	14,575	13,250	15,900	19,875	26,500	33,125	39,750	46,375	322,475
Cumulative		80,000	81,325	85,300	91,925	113,125	127,700	140,950	156,850	176,725	203,225	236,350	276,100	322,475	
CASH OUT															Cash Out
COG Standard $0.16/card+envelope			160	480	800	2,560	1,760	1,600	1,920	2,400	3,200	4,000	4,800	5,600	29,280
COG Celebrity $0.16/card+envelope			80	240	400	1,280	880	800	960	1,200	1,600	2,000	2,400	2,800	14,640
Picture Fees avg. $500		15,000	3,000	3,000	3,000	2,000	2,000	2,000	2,000	2,000	2,000	1,500	1,500	1,500	40,500
Royalties $0.10/celebrity card			48	143	238	760	523	475	570	713	950	1,188	1,425	1,663	8,693
Rep Commissions 20%		0	133	398	663	2,120	1,458	1,325	1,590	1,988	2,650	3,313	3,975	4,638	24,248
Delivery $0.03/card		0	40	119	199	636	437	398	477	596	795	994	1,193	1,391	7,274
Supplies & Equip		10,000	2,500	500	500	500	500	500	10,000	1,000	600	600	600	700	28,500
Catalogs & Ads Fixed		2,000	300	2,500	1,000	3,000	2,000	1,000	3,000	500	500	500	500	500	17,300
Travel		2,000	3,500	3,500	3,000	2,000	1,500	1,000	500	500	500	500	500	500	19,500
Rent 1993:$3000		0	0	0	0	0	0	0	6,000	3,000	3,000	3,000	3,000	3,000	21,000
Phone & Utilities		2,000	500	500	500	800	800	700	600	500	500	500	500	500	8,900
Wages & Tax $8/hr		0	0	0	0	1,200	1,200	1,200	1,600	1,600	2,000	2,000	2,200	2,200	15,200
Miscellaneous		2,500	1,000	1,000	1,000	1,000	1,000	1,200	1,200	1,200	1,200	1,200	1,200	1,200	15,900
Dividends		0	0	0	3,000	0	0	3,000	0	0	3,000	0	0	3,000	12,000
Debt Service		0	0	0	0	0	0	0	0	0	0	0	20,000	20,000	40,000
Total Cash Out		33,500	11,260	12,379	14,299	17,856	14,057	15,198	30,417	17,196	22,495	21,294	43,793	49,191	302,934
Cumulative		33,500	44,760	57,139	71,438	89,294	103,351	118,549	148,966	166,162	188,657	209,951	253,743	302,934	
NET CASH		46,500	36,565	28,161	20,487	23,831	24,349	22,402	7,885	10,563	14,568	26,400	22,357	19,541	19,541

MUDVILLE
SECOND YEAR SALES & CASH FLOW PROJECTION

Description	Premise	1st year	July	August	September	October	November	December	January	February	March	April	May	June	Totals
			1993---------------->						1994---------------->						
Units Sold															Units Sold
Standard		183,000	36,000	37,000	37,000	110,000	50,000	40,000	38,000	40,000	42,000	44,000	46,000	49,000	752,000
Celebrity		91,500	18,000	18,500	18,500	55,000	25,000	20,000	19,000	20,000	21,000	22,000	23,000	24,500	376,000
CASH IN															Cash In
Standard $0.85/card		155,550	30,600	31,450	31,450	93,500	42,500	34,000	32,300	34,000	35,700	37,400	39,100	41,650	639,200
Celebrity $0.95/card		86,925	17,100	17,575	17,575	52,250	23,750	19,000	18,050	19,000	19,950	20,900	21,850	23,275	357,200
Investment		80,000	0	0	0	0	0	0	0	0	0	0	0	0	80,000
Total Cash In		322,475	47,700	49,025	49,025	145,750	66,250	53,000	50,350	53,000	55,650	58,300	60,950	64,925	1,076,400
Cumulative		322,475	370,175	419,200	468,225	613,975	680,225	733,225	783,575	836,575	892,225	950,525	1,011,475	1,076,400	
CASH OUT															Cash Out
COG Standard $0.16/card		29,280	5,760	5,920	5,920	17,600	8,000	6,400	6,080	6,400	6,720	7,040	7,360	7,840	120,320
COG Celebrity $0.16/card		14,640	2,880	2,960	2,960	8,800	4,000	3,200	3,040	3,200	3,360	3,520	3,680	3,920	60,160
Picture Fees avg. $500		40,500	1,500	1,500	1,500	1,500	1,500	1,500	2,000	2,000	2,000	2,000	2,000	2,000	61,500
Royalties $0.10		8,693	1,710	1,758	1,758	5,225	2,375	1,900	1,805	1,900	1,995	2,090	2,185	2,328	35,720
Rep Commissions 20%		24,248	4,770	4,903	4,903	14,575	6,625	5,300	5,035	5,300	5,565	5,830	6,095	6,493	99,640
Delivery $0.03/card		7,274	1,431	1,471	1,471	4,373	1,988	1,590	1,511	1,590	1,670	1,749	1,829	1,948	29,892
Supplies & Equip		28,500	2,500	500	500	500	500	500	10,000	1,000	600	600	600	700	47,000
Catalogs & Ads Fixed		17,300	1,000	1,000	2,000	3,000	4,000	3,000	3,000	3,000	2,000	2,000	3,000	3,000	47,300
Travel		19,500	700	700	700	800	800	900	800	800	900	800	800	900	29,100
Rent 1993:$3000		21,000	3,000	3,000	3,000	3,000	3,000	3,000	3,000	3,000	3,000	3,000	3,000	3,000	57,000
Phone & Utilities		8,900	500	600	600	800	600	500	600	600	600	600	600	600	16,100
Wages & Tax		15,200	4,000	4,000	4,000	8,000	7,000	5,000	6,000	7,000	7,000	7,000	7,000	6,000	87,200
Miscellaneous		15,900	1,500	1,500	2,000	4,000	2,000	2,000	2,000	2,500	2,500	2,500	2,500	3,000	43,900
Dividends		12,000	3,000	3,000	3,000	5,000	5,000	60,000	20,000	20,000	20,000	20,000	20,000	20,000	211,000
Debt Service		40,000	0	0	40,000	0	0	0	0	0	0	0	0	0	80,000
Total Cash Out		302,934	34,251	32,811	74,311	77,173	47,388	94,790	64,871	58,290	57,910	58,729	60,649	61,728	1,025,832
Cumulative		302,934	337,185	369,996	444,307	521,479	568,867	663,657	728,527	786,817	844,727	903,456	964,104	1,025,832	
NET CASH			19,541	32,990	49,204	23,918	92,496	111,358	69,568	55,048	49,758	47,498	47,069	47,371	50,568

MUDVILLE
THIRD YEAR SALES & CASH FLOW PROJECTION

Description	Premise	2nd year	July	August	September	October	November	December	January	February	March	April	May	June	Totals
			1994--------------->						1995--------------->						
Units Sold															Units Sold
Standard		752,000	46,000	46,000	48,000	130,000	70,000	50,000	48,000	48,000	49,000	49,000	50,000	50,000	1,436,000
Celebrity		376,000	23,000	23,000	24,000	65,000	35,000	25,000	24,000	24,000	24,500	24,500	25,000	25,000	718,000
CASH IN															Cash In
Standard $0.85/card		639,200	39,100	39,100	40,800	110,500	59,500	42,500	40,800	40,800	41,650	41,650	42,500	42,500	1,220,600
Celebrity $0.95/card		357,200	21,850	21,850	22,800	61,750	33,250	23,750	22,800	22,800	23,275	23,275	23,750	23,750	682,100
Investment		80,000	0	0	0	0	0	0	0	0	0	0	0	0	80,000
Total Cash In		1,076,400	60,950	60,950	63,600	172,250	92,750	66,250	63,600	63,600	64,925	64,925	66,250	66,250	1,982,700
Cumulative		1,076,400	1,137,350	1,198,300	1,261,900	1,434,150	1,526,900	1,593,150	1,656,750	1,720,350	1,785,275	1,850,200	1,916,450	1,982,700	
CASH OUT															Cash Out
COG Standard $0.16/card		120,320	7,360	7,360	7,680	20,800	11,200	8,000	7,680	7,680	7,840	7,840	8,000	8,000	109,440
COG Celebrity $0.16/card		60,160	3,680	3,680	3,840	10,400	5,600	4,000	3,840	3,840	3,920	3,920	4,000	4,000	54,720
Picture Fees avg. $500		61,500	2,000	2,000	2,000	2,000	2,000	2,000	2,000	3,000	3,000	2,000	3,000	3,000	28,000
Royalties $0.10		35,720	2,185	2,185	2,280	6,175	3,325	2,375	2,280	2,280	2,328	2,328	2,375	2,375	32,490
Rep Commissions 20%		99,640	6,095	6,095	6,360	17,225	9,275	6,625	6,360	6,360	6,493	6,493	6,625	6,625	90,630
Delivery $0.03/card		29,892	1,829	1,829	1,908	5,168	2,783	1,988	1,908	1,908	1,948	1,948	1,988	1,988	27,189
Supplies & Equip.		47,000	1,000	500	500	500	500	1,000	700	700	600	600	700	700	8,000
Catalogs & Ads Fixed		47,300	6,000	4,000	4,000	10,000	6,000	6,000	6,000	6,000	6,000	6,000	6,000	6,000	72,000
Travel		29,100	800	700	1,000	1,200	1,000	600	1,000	900	900	900	1,000	900	10,900
Rent 1995:$4000		57,000	3,000	3,000	3,000	4,000	4,000	4,000	4,000	4,000	4,000	4,000	4,000	4,000	45,000
Phone & Utilities		16,100	600	600	600	800	600	600	600	600	600	600	600	600	7,400
Wages & Tax		87,200	6,000	6,000	8,000	8,000	8,000	6,000	6,000	6,000	7,000	6,000	6,000	7,000	80,000
Miscellaneous		43,900	3,000	3,000	4,000	6,000	4,000	4,000	4,000	4,000	5,000	5,000	5,000	5,000	52,000
Dividends		211,000	20,000	20,000	20,000	20,000	20,000	40,000	20,000	20,000	20,000	20,000	20,000	20,000	471,000
Debt Service		80,000	0	0	0	0	0	0	0	0	0	0	0	0	80,000
Total Cash Out		1,025,832	63,549	60,949	65,168	112,268	78,283	87,188	66,368	68,268	68,628	67,628	69,288	70,188	1,903,601
Cumulative		1,025,832	1,089,381	1,150,329	1,215,497	1,327,765	1,406,047	1,493,235	1,559,603	1,627,871	1,696,498	1,764,126	1,833,414	1,903,601	
NET CASH		50,568	47,970	47,971	46,403	106,386	120,853	99,916	97,148	92,480	88,777	86,074	83,037	79,099	79,099

MUDVILLE
Income Statements
For The Year ending ...

	1992	1993	1994
Sales	$60,950	$596,525	$848,000
Less Variable Expenses			
Cost of Goods Sold	11,040	108,080	153,600
Royalties	2,185	21,233	30,400
Commission	6,010	59,653	84,800
Delivery	2,185	17,896	25,440
Total Variable Expenses	21,420	206,861	294,240
Contribution Margin	39,530	389,664	553,760
Less Fixed Expenses			
Pictures	30,000	21,000	24,000
Supplies and Equipment	15,000	17,900	36,000
Advertising	11,800	19,500	52,000
Travel	16,500	7,600	10,300
Rent	0	39,000	39,000
Utilities	5,800	6,900	7,400
Wages	3,600	43,600	82,000
Miscellaneous	8,700	20,200	39,000
Total Fixed Expenses	91,400	175,700	289,700
Net Income	($51,870)	$213,964	$264,050

MUDVILLE
Balance Sheet
For the Year Ending...

		1992	1993	1994
Assets				
	Cash	22,500	70,000	85,000
	Accts Receivable	0	0	0
	Equipment	15,000	30,000	50,000
	Inventory	1,000	12,000	16,000
	Other	44,440	60,000	70,000
Less				
	Depreciation	3,000	6,000	10,000
Total Assets		79,940	166,000	211,000
Liabilities				
	Accts Payable	0	0	0
	Long Term Debt	80,000	0	0
Capital				
	Retained Earnings	0	166,000	211,000
Total Liabilities and Capital		80,000	166,000	211,000

It will be assumed that all of Mudville's customers will adhere to industry standards and pay their entire bill at the time of ordering. It will also be assumed that Mudville will have no debts, paying for all its expenses up front.

OPERATING AND CONTROL SYSTEM

Administrative Policies, Procedures, and Controls

Mudville will use a computer program to handle inventory and to fill customer orders. Most orders will likely be received by mail. For large orders, customers are encouraged to phone in to assure availability. Customers may place an order over the phone but the order will not be delivered until payments are received. After a customer places an order, the order will be entered into Mudville's computer, which will indicate whether or not the cards are available. The computer will print out shipping instructions to be handed to the president along with the payment. The president will sign the instruction slip to indicate that the order has been paid and okay to deliver. The shipping instructions will then be handed to the shipping department.

At the end of each working day, the computer will print a list of available inventory along with a list of unfilled orders. The lists will be evaluated by the president, who is responsible for restocking inventory.

Almost all of Mudville's payments will be drawn by the president. Mudville will open two bank accounts, a main account and a petty cash account. On the bank records, all three Mudville executives will be authorized signers of the main account, but the company policy will allow only the president to perform transactions unless special instructions were passed out by the president. The petty cash account will be available for all of Mudville executives to pay for small immediate expenses.

Budgets of each executive will not be formally monitored. Executives will have access to unlimited phone usage, supplies, car allowances, and other operating necessities. There is enough trust among the executives to feel confident that spending privileges will not be abused.

Employee theft is not expected to be a concern, and virtually no precautions will be taken besides the hiring of seemingly trustworthy individuals. Because cards only cost approximately 15 cents each, it would not be worth the effort to place tight controls. It is unlikely that someone would have use for large quantities of greeting cards, and with less than two employees, tracing theft would be easy. Requests for reasonable amounts of cards will be granted to employees at no charge.

SCHEDULE

Mudville's management team will begin their preoperations activities in April 1992. The first thing they will do is convert their home into an office. After that the management team will begin searching for photographers and artists to provide pictures for Mudville cards. At the same time, sport celebrities and their agents will be contacted to negotiate contracts for use of the celebrities' pictures. When the first picture is acquired, David Yang will begin designing cards. By June, at least six card designs should be printed and ready to be shown to prospective customers. Jenny and Sophia Yang will show the available cards, but continue their search for more pictures. The first Mudville catalog, featuring 16 to 20 cards, will be printed just before the sports trade show in the middle of July. An updated catalog, featuring at least 36 cards will be printed before the gift show at the end of August. Mudville cards should be available in stores by September.

WHO IS RESPONSIBLE

Preparing Facilities	David Yang
Finding Pictures	Sophia Yang
Negotiating Rights to Pictures	David Yang
Designing and Printing Cards	David Yang
Generating Sales	Jenny Yang
Delivering Orders	Sophia Yang
Arranging Trade Shows	Jenny Yang
Hiring and Training Employees	Sophia Yang

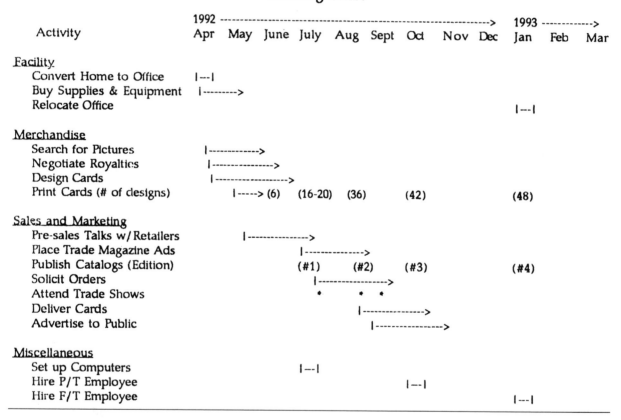

Mudville
Planning Chart

Activity	1992 -->								1993 ------------>		
	Apr	May	June	July	Aug	Sept	Oct	Nov Dec	Jan	Feb	Mar
Facility											
Convert Home to Office	|--|										
Buy Supplies & Equipment	|------->										
Relocate Office									|--|		
Merchandise											
Search for Pictures		|---------->									
Negotiate Royalties		|------------>									
Design Cards		|----------------->									
Print Cards (# of designs)		|----> (6)	(16-20)	(36)		(42)			(48)		
Sales and Marketing											
Pre-sales Talks w/ Retailers		|------------->									
Place Trade Magazine Ads			|------------->								
Publish Catalogs (Edition)			(#1)		(#2)	(#3)			(#4)		
Solicit Orders			|---------------->								
Attend Trade Shows				•	• •						
Deliver Cards						|-------------->					
Advertise to Public						|---------------->					
Miscellaneous											
Set up Computers			|--|								
Hire P/T Employee							|--|				
Hire F/T Employee									|--|		

GROWTH PLAN

New Offerings to Market

Mudville will on a continuous basis introduce new greeting cards while retiring stagnant cards. While concentrating on sales in Southern California, Mudville will attempt to expand its sales throughout the entire country with manufacturers' representatives. It is possible that Mudville will open new offices in other major "sports cities." The decision would depend on the degree of initial success Mudville cards encounter in the market.

If Mudville greeting cards are a major success, Mudville may introduce other sports theme gift items, such as calendars, gift wrap, mugs, figurines, and apparel. Wanting to first establish stability, Mudville will not begin planning for new products at least until 1995. One limitation of the new products is that sports miscellany stores may be reluctant to carry them due to lack of space or to inconsistencies with their current product lines. The new Mudville products may have a better chance of penetration at greeting card stores, department stores, and drug stores.

Opening additional offices or adopting the new products is expected to be costly, as new facilities, vehicles, computers, and personnel would be needed. Opening an office in another city would require investments of approximately $200,000.

Capital Requirements

New offices or new products offerings would likely be financed by Mudville's earnings. If that amount is insufficient, the remaining funds would be financed through loans from financial institutions. There is also the option to obtain additional funds from Charles Yang.

Personnel Requirements

Mudville anticipates hiring one additional management personnel during the second year of operations to support the projected growth. The title of the new hiree has not yet been determined; however, like existing management personnel, the individual will be involved in almost all aspects of the business. One purpose of hiring an additional management personnel is to make it possible for other management personnel to take vacations.

If Mudville decides to open new offices, three or four management personnel would be needed at each new office. The structure would be similar to those at the Southern California office.

Exit Strategy

Presently, the owner of Mudville, David Yang, has no desires to exit from the business until his retirement age. However, if a better business opportunity arises, the company will be sold for cash.

CONTINGENCY PLAN

If not enough retailers are willing to carry Mudville cards, Mudville will offer the cards on a consignment basis until they prove to be in demand. Stores that carry Mudville cards on consignment will have to pay a higher price than stores that prepay. Instead of 85 cents and 95 cents per card, those stores would be required to pay $1.15 and $1.25 per card.

If retail sales are not nearly as high as projected, extensive customer surveys would be performed to reevaluate the potentials of Mudville's products. The surveys would also serve to determine if more advertisements or promotions are needed and, if so, what types. One promotional possibility is passing out free Mudville cards in crowded shopping centers.

If after the first year of operations, Mudville's sales are much less than projected and there appears to be no possibilities of substantial improvement, Mudville may liquidate its inventory to bargain retailers such as 99¢ Only stores or swap meet merchants. If there is a demand for Mudville cards at bargain retailers, Mudville may continue to print and distribute its cards, but not stay in operation on a full-scale basis. No new products would be introduced, no office would be maintained, and sales and marketing activity would be limited to approaching local bargain retailers. One part-time personnel would be sufficient to upkeep such a venture, and virtually no overhead expenses would be required.

If competitors enter the sports greeting card market and offer lower prices to retailers or end users, Mudville most likely will not counter by lowering its prices. Mudville will instead compete by offering high-quality products at a reasonable price. However, if competitors are able to produce same or better quality products and offer them at a lower price, Mudville would then match the competitor's prices.

Though highly unlikely, if the cards David Yang designs are not recognized by customers as high quality, an outside designer may be contracted to design Mudville cards. An outside artist may also be contracted when David Yang's time constraints make it difficult for Mudville to stay on its production schedule. An outside designer would be paid on a piecework basis.

If either Jenny or Sophia Yang do not display enough competency to carry out their duties, they would be reassigned to less challenging duties. New management personnel would then be hired to burden the surrendered duties.

If Charles Yang, the father of David, Jenny, and Sophia refuses to fund the venture, Mudville will have to seek other investors. Because David Yang desires total control of the company, Mudville would be set up as a limited partnership. To be more attractive to investors, Mudville's exit strategy would include plans to sell the company not more than five years into the future. If not enough investors can be found, David Yang would take his business plan to an existing card company that would be willing to hire him to head the project.

THE DEAL

Money Needed

An investment of $80,000 is needed by Mudville at the start-up stage to pay for equipment, supplies, pictures, travel expenses, utilities, and inventory. No additional funding will be needed after that.

Source of Money

Because David Yang wants to maintain full control of Mudville, the venture will be financed exclusively through debt. David Yang will attempt to get an $80,000 unsecured interest-free loan from his father, Charles Yang. In return for the loan, David will make a verbal promise to provide employment for his sisters, Jenny and Sophia, as well as share profits with them (30 percent each). Furthermore, David will promise to provide a luxurious living for his parents, Charles and Becky, after they retire, if they are unable to provide one by themselves.

Payback

The loan will be paid back to Charles Yang after Mudville is able to maintain a positive yield. Charles will receive sporadic payments from what is left of the profit after David, Jenny, and

Sophia take what they need to pay their living expenses. The entire loan is projected to be paid back during the second year of operation.

BIBLIOGRAPHY

Levine, Joshua. "Love Means Never Having to Say Anything," *Forbes,* April 1, 1991.

Maloney, Lawrence. "Sports-Crazy Americans," *U.S. News and World Report,* August 13, 1984.

Weiner, Steve. "Do They Speak Spanish in Kansas City?" *Forbes,* January 25, 1988.

Weisman, Adam. "The Business of Staying Fit," *U.S. News and World Report,* August 11, 1986.

6

BUSINESS PLAN FOR ONYX MARKETING GROUP

Developed by
Anthony Coleman

Used with the Permission of the Author

JAMAKO AND THE BEANSTALK

Retold and Illustrated by Fred Crump, Jr.

Table of Contents

INTRODUCTION . . . . 6 · 4

BACKGROUND . . . . 6 · 4

EXECUTIVE DIGEST . . . . 6 · 4

COMPANY MISSION, SCOPE,
AND GOALS . . . . 6 · 4

SITUATION ANALYSIS . . . . 6 · 5

Market Characteristics . . . . 6 · 5
Key Success Factors . . . . 6 · 6
Competition . . . . 6 · 6
Market Potential . . . . 6 · 9
Environmental Factors . . . . 6 · 9
Internal Resources . . . . 6 · 9
Problems and Opportunities . . . . . 6 · 9

MARKET OBJECTIVES . . . . 6 · 10

Target Market . . . . 6 · 10
Target Volume . . . . 6 · 10

PROFIT ANALYSIS . . . . 6 · 10

MARKETING STRATEGY . . . . . . 6 · 11

The Product . . . . 6 · 11
The Price . . . . 6 · 11
The Promotion . . . . 6 · 12
The Place . . . . 6 · 12

TASKS . . . . 6 · 15

CONTROL AND CONTINUITY . . . 6 · 15

CONCLUSION . . . . 6 · 17

REFERENCES . . . . 6 · 17

INTRODUCTION

The purpose of this business plan is two-fold: (1) to show potential partners (investors) how Onyx Marketing Group will operate, why it will be successful, and how the profit structure is determined, and (2) to act as a guiding, measuring, and evaluating vehicle in the implementation of all aspects of Onyx Marketing Group.

BACKGROUND

Onyx Marketing Group (OMG) is a dynamic, new marketing company designed to offer new ways to purchase reading materials in the African American community. These reading materials will consist exclusively of children's books at the outset with concentration in other areas in the immediate future. As African Americans continue to search out ways of broadening their black history base, more reading materials are needed from the Afrocentric perspective. Over 60 percent of black teenagers have read books concerning their unique culture and history in the past year. The dress and hairstyles of many African Americans have reflected a sense of "blackness" more than any other time in history (Jacobs, 1991, p. 33). Black mothers and fathers are also in the search for teaching their children from a black perspective. Less than 18 percent of black parents read the traditional Mother Goose bedtime stories to their children, choosing rather to tell "stories" of great black men and women in history (Smith, 1991, p. 67). There is always the endless search to find dolls, toy soldiers, puppets, etc. with black faces, wrote John Hall of *Heritage Magazine*. Although there may be difficulties in finding toys, black publications are having success. The traditional black press has enjoyed record levels of readership over the last four years. Magazines such as *Ebony, Jet,* and *Black Enterprise* have increased their subscriber base by over 34% during this time (Jones, 1992, pp. 44–45). New magazines such as *Emerge, Talent,* and *Ebony Man* are doing very well since their inception in the last two years. The African American population craves products targeted and easily accessible to them. These

factors present a significant business opportunity for literature from the black perspective.

The ideas for OMG are new. It will provide easily accessible literature on a continuous basis. Some bookstores will offer some of the products; however no one will make them as easy to purchase.

EXECUTIVE DIGEST

Onyx Marketing Group has conducted market research and analysis and has identified a need for the marketing of reading materials of an Afrocentric perspective. In response to this need, Onyx Marketing Group will initially market a set of children's books specifically directed to the black community. This set of children's books contains thirteen well known stories. The price of the books is $11.95 per copy, and they will be distributed via mail order. Advertising will be conducted through the black press with primary promotional emphasis based on coupons.

The financial analysis shows that the project requires a small amount of start-up capital and has a high rate of return on investment with extremely low overhead costs.

The company is owned by Anthony and Andrea Coleman. Anthony is pursuing a Masters of Business Administration degree and has much applicable professional experience. Andrea will develop and implement all administrative procedures after having done this as a consultant for the Metro Rail Project in Los Angeles, California.

The company is fortunate to have Fred Crump, Jr., the creator and illustrator of the children's books, and Dennis DeLoach, owner of Delco Publishing Company, as advisory board members. Their expertise in the field of book sales to the African American community is appreciated by everyone in the industry.

COMPANY MISSION, SCOPE, AND GOALS

Onyx Marketing Group (OMG) is in the literature marketing business. Initially, OMG will strive to market books through the black medium locally. In the first nine months of operation, OMG seeks to sell 7,505 children's books in the Los Angeles market. Although Los Angeles has been chosen as the initial target area, OMG will expand after the introduction stage of the product life cycle. At the end of this period, OMG will determine the feasibility of expanding into selected other markets. If the evaluation proves positive, expansion into the San Francisco/Oakland and Seattle markets will be formulated by the end of the first year of business. California and the West coast have been chosen because of size, convenience, and market familiarity. If this expansion proves successful, OMG will then market literature in every urban metropolis in the United States in a 3-year period of time through the black press.

In addition to possibly expanding the children's book division, other areas of self-help literature will be investigated by OMG to determine the validity of entering such markets.

The company philosophy is to operate with a minimum amount of required capital and overhead as well as with a maximum of quality products and service.

SITUATION ANALYSIS

This section reviews the factors in the present and future business environment. It includes examination of market characteristics, key success factors, competition, market potential, environmental factors, internal resources, problems, and opportunities. Much of the research was gathered by questionnaires with a sample size of 214 respondents.

Market Characteristics

Because the product that we are proposing is literature, it may be available but not readily accessible to our market. Thus, the characteristics of our market are not as clear as we would like. The information we came across in our research effort, however, has presented us with some very useful data.

Geographic segmentation is nationwide. It includes major cities in the United States. The targeted markets include major metropolitan areas and capital cities. Areas of concentration initially to be focused on include the greater Los Angeles area, including Inglewood, Lenox, Compton, Lynwood, Culver City, Hawthorne, Lemiert Park, Baldwin Hills, Windsor Hills, Ladera Heights, and Watts. This geographic area comprises over 1.2 million blacks.

Demographically, market segmentation includes mothers with small children, grandparents, uncles and aunts, friends of families, churches, community groups, and nursery schools. The majority of this market will be adults that come in contact with small children on a frequent basis. The average customer will be conscious of the literature read to a child and will be responsive to books with black illustrations. The age of the consumer is not really significant when specifying this market, although the ages 21 to 31 and 50 to 60 gave an overwhelming response when OMG conducted their research. These age groups consist of the early civil rights participants and the new pro-black regimen that is now politicking in the black community. Generally, older consumers would have no interest in a product such as this, but their relationship with a child, whether friend or family, can make them a viable customer. The age of the end user or the child plays an important role. There are currently over 190,000 black school-age children from the grades of kindergarten through sixth grade (James, 1990, pp. 5–7). This number is significant to the potential number of consumers in the target market.

Psychologically, the consumers have a preoccupation with teaching the virtues of the black race and a pursuit of excellent black literature. They care about the image and reputation portrayed to an African American child. These consumers read positive literature concerning their race. They read such publications as *Essence, Ebony, Black Enterprise, Image,* and *Ebony Man.* They are concerned about the community in which they live. They are kept abreast of what is going on in their community by reading newspapers such as the *Los Angeles Sentinel, Watts Times, Communique, The Florence News, The Scoop,* and *The Black Chronicle.* They are concerned about the neighborhood in which they reside. They are affiliated in many healthy community organizations such as the NAACP, neighborhood block clubs, neighborhood crime watch, graffiti cleanup crews, and other prominent civic groups. However, other consumers of the target market may not read these newspapers and publications or be involved in these types of civic groups. Onyx Marketing Group's products help these consumers and end users feel more important, and will boost self-images.

Income is an important determinant of purchasing power and thus would be of concern to OMG as well. Literature purchases are more prominent in higher-income households. In 1982, 46% of all black households earning incomes of $26,500 or more annually purchased a book within the preceding 30-day period. In the same year, 16% of all black households earning incomes of less than $13,750 annually purchased a book within the preceding 30-day period (Perkins, 1984, p. 43).

Equally important is the fact that 44% of all black families are single-parent households with almost 92% of these households run by women (Perkins, 1984, pp. 44–45).

Black households in which the head has had some college education or more dominated total expenditures on literature. The 47% where this was the case was responsible for 88% of the literature purchases (Perkins, 1984, p. 47).

Finally, households headed by someone in a professional or managerial position were the primary contributors to total expenditures on literature. These two occupational groups made up 51% of the black magazines sold, 43% of the black newspapers sold, and 69% of all African American literature sold (Perkins, 1984, p. 49).

Examination of purchase patterns to determine where purchases of literature were made, by type of store, found that the majority of purchases were made at liquor stores, followed by newsstands, large chain bookstores, black bookstores, and others (Perkins, 1984, p. 51). The following chart breaks down the specific place of purchase by publication type:

	Newspapers (%)	Magazines (%)	Books (%)
Newsstands	8.1	12.5	1.2
Major bookstore	1.3	17.8	66.4
Liquor store	88.8	61.3	5.3
Black bookstore	2.2	9.9	23.6
Other	0.5	1.8	4.2
Don't know	1.6	0.4	0.8

The African American market is concerned about what is taught their children, more now than any time in the past. These consumers are seeking help in specific or general areas that they may have defined or that they have not yet identified.

Key Success Factors

Onyx Marketing Group has defined certain criteria to be very important to the success of its business. In a recent consumer survey conducted by *Black Enterprise* magazine in 1990, the three primary reasons African Americans purchase black reading literature is for identification with other blacks, support for the black authors or writers, and to understand the current events from the black perspective. Therefore, if the consumer values these factors in reading black literature, the key success factors for OMG are creations and illustrations that identify with the target market, stories solely authored and written by African Americans, and words and phrases from the Afrocentric perspective.

Competition

Two kinds of competition to Onyx Marketing Group's product line exist to some degree: direct enterprise competition and product competition.

Direct enterprise competition is the most concrete of the two. Direct enterprise competition is established before the company has made its entrance into the market. Many large bookstore chains, such as Waldenbooks, Crown, and B. Dalton are located throughout the African American community. In each one of these stores, there are sections for children and black books. Although the sections are small, they have the visibility and the name to be a viable competitor. There are also other bookstores throughout the community that have the ability to compete. These stores are children's bookstores such as Children's Book & Music Center, Children's Book World, Happily Ever After-Children's Book Store, and Prince and the Pauper Book Store. Finally, there are the ethnic or black bookstores, such as Aquarian, Dawah Book Shop, and Third World Ethnic Books.

Questionnaire

Name of Respondent _____

Address _____ Date _____

Location of Interview _____

This questionnaire is part of a marketing study to determine whether or not to introduce our new product to the general public. A few minutes of your time will be of great benefit to us.

These books retell Mother Goose Stories, using black illustrations. The benefits of this product are

_____

_____

1. What is your immediate reaction to this idea?

   Positive   *Negative*

   Great   _____   So-so   _____

   Like it very much _____   I can do without it   _____

   I like it somewhat _____   I do not like it at all _____

   Why do you say this? Explain _____

   _____

2. Which of the following best expresses your feeling about buying this product if it were available to you?

   Positive   *Negative*

   I'm absolutely sure I would buy _____   I probably would not buy it _____

   I'm almost sure I would buy   _____   I'm almost sure not to buy _____

   I probably would buy it   _____   Absolutely I would not buy _____

   Why do you say this? Explain _____

   _____

   IF YOUR LAST ANSWER WAS IN THE POSITIVE COLUMN PLEASE CONTINUE

3. Please tell me, all things considered, what is there about this product that appeals to you most? What do you consider its most important advantages?

   Appeal to most   *Advantages*

   1. _____   1. _____

   2. _____   2. _____

   3. _____   3. _____

4. Would you buy this product for?

   Your child   _____   Nephew/Niece _____

   Grandchild _____   Other   _____

5. How much do you think such a product would cost? _____

6. Would you purchase this product through the mail? _____

Questionnaire (*Continued*)

7. Do you shop at black bookstores? _____

8. Do you read the following newspapers? How often?

    The Wave _____ Weekly? _____ Monthly? _____ Other _____

    The Los Angeles Sentinel _____ Weekly? _____ Monthly? _____ Other _____

    Scoop _____ Weekly? _____ Monthly? _____ Other _____

    The Communique _____ Weekly? _____ Monthly? _____ Other _____

    I do not read these newspapers _____

Classification Data

Check One in Each Category

Age		*Number of Children*	
18–21 _____		1 _____	
21–30 _____		2 _____	
31–49 _____		3 _____	
50–60 _____		4+ _____	
over 60 _____		none _____	

Income		*Sex/Marital Status*	
0–$15,000 _____		Female - Single ____ Married ____	
$16,000–$30,000 _____		Male - Single ____ Married ____	
$31,000–$49,000 _____			
$50,000 - Above _____			

Occupation		*Formal Education* (Check Highest)	
Blue Collar/Trade _____		High School _____	
Office Worker _____		High School Graduate _____	
Manager _____		Tech School Graduate _____	
Professional (Lawyer Doctor, Professor) _____		AA (two years) of College _____	
Student _____		College Graduate _____	
Housewife _____		Master Degree _____	
Entrepreneur (Small business owner) _____		Doctorate _____	

Thank You

Each one of these stores has the ability to compete in a direct manner for the same market OMG has targeted, but none of them offer and are specifically geared to the selling of books via mail order.

Product competition varies from the other types of competition. Product competition refers to other types of children's books designed specifically with the black child in mind. There is no cause for alarm with this competition because there is no series of books directed at this market. One cannot discount this type of competition, but the primary concern is to identify the alternatives, know they exist (when they do), and then create a need in the consumer to be inclined to purchase from a reputable African American company rather than a myopic business that focuses only on the bottom line. Product competition includes personal needs, preferences, and decision. OMG provides quality service, expertise in black literature, and fair market price versus similar products.

Onyx Marketing Group looks forward to distinguishing itself from any competition with a quality product or extraordinary service.

Market Potential

The market potential for products offered by OMG is extremely positive. As mentioned earlier in the background section, African Americans are becoming more attuned to their heritage and more inclined to purchase clothes, literature, and so on that show it. Marketers are putting forth more effort than ever before to capitalize on the vast resources in the black community. This is seen every day in the advertising medium. Although resources are more scarce in this market, research has shown that dollars are more apt to stay in the community than any time before. Organizations such as Recycling Black Dollars estimate that the purchasing power of the black community in the black community has reached an all-time high. This leaves a great amount of potential for those organizations willing to do business with this market in the future. OMG looks forward to realizing this potential.

Environmental Factors

Environmental factors will have no significance in the business of Onyx Marketing Group in the immediate future. All of our children's books are published by Winston-Derek Publishers of Nashville, Tennessee, which uses recycled paper for all of its publications. OMG foresees no repercussions from environmental concerns in the future.

Internal Resources

Onyx Marketing Group draws on the marketing expertise of Anthony Coleman and the administrative expertise of Andrea Coleman. Anthony has a Bachelor's degree in business marketing and is a Masters of Business Administration candidate. He has formal academic training in mail order marketing, marketing research, and consumer behavior. In addition, Andrea possesses two Bachelor degrees in the health field along with a vast amount of experience in administrative work for the Los Angeles Metro Rail Project.

OMG will also be assisted by an advisory board consisting of Fred Crump, Jr., and Dennis DeLoach. Mr. Crump has over 20 years of experience in creating and illustrating books targeted toward the African American market. Mr. DeLoach, owner of Delco Publishing, has a vast amount of experience serving the black community.

Problems and Opportunities

1. *Market Characteristics*

Problem	The actual product demand is unknown.
Opportunity	The geographic areas targeted (urban metropolitan) are densely populated by African Americans.
Problem	Resources are limited in this market.
Opportunity	The target market is searching for any and all materials that portray a black perspective.

2. *Competition*

Problem	The ideas of the literature may be duplicated.

Opportunity   Being a leader in the market with the quality product via mail order maximizes the chances of doing well. The consumer market is currently ignored by the competition.

3. *Market Potential*

Problem   Potential is virtually unknown because no one is currently marketing these types of products through this type of channel.

Opportunity   Marketing strategy is ripe for exploitation.

4. *Internal Resources*

Problem   Owners will be embarking on their first venture into entrepreneurism.

Opportunity   Introduction and start-up costs are minimal. Advisory board will assist in all aspects of the business to ensure a smooth operation.

MARKET OBJECTIVES

Onyx Marketing Group's goal is to initially obtain a medium niche for quality African American children's books. The initial communication vehicle selected is the black press. This will include both large and small newspapers. The marketing campaign will begin June 1992 in weekly, biweekly, and monthly newspapers. Objectives in the first nine months are to sell 7,505 books at an average cost of $11.95. This would yield $89,684 in revenues in the nine-month period.

Following the first nine months of operations, OMG plans to expand its market and penetrate other geographic areas beyond Los Angeles, in and out of the state of California. (See the tables at the end of this business plan.)

Target Market

The target market, as previously stated in the section entitled Market Characteristics, is mothers with small children, grandparents, uncles and aunts, friends of families, churches, community groups, and nursery schools. In addition, the ideal consumer would read the black press and could be either male or female. The basic "want-satisfying power" or utility (OMG provides) is to make black literature (initially for children) available in an easily accessible manner.

Target Volume

Once again, on the basis of the information presented in the Market Characteristics, we project the sales volume at 7,505 in the first nine months. This is based on the projection of the total number of black school-age children from kindergarten to sixth grade in the Los Angeles target market and an estimated percentage that we believe can be reached times the average number of the different stories wanted for purchase. The total number of school-age children in the Los Angeles area is 190,000. This total is large enough to create a vast amount of revenue. If the response rate from the advertising campaign can produce 1% of the total market, OMG will have 1,900 potential end users of the product.

Target volume in dollars is based upon projections forecasted from the response rate of the advertising campaign (or 1,900 end users). Revenue of $89,684 is based on 1,900 end users times a 3.95 average of books sold to each user times the average price of $11.95 for each book. This does not imply that 1,900 end users will each purchase 3.95 books; rather the number of consumers will range from 1 to 1,900 and the overall average expenditure will be $47.20. These estimates may be conservative because the average number of books purchased per end user may be higher.

The break-even analysis is included in the Profit Analysis section immediately following.

PROFIT ANALYSIS

OMG's profitability for the first three years of operations is revealed next. This analysis will include breakeven analysis at start-up and cash flow analysis. A three-year income statement is also included. Cost analysis can be slanted pending additional information on tactics, involvement, and resources. Please note that estimates become more reliable the closer they are to implementation.

MARKETING STRATEGY

This is a detailed specification of the marketing program proposed for Onyx Marketing Group. It is divided into four main parts: the product, the price, the promotion, and the place. The basic strategy for marketing OMG's products in the industry is to concentrate on quality, professional image, consumer satisfaction, and personal improvement.

The Product

Onyx Marketing Group has a full line of children's fairy tales. The product is of high quality and is well illustrated. The product package is very unique from other children's books, in that all illustrations are very vivid with an array of colors. All human-like characters are of African American decent with exaggerated facial and bodily features. Each two-page spread is arranged with one side that has the fairy tale enclosed on a colorfully decorated scroll. The other side embraces a whole sheet illustrated magnificently from top to bottom with that part of the story being told on the other side. This is done throughout each one of the 14 books, which makes this product most enticing for the target market selected by OMG.

As mentioned earlier, the product is a mix of children's fairy tales. Some of the names have been altered to identify with the target market, but all of the names of the stories are recognizable. The 14 books in the initial product line of OMG are the following (the first column is the standard name with the OMG story name in the second column):

Standard	OMG
Sambo and the Tigers	Mgambo and the Tigers
Beauty and the Beast	Beauty and the Beast
Hansel and Gretchel	Hakim and Grenita
Thumbelina	Thumbelina
Mother Goose	Mother Goose
Cinderella	Cinderella
A Rose for Zemira	A Rose for Zemira
Little Red Riding Hood	Little Red Riding Hood
Sleeping Beauty	Sleeping Beauty
Jack and the Beanstalk	Jamako and the Beanstalk
Goldilocks and the 3 Bears	Afrotina and the 3 Bears
Rapunzel	Rapunzel
Rumpelstiltskin	Rumpelstiltskin
The Ugly Duckling	The Ebony Duckling

Each book is approximately 8.5 inches wide by 10 inches long. There is an average of 25 pages for each story. These dimensions make the product easy to package and to ship with little outlay in cost.

The attractiveness of the books will undoubtedly make the demand very high for this product.

The Price

The quality and image of the product will allow OMG to realize profit maximization. OMG has estimated the demand and costs associated with other prices and chose the price that produces maximum current profit and cash flow. OMG is emphasizing current financial performance rather than long-run performance and is ignoring the effects of competitor's reactions and legal restraints on price.

OMG favors the high price or market-skimming strategy because the comparative benefits of the product versus any available substitutes is very extreme. This strategy makes sense because OMG believes a sufficient number of buyers have a high current demand, the total costs of selling a small volume are not so much higher that they cancel the advantage of charging what the traffic will bear, the high price does not attract more competitors, and the high price supports the image of a superior product.

We believe the target market will be less price sensitive to our product because of the following reasons: (1) The product is very unique; (2) there is very little product substitution; (3) it is not easily comparable to the quality of substitutes; (4) the product has more quality, prestige, and exclusiveness.

Because of the perceived insensitivity to price, OMG believes the strategy selected will benefit the firm in the short term by outweighing costs and in the long term when introduction of new products yield less operating revenue. Therefore, the $11.95 per book will yield a substantial margin in relation to the fixed and variable costs.

The Promotion

The advertising time frame for OMG will begin in June 1992. These advertisements will run in black newspapers all over the black community in Los Angeles, CA. These advertisements mark the introduction of Onyx Marketing Group to the market. Ads will run continuously throughout the month. For those newspapers that run weekly, bi-weekly, and even monthly, OMG will run an advertisement. The advertisement will contain a headline announcing the introduction of the product along with a brief column of copy down the right side of the page. A beautiful picture of one of the books will be set in the middle of the ad with the address and telephone number of OMG listed for the order. A number system will be used for the different stories to make the ordering procedure systematic. Thus, any customer can choose to order more than one book or any number of copies of any book. This system will make ordering effortless and uncomplicated for potential customers.

All advertisements will require the same amount of space in each newspaper. One-fourth of a page has been chosen as the size. The ad will be located in the social or entertainment section of all papers, preferably on the third page. This strategy will allow the customer to see the advertisement immediately after opening the section.

OMG will also implement a follow-up campaign. This campaign will immediately follow the shipment of the initial purchase. All names and addresses will be installed into the customer database. Two weeks following the shipment, a letter will be sent to each customer inquiring his or her satisfaction with the product. Included in this letter will be a list of the available books for future purchase along with an order form. OMG has not decided if the development of a dollars-off coupon is necessary for the repeat purchase. This will be taken into account in the immediate future.

Other promotions may also be used. A direct mail campaign announcing the introduction with dollars off will also be considered in the future. This campaign will consist of a mailer to many of the neighborhoods in the black community. This campaign along with door knobbers can run into considerable costs. If the response rate is not what is initially forecasted these promotions will be considered for further penetration.

If successful, all promotions will be run exactly the same in other geographic markets. Costs of these campaigns cannot be accurately calculated because the future costs of advertising rates are not currently available. Research indicates that most urban black newspapers operate with a similar advertising costs structure.

The Place

The channel of distribution is very important in any business. The Onyx Marketing Group will use a three-level distribution:

Winston-Derek Publisher   OMG   Consumer

Winston-Derek Publishers is located in Nashville, TN. It is owned by Dr. James Peoples, a personal friend of the officers of OMG. He is responsible for the extremely low product cost and has assured OMG of prompt movement of the product through the first phase of the distribution channel. The process of the product moving through the distribution channel is as follows:

1. Orders will be received by OMG through the P.O. box daily.
2. Orders will be assorted with the number of each product tallied.
3. Total numbers of each product will be faxed to Nashville at 12 noon the Firday of each week.
4. A check will be sent to Nashville the following Tuesday after assurance that the order has been received and to insure delivery of the ordered product.
5. Product will be packed and shipped to Los Angeles via UPS 8–10 days after the receipt of the order in Nashville.

By Popular Demand.....The Hottest Children's Books in many decades !!!!!!

Only $11.95 each

These dynamic books take a revolutionary approach to retelling children's stories, using Black illustrations of the characters. The color drawings are especially vivid and extract chuckles from children and adults alike.

Created and illustrated by Fred Crump Jr. (Winner of several major award for his work), it is:

The Perfect Gift for a Child at
BIRTHDAY   BEGINNING
HOLIDAY   PRESCHOOL
KINDERGARTEN
OR JUST TO SAY I LOVE
YOU

SEND ORDERS TO:

Onxy Marketing Group
P.O. Box 3472
Los Angeles, CA 90043
(213) 296-1076

Price: $11.95

Pick one or all of the following stories:

1 THE EBONY DUCKLING
2 RAPUMZEL
3 CINDERELLA
4 SLEEPING BEAUTY
5 LITTLE RED RIDING HOOD
6 MOTHER GOOSE
7 THUMBELINA
8 HAKIM AND GRENITA
9 JAMAKI AND THE BEANSTALK
10 AFROTINA AN THE THREE BEARS
11 MGAMBO AND THE TIGERS
12 RUMPELSTILTSKIN
13 BEAUTY AND THE BEAST

ORDER FORM
Indicate the story by the number:

Please send ____ copy(s) of number(s)____
remittance of $_____ is enclosed.
(CA residents add 8.25% sales tax.)

Name_____

Address_____

City/State/Zip_____

Visa/MC #_____Exp. Date_____

By Popular Demand.....The Hottest Children's Books in many decades !!!!!!
Only $11.95 each

SEND ORDERS TO:

Onxy Marketing Group
P.O. Box 3472
Los Angeles, CA 90043
(213) 296-1076

Price: $11.95

ORDER FORM
Indicate the story by the number:

Please send ____ copy(s) of number(s)___
remittance of $_____ is enclosed.
(CA residents add 8.25% sales tax.)

Name_____
Address_____
City/State/Zip_____

Visa/MC #_____Exp. Date_____

These dynamic books take a revolutionary approach to retelling children's stories, using Black illustrations of the characters. The color drawings are especially vivid and extract chuckles from children and adults alike.

Created and illustrated by Fred Crump Jr. (Winner of several major award for his work), it is:

The Perfect Gift for a Child at
BIRTHDAY BEGINNING
HOLIDAY PRESCHOOL
KINDERGARTEN
OR JUST TO SAY I LOVE
YOU

Pick one or all of the following stories:

1 THE EBONY DUCKLING
2 RAPUMZEL
3 CINDERELLA
4 SLEEPING BEAUTY
5 LITTLE RED RIDING HOOD
6 MOTHER GOOSE
7 THUMBELINA
8 HAKIM AND GRENITA
9 JAMAKI AND THE BEANSTALK
10 AFROTINA AN THE THREE BEARS
11 MGAMBO AND THE TIGERS
12 RUMPELSTILTSKIN
13 BEAUTY AND THE BEAST

6. Order will be shipped to the customer 5–7 days after received from Nashville.

This distribution channel procedure set forth by OMG is compatible with any mail-order business. The efficiency of this process will make the product available to the consumer in a very short period of time.

TASKS

OMG will have a post office box as its mailing address. All correspondence will be sent through the mail, fax, or telephone. Therefore, there is no rental cost for business offices at this time.

OMG is a full-service firm that will be responsible for the following:

1. Receiving, recording, and following up on orders daily.
2. Packaging and shipping all products.
3. Installing all names and addresses into the customer base.
4. Supplemental cost of running OMG.
5. Any and all legal aspects.

All phases of the business will be shared by the owners. The expertise of each owner will maximize operations for better productivity. It will be the responsibility of each owner to delegate work and define needs that the other owner can fulfill.

CONTROL AND CONTINUITY

Formal records of actual results as compared with forecasted results will be compiled monthly for evaluation purposes. This will allow Onyx Marketing Group to react to small fluctuations and unexpected occurrences in the market.

Biannually, near the end of December and June, this business plan will be reviewed in its entirety. Using primary and secondary data, appropriate changes will be made. By February 28th of each year, a written supplement will be submitted identifying necessary amendments in the original business plan.

Controlling and reviewing the continuity of this plan will investigate company progress and the feasibility of expansion of more products. Medium- and long-range goals and objectives will be determined and evaluated.

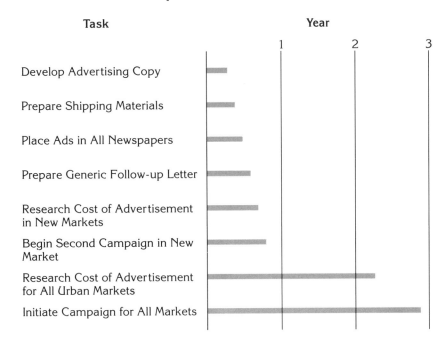

Implementation Schedule

Retold and Illustrated by
Fred Crump, Jr.

CONCLUSION

Onyx Marketing Group strongly believes that with an initial investment of $2,000 to roughly cover fixed costs, and careful and persistent administration of its marketing plan, it will become a successful, growing concern.

REFERENCES

Hall, M. (1992, January). Toys for your child. *Heritage Magazine,* p. 16.

Jacobs, A. (1991, December). African Americans in the 90's. *Black Enterprise,* p. 33.

James, M. (1990, September). Are the schools teaching our children? *Ebony,* pp 5–7.

Jones, H. (1992, January). The black press in America. *Black Enterprise,* pp. 44–45.

Perkins, L. (1984, January). Do black people read? *Jet Magazine,* pp. 42–53.

Smith, P. (1991, August). Bring up a child in the way he should go. *Emerge,* pp. 67–69.

Variable and Fixed Cost Start-Up and Introduction

Variable Cost/Unit		Fixed Cost	
Description	Cost/Unit	Description	Total Cost
Packaging	$0.43	Advertising	$ 850.00
Mastercard/Visa	0.02	Registration	60.00
Shipping	1.52	P.O. Box	34.00
Follow up	0.32	Resale number	150.00
Miscellaneous	0.10	Credit card setup	200.00
Product cost/unit	3.95	DBA (Adv)	65.00
Total variable cost	$6.34	Total fixed cost	$1,359.00

Breakeven Analysis Start-Up and Introduction

Fixed Cost $1,359.00	Variable Cost/Unit $6.34		Selling Price/Unit $11.95	
Units Sold	242	900	3,600	7,505
Total sales	$2,891.90	$10,755.00	$43,020.00	$89,684.75
Variable cost	1,534.28	5,706.00	22,824.00	47,581.70
Total cost	2,893.28	7,065.00	24,183.00	48,940.70
Profit (loss)	$ (1.38)	$ 3,690.00	$18,837.00	$40,744.05

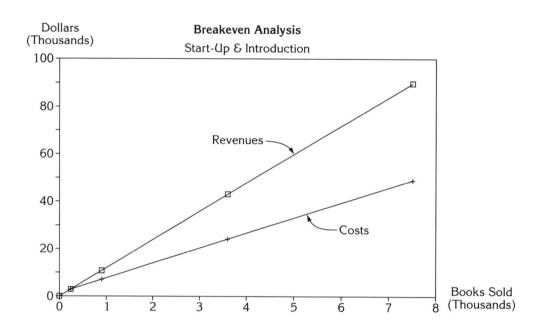

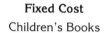

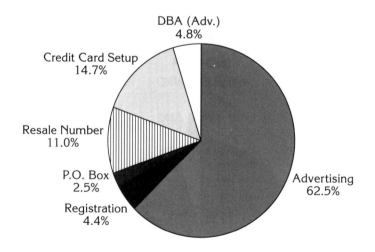

Financial Analysis Projected Years 1, 2, and 3 Income Statements
(Projected in 1992 Dollars)

	Year		
	1	2	3
Total net sales	$113,525	$256,925	$352,525
Cost of goods sold	37,525	84,925	116,525
Gross profit	$076,000	$172,000	$236,000
Expenses			
Advertising	10,200	23,400	36,000
Business registration	60	50	50
Post office box	408	408	408
Packaging	4,085	9,245	12,685
MC/Visa percentage	190	430	590
Shipping	14,440	32,680	44,840
Follow-up	3,040	6,880	9,440
Miscellaneous	950	2,150	2,950
Credit card setup	200	0	0
Total expenses	$ 33,573	$ 75,243	$106,963
Net profit (loss) before tax	$ 42,472	$ 96,757	$129,037

Profitability Statement Cash Flow Analysis Three-Year Period

	June 1992	2	3	4	5	6
Sales (qu)	840	800	860	700	830	800
Price	$ 11.95	$11.95	$ 11.95	$11.95	$ 11.95	$11.95
Sales (vl)	10,038	9,560	10,277	8,365	9,918.5	9,560
Cost	3.95	3.95	3.95	3.95	3.95	3.95
Product (cst)	3,318	3,160	3,397	2,765	3,278.5	3,160
Variable expenses						
pkg	0.43	0.43	0.43	0.43	0.43	0.43
mc/visa	0.02	0.02	0.02	0.02	0.02	0.02
shipping	1.52	1.52	1.52	1.52	1.52	1.52
fol-up	0.32	0.32	0.32	0.32	0.32	0.32
misc	0.1	0.1	0.1	0.1	0.1	0.1
Expenses	2.39	2.39	2.39	2.39	2.39	2.39
Total Variable Expenses	$2,007.6	$1,912	$2,055.4	$1,673	$1,983.7	$1,912
Fixed Expenses						
adv	850	850	850	850	850	850
regis	60	0	0	0	0	0
p.o. box	34	34	34	34	34	34
resale #	150	0	0	0	0	0
cc-setup	200	0	0	0	0	0
dba-adv	65	0	0	0	0	0'
Total Fixed Expenses	$ 1,359	$ 884	$ 884	$ 884	$ 884	$ 884
Total Expenses	$3,366.6	$2,796	$2,939.4	$2,557	$2,867.7	$2,796
Net Profit	$3,353.4	$3,604	$3,940.6	$3,043	$3,772.3	$3,604

	7	8	9	10	11	12
Sales (qu)	900	900	870	670	700	630
Price	$ 11.95	$ 11.95	$ 11.95	$ 11.95	$11.95	$ 11.95
Sales (vl)	10,755	10,755	10,396.5	8,006.5	8,365	7,528.5
Cost	3.95	3.95	3.95	3.95	3.95	3.95
Product (cst)	3,555	3,555	3,436.5	2,646.5	2,765	2,488.5
Variable expenses						
pkg	0.43	0.43	0.43	0.43	0.43	0.43
mc/visa	0.02	0.02	0.02	0.02	0.02	0.02
shipping	1.52	1.52	1.52	1.52	1.52	1.52
fol-up	0.32	0.32	0.32	0.32	0.32	0.32
misc	0.1	0.1	0.1	0.1	0.1	0.1
Expenses	2.39	2.39	2.39	2.39	2.39	
Total Variable Expenses	$ 2,151	$ 2,151	$ 2,079.3	$1,601.3	$1,673	$1,505.7
Fixed Expenses						
adv	850	850	850	850	850	850
regis	0	0	0	0	0	0
p.o. box	34	34	34	34	34	34
resale #	0	0	0	0	0	0
cc-setup	0	0	0	0	0	0
dba-adv	0	0	0	0	0	0
Total Fixed Expenses	$ 884	$ 884	$ 884	$ 884	$ 884	$ 884
Total Expenses	$ 3,035	$ 3,035	$ 2,963.3	$2,485.3	$2,557	$2,389.7
Net Profit	$ 4,165	$ 4,165	$ 3,996.7	$2,874.7	$3,043	$2,650.3

Profitability Statement Cash Flow Analysis Three-Year Period (*Continued*)

	13	14	15	16	17	18
Sales (qu)	1,900	1,975	1,925	1,850	1,755	1,965
Price	$ 11.95	$ 11.95	$ 11.95	$ 11.95	$ 11.95	$ 11.95
Sales (vl)	22,705	23,601.25	23,003.75	22,107.5	20,972.25	23,481.75
Cost	3.95	3.95	3.95	3.95	3.95	3.95
Product (cst)	7,505	7,801.25	7,603.75	7,307.5	6,932.25	7,761.75
Variable expenses						
pkg	0.43	0.43	0.43	0.43	0.43	0.43
mc/visa	0.02	0.02	0.02	0.02	0.02	0.02
shipping	1.52	1.52	1.52	1.52	1.52	1.52
fol-up	0.32	0.32	0.32	0.32	0.32	0.32
misc	0.1	0.1	0.1	0.1	0.1	0.1
Expenses	2.39	2.39	2.39	2.39	2.39	2.39
Total Variable Expenses	$ 4,541	$ 4,720.25	$ 4,600.75	$ 4,421.5	$ 4,194.45	$ 4,696.35
Fixed Expenses						
adv	1950	1950	1950	1950	1950	1950
regis	50	0	0	0	0	0
p.o. box	34	34	34	34	34	34
resale #	0	0	0	0	0	0
cc-setup	0	0	0	0	0	0
dba-adv	0	0	0	0	0	0
Total Fixed Expenses	$ 2,034	$ 1,984	$ 1,984	$ 1,984	$ 1,984	$ 1,984
Total Expenses	$ 6,575	$ 6,704.25	$ 6,584.75	$ 6,405.5	$ 6,178.45	$ 6,680.35
Net Profit	$ 8,625	$ 9,095.75	$ 8,815.25	$ 8,394.5	$ 7,861.55	$ 9,039.65

	19	20	21	22	23	24
Sales (qu)	1,800	1,995	1,570	1,675	1,535	1,555
Price	$ 11.95	$ 11.95	$ 11.95	$ 11.95	$ 11.95	$ 11.95
Sales (vl)	21,510	23,840.25	18,761.5	20,016.25	18,343.25	18,582.25
Cost	3.95	3.95	3.95	3.95	3.95	3.95
Product (cst)	7,110	7,880.25	6,201.5	6,616.25	6,063.25	6,142.25
Variable expenses						
pkg	0.43	0.43	0.43	0.43	0.43	0.43
mc/visa	0.02	0.02	0.02	0.02	0.02	0.02
shipping	1.52	1.52	1.52	1.52	1.52	1.52
fol-up	0.32	0.32	0.32	0.32	0.32	0.32
misc	0.1	0.1	0.1	0.1	0.1	0.1
Expenses	2.39	2.39	2.39	2.39	2.39	2.39
Total Variable Expenses	$ 4,302	$ 4,768.05	$ 3,752.3	$ 4,003.25	$ 3,668.65	$ 3,716.45
Fixed Expenses						
adv	1950	1950	1950	1950	1950	1950
regis	0	0	0	0	0	0
p.o. box	34	34	34	34	34	34
resale #	0	0	0	0	0	0
cc-setup	0	0	0	0	0	0
dba-adv	0	0	0	0	0	0
Total Fixed Expenses	$ 1,984	$ 1,984	$ 1,984	$ 1,984	$ 1,984	$ 1,984
Total Expenses	$ 6,286	$ 6,752.05	$ 5,736.3	$ 5,987.25	$ 5,652.65	$ 5,700.45
Net Profit	$ 8,114	$ 9,207.95	$ 6,823.7	$ 7,412.75	$ 6,627.35	$ 6,739.55

Profitability Statement Cash Flow Analysis Three-Year Period (*Continued*)

	25	26	27	28	29	30
Sales (qu)	2,890	2,750	2,785	2,800	2,735	2,400
Price	$ 11.95	$ 11.95	$ 11.95	$ 11.95	$ 11.95	$ 11.95
Sales (vl)	34,535.5	32,862.5	33,280.75	33,460	32,683.25	28,680
Cost	3.95	3.95	3.95	3.95	3.95	3.95
Product (cst)	11,415.5	10,862.5	11,000.75	11,060	10,803.25	9,480
Variable expenses						
pkg	0.43	0.43	0.43	0.43	0.43	0.43
mc/visa	0.02	0.02	0.02	0.02	0.02	0.02
shipping	1.52	1.52	1.52	1.52	1.52	1.52
fol-up	0.32	0.32	0.32	0.32	0.32	0.32
misc	0.1	0.1	0.1	0.1	0.1	0.1
Expenses	2.39	2.39	2.39	2.39	2.39	2.39
Total Variable Expenses	$ 6,907.1	$ 6,572.5	$ 6,656.15	$ 6,692	$ 6,536.65	$ 5,736
Fixed Expenses						
adv	3000	3,000	3,000	3,000	3000	3,000
regis	50	0	0	0	0	0
p.o. box	34	34	34	34	34	34
resale #	0	0	0	0	0	0
cc-setup	0	0	0	0	0	0
dba-adv	0	0	0	0	0	0
Total Fixed Expenses	$ 3,084	$ 3,034	$ 3,034	$ 3,084	$ 3,034	$ 3,034
Total Expenses	$ 9,991.1	$ 9,606.5	$ 9,690.15	$ 9,726	$ 9,570.65	$ 8,770
Net Profit	$13,128.9	$12,393.5	$12,589.85	$12,674	$12,309.35	$10,430

	31	32	33	34	35	36
Sales (qu)	2,600	2,350	2,215	2,110	1,900	1,965
Price	$ 11.95	$ 11.95	$ 11.95	$ 11.95	$ 11.95	$ 11.95
Sales (vl)	31,070	28,082.5	26,469.25	25,214.5	22,705	23,481.75
Cost	3.95	3.95	3.95	3.95	3.95	3.95
Product (cst)	10,270	9,282.5	8,749.25	8,334.5	7,505	7,761.75
Variable expenses						
pkg	0.43	0.43	0.43	0.43	0.43	0.43
mc/visa	0.02	0.02	0.02	0.02	0.02	0.02
shipping	1.52	1.52	1.52	1.52	1.52	1.52
fol-up	0.32	0.32	0.32	0.32	0.32	0.32
misc	0.1	0.1	0.1	0.1	0.1	0.1
Expenses	2.39	2.39	2.39	2.39	2.39	
Total Variable Expenses	$ 6,214	$ 5,616.5	$ 5,296.85	$ 5,042.9	$ 4,541	$ 4,696.35
Fixed Expenses						
adv	3,000	3,000	3000	3,000	3,000	3,000
regis	0	0	0	0	0	0
p.o. box	34	34	34	34	34	34
resale #	0	0	0	0	0	0
cc-setup	0	0	0	0	0	0
dba-adv	0	0	0	0	0	0
Total Fixed Expenses	$ 3,084	$ 3,034	$ 3,034	$ 3,084	$ 3,034	$ 3,034
Total Expenses	$ 9,248	$ 8,650.5	$ 8,327.85	$ 8,076.9	$ 7,575	$ 7,730.35
Net Profit	$11,552	$10,149.5	$ 9,392.15	$ 8,803.1	$ 7,625	$ 7,989.65

7

BUSINESS PLAN FOR MISCHA'S SILVERLAKE COOKIES

Developed by
JulieAnn Peterson

Used with the Permission of the Author

Summary

Mischa's Silverlake Cookies will begin business operations and will market cookie gift baskets. The product has several benefits. It is convenient, carries premium quality prestige, and is a niche of an industry experiencing rapid growth. The cookie baskets will be advertised as a specialty service item. The business plan has two phases, in the first phase, the local Silverlake area will serve as the initial testing location. The product will be advertised via display ads in local publications. The second phase enlarges the geographical and target market.

Mr. H., the proposed proprietor, has previous experience in advertising and graphic arts. He will be able to use his artistic talents in the specialty packaging, arrangements, and personalized gift cards. Breakeven sales are estimated at 50 units a month, with forecasted sales of 70 units. Implementation of the entire plan will take five months, after which evaluation of problems and successes is recommended.

Table of Contents

LIST OF TABLES . . . . **7 · 4**

LIST OF FIGURES . . . . **7 · 5**

I.   INTRODUCTION . . . . **7 · 6**

II. SITUATIONAL ANALYSIS . . . . **7 · 6**

    Situational Environment . . . . 7 · 6
    Neutral Environment . . . . 7 · 6
    Competitive Environment . . . . 7 · 8
    Company Environment . . . . 7 · 11

III. TARGET MARKET . . . . **7 · 12**

    Marketing Objectives and Goals . . . . 7 · 13

IV. PROBLEMS AND OPPORTUNITIES . . . . **7 · 14**

    Problems . . . . 7 · 15

V.   MARKETING STRATEGY . . . . **7 · 15**

    Product . . . . 7 · 16
    Price . . . . 7 · 16
    Promotion and Place . . . . 7 · 17

VI. CONTROL AND IMPLEMENTATION . . . . **7 · 19**

    Control . . . . 7 · 19
    Implementation . . . . 7 · 21

ENDNOTES . . . . **7 · 23**

REFERENCES . . . . **7 · 24**

List of Tables

1. SIC Code 2052 Sales . . . . 7 · 8
2. Per Capita Cookie Consumption . . . . 7 · 9
3. Leading Brand Sales . . . . 7 · 9
4. Strengths and Weaknesses Analysis . . . . 7 · 11
5. Direct Response Criteria . . . . 7 · 17
6. Population and Income . . . . 7 · 18

List of Figures

1. Growth Rate of Cookie Sales Vs. GDP . . . . 7 · 7
2. Per Capita Cookie Consumption . . . . 7 · 9
3. Q = nqp . . . . 7 · 12
4. Breakeven Analysis . . . . 7 · 14
5. Silverlake Area . . . . 7 · 18
6. Income Statement . . . . 7 · 20
7. Balance Statement . . . . 7 · 22
8. Implementation Schedule . . . . 7 · 23

I. INTRODUCTION

Mr. H., of Silverlake Los Angeles, is interested in an entrepreneurial adventure into the realm of cookies. He is a talented baker, with recipes borrowed from his mother, and personal creations which people continually demand. Mr. H. is exploring the possibilities of introducing his cookies, cakes, and bread to an audience larger than his local friends and relatives. He would like to begin by producing and selling cookie gift baskets. He is looking for directions and details of marketing alternatives available to him before he commits to this enterprise. He is also interested in the tax benefits the company can offer him. He chose *Mischa's Silverlake Cookies* as a company name, perfected the recipes, engaged in a modest amount of neighborly trade, and began research. He needs a business plan for his potential company. Mr. H. is primarily an artist and a teacher; he teaches computer graphics at a variety of forums, including many of the local universities. He will be able to use his experience and skills in both promotional and packaging efforts. This plan evaluates the possibilities open to Mr. H., particularly with his baskets of cookies, the problems he may likely encounter, and a strategy for success.

II. SITUATIONAL ANALYSIS

Analysis of *Mischa's Silverlake Cookies'* potential consists of four environmental aspects. We first examine the situational or the general business environment, next the neutral environment of organizations, such as the regulatory agencies in California, then the competitive environment of the snack industry, and finally, the future company environment.

Situational Environment

New product ventures face a myriad of national and regional problems: consumer uncertainty about President Clinton's economic plan, a general growth slump in the California economy, a foreign trade deficit in excess of $100 billion a year,[1] and federal and state budget deficits. However, despite economic concerns, people continue to eat, and they continue to snack.

As depicted in Figure 1, the annual growth rate of the cookie industry usually more than triples the growth rate of Gross Domestic Products (GDP). The cookie market average growth during the period 1989 to 1992 was 10.68 percent; the GDP average growth rate during the same period was 2.79 percent.[2] In a quarterly analysis, it is also evident that the cookie markets are not subject to the cyclical turns of the overall GDP.[3]

The cookie market is performing better than the economy and is doing so with negligible help from imports or foreign producers, as imports represent only 1.5 percent of all domestic cookie consumption. Imports of bakery products including cookies, in 1992 rose 6.9 percent to $376.1 million, exports were $209.2 million. Cookie exports represented eight percent of aggregate product shipment value. The total value of all products in the bakery industry is estimated at $24.3 billion, cookies account for $9.672 million or around 40 percent.[4]

Neutral Environment

The maze of regulations and permits required to market a product and run a business in Southern California make the neutral environment appear hostile, not neutral, to new products. This aspect of the marketing plan summarizes federal and state regulations, and pertinent local codes.

**Figure 1   Growth Rate of Cookie Sales versus
Gross Domestic Product**

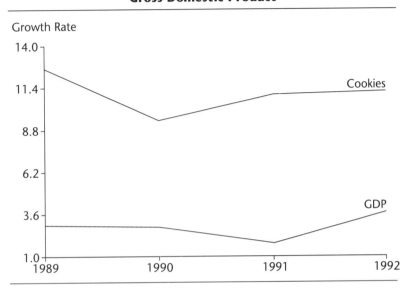

Federal Laws

Although there are no explicit laws on ownership or licenses, various federal laws may apply to a cookie company.

> The Food and Drug Act of 1906 prohibits the sale or transport of adulterated or fraudulently labeled food and drugs in interstate commerce.
>
> The Fair Packaging and Labelling Act of 1966 provides the regulation of the packaging and labeling of consumer goods. It requires manufacturer to state what the package contains, who made it, and how much it contains.[5]

The Internal Revenue Service treats an individual and a sole proprietorship as one. This may be beneficial in tax returns if the operation loses money at first because the individual may deduct losses against income earned in other enterprises. In Mr. H.'s case, this would lessen the tax burden from his teaching salary. However, a sole proprietor assumes all liability from the business, should anything occur to inspire lawsuits.

State Laws

A retail business license is required in California and is easily obtained for the cost of $119. However, to operate as *Mischa's Silverlake Cookies,* a fictitious business name statement must be filed with the Los Angeles County Clerk, and intent must be published once a week for four consecutive weeks after filing the statement. Prior to publication, one should research the fictitious business name with the county clerk to verify the name is not already in use. Proof of publication must be provided to the county clerk 30 days after publication. The filing fee is $10, and the least expensive publication fee was located at the *Daily News* at $130. The *Los Angeles Times* was willing to complete the requirements for $525. The fictitious business name statement expires in five years.

A commercial kitchen is necessary, as no one is allowed to bake items for commercial sale in home kitchens. The California Department of Health is keenly interested in food quality, and conducts regular inspections of commercial kitchens to ensure quality control standards. It is possible, although rare, to lease commercial kitchens, with a release of liability contract for the owner. Mr. H. is not currently leasing, nor does he own a commercial kitchen; however, he is confident in a potential source, and not interested in further analysis of the topic.

Operating commercial ovens in California requires approval and release from the SCAQMD, the South Coast Air Quality Management District. Local bakeries are required to comply with varying regulations, depending on their size, output, and experience. Rule 1153, available from public information services, explains in detail the requirement for this venture. The engineers at the SCAQMD will readily answer questions and provide purchase recommendations.

With the recent passage of Proposition 163, several changes have been made to California's Sales and Use Tax law. Proposition 163 amends Section 6359 of the Sales and Use Tax law to expand the tax exemptions for food products which were rescinded effective July 1, 1991, by the Assembly Bill 2181 and Senate Bill 179, commonly known as the "Twinkie Tax." Consequently, cookies, crackers, chips, pretzels, cakes and pies, and other snack foods are no longer subject to sales and use tax. This absence of taxation frees a cookie company from obtaining a sellers permit or remitting sales taxes to the State Board of Equalization. This will be true for the gift packages of cookies as long as the packaging costs do not exceed one tenth of the total food costs.

Competitive Environment

The competitive environment of *Mischa's Silverlake Cookies* consists of all the bakers and companies pursuing snack sales dollars. The cookie market is part of the snack and dessert market. It can be defined by the overall market size, annual growth rate, historical profit margin, the industry leaders and specialized niches, and the dynamics of product cycles.

Market Size

One way to classify the cookie market is to use the Standard Industrial Classification (SIC) codes. The SIC codes, developed by the Census Bureau, classify all manufacturing into 20 major industry groups; then each group is divided into subgroups and product categories. Food and Kindred products is code 20, Wholesale Baked Goods is number 205, and Cookies is product category 2052. Table 1 is a list of cookie sales over the last four years, and indexed against 1987 dollar values.

Cookies and exhibited have the highest growth rate in the SIC 205 group, although crackers appeared to be gaining ground in 1992.

In 1992, combined per capita consumption of cookies rose 4 percent, outpacing the 3.8 percent growth rate of crackers consumption. This growth in the cookie market has been across the board, except for the marshmallow cookie products, where consumption is weakening. This weakening follows the trend of healthy cookies, as we see companies targeting many new premium brand cookies often containing honey and fruit juices as alternative sweeteners, aimed at health conscious consumers. Approximately

Table 1   SIC Code 2052 Sales (Billions)

	1989	1990	1991	1992
Value	7.296	7.950	8.793	9.672
1987 dollars	6.350	6.516	6.743	6.934

Source: U.S. Industrial Outlook, January 1992.

Figure 2   Per Capita Cookie Consumption

Sandwich Cookies
3.35 lbs.
Graham Crackers
.32 lbs.
Marshmallow Cookies
.21 lbs.
All Other Cookies
10.49 lbs.

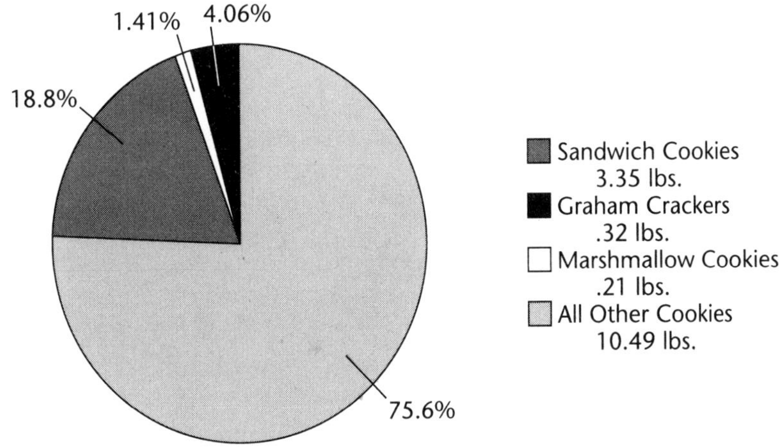

Source: Compiled by the author from Predicasts Forecasts, SIC groups 20520000, 2052123, 2052213, 2052215 and 2052210.

1,000 new products are introduced in the cookie market each year.[6] Fruit and nuts are increasingly popular cookie ingredients, although chocolate remains a favorite. Chocolate chip cookies accounted for $1.5 billion in sales in 1991.[7] As illustrated in Figure 2 and Table 2, Americans ate 14.37 pounds of cookies per capita in 1992.

Industry Leaders

While per capita consumption increases, cookie companies tend to expand and break apart. This is for managerial and financial reasons. There were 374 cookie companies in the United States in 1992. Of the top 50 U.S. cookie companies, 17 are divisions of the three major conglomerates: Nabisco, Keebler, and Sunshine. Sales from these three companies are listed in Table 3. The top 50 companies in this industry account for half of the

Table 2   Per Capita Cookie Consumption
(Pounds per Person)

	1989	1990	1991	1992
All cookies	13.17	13.67	13.92	14.37
Sandwich	3.14	3.18	3.29	3.35
Marshmallow	.26	.24	.23	.21
Wafers	.31	.31	.31.	.32
All others	9.46	9.94	10.09	10.49

Source: Predicasts Forecasts 1992.

Table 3   1991 Leading Brand Sales

Company	Estimated Sales ($ mill.)
Nabisco	7,755
Keebler	1,355
Sunshine	612
Total top 50	12,291

$24.3 billion in sales of the industry and Nabisco controls almost a third of the industry sales. None of the top 50 companies are located in Los Angeles. The industry employs 34 million people, who earn an average wage of $11.45 an hour. Nabisco, as the industry leader, supplies the trends in the industry. As mentioned, various changes are taking place in the cookie industry. These changes involve both cookie content and cookie size.

Healthy Cookies

In 1989, 15 percent of the new cookie introductions displayed health claims on the label, while by 1992, the health claim had risen to 30 percent for new products. In response to health conscious consumers, manufacturers are replacing tropical oils and white flour with soybean oil and whole wheat flour. There is a growing market of consumers who are concerned about their own eating habits, as well as their children's. Nabisco's share of this $3.2 billion category was 36 percent in 1991, and its closest competitor was Keebler, with a 15 percent share.[8] Nabisco has addressed this group by building on their core of products. As a new niche category, healthy cookies and desserts have shown mixed results. Pepperidge Farm's Wholesome Choice hit $14.6 million in its first year out, and in 1991, Health Valley Natural Foods saw its cookie sales jump 173 percent to $23.7 million. Nabisco's line of healthy cookies and crackers called Snack Well, was presented in August of 1992 and appears to be performing to Nabisco standards.[9] However, sales of Frookies fell 30 percent to about $13 million in 1992. Frookies are sold in 63 percent of all supermarkets, and sell at a premium price. Frookies are made from whole grains and fruit juice sweeteners instead of sugar. Richard Worth, an ex-hippie blueberry farmer, built the Frookie company in a few years starting with nothing but a business plan, and contractors to bake, package, and distribute his goods.[10] Like many of these products, Mr. H.'s products contain a variety of whole grains and natural sweeteners that will appeal to this growing consumer group.

Miniature Cookies

Nabisco Food Group's recent string of cookies (Teddy Grahams, Teddy Graham Rockin Bears, Beach Bears, and T.G. Bearwich Graham Sandwiches) capitalize on the phenomena of miniature cookies and crackers. Nabisco also reduced the size of some of their older stodgier, brands and produced Mini Chips Ahoy and Ritz Bits.[11] These products are the first successful innovations by Nabisco since the late 1800s, when they created Fig Newton, Saltine, Animal Crackers, Lorna Doone Shortbread, and the Oreo. The "mini revolution" began in the 1980s when Nabisco produced the easier to handle, fun shaped Teddy Graham for MTV generation's toddlers, who had outgrown graham crackers and wanted racier snacks.

Keith Lively, president of famous Amos Cookies, producers of another miniature cookie, has been successful doing things much differently than Nabisco, because he could not afford to use Nabisco's distribution tactics.[12] Sales of Famous Amos Cookies were around $91 million in 1992 compared to $5 million in 1987. The key for Famous Amos has been specialized packaging and the selection of distribution channels. They first selected club stores, such as Pace and Price Club in California, where their larger competitors weren't entrenched, and where they could avoid the battle for supermarket shelf space, which they couldn't afford to enter. They made their next move with a 2 oz. "vend pack." It wasn't easy to convince vending distributors that a 2 oz. bag of cookies selling for 50–60 cents a pack would sell. However, by promoting the cookie as an upscale, quality product, they succeeded. From this base, and after achieving name recognition in more mass markets, Amos Cookies expanded into more competitive channels.[13]

Company Environment

Mr. H.'s primary assets are a quality product, a visionary idea of potential, and superior artistic abilities which he can use in promotion and packaging. He also has a flexible schedule and the ambition to allow him to use these assets. As exhibited in Table 4, *Mischa's Silverlake Cookies* can be evaluated in terms of its potential strengths and weaknesses in the cookie gift basket environment.

Mr. H.'s analysis of his position is subjective. Another person may list different qualities or strengths, or perceive weaknesses listed here as strengths. Company reputation is considered neutral, as consumer concerns of ordering items through the mail or from advertisements and not receiving satisfaction, is offset by the advantages of not having a negative reputation with anyone. Market share is a major weakness of high importance obviously, when there are no sales, there are no revenues. Manufacturing costs are another weakness, as the packages are essentially handwrapped, stuffed, and delivered, manufacturing costs will be high; however, the premium price charged for the product will cover these costs and be a benefit in customer perception of high quality. Distribution costs are

Table 4   Strengths and Weaknesses Analysis

Mischa's Silverlake Cookies

	Performance			Importance		
	Strength	Neutral	Weakness	High	Medium	Low
Marketing						
Reputation		✓			✓	
Market Share			✓	✓		
Mfg. Costs			✓		✓	
Distribution	✓				✓	
Effectiveness	✓			✓		
Innovation	✓					✓
Coverage	✓				✓	
Finance						
Capital			✓	✓		
Stability			✓		✓	
Manufacturing						
Econ. of Scale		✓			✓	
Capacity			✓			✓
Time			✓		✓	
Organization						
Creative	✓					✓
Flexible	✓			✓		

a major strength, as the many package and postal companies are far less expensive than shelving space, or wholesalers' fees, traditional methods of cookie distribution.

Promotional effectiveness is expected to be high, and a minor strength, as Mr. H. is associated with a variety of advertising professionals who have offered advice and assistance, on promotions. This will be important, as the lack of a solid customer base requires highly effective promotions. Marketing innovation, or the channels used in this plan are a minor strength. This is based on the assumption that they will be effective. Geographical coverage is a major strength of the marketing plan, as the promotional methods to be employed will cover a far larger area group than typically handled by one person. The lack of capital, the high cost of capital, and the instability of company capital are weaknesses, of medium importance; obviously, the company can't operate forever as a losing proposition, but in the short range, personal capital will be sufficient to cover the needs of the operation. The economies of scale from commercial convection ovens are important, as bake times tend to occupy the majority of preparation time. Capacity and delivery times are both major strengths as, initially, the products will be essentially baked to order and only promoted on the scale of available time. The flexible and entrepreneurial orientation of the company are perceived as strengths because it will be so small that it will be able to adapt almost instantly to changes in the market and shift strategies as rapidly as needed.

III. TARGET MARKET

The cookie market is the set of all actual and potential cookie buyers, not just those who eat cookies, although there may be considerable overlap. The potential market is the set of consumers who profess a sufficient level of interest in a defined cookie offer. The available market is the set of consumers who have interest, income, and access to a particular market offer, and the target market is the qualified available market we pursue. To determine market demand, we must determine the total volume that would be purchased by a defined customer group in a defined geographical area in a defined time period, in a defined marketing environment under a defined marketing program. The Los Angeles-Long Beach area ranks number one in the nation in grocery and other food sales.[14] In 1989, regional sales of groceries and other food items was $34,584,948,000. The projected population in this area is 9,564,400. In determining the potential market in this area, we assume that all people would be sufficiently interested in buying *Mischa's Silverlake Cookies* according to the national per capita consumption figures. As depicted in Figure 3, the total market in the Los Angeles-Long Beach Area is a function of

Figure 3

	$Q = nqp$
where:	Q = total potential market
	n = population in the market
	q = quantity consumed
	p = price per unit
	Substituting values:
	n = 9,564,400 people
	q = 14.37 lbs./person
	p = $15/lb.
	Q = $2,061,606,300

the population, the quantity consumed, and the price. This number assumes that no other brands of cookies are purchased, and our selling price is constant regardless of volume. These assumptions are highly suspect, but they allow us to start estimating our market and its size.

Another method to determine demand is a multiple factor index method. One of the best known indices is the "Annual Survey of Buying Power" published by *Sales and Marketing Management*.[15] This index reflects the relative buying power in various regional areas. Effective buying power is classified as all personal income less personal tax and nontax payments, a number often referred to as disposable or after-tax income. The buying power index is a weighted index that converts the survey's three basic elements: population, effective buying income, and retail sales (demographic, economic, and distribution) into a measurement of a market's ability to buy, expressing it as a percentage of the national total. The buying power factor variables—income, population, and the percentage of national retail sales in the area—are believed to be related to the level of demand. Each variable is assigned a coefficient. The coefficient values are arbitrary estimates of the importance of the factor. The Los Angeles-Long Beach area has a projected buying power index for food products of 3.8813, and the Los Angeles, Riverside, Anaheim area is indexed at 6.4120. This tool estimates potential of mass-marketed items sold at popular prices. Thus 3.8813 or $376 million of the nation's cookie sales may be expected to come from this area. In the wider, Los Angeles, Riverside, Anaheim area, sales may be $626 million. These numbers are greatly less than the two billion from the previous estimation method. This is easily explained by the premium price used in the earlier equation. The vast middle market of cookies averages around $4 a pound, not $15. Using this average price does yield the same sales estimate.

It is easy to isolate the market segment of a particular product, but other segments compete against that segment for snack purchase dollars. For example, Oreos are in the sandwich segment of the market, but their competition is all types of cookies, (plain, chocolate chip, mallow, fruit filled, etc.), as well as noncookie snacks.[16]

Because these figures represent the overall cookie market, we must reduce them for our specific product. Our target market is people who buy homemade, premium cookies. They may buy them for any of the following reasons:

- Personal gifts, ease of sending, always appropriate.
- Corporate gifts to recognize service anniversaries or birthdays.
- They do not have the time to assemble packages themselves.
- They wish to give a gift to a health-conscious consumer.

Future markets may also include catering, film industry catering in particular, or other groups that engage large buffets and would want bulk cookies. One local cookie company currently operates solely in this market, and their customers are part of the target market. Corporate Cookie in Los Angeles has been in business seven years, employs 13 people, and has estimated annual sales of $250,000.[17] They advertise on a limited basis, and eschew rapid growth.

Marketing Objectives and Goals

One necessary goal is to increase market share, but to how much? Computation of market share raises three problems: the measure of sales, the exact market are we in, and the brands our product is competing against.[18] In our target market we are competing against all other companies that offer a similar product as well as all substitutes. For example, if someone sends a box of cookies as a thank-you gift, flowers may be an

Figure 4   Breakeven Analysis for Mischa's Silverlake

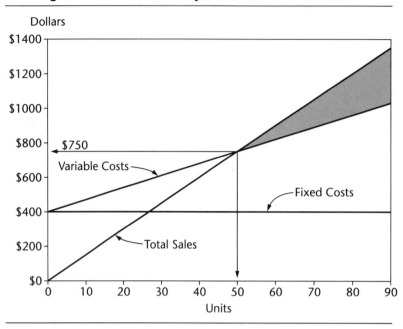

appropriate substitute. In new-product situations, market share goals may be preferred to return on investment targets, as development and introduction can be limited by short-term ROI figures. However, to express our market share goal as .0002 of the Los Angeles cookie market actually holds little meaning. Profitability goals are not completely appropriate either. There is a clear relationship between the size and power of the market, the economies of scale obtained, and the profitability of the firm in a given sector. Gaining market share is a long-term investment that might provide negative results in the short run.[19] Therefore, the initial objectives are to survive in the industry, and gain experience in direct response marketing.

Breakeven analysis is a tool commonly used to avoid or delay the problems of computing market share. Breakeven analysis is a method to determine what level of sales are necessary to cover costs, both fixed and variable. In estimating breakeven sales, various levels of fixed expenses are uncertain. Figure 4 is an estimate of the breakeven level of the gift baskets, with the initial level of local advertising, and fixed costs. As charted, the breakeven level of sales is 50 units in a month. Should sales reach beyond 50 units, the extra units are profit. Any changes to the cost calculations will change the slope of the lines, and then the new breakeven point should be calculated.

IV.   PROBLEMS AND OPPORTUNITIES

More than 70 percent of new products fail.[20] New products are a disaster area for marketeers. A study analyzing new grocery brands found formulas for success.[21] The new brand must be significantly different from existing brands, or have a radically different appearance or performance that would be immediately apparent to consumers before they used the brand. Brands that are merely very different, would have differences that would not be fully apparent until they used the products, and marginally different brands would have small differences in areas of little importance. A significant difference may be in price or performance, or an untried idea. Many brands have failed because the company simply lacked objectivity in evaluating the product. The most important factor in new product marketing is planning; if planning is inaccurate, the plan will not reflect the market or internal reality. As exhibited in this report, Mr. H., because of his careful planning and willingness to seek assistance, has an excellent opportunity to edge out competition that has not planned as well as he. He also faces challenging problems.

Problems

The regulatory environment described in Section II is one of the biggest potential problems. The Department of Health, and the SCAQMD, although established for consumer protection, provide a bureaucratic wasteland of procedures that will consume scarce resources of time and effort. However, these problems are surmountable, and the key offered by an inspector is to include the health department in every step. They feel that many costly errors companies have made in the past resulted from not checking in advance on proper procedures and requirements.

Another obvious problem is the lack of experience in running a business. This will be felt in two ways, first of all, in obtaining capital for start-up costs. Financial institutions prefer to lend to individuals with any kind of track record than to an unknown. It is easier to obtain loans if one has already failed in a business than if one has never tried. This is partly due to the problems of risk assessment. Mr. H. has two alternative solutions to this problem. On one hand, he may use his personal finances with his bank, and borrow against his savings account, and as proof of his commitment, provide the bank with his detailed business plan to assist them in risk assessment. Other possibilities are borrowing against life insurance, or seeking a loan company or a venture capital company: a Small Business Administration, or a Small Business Investment Corporation or Business Development Corporation. For a finder's fee, a financial broker may be able to locate a loan. But the most often recommended method of financing a new business is to borrow it from close friends and relatives.[22] However, Mr. H. should not include them in the business, as these type of financiers are difficult to control and may wish to have a larger role in the business decisions.

The second problem with lack of experience is the possibility of fatal errors. A wrong choice with perfect timing can end the business. The best solution to this problem is to recognize that even with a great deal of experience, companies make poor choices all of the time, and that bad decisions are not necessarily limited to the inexperienced. Advice from professionals (suppliers, vendors, other business people, or interested bystanders) can also help. To his favor, his recent round of gift boxes, distributed during December, provided Mr. H. with a level of expertise in planning, packaging, distribution, financing, and cost control. He also gained experience when he worked with a local yogurt shop coordinating his cookie recipes which were used as side items to yogurt sales.

V. MARKETING STRATEGY

Despite the variety of products planned for *Mischa's Silverlake Cookies,* the marketing strategy in this document is limited to the business plan for the gift boxes. The other products, bread, cakes, bulk cookies, catering supplies, and wholesale goods each have their own markets and their own tactics for success. The tactics Mr. H. will use for the gift boxes are divided into four traditional areas, Product, Price, Place, and Promotion.

Product

Mischa's Silverlake Cookies will produce four types of cookies: Chocolate chip, Chocolate fudge with yogurt chips, Butterscotch pecan, and Old-fashioned oatmeal raisin. The products have been taste tested by more than 100 of Mr. H.'s relatives and friends, and were all favorably received. They are not too rich, nor too gooey, and have a texture that holds together for minimal crumbling without being hard. The tested shelf life is six months, although Mr. H. believes that two weeks is the best length for fresh quality. The products will be compiled in gift baskets attractively arranged and wrapped in varying sizes, from the quantity one person could eat in few days to enough for 20 people. However, the cookie baskets themselves are not the sum of the product. In that a gift basket relieves the purchaser from shopping for ingredients, mixing and baking, finding a suitable manner of presentation (decorative tin, baskets, bags, boxes, etc.), wrapping, and delivery, the product is also a timesaving service. This aspect of the product is the factor that will produce sales. It is more difficult to sell staple items unless there is something unique about it. In this case, the originality is that it is homemade, kept fresh, difficult to obtain, and convenient. The advertising and promotion about the product will stress the different benefits, how important they are, why the product is superior, but still affordable.

Price

Pricing theory is an extensive topic, and crucial to business success. The fundamental objective is to price according to the need-satisfying benefits of the products. In the Cookie Gift basket realm, these benefits may be in various forms, such as enhanced reputation, more time, and ease of giving. In examining the pricing for the initial product offering the objective is to achieve maximum sales growth, company survival in the short term, and return on investment in a longer range. Various pricing tactics are available; one possibility is cost-oriented pricing, often used to counter lack of demand. As with breakeven analysis, the cost estimates are the crucial elements. The variable costs are:

- Ingredients ($4.00).
- Packaging ($.40).
- Distribution ($.60).
- Selling (phone, advertising costs, credit card fees, etc.) ($3.00).

The costs of ingredients are merely one of the costs attributed to variable costs. Packaging is another element. The baskets could be a very crucial cost if the prices were to rise. As mentioned, the container cannot exceed 10 percent of the product value and remain free from sales tax. To reduce costs of this element, an inexpensive source of baskets is necessary. Importing a container from Hong Kong is the usual answer.[23] A container is large and would hold approximately 2,000 baskets, thus in addition to storage fees to hold the product in a clean and dry facility, we would need to pay duties and importer's fees. The other variable costs, distribution and advertising, include items such as delivery, printing, display ads, and extra telephone service, that will vary with the level of sales. Fixed expenses of kitchens, licensing, insurance, utilities, office supplies, attorney's fees, and more will not vary, once the business is established, with the level of sales.

In demand-oriented pricing, determining the sensitivity of the price is essential. The sensitivity depends on the number and availability of substitutes for the product, and the perceived price quality effect, and how rapidly customers will change to a different product. By charging premium prices, we can tap consumers who believe they must pay a lot to get good quality. However, setting the prices too high will send these same customers value hunting elsewhere. The traditional approach to direct response marketing of food products is double to triple the costs,[24] and to direct response marketing in general, three to four times the cost.[25]

In choosing the exact numbers of pricing, we look at odd-even pricing; for example, if the price ends in an odd number it is perceived as a bargain. The price, $19.99 appears to be less expensive than $20, although everyone knows that it isn't. Another option is to elevate the costs, and claim to have a unique product that people should be willing to pay more for, then issue coupons to enhance the appearance of value.

Mischa's Silverlake Cookies will be sold initially in a variety of basket sizes ranging from $15 to $100 at a markup of three times costs.

Payment methods are also a part of pricing. Mr. H. has ruled out COD (cash on delivery) as a feasible option. Billing small accounts for one-time sales is not feasible, as bad debts and high receivables could finish the business. Credit card sales are the usual and standard procedure in the business. Credit card companies charge the seller a percentage of sales, usually 2 to 4 percent, depending on the volume. Naturally, for large sales, or accounts of a continuing nature, price discounts and payment options will be offered.

Promotion and Place

Promotion and place are combined in this marketing plan, as the direct mail campaign offered requires no retail outlet. The promotion strategy of direct advertising and direct response marketing has been growing rapidly in the last 10 years. Many societal changes encourage direct mail marketing; for example, more dual career relationships may mean that people now have less opportunity or the time to shop. This change has extended the range of products people are willing to buy through the mail. Promoters are also encouraged by such campaigns for many reasons, for example, low barriers to entry. The U.S. Post Office is delighted to increase business and no special permission is needed to send items in the mail. Compared to establishing retail outlets, direct response marketing has low capital requirements and provides the investor with fast appraisal of investments.

Consumers purchase items from direct response marketing offers for a variety of reasons. Table 5 is a comparison of the most commonly cited reasons for purchase and analysis of how *Mischa's Silverlake Cookies* apply to those reasons. They are rated on a scale of one to four stars, four being the highest. The initial campaign will be conducted locally, in the Silverlake area, and in the Los Angeles area. The limited locality of the initial offering allows Mr. H. to determine the success of his venture, and resolve problems prior to being committed on a national scale. As depicted in Figure 5, the Silverlake area is a small area of approximately fifteen square miles. The medium of promotion will be

Table 5   Mischa's Cookies and Direct Response Criteria

Unable to find elsewhere	**	Although the product is rare, it is not one of a kind, and with some trouble it could be located elsewhere, but most consumers do not have time to comparison shop cookie baskets.
Convenience	****	A more convenient way to send a basket of cookies does not exist.
Fun	*	Some may feel that baking is more fun than buying, but not have the time, however many people believe that sending gifts is fun.
Relatively low price	*	The product has a premium price.
Specialty item	****	The product is completely a specialty item.

Figure 5   The Silverlake Area

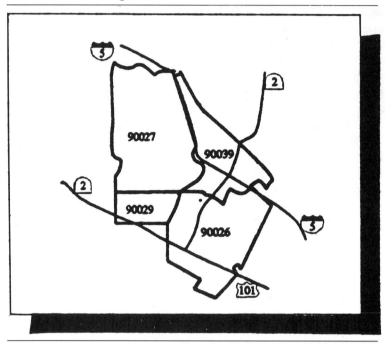

display advertising, placed in local newsletters, magazines, and newspapers. National advertising would require extensive delivery arrangements, and contracted kitchens throughout the nation to ensure product freshness. Mr. H. has a goal of delivery of the product within two days of the baking to ensure initial freshness and maximum customer satisfaction, as he hopes to limit advertising costs with repeat business. However, it is likely that some purchases will be for gifts outside of the local area, and the shipping will take an additional three days. As depicted in Figure 5, the Silverlake area consists of four Zip Code areas, with population and income as listed in Table 6. The population of these four Zip codes, combined with our target market figures from Section III, provide us with expected sales of $7,247 assuming a .001 response rate of display advertising and average size sales.[26]

Marketing efforts will begin primarily with the "throwaways." Throwaways are free newsletters, newspapers, and magazines obtained by interested parties in grocery stores and convenience stores. Pricing of display ads in throwaways varies from $50 to $400, depending on the size of the advertisement and the circulation of the publication. With the exception of full-page color ads, prices seem commensurate with what you get. For

Table 6   Silverlake Population and Income

Zip Code	1990 Population	Income* (Dollars)
90026	72,158	24,129/8,333
90027	61,475	31,504/14,939
90029	33,676	23,870/9,628
90039	41,195	28,262/10,491
Total	208,504	NA

*Average household income/per capita income.

Silverlake area marketing, among the recommended publications are: *Small Business Report, The Independent, Vanguard Newspaper, Hollywood Today, West Hollywood Today, The L.A. Reader, Hollywood Reporter,* and the *Hollywood Gazette.* These particular publications are recommended because they are frequently seen in the area shops and passed around offices. The various display ads will be created by Mr. H., and coded for response to assist Mr. H. in assessing the value of the ads. There are currently 210 local publications that claim the Los Angeles area in readership. The largest, the *Los Angeles Times,* has a circulation of 1.5 million. Advertising in the *Los Angeles Times* is charged on a per-column-inch basis and costs $482, per column inch Monday through Saturday, and $492 per column inch on Sundays.

The second phase of the marketing plan, after the initial local area learning period is complete, will be to select a national paper or magazine and advertise in that. Selection of the publication will be based on results from the local tests, but it is expected to be aimed at working professionals. The costs of a two-inch ad in small (circulation 800,000) publication are around $2,500, and a full-page color ad is $21,000.[27]

An integral element of the advertisement will be the phone number. It is important to provide a phone number for the people who wish to order immediately. Very few people choose to mail an order for specialty items. Answering services are a way to lower the costs and free time for Mr. H. to perform more essential functions. Prices of such services vary, as does quality. It will behoove Mr. H., if he chooses this method, to occasionally call the service and evaluate the quality of the services he receives. Another option for Mr. H. is to use his phone number, or a second phone installed in his residence. He would have to be available to answer as much as he could, and leave a message on a machine during the times that he cannot answer the phone. An answering machine will turn a certain amount of people away; it will be up to Mr. H. to determine if the costs of a service can be offset by lost sales from an answering machine. Naturally, as orders increase, a more permanent solution will be necessary. Toll-free, or "1-800" numbers are available. The costs vary, depending on usage, but in the local area, installation is $50, and then a $15 a month service charge is added to the rate of $11 an hour, with a minimum of 25 hours. This is somewhat expensive, and an increasingly popular alternative is number sharing. In this situation, numerous small businesses share the costs and usage of one number. In the initial phases, all calls are expected to be local.

Delivery via personal vehicle will be the least expensive method for orders in the Silverlake area. Security issues are a concern, and Mr. H. will need documentation of all stops for his protection. Delivery in the downtown area is another matter. There is no free parking downtown, and a half hour parking to drop off a package will cost at least five dollars. A commercial tag on the delivery vehicle is an option, this would allow parking in loading zones. There are also delivery companies that would solve these problems.

VI. CONTROL AND IMPLEMENTATION

Control is the means of measuring progress and shortfalls of the marketing plan, while implementation is the schedule of timing.

Control

The IRS and generally accepted accounting principles require a system of record keeping that is accurate. An accurate system is also the way to determine progress towards goals, and what particular problems one is having. A single entry accounting method is appropriate and simplest for small business to maintain. This system is based on the income

Figure 6   Mischa's Silverlake Cookies

Income statement
For the Year Ended December 31, 1993-

Revenues
  Sales
  Less: Sales Discounts
  Net sales

Cost of Goods Sold
  Beginning Inventory
  Add: Purchases
    Freight In
  Less: Purchase Returns
  Net Purchases
  Goods Available For sale
  Less: Ending Inventory, December 31
  Cost of Goods Sold
Gross Profit

Operating Expenses
  Selling Expenses
      Advertising
      Depreciation
      Miscellaneous
    Total Selling Expenses
  General and administrative Expenses
      Salaries
      Insurance
      Miscellaneous
    Total General and Administrative expenses
      Total Operating Expenses

Income from Operations

Interest Expense
net Income before Taxes
    Income taxes
Net Income

statement and includes only business income and expenses. Figure 6 shows a recommended format for the income statement.

An excellent means of record keeping is to separate personal records from business and maintain separate accounts for business receipts and disbursements.[28] Financial accounts can be classified into five groups: income, expenses, assets, liabilities, and equity. Asset accounts shall include date of acquisition, cost or basis, depreciation, and depletion. Expenses are typically categorized as follows: Cost of Goods Sold, Selling Expenses, General and Administrative Expenses, Nonoperating Expenses, and Income Tax Expense. The calendar year is required for tax purposes, as establishing an accounting period would not be worth the effort. An accounting method is a one-time choice; it must remain consistent from year to year unless the IRS has granted permission to change it.[29] Because of a limited amount of inventory that is necessary (baking supplies and spare baskets), the accrual method may be necessary. In the accrual method, all income items are included in gross income when earned, even if payment occurs in a later period. Expenses are capitalized when you become liable for them whether or not paid in the same year.

Three types of costs must be capitalized: The costs of going into business, such as advertising, travel, and utilities; business assets; and the cost of any assets used for more than one year. The full cost must be capitalized, including freight and installation. The costs of making improvements, unlike the costs of repairs, also must be capitalized. The recovery must be in one of the following ways: depreciation, amortization, or depletion.

The balance sheet provides information about a company's assets, existing liabilities, and the capital provided by the owner. Balance sheet information may be useful in many ways to many different groups. For example, Mr. H. can study the level of merchandise inventory at the end of an accounting period to judge the effectiveness of ordering policies. Creditors may review the asset and liability relationships on a balance sheet to determine if the owners are investing their own capital or relying on other creditors. Lenders want the owner to have a sizable stake in the business should financial problems develop. Figure 7 shows the suggested format for *Mischa's Silverlake Cookies* balance sheet.

In addition to basic financial statements, and their value to control activities, other data will be useful for control. Complaints are a key to improving methods or products. Often the complainer has an idea in mind that would serve the company's interests better than present procedures. Recording and acting on complaints in a timely manner can be an enlightening activity. Careful records of all inquiries from the ads, the percentage purchased from each ad inquiry group, the frequency of purchases, in addition to the size of the purchase, are all part of the task of determining what ads work the best, but these records will also provide future mailing lists, sales calls, and test markets for new products.

Implementation

The implementation schedule of this plan is presented in Figure 8. This is an initial schedule and will need revision as time slippage occurs. Slippage most commonly occurs due to unforeseen events, and Mr. H. should not see slippage as a failure, but an opportunity to revise his schedules. In the first three months, the schedule is rather rigorous, and a slippage of two weeks or a month may not be extreme, however, spans longer than a month call for evaluation of the plan with respect to costs and feasibility, and possible revision of the marketing strategy. Note that in the chart, the initial two months are business activities that must be mostly complete prior to implementation of the marketing plan.

Figure 7   Mischa's Silverlake Cookies

Balance Sheet
December 31, 1993

ASSETS

Current assets
  Cash
  Other funds
  Accounts receivable
  Merchandise Inventory
  Prepaid expenses
    Total current assets
Long term investments
Property, plant Equipment
  Land, buildings and Equipment
  Less: Accumulated depreciation
  Vehicles
  Less: Accumulated depreciation
    Total property , plant, and equipment
Other assets
    Total assets

LIABILITIES &OWNER'S EQUITY

Current liabilities
  Accounts payable
  Taxes payable
  Salary payable
  other payable
    Total current liabilities
Long Term liabilities
    Total Liabilities

Owner's Equity
  Michael Henderson, capital

    Total liabilities & owners equity

Figure 8   Implementation Schedule

Activity	Month 1	Month 2	Month 3	Month 4	Month 4
Business					
License	▓▓▓▓▓▓▲				
Registration	▓▓▓▓▓▓▲				
Kitchen	▓▓▓▓▓▓▲				
AQMD	▓▓▓▓▓▓▲				
Health Dept.	▓▓▓▓▓▓▲				
Phone	▓▓▓▓▓▓▲				
Delivery	▓▓▓▓▓▓▲				
Credit Card	▓▓▓▓▓▓▲				
Promotion					
Create Ads		▓▓▓▓▓			
Evaluate					
Silverlake Publications		▓▓▓▓▓			
Los Angeles Publications			▓▓▓▓▓		
Run Ads					
Silverlake			▓▓		
Los Angeles				▓▓	
Delivery			▓▓▓▓▓▓▓▓		
Evaluation			▓▓▓▓▓▓▓▲		

ENDNOTES

1 Philip Kotler, *Marketing Management* (Englewood Cliffs, NJ: Prentice Hall, 1991), p. 23.

2 United States Department of Commerce, *U.S. Industrial Outlook* (Washington, DC, 1992), pp. 3-21:3-26.

3 United States Department of Commerce, loc. cit.

4 Predicast, *Predicasts F&S Index, U.S. Annual Edition* (New York: Predicast, 1992), pp. B162–164.

5 Kotler, op. cit., p. 147.

6 United States Department of Labor, *Consumer and Producer Price Indexes,* (Washington, DC, 1990), p. 278.

7 United States Department of Commerce, op. cit., p. 3-2.

8 John Berry, "Inside Nabisco's Cookie Machine," *AdWeek's Marketing Week,* Vol. 32, March 18, 1991, p. 22.

9 John Sinisi, "Health Line Intro Gets $20 Million," *Brandweek,* Vol. 33, July 1992, p. 14.

10 Alyssa A. Lappen, "Meet the Frookie Man," *Forbes,* Vol. 146, No. 7, October 1, 1990, p. 193.

11 Robert McMath, "The Cookie Market Gets in Shape," *Brandweek,* Vol. 33, No. 28, July 20, 1992, p. 28.

12 "Putting the Aim Back into Famous Amos," *Sales and Marketing Management,* Vol. 144, No. 6, June 1992, p. 32.

13 Robert C. Prus, *Pursuing Customers* (Newbury Park, CA: Sage Publications, 1989), p. 41.

14 "Annual Survey of Buying Power," *Sales and Marketing Management,* November 13, 1990, pp. 14–57.

15 *Sales and Marketing Management,* loc. cit.

16 Jim McElgunn, "Colorful Cookie Campaign," *Marketing,* Vol. 95, June 18, 1990, p. 1.

17 Valerie Ford, "Quick and Easy," *Small Business Report,* Vol. 2, No. 1, January 1993, p. 2.

[18] Bernard Catry and Michael Chevailier, "Market Share Strategy and the Product Life Cycle," *Journal of Marketing,* Vol. 38, October, 1974, p. 29.

[19] Catry, op. cit. p. 34.

[20] J. Hugh Davidson, "Why Most New Consumer Brands Fail," *Harvard Business Review,* Vol. 54, No. 2, March–April 1976, p. 117.

[21] Davidson, op. cit., p. 122.

[22] William A. Cohen, *Direct Response Marketing* (New York: John Wiley & Sons, 1984), p. 103.

[23] Personal interview with Sue Finn, Marketing Products Control Manager, Fingerhut Corp., American Wholesale Manufacturers Trade Show, Los Angeles, CA, February 27, 1993.

[24] Finn, loc. cit.

[25] Cohen, op. cit., p. 61.

[26] Finn, loc. cit.

[27] David Masello, "What's New," *Food and Wine,* March 1992, p. 8.

[28] Lanny M. Solomon, *Accounting Principles* (New York: Harper & Row, 1983), pp. 217–224.

REFERENCES

Bucklin, Randolph E., "Brand Choice, Purchase Incidence, and Segmentation: An Integrated Modeling Approach," *Journal of Marketing Research,* Vol. 24, May 1992, pp. 201–15.

Buzzell, Robert D., "Market Share—A Key to Profitability," *Harvard Business Review,* Vol. 53, No. 1, January–February 1975, pp. 97–107.

Catry, Bernard, and Michael Chevailier, "Market Share Strategy and the Product Life Cycle," *Journal of Marketing,* Vol. 38, October, 1974, pp. 29–34.

Chiasson, Gail, "Familiar Cookie Takes on New Sensuous Image," *Marketing,* Vol. 96, April 8, 1991, p. 18.

Cohen, William A., *Direct Response Marketing* (New York: John Wiley & Sons, 1984).

Cooper, Lee, *Market Share Analysis* (Boston, MA: Kluwer Academic Publishers, 1988).

Davidson, J. Hugh, "Why Most New Consumer Brands Fail," *Harvard Business Review,* Vol. 54, No. 2, March–April 1976, pp. 117–122.

Ehrenberg, A. S., "New Brands and the Existing Market," *Journal of Marketing Research,* Vol. 33, No. 4, October 1991, pp. 285–299.

Fogg, C. D., "Planning Gains in Market Share," *Journal of Marketing,* Vol. 38, No. 3, pp. 30–38.

Gannes, Stuart, "The Riches in Market Niches," *Fortune,* Vol. 115, No. 9, April 27, 1987, pp. 227–230.

Ginter, James, "An Experimental Investigation of Attitude Change and Choice of a New Brand," *Journal of Marketing Research,* Vol. 11, February 1974, pp. 30–40.

Hamermesh, R. G., "Strategies for Low Market Share Businesses," *Harvard Business Review,* Vol. 56, No. 3, May–June 1978, pp. 95–103.

Kincannon, C. L., *County Business Patterns,* Table 2, SIC code, 2051, 2052, p. 76.

Kotler, Phillip, *Marketing Management* (Englewood Cliffs, NJ: Prentice Hall, 1991).

Lammers, H. Bruce, "The Effect of Free Samples on Immediate Consumer Purchase," *Journal of Consumer Marketing,* Vol. 8, Spring 1991, pp. 31–37.

Lappen, Alyssa A., "Meet the Frookie Man," *Forbes,* Vol. 146, No. 7, October 1, 1990, pp. 192–193.

McElgunn, Jim, "Colorful Cookie Campaign," *Marketing,* Vol. 95, June 18, 1990, p. 1.

McMath, Robert, "The Cookie Market Gets in Shape," *Brandweek,* Vol. 33, No. 28, July 20, 1992, pp. 28–29.

Personal interview with Sue Finn, Marketing Products Control Manager, Fingerhut Corp., American Wholesale Manufacturers Trade Show, Los Angeles, CA, February 27, 1993.

Prendergast, Alan, "Learning to Let Go," *Working Woman,* January 1992, p. 42.

"Putting the Aim Back into Famous Amos," *Sales and Marketing Management,* Vol. 144, No. 6, June 1992, pp. 31–32.

Sinisi, John, "Health Line Intro Gets $20 Million," *Brandweek,* Vol. 33, July 1992, pp. 13–14.

Sommers, Michael, "The Prospects for Innovation," *Marketing and Research Today,* Vol. 19, No. 1, February 1991, pp. 35–42.

Source book of Zip Code Demographics 1990. CACI Marketing Systems.

United States Department of Commerce, *U.S. Industrial Outlook* (Washington, DC, 1992), pp. 3–21:3–26.

United States Department of Labor, *Consumer and Producer Price Indexes* (Washington, DC, 1990), p. 278.

Weisman, Katherine, "Succeeding by Failing," *Forbes,* Vol. 145, No. 13, June 25, 1990, p. 46.

8

BUSINESS PLAN FOR VENCHERTECH INDUSTRIES, INC.

Developed by

**Yam Kim Lian, Gunadi Gunadi,
Trent Kwan, Duc Hinh, and Louis Cheng**

Used with the Permission of the Authors

EXECUTIVE SUMMARY

In the past two years, the AIDS crisis has created an unprecedented demand for rubber latex gloves. In 1988 alone, sales increased 20% from $118.8 million to $142.6 million, or 10.3 billion latex gloves.

Based on our research study, sales will increase at a continuous rate of 5% per year from 1989 until 1993. This could be an underestimated figure, since the market for latex gloves is expanding from the health community into the service industry.

In 1989, the FDA and ASTM raised their standards for the latex gloves to ensure safety. In turn, importers who failed the FDA and ASTM test tried to dump gloves that nobody wants in the market. Although there was a glut in 1989 as importers flooded the market with gloves of inferior quality, prospect for sales of superior gloves is excellent.

In the following report, we will state our objectives and goals, and describe strategies which will be used to attain those objectives and goals.

TABLE OF CONTENTS

INTRODUCTION . . . . **8 · 5**

SITUATION ANALYSIS . . . . **8 · 5**

    A. The Situational Environment . . . . 8 · 5
    B. The Neutral Environment . . . . 8 · 7
    C. The Competitor Environment . . . . 8 · 7
    D. The Company Environment . . . . 8 · 9

TARGET MARKET . . . . **8 · 10**

SWOT ANALYSIS . . . . **8 · 11**

    A. Strengths . . . . 8 · 11
    B. Weaknesses . . . . 8 · 11
    C. Opportunities . . . . 8 · 12
    D. Threats . . . . 8 · 12

BUSINESS OBJECTIVE AND GOAL . . . . **8 · 12**

    A. Differential Advantage . . . . 8 · 12

MARKETING STRATEGY . . . . **8 · 13**

MARKETING TACTICS . . . . **8 · 13**

    A. Product . . . . 8 · 13
    B. Price . . . . 8 · 13
    C. Promotion . . . . 8 · 14
    D. Distribution . . . . 8 · 15

CONTROL AND IMPLEMENTATION . . . . **8 · 15**

SUMMARY . . . . **8 · 16**

ENDNOTES . . . . **8 · 16**

LIST OF TABLES

Table I	Market Growth in the United States (Revenue)	8 · 7
Table II	Market Growth in the United States (Volume)	8 · 8
Table III	Market Share, Latex Glove	8 · 9
Table IV	Latex Glove Importers (Cost Per Container)	8 · 9
Table V	Estimated 1991 Demand in the United States for Latex Gloves	8 · 10
Table VI	U.S. Latex Gloves Demand (Projected 1991)	8 · 11
Table VII	Market Cost for Latex Gloves	8 · 14
Table VIII	Financial Analysis Projected Income Statement for 1990, 1991, and 1992	8 · 15
Table IX	Break-Even Analysis	8 · 16

INTRODUCTION

Venchertech, Inc. is a subsidiary of Arista Latindo Industrial Ltd., a privately owned manufacturer based in Indonesia. A distribution plan began when demand for latex gloves increased around the world. California was chosen to be the first export site. There are two divisions located in California at the present time.

The company is not looking for a sales force, but collaborators (such as brokers), who will sell on a 50% commission basis. As of January 1, 1990, Venchertech has begun a business plan to expand beyond the state of California. The company presently has 15 people standing by to take on different parts of the country. The following is a list of overviews on the business Venchertech is involved in:

- Competition is fierce from China, Hong Kong, and Taiwan, as far as imports are concerned.
- Objective is to create a market niche in the United States and possibly expand into Canada.
- Philosophy is direct selling to the customers without funneling our products through wholesalers.
- Targets are hospitals, police stations, food production centers, and medical labs.
- Control of sales is done by holding monthly meetings with the sales force to discuss progress and problems.
- Marketing is done by direct mailings with sample gloves included, and our sales force do personal selling in various states.
- The product has been approved by the FDA. The gloves are made of high-grade resistant rubber.

There is a need to define the number of hospitals in each state; this can be done by researching government publications, the American Dental Association (ADA), the American Medical Association (AMA), pharmaceutical associations, and various periodical sources.

SITUATION ANALYSIS

A. The Situational Environment

Demand

During the past years, concern about AIDS has been growing, and fears of the AIDS virus contamination will continue in an upward trend.[1] The following table shows what 100 Americans think about AIDS:

Do you think that anyone could catch AIDS:

	Yes	No	Don't Know
From touching what carriers touched?	38	51	11
From touching a carrier?	23	69	8
From being spat upon by a carrier?	36	47	17

Source: Advertising Age, 1988.

The following table shows the AIDS cases as an annual incidence per 100,000 people, by state, reported May 1987 through April 1988, and May 1988 through April 1989:

AIDS Cases in the United States from 1987 to 1989

States	May 1987–April 1988	May 1988–April 1989
California	5,238	5,865
New York	5,057	6,613
New Jersey	1,933	2,441
Florida	1,898	2,987
Texas	1,851	2,353
Illinois	797	1,002
Pennsylvania	778	965
Massachusetts	529	771
Washington, DC	510	526
Georgia	549	968

Source: Medical World News, 1989.

AIDS is the number one public health enemy today.[2] By the end of 1991, it is projected that a total of 324,000 cases of AIDS, including 234,000 deaths, will be reported in the United States.

The increased awareness of both the public and health care providers has accelerated the demand for latex disposable gloves.[3] The effect of the AIDS crisis on the latex consumer market are:

- A surge in demand for latex gloves.
- A doubling of prices.
- A growing shortage of latex gloves.

Economic Business Conditions

During the latex shortage crisis in 1988 and 1989, hospitals were taking gloves from just about anywhere. Also, hospitals and medical and dental offices were willing to pay hefty premiums for gloves from new suppliers or to accept gloves of a lesser quality.[4] As a result, orders were outstripping the supply as manufacturers scrambled to add production capacity. Suppliers struggled to fill the gap by importing gloves made in Taiwan, China, Thailand, Malaysia, and Indonesia, where rubber trees are the world's major source of supply.[5]

Medical industry observers predict that the glove shortage will perhaps last more than two years.[6] Its duration will depend in part on how many other service workers, such as restaurant and cafeteria employees, grocers, and police officers will be required to wear gloves.

Sales of latex gloves were $142.6 million or 10.3 billion gloves in 1988 (see Table I). This represented a 20% increase from 1987 sales of $118.8 million. Sales in 1989 grew 10% to $156.8 million. The U.S. latex market is expected to grow at a rate of 5% per year, and reach $176.5 million by 1993 (see Table I).

Laws and Regulations

The Occupational Safety and Health Administration has endorsed the CDC (Centers for Disease Control) guidelines, which called for the use of gloves and other "barrier" precautions such as masks and gowns. In response, hospitals that once required personnel to wear examination gloves only when treating patients with diagnosis of infectious diseases now require personnel to wear gloves routinely at all times.

Table I Market Growth in the United States (Revenue)

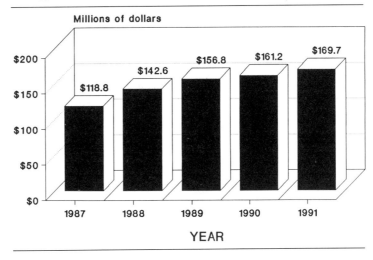

CDC recommended three important aspects of routine examinations:

1. Use either latex or examination gloves.
2. Apply universal precautions (gowns, gloves, masks, and goggles) only when handling certain bodily fluids.
3. Change gloves after drawing blood samples from each patient.

B. The Neutral Environment

Beginning April 13, 1989, examination glove manufacturers will have to notify the government before their products go on the market and submit to federal inspection of workplaces. With the heavy reliance on gloves as a barrier, and with concerns in the medical community, it seemed appropriate for the FDA to make absolutely certain that the products being sold are of the highest quality.[7]

The FDA revoked the medical exam glove industry's exemption from usual federal premarket notification requirements because of concerns over AIDS. All glove makers and importers must submit notification forms to the FDA and make gloves according to the general quality standards demanded by the government.

With the U.S. customs detaining countless containers of imported gloves at ports of entry, this could mean trouble for some foreign glove producers where technology and sanitation may be lacking.

C. The Competitor Environment

In response to the demand surge of latex gloves, major American manufacturers are adding capacities both in the United States and Asia.

Baxter, the biggest glove manufacturer, built a plant in Malaysia that will produce 500 million latex gloves annually. Ansell Inc., another latex giant, has built a plant in Thailand. Johnson & Johnson added two new machines which operate 24 hours a day. Smith & Nephew, Chicago, added two product lines and more high-volume, high-speed equipment in their two Ohio plants.

Smith and Nephew Associated Companies increased capacity in three North American facilities to keep pace with the growing demand. The fear of AIDS and concerns of other communicable diseases have boosted their sales significantly. Two of their executives believe the strong demand for gloves will persist.[8] Phoenix Medical Technology Inc. entered the latex arena because more and more of their customers indicated a need for a high-quality U.S. producer. They have recently built an ample capacity of producing 250 million gloves a year.

Based on a survey in 1989, the market is now divided among the following companies according to their known market shares:

Share of Market (1989)

Baxter Travenol Laboratories, Inc.	36.5%
Becton-Dickinson	23.6
Johnson & Johnson	23.0
Others	16.9
Total	100.0%

Source: Rubber and Plastic News, 1989.

Baxter will continue to dominate for the next five years because of its strengths in distribution, product availability, and competitive pricing.[9]

Many glove sellers have turned to imports to keep up with demand (see Table IV). However, the majority of foreign glove manufacturers failed to meet the U.S. standards because of poor quality. In fact, all of the gloves could not be counted on as effective barriers to AIDS because they have tiny holes on the surface.[10] Since the tougher FDA regulation began on April 13, 1989, some importers started canceling orders of foreign latex gloves. Consequently, they attempted to dump what was left of their inventory for any return they could get and created a short-term glut in the market. Many foreign glove manufacturers have folded their businesses as a result of canceled orders.

Table II   Market Growth in the United States (Volume)

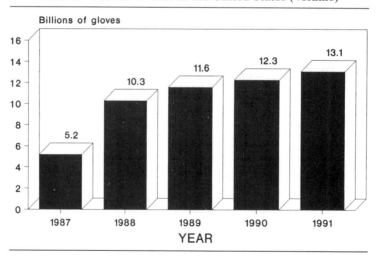

D. The Company Environment

Venchertech, Inc., is a direct manufacturer representative from Indonesia. Their main product line is the latex exam gloves. The gloves are made from the finest grade rubber utilizing state-of-the-art technology. The gloves offer tactile sensitivity so doctors can get a better feel of the patients' veins. The gloves also have roll cuffs for easy removal, and provide the necessary strength to ensure maximum safety.

Venchertech, Inc., caters to the health professionals, giving them the comfort of working in safety, while concentrating on the health care of their patients.

Table III   Market Share, Latex Glove

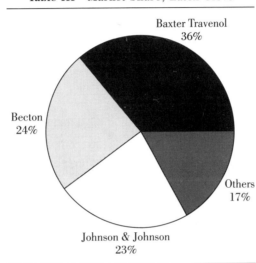

Source: Rubber & Plastics News, 1989.

Table IV   Latex Glove Importers (Cost Per Container)

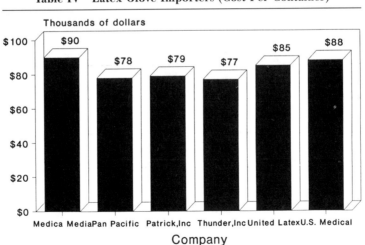

The basic selling concept is as follows:

1. Provide the best quality products.
2. Provide superior services.
3. Provide factory prices straight to the consumer without the middleman cost.

The factory uses an immaculate facility and imposes strict quality control. Each glove has been individually tested to make sure all the gloves have exceeded the FDA and ASTM standards. Here are some of the qualities which Venchertech offers:

1. Finest grade rubber.
2. High-grade absorbent powder.
3. Superior tactile sensitivity.
4. Prompt delivery and services.

TARGET MARKET

We will target our market mainly towards hospitals and clinics in major cities and adjacent suburbs beginning in California. The reason for targeting the suburbs is that large firms have a tendency to take only the high profit buyers of a market and ignore the smaller users. We would have a better advantage in capturing sales of the smaller users. Representatives of glove manufacturers in the United States do a majority of their business with high margin buyers only. They include city hospitals, buyers for multiple hospitals, and dentist organizations.[11] Our consumers will basically be doctors, dentists, nurses, and other health care workers who often perform physical examinations, take blood samples, and take bodily fluids from patients.

A physician uses an average of 7 gloves a day, a registered nurse working in a hospital uses 20, and a dentist uses 22 pairs, based upon an estimated number of patients they see each day (see Table V). According to the American Medical Association, there are roughly 3.5 million health care providers in the nation. They include doctors, nurses, dental hygienists, and lab technicians.

Table V Estimated 1991 Demand in the United States for Latex Gloves

User	Number	# Used	Workdays	Total
Physicians	569,160	7	261	1,039,855,320
Physician assistants	25,000	4	261	26,100,000
RN—Hospital	884,000	20	261	4,614,480,000
RN—Non-hospital	647,200	10	261	1,689,192,000
LPN	602,000	10	261	1,571,220,000
Dentists	156,000	22	261	895,572,000
Dental hygienists	76,000	18	261	357,048,000
Dental assistants	76,000	18	261	357,048,000
Emergency medical technicians	133,000	12	122	194,712,000
Respiratory therapists	55,000	16	261	229,680,000
Lab/medical technicians	236,000	8	261	492,768,000
Industry & others				2,866,963,830
Total	3,459,360	145	2,732	14,334,819,150

Table VI   United States Latex Gloves Demand
(Projected 1991)

RN's & LPN's
55.0%

Physician Offices
7.0%

Lab & Med Tech
3.0%

Industrial & Other
20.0%

Emer. & Respir. Tech
3.0%

Dental Offices
11.0%

Source: American Medical Association.

SWOT ANALYSIS

A.   Strengths

Quality control measures used by manufacturers on product testing are of special interest to the FDA. Venchertech, Inc., submitted to FDA a detailed description of the product testing procedures, standards employed, and the acceptable quality level. The quality level of our latex gloves is determined by FDA to be satisfactory, and the risk of glove defects is minimal. Indonesia is one of the leaders in the world's quality rubber-producing industry. Demand for quality gloves will continue to flourish as the breadth of variety users will expand from medical technicians to public health care and service workers. Our strength is in providing customer satisfaction. We can promptly meet our customers' needs through our distribution warehouse in California. The customers won't have to wait two months before receiving shipments from Indonesia. We can deliver within 48 hours to anywhere in the United States. The major strength we have is inherent in our quality control. We can monitor our quality better than any of our counterparts in the market because we can afford to hire more quality controllers and inspectors to supervise the quality of our output.

As an overseas manufacturer, our cost of production is lower compared to the firms in the United States. These costs include labor, plant construction, and licensing. In addition, there is no import tax on our goods as opposed to taxes levied on products from Taiwan, because Indonesia falls under the Generalized System of Preferences. These combined strengths will enhance our position as a seller of latex gloves in the U.S. market.

B.   Weaknesses

Venchertech, Inc., lacks brand image. Since we are a privately owned company from overseas, we have not yet established a corporate image as prominent as some of the domestic producers such as Johnson & Johnson, and Baxter.

As a company that is in the initial stage of product introduction in the United States, it will take us some time and effort to convince consumers of the reliability of our brand.

C. Opportunities

The concerns about contamination by the AIDS virus has created an exploding market for thin-gauge surgical and medical examination gloves. This has opened some new areas of business for raw material producers.

The U.S. latex glove market is expected to grow 5% per year until 1993 according to a market study on hospital room supplies. Many analysts originally expected a sharp rise in demand for condoms; while there has been an increase, demand for latex gloves has caused the largest shortage.

Current health needs and recommendations from health authorities suggest the use of latex gloves as the remedy for preventing the transmission of HIV from patients to health care practitioners. Even if a cure for AIDS is found, most medical industry observers believe that gloves have become a permanent part of hospital's garb to guard against the spread of AIDS.

D. Threats

Domestic glove producers have increased production to the point where they can fill most back orders themselves. A major threat is that more and more companies are building plants across the nation and overseas to fill the demand caused by the AIDS scare. As more plants are built, more gloves will be available and this will saturate the market; therefore, the price of latex gloves may drop steadily.

Most of the materials used in producing latex gloves come from natural latex rubber trees which take seven years to reach maturity. Chemical stimulation of older trees has not been successful, so there may be a shortage of rubber trees in the future.

BUSINESS OBJECTIVE AND GOAL

The objective of Venchertech is to introduce its products in the United States, and capture 0.1% of the market at the end of 1991. The goal is to retain at least 350 customers with each purchasing a minimum of 9 cases a year by 1991.

A. Differential Advantage

Venchertech's competitive advantage lies in high product quality, and low market price. Most of the latex gloves imported from Asia were dumped below market price, but they were in such poor conditions that the FDA had to come up with strict quality measures to screen them out.

We will be facing stiff competitions in the future from domestic as well as foreign producers. However, we have a clear advantage in that other companies who sell to wholesalers and distributors must sell a large volume in order to realize profit. At Venchertech, we believe in selling directly to the consumers through our own channels of distribution, thereby cutting out the middlemen markups. This will allow us to sell at a lower price in the market, and still maintain as high a profit margin as our competitors.

Venchertech, Inc., can afford a lower-than-market price because of three reasons; Venchertech is not required to pay import taxes; production costs are much cheaper in Indonesia (since trees and laborers are abundant in Indonesia); Venchertech employs direct channels of distribution rather than using wholesalers.

MARKETING STRATEGY

The objective and the goal can best be accomplished by market penetration, and market segmentation. By market penetration, the company is looking to create a bond with the consumers by establishing credibility in the marketplace. By market segmentation, the company will be able to focus on several market segments at a time, so when more competition enters the market, we can respond swiftly by diversifying into other segments of the market. And to further stay ahead of the competition, we will invest extensively in R&D so as to premiere a new product every 2 years.

MARKETING TACTICS

A. Product

Venchertech, Inc., is offering a high-quality latex examination glove. The raw material used in producing these premium gloves comes fresh off the local rubber trees in Indonesia. This is important in that if the raw material had to be imported, it would be subjected to the risk of spoilage. Each glove is then hand inspected and tested for defects before leaving the plant.

The message "high quality" will be stressed on all packages of gloves. The use of graphics, print size, wordings, package design, and modern styling will enhance the overall image of the product. How the gloves are placed within the packages makes a difference. For example, we arrange all of the gloves neatly into layers like a tissue box, so only one glove comes out at a time. This promotes easy usage of the product. Most imported gloves are bunched together in a ball and have been shoved into the boxes.

B. Price

Price is the key factor in business tactics which can determine the decision to purchase. Since we are introducing a product in a mature market, the penetration pricing policy should be adopted. This tactic will help us enter the market by offering lower prices to our customers and those consumers who are very price conscious.

To price our products as high as our competitors will not work because, presently, we need something other than superior quality to set us apart from the rest, namely, at a cheaper price. Price incentive will be the best way to entice prospective buyers.

Price skimming would be inappropriate since we are not introducing something that is new.

The most effective pricing tactic would be penetration pricing, and we have the best resources to compliment this method of pricing. Once we have gained a market share, we can then increase our price in small margins.

Our price in 1990 is cheaper than the market price in 1989, as the graph on the next page illustrates. Our price is $52.50 as opposed to $62.00 in the market. Should a customer decide to purchase a minimum of 5 cases, we can offer a 5% discount. If the customer buys a total of 10 cases, a further discount may be negotiated.

Table VII   Market Cost for Latex Gloves

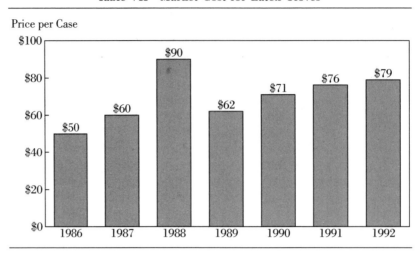

The market price is expected to rise as the FDA tightens up regulations in the future, but the price increase will level off as the market starts to saturate.

C.   Promotion

Several factors need to be considered when dealing with promotion. First is how to attract new customers to try our product. The second consideration is how to keep our existing clients.

One of the primary objectives of most firms is to increase their total sales. This usually means finding new customers to use the product. We want other doctors, dentists, nurses, clinics, and health care providers to be familiar with our product, or be willing at least to try it. We can let them know about our product by first sending out flyers. In the flyers we'll tell them about our quality, explain to them why we are better than the rest, and address the benefits of using our gloves. We will then follow up with a sample of our product so they can see, feel, and test our gloves. Since we are coming out with "strawberry scented" gloves, the customers can even smell the gloves.

We will also include a price list for our customers to review. In the price list, we will compare our prices with the competitor who has the lowest prices. The customers will then realize the bargain. Subsequently, we will follow up again with customers who have actually placed an order using a questionnaire. The purpose of the questionnaire is to find out what areas of improvements might be needed and how satisfied the patrons were with our products and services.

The important thing is to familiarize them with our product or at least make them aware of our existence before we mount a sales campaign. The advantage of doing this is that they will be more receptive to our product.

To keep our existing clients, we will offer premiums much like the ones offered by major airlines, such as "the more miles you fly with us, the better your chances are of getting a free air fare." In our case, "the more orders you place with us, the greater your chances are of receiving an extra free case of latex gloves."

D.   Distribution

Venchertech's gloves are shipped in large containers from Indonesia. Once in the United States, they are stored in a central warehouse in Los Angeles and are ready for delivery to customers.

We will use the service of UPS to ship boxes or cases. This is the most convenient and cost-effective means of delivery. In case a customer orders more than 30 cases, we will ship the products using a trucking company. If the customer is in the local area (L.A. vicinity), we will personally deliver the shipments.

CONTROL AND IMPLEMENTATION

Total net sales is projected to increase 60% between 1990 and 1991; and it will subside to 12% between 1991 and 1992 (see projected income statement). The increasing rate reflects the annual increase in demand at 5% per year. But the decline in the rate of increase is due to saturation in the marketplace. Nevertheless, our net profit will continue to grow at an increasing rate, because there is no middleman cost, we have a better control over our operating costs. We will be constantly putting pressure on those costs, so as to get a bigger profit every year. The net profit is expected to outgrow the total revenue in percentage rates.

The break-even point is set at 319 cases, or $100,000. Profit will be realized in 1991, as we break even in that year. The break-even point is calculated by dividing the total fixed cost by the unit gross profit. The reason our break-even point is so low is that Venchertech is a subsidiary company; therefore, there are no plant and equipment costs in considerations of fixed costs (see Break-Even Analysis).

Table VIII   Financial Analysis
Projected Income Statement for 1990, 1991, and 1992

	1990	*1991*	*1992*
Total net sales	$100,000	$160,000	$180,000
Cost of goods sold	64,760	103,619	116,571
Gross Profit	$ 35,240	$ 56,381	$ 63,429
Expenses			
Warehouse	$ 10,800	$10,800	$10,800
Phone bills	550	630	600
P.O. Box	39	39	39
Postage	1,500	1,800	2,000
Stationaries	1,250	1,550	1,700
Brochures	750	880	1,000
Reorder cards	360	450	520
Miscellaneous	250	320	370
Total Expenses	$ 15,499	$ 16,469	$ 17,029
Net Profit (Loss) before Taxes	$ 19,741	$ 39,912	$ 46,400

Table IX   Break-Even Analysis

Selling price	$	52.25
Variable Cost		
State sales tax		3.26
Gross Profit per Unit	$	48.63
Fixed Costs		
Warehouse		10,800.00
Phone bills		550.00
P.O. Box		39.00
Postage		1,500.00
Stationery		1,250.00
Brochures		750.00
Reorder cards		360.00
Miscellaneous		250.00
Total Fixed Cost		$15,499.00

Break-Even Quantity:
$15,499.00/$48.63 = 319 Units

SUMMARY

The future looks bright for Venchertech, Inc. Our quality can match the standards of the FDA many times over. Since health and safety are primary concerns to our consumers, our gloves will be in demand.

Our price is very competitive, so our competitors will not be able to match our price without significantly sacrificing the profit margin.

We have a high leverage in terms of reaping maximal profit with minimal investments.

We can set the price floor in the market and still be as profitable as our foreign competitors.

We have made it possible to produce inexpensive, but quality gloves for a demanding market.

ENDNOTES

[1] Davis, Bruce; "Market for Latex Gloves to Escalate"; *Rubber and Plastic News:* June 5, 1989, p. 2.

[2] Higgins, Linda; "Reports of Leaky Gloves Spur FDA to Take Action"; *Medical World News:* Jan. 23, 1989, p. 43.

[3] Moore, Miles; "Tougher Exam Glove Regulations Begin April 13"; *Rubber and Plastic News:* March 27, 1989, p. 3.

[4] Brightbill, Tim; "Use Caution and Clear Contracts to Purchase Imported Gloves"; *Hospitals Materials Management:* Sept. 1988, p. 12.

[5] Berkman, Leslie; "Latex Medical Emergency at Hand"; *Los Angeles Times:* Dec. 10, 1987, p. 1:7.

[6] Puster, Todd; "Rubbermaid Expanding Glove Lines"; *Rubber and Plastic News:* Feb. 6, 1989, p. 6.

[7] Pritchard, Ed; "Another Glove Maker Expanding"; *Rubber and Plastic News:* April 25, 1988, p. 7.

[8] Marcial, Gene; "Gloves for Profit and Protection"; *Business Week:* Feb. 1, 1988, p. 76.

[9] Chambers, Robert; "Running Out of Gloves"; *Los Angeles Times:* Jan. 18, 1988, p. 27.

[10] Truell, Peter; "Demand for Rubber Gloves Skyrockets"; *The Wall Street Journal:* Jan. 9, 1988, p. 6:7.

[11] Slakter, Ann; "AIDS Fears Boost Thin Gloves"; *Chemical Week:* March 2, 1988, p. 16.

9

BUSINESS PLAN FOR COMPACT DISC STORE SPECIALIZING IN USED CDs

Developed by
Kevin M. Krahn

Used with the Permission of the Author

Table of Contents

I. EXECUTIVE SUMMARY . . . 9 · 3

II. CURRENT MARKETING
SITUATION . . . . 9 · 3

III. OPPORTUNITY AND ISSUE
ANALYSIS . . . . 9 · 14

IV. OBJECTIVES . . . . 9 · 18

V. MARKETING STRATEGY . . . 9 · 18

VI. ACTION PROGRAMS . . . . . 9 · 19

VII. FINANCIAL STATEMENTS . . 9 · 21

VIII. CONTROLS . . . . 9 · 22

BIBLIOGRAPHY . . . . 9 · 22

I. EXECUTIVE SUMMARY

This business plan focuses on the establishment of a medium-size compact disc (CD) store in Long Beach, California. The location will be a neighborhood shopping mall anchored by a grocery store. The store will primarily sell used CDs as opposed to new CDs. This is a new area of the CD retail business, and the growth potential is excellent. After nearly 10 years of CD sales, many consumers now want to exchange their old CDs for new CDs or even other used CDs. The used market is huge as potentially every CD ever sold could become a part of this ever-expanding market.

The store will also sell other music-related products such as new cassettes, music videos, and books. Sales of CD-ROM discs is a new market that will also be explored.

The advantages of the small CD store over the larger chains include the ability to offer a better selection in more categories of music in a friendlier, more intimate environment. Many people are put off by huge, loud, and commercial stores.

The appeal of this plan is the low start-up cost, which is expected to range from $65,000 to $86,000 (see Start-up Cost Schedule in Section VII for detail). A couple could easily run this business with minimal help (one or two part-time employees).

Under the most conservative scenarios, the store is expected to earn a minimum of about $48,000 after taxes in the first year and to increase net profits each subsequent year by 4% to 5%.

The store could easily provide significantly higher profits, especially if CD-ROM sales take off. This plan conservatively projects only very modest sales for this new and potentially very profitable product.

Projected profit improvement after the first year is expected as a result of improved experience with marketing strategies and also because the economy in Southern California is expected to turn upward during the mid-1990s. As a result, it is expected that there is only a moderate risk factor in the success of this plan.

II. CURRENT MARKETING SITUATION

Market Situation

The target market for this business plan will be the local populace near the neighborhood shopping center. Typical buyers of CDs and tapes range from young teenagers to aging baby boomers in their early 50s.

"According to a '1990 Consumer Profile' published by the Recording Industry Assn. of America, the percentage of dollars spent on prerecorded music that year by those aged 35-plus rose to 29.1% from 22.7% in 1986. In contrast, those aged 15–19 accounted for only 18.3% of dollars spent on music in 1990, compared with 23.6% in 1986; 10–14-year-olds spent only 7.6% of the total in 1990, down from 9.6% in 1986."[1]

The very latest figures for 1993 show that "recorded music sales to boomers aged 30 to 39 increased 6.4 percent over the last five years, while sales to people aged 24 or under fell 12 percent. Boomers make up a larger share of the market than they did in 1988. In that year, boomers were aged 24 to 42 and accounted for about 34 percent of recorded music sales. In 1992, however, boomers accounted for roughly 44% of sales."[2]

There are subcategories that define particular musical preferences for the general population. According to a survey by Chilton Research Services, the percentages of types of music purchased based on dollar volume in 1985 were as follows: rock—43%, pop—17%, black/dance—10%, country—10%, other—8%, classical—5%, gospel—4%, and jazz—3%.[3]

According to the most recent 1993 information, musical tastes have shifted moderately from the trend in the 1985 survey. "The type of music most often sold reflects boomer tastes. Rock accounts for one-third of recorded music purchases, despite a 3.1 percent drop from last year. Country music sales increased 4 percent to 16.5 percent of all music sold. Classical and

[1] *Billboard* (Jan. 18, 1992), p. 49.
[2] *Entertainment* (June 15, 1993), p. 6.
[3] *American Entrepreneur Association Business Manual No. X1308*, p. 8.

children's music sales also increased. The second most popular genre, after rock, is urban contemporary, but its market share declined 1.5 percent to 16.7 percent."[4]

It is obvious that rock music is one type of music that should not be ignored. A survey noted that "most people who buy rock are between the ages of 10 and 25" and they tend to come from blue-collar, middle-class, and upper-middle-class families.[5]

Pop audiences include teenagers, college students, young professionals, and some older adults.[6]

Country is enjoyed mostly by those in the southern and southwestern states ages 20 to 40 who are in agricultural or blue-collar lines of work.[7] It should be noted, however, that in recent years a crossover of certain country artists into the rock audience has often occurred. For example, the number one selling artist in 1992 was country artist, Garth Brooks.

Classical music tends to draw older, more affluent adults, while gospel is favored by both younger and older families. Jazz is listened to by ages 30 to 35 with modest to affluent incomes and at least a college degree.[8]

The survey also revealed that for CD sales in the late 1980s, "virtually every retailer we interviewed claimed that professional males between the ages of 20 and 50 make up more than 90 percent of their customer base."[9] Since the time of that survey those percentages have probably lowered somewhat, but men are still the primary CD buyers for several reasons. Men tend to buy more audio equipment, especially high-end products, than women. CDs were first introduced into the marketplace as an expensive audio accessory and mostly men bought the first CD players. Men also tend to read more audio-related magazines that advertise audio equipment, CD players, and music than do women.

In addition, current chart rankings of the best selling CDs by category are always available in *Billboard* magazine.

Based on the above information, this store will target a fairly wide group from college age to aging baby boomers in their early 50s. However, the primary focus will be on the rock audience because of their large market share. This group is primarily comprised of teenagers and the college age group, with significant sales also coming from the baby boomers. This is one of the most important subgroups as they tend to buy the latest popular titles which accounts for a large percentage of total sales.

This plan also employs a survey (see Section V, Marketing Strategy) to further pinpoint the musical tastes of the potential customer base in the Bixby Knolls area.

In addition, since this store is concerned with the used CD market, to a certain extent the types of rock music that the consumer wants will become apparent as CDs are brought in for trade. In other words, the retailer should be able to see what the target consumers have bought in the past by observing what types of music they are bringing in for trade.

Market Share

In 1986, market share and sales by dollar value of the various prerecorded mediums were as follows:

CDs 20.0% ($930,000,000)
LPs 21.1% ($983,000,000)
Cassettes 53.7% ($2,499,500,000), and
Other 5.2% ($238,600,000).[10]

In 1987, CD sales exceeded LP sales for the first time. "Since they were introduced in 1983, compact disc sales have mushroomed. According to the Recording Industry of America, sales have gone from $17.2 million (a 0.45-percent market share) in 1983, to $930 million, or 20 percent of overall dollars spent on the audio industry, in 1986. At the same time, LP sales have decreased from 30 percent of the market share in 1985 to 20 percent in 1986. Cassettes are still going strong at an average of 50–60 percent market share every year, but they're getting a run for their money from compact discs."[11]

---

[4] *Entertainment* (June 15, 1993), p. 6.
[5] Ibid., p. 10.
[6] Ibid.
[7] Ibid.
[8] Ibid.
[9] Ibid.

[10] Ibid., p. 2.
[11] Ibid., p. 3.

Today, CDs have more than fulfilled the predictions made in 1987, "CDs are the most popular format, accounting for 56 percent of the market; cassettes have 37 percent of the album length market. CD sales will continue to increase, says the RIAA, since only 42% of American households currently own CD players."[12] This widespread acceptance of CDs and rapid growth, from a 20 percent market share to 56 percent in just five years, lends further support to the concept of specializing in the ever-expanding used CD market.

Part of the increased popularity of CDs is attributable to sharply lower prices as a result of increased production capacity. In addition, CD players dropped significantly in cost to about $150 and relatively inexpensive CD players for the car are also now available.

Location

Because CDs are bought with disposable income, the store will be ideally situated in a high-income area. The specific location targeted in Long Beach is the Bixby Knolls area which is of interest because of the high income per household according to the demographics chart provided by the city of Long Beach. This location also has easy access to the Long Beach and San Diego freeways as well as close proximity to the Artesia (91) freeway.

The target retail location will be in a neighborhood shopping center on Atlantic Blvd. near Del Amo Blvd. in Long Beach, California. The advantage of this shopping center location is that it is well anchored by a popular grocery store chain, the U.S. post office, a Home Depot, and two well-known drug store chains. Each of these anchors brings in local foot traffic on a regular basis.

A location near a community college was considered but rejected. School is often closed for extended periods of time during summer vacation and the holidays; also many students probably park and go directly to class and then leave to go home without lingering in the area, as they probably live within a few miles of the college.

There is also a redevelopment area adjacent to the Bixby Knolls area which offers retailers incentives in the form of tax rebates from the city and financial aid, as well as a very low cost per square foot. It is expected that this area will gradually improve over a period of 40 years as the redevelopment plan progresses. This area was rejected for the current plan but is of interest because it is adjacent to the Bixby Knolls area and its success in revitalizing the area will cause property values in the surrounding areas to rise and thereby increase the disposable income level in the area. It is also possible that a second expansion store could be located in the redevelopment area after the project begins to improve the area demographics.

The nearest chain competitors are a Wherehouse and Music Plus in the Lakewood shopping mall about six miles away and an independent used CD store about eight miles away. In addition, there is another Wherehouse in the Long Beach shopping mall about five miles away in an undesirable demographic area. Also, there is a small independent store about four miles away that does not sell used CDs, but rather specializes in selling new CDs, primarily of blues artists.

The Store

The store itself is about 1,200 square feet and faces the only entrance to the supermarket anchor across a large parking lot that could accommodate about 800 cars. There are Vons, Thrifty's, Home Depot, and Kentucky Fried Chicken outlets within the shopping center. There is also a Savon Drug store and U.S. Post Office across the street in an adjacent small shopping complex.

The store's hours are from 10 A.M. to 8 P.M. or 9 P.M. (it will be open later on Fridays and Saturdays than during the rest of the week). Initially, the store will be open seven days a week.

The store's internal space will be divided into retail space (about 80%) and storage space (about 20%). The checkout area would be near the door and the rest of the retail area arranged such that the consumer will see the most desirable items as soon as he or she walks in. The lowest volume items should be near the back of the store. The lighting,

---

[12] *Entertainment* (June 15, 1993), p. 6.

carpeting, displays, and atmosphere should be comforting to the consumer so that he or she feels at home in the store. A CD player will be prominently displayed where consumers can play used CDs before they buy them. Office space and storage will occupy the back portion of the store. Security precautions should include some one-way mirrors between the back of the store and the retail area to discourage shoplifters. For security reasons the store should also have low displays so that hidden areas are minimized. The store will also have a music system that plays the latest CDs so that customers will be aware of what is now for sale.

To avoid consumer conflicts, signs clearly stating the store policies on returns and guarantees will be posted above the checkout area.

Leases

The cost for retail space per square foot per month in Long Beach, as well as throughout the Los Angeles area, varies, depending on size and location of the shopping center, from $1.35 to $2.00.[13] Another $.15 to $.18 should be added to those figures to cover "triple net pay all"—this is the retail business terminology referring to the shopping center maintenance, insurance and tax expenses that will have to be paid in addition to the rent or lease. It is important to be sure that the lease is easily assignable to another retailer should the store owner decide to go out of the business before the lease expires.

Product Situation

Profit Margin

The typical retail markup on new CDs by the large chains probably approaches 50% to 100%. It is extremely difficult to be more specific because it is a trade secret and because advertising credits, return policies and special deals on new titles are all factored into the revenues and costs. The kind of arrangement that Capital Records, for example, has with the Wherehouse is often substantially different

from the deal that that same label would have with Tower Records. Further, Warner Brothers Records would not follow Capital's lead in how they do business with the chains. Also, because the chains can get substantial volume discounts from the labels, an outsider can only guess at how much the chains really make on CD sales. The most important factor here is that the chains have a distinct advantage over the small retailer in the sale of new CDs.

I conducted an interview with a former buyer for Music Plus, who is now the owner of a small CD store in Pasadena, about how business is conducted in the prerecorded music business. According to this buyer, even employees inside the large chains would have difficulty pinpointing profit margins because there are no set rules on cost structures. Apparently, the chains constantly make unique deals on particular titles, especially new popular titles. This could mean, for example, that a chain could agree to receive perhaps 20,000 CDs of a new title, but will not pay for the inventory until it has been sold in three months. Part of the deal might include a clause that the labels will agree to accept perhaps 10% of these CDs back as opened returns for full credit. The chain might also negotiate that the label will also accept perhaps 5,000 other opened returns of different titles if they have perhaps less than 5% returns of the new title. Further, since the chains are allowed to subtract a certain percentage of their advertising costs from the cost of the CD purchases from the labels—this percentage is also subject to negotiation. "The labels have always used advertising dollars to control the behavior of the chains."[14]

It was very clear from the interview with the buyer that this is a dynamic rather than a static process. According to the buyer, the chains will often pay off their outstanding payables to the record labels early if they can get other concessions related to CD purchases.

The profit margin situation on new CDs is only slightly clearer for the small retailer. The small retailer does not concern himself with advertising credits as he usually buys from a distributor rather than directly from the labels. The buyer I spoke with said that he often saw a 12% markup passed on to the retailer by the

[13] Per telephone interview with a representative of CB Commercial Property Co. in Long Beach, CA.

[14] *Billboard* (Mar. 20, 1993), p. 84.

distributor. It is easy to see that the chains have a distinct advantage with a 12% lower cost off the bat and advertising credits as well as volume discounts.

The small CD retail store makes most of his profit on used product where he can get at least a 100% markup. Typically, the small retailer will buy used CDs for $3 to $5 and sell them for $6 to $10. It is this market that this plan targets.

Inventory Control

One advantage the small retailer has over the larger chains is tighter inventory control. The small operation is often run by one or two very knowledgeable individuals who know what their customers buy. Often they have established a particular niche in the business and they can quickly filter out the CDs they know won't sell. Undesirable CDs are either not bought or are bought only for a very low price. According to the buyer I interviewed, this level of product differentiation is not at all seen at the large chains where inexperienced staff often buy undifferentiated used product that is often difficult to sell later.

Also, the smaller operation can easily stop and start buying inventory to adjust to recent business trends. The chains, however, have a set policy that has been extensively advertised for months; and they would have difficulty stopping or slowing return sales. As a result of this lack of control and the lack of differentiation of purchased used product, the chains could easily build up large inventories of CDs that have low resale value. At the end of the year, the chains may have to sell their excess used product at cost to avoid taxation on unsold inventory.

The Competitive Situation

Used CD Sales

Until early this year, the used CD market was limited to small independent CD store owners. The major chains did not sell used CDs. This meant that the small owner didn't need to worry about competition from the larger chains. The new CD business and the used CD business could be mixed together with the owner profiting from both markets. The Wherehouse chain however, is threatening to break into the used market. For the first time (beginning in Spring 1993), they are selling used CDs in addition to new CDs. Two other major chains are also selling used CDs in other parts of the country, Western Merchandising in Texas and Strawberries in Massachusetts. The record companies do not want retailers to mix used and new CDs because they are afraid the consumer will buy the used CDs instead—the record companies receive no reimbursement on used CD sales. A major country artist, Garth Brooks, recently stated that he did not want his CDs sold in any stores that also sold used CDs.[15]

CDs last nearly forever and now that the CD market has flourished for nearly a decade there are lots of used CDs available. In the past, record labels were willing to ignore the smaller retailer selling used product on a smaller scale—but because of the large market share that the Wherehouse enjoys in Southern California and because the record labels have significant financial leverage on the Wherehouse, they have decided to fight this new development.

In an attempt to prevent the Wherehouse and other chains from entering into the used CD business, four of the six major music conglomerates cut off millions of dollars in advertising money that the Wherehouse would normally use to promote artists.[16] Also, the major labels have threatened to cut the chains off from direct buying. A spokesman for the major labels said, "We will do anything we can to discourage the [used CD] business up to and including cutting [retailers] off if necessary."[17]

As a result of these actions, the Wherehouse has filed an antitrust lawsuit against those companies. According to the Wherehouse, they are simply responding to customer complaints about the high price of CDs. They are also attempting to enter a lucrative market where the profits are 100% on used CD sales. The major labels, however, are saying that the artist gets paid once when the initial CD is sold, but then he receives nothing after the CD is taped and then resold to the CD store, which then sells it to another customer, who buys the cheaper used CD instead of the same higher

[15] Ibid.
[16] *Los Angeles Times* (July 23, 1993), p. D1.
[17] *Billboard* (Mar. 20, 1993), p. 84.

priced new CD. Essentially, the business begins to resemble a rental business where the artist is not paid after the first transaction occurs.[18]

The Wherehouse has responded to these criticisms by stating that so far 75% of the credits for resales have been spent on new CD sales.[19] But, that may simply be because the Wherehouse has only been buying used CDs for a few months and has not built up a sufficient inventory of used product yet. At the Wherehouse near my home, I have observed that the space devoted to used CDs has more than doubled since the 75% figure was quoted in the March *Billboard* article. And of course, any retail space devoted to used CDs comes at the expense of space that could be devoted to new product. All stores do, however, separate the CDs into separate sections of old and new—never are they side by side. Undoubtedly, this separate arrangement was influenced by the record companies.

The concern here for the small retailer is that the large chains will advance into the used CD business. If that should happen the competition would undoubtedly shake out the inefficient retailers.

On the other hand, if the court rules against the Wherehouse, it could be a blessing to the small CD stores as they would not have to worry about competition from the large chains—the used business would be their exclusive domain.

Obviously, since the CD practically never wears out, the used market is a very important and growing business. It is entirely possible that a majority of the millions of CDs sold in this country over the last 10 years will eventually be resold to small CD stores. If that turns out to be the case, then the used CD business will be a very good business opportunity. It is no wonder that the Wherehouse wants to get into the used market.

Small CD Stores

Small CD stores are another source of competition. Currently there are about 200 used CD stores in the greater Los Angeles area.[20] However, since they are scattered across the county, it is unlikely that most of them pose a threat to the proposed Long Beach store. The nearest independent used CD store is located about 8 miles from the proposed Bixby Knolls location. This is too far away to be of much concern to this market plan.

The fact that there are so many used CD stores in Los Angeles shows how viable the business can be. Some independents that specialize in used CDs have done so well that they have become chains. Record City, based in Las Vegas, Nevada, for example, has grown from five stores in 1990 to 11 stores this year.[21]

Mail-Order Competition

According to a recent article in the *Los Angeles Times,* music buyers are gradually buying more of their music through mail order. This is not a surprising trend as "throughout the '80s, U.S. mail-order sales grew at an annual rate of 10%."[22] In 1992, about 11% of music purchases were through mail order compared with 7% in 1988. Tape or record club sales also grew to 23% in 1992 from 19% in 1988. This growth largely came at the expense of the record stores, which suffered a decline to 62% in 1992 from 70% in 1988.[23]

Three of the six major record labels, Sony, Capital/EMI, and the Warner Music group, are currently involved in mail order through 800-numbers, which is a different approach than the CD clubs.[24] Some operations offer the consumer the ability to call a 900-number to hear excerpts from the catalog for 99 cents a minute.[25]

The labels are also trying direct marketing of specific titles. For example, "Capital took half-page ads in *Modern Maturity* magazine for its Frank Sinatra boxed set. 'We're having incredible results,' says Lou Mann, senior VP of sales for Capital. 'That's our first real attempt to go direct to the consumer that will probably not go to the record store. You rarely find people of 55-plus in Tower Record."[26]

"The Sound Exchange" mail-order unit is a joint venture operation of Sony Corp. and Time

---

[18] Ibid.
[19] Ibid.
[20] Ibid.
[21] Ibid.
[22] *Billboard* (Jan. 18, 1992), p. 49.
[23] *Los Angeles Times* (July 23, 1993), p. D1.
[24] Ibid.
[25] *Billboard* (Jan. 18, 1992), p. 49.
[26] Ibid.

Warner Inc. which has a mailing list of about 1 million people culled from upscale magazine subscriber lists. Basically, this publication is aimed at ages 35 and older, with an annual income above $50,000 a year. Currently, however, these mail-order operations typically sell at a premium over discount prices at a CD store. For example, a CD which sells for $12 to $14 at the Wherehouse, sells for $17 in the mail-order catalog (not including tax and shipping and handling charges).[27]

Rhino Records, a major reissue record label and distributor, utilizes direct mailings to its customers each quarter to distribute an extensive mail-order catalog. Another company that relies exclusively on mail order is Mosaic Records. They specialize exclusively in the Jazz reissue market and most of their sales are generated from favorable magazine reviews and word of mouth.

The CD retailers have also experimented with direct marketing efforts. Tower Records has an in-store magazine, *Pulse!* which contains an 800-number for consumers to call to order directly from Tower.[28]

For now though, many of these direct marketing efforts seem to be just testing the water. Obviously, for a certain limited segment of the population, the convenience of mail order outweighs the two- or three-week delay in receiving the product and the higher price. While this segment has clearly grown recently at the expense of the walk-in sales at CD stores, it is not clear that it will grow significantly more in the future considering the high prices charged for the product. It is also not clear that the mail-order business could cut prices to be more competitive and remain profitable because of the high cost of shipping and handling. At Warner Brothers, a key executive said, "going through the retail market is the most profitable way to sell music,' He maintains that—even though the company is charging list price—it is more expensive to ship, handle bill, and advertise a cassette or CD directly to the customer than to sell it via retail stores."[29] This same executive also said, "The only reason to get into involved in direct marketing is with

the idea of reaching people who care about music but don't shop at retail—and we think that the population is out there in significant numbers."[30]

Department Stores

The CD marketing plans of department stores, such as the Broadway or May Company, appear to be unaffected by the activities of the Wherehouse and other large record stores as they tend to treat CDs and tapes as a side commodity that is fairly profitable, but perhaps not very important. Their sales approach has not changed over the years and they continue to offer the same limited selections of hit records at prices slightly higher than the chain stores. Their selection is extremely limited and prices are not very competitive.

Distribution Situation

The proposed CD store is a walk-in business where customers have to come to the store to buy CDs. It is possible to conduct some business over the phone to special order requested titles, but the customer would still have to pick up the order at the store.

Based on a 100% markup for used CDs, the small retailer would have to sell roughly 16,000 to 17,000 used CDs each year from walk-in business to achieve the gross income figures noted in the projected Income Statement (see Section VII). This means that on average at least about 330 used CDs need to be sold each week (this does not take into account the number of new CDs, cassettes, and other products that must also be sold).

Sources of used CDs are walk-in customers and cutout sales from the record companies and distributors. Cutouts are CDs that are sold by record companies at lower than new cost because of overstock or discontinued titles. The cutouts are typically identified by a small hole drilled into the CD jewel case to distinguish them from new CDs. Obviously, the record companies wouldn't want low-margin cutouts sold as new product as that practice would cut into the more profitable sales of new product.

---

[27] *Los Angeles Times* (July 23, 1993), p. D1.
[28] *Billboard* (Jan. 18, 1992), p. 49.
[29] Ibid.

[30] Ibid.

The following is a list of Compact Disc manufacturers and distributors:

A & M Records, 1416 N. La Brea, Los Angeles, CA 90028, (213)469-2411

Atlantic Recording Corp., 75 Rockefeller Plaza, New York, NY 10019, (212)484-6000

The Benson Co., 365 Great Circle Rd., Nashville, TN 37228, (615)742-6800

CBS Records Group, 51 W. 52nd St., New York, NY 10019, (212)975-4321

California Records, P.O. Box 6367, Glendale, CA 91205-0367, (818)246-8228

Capital Record, Inc., 1750 Vine, Hollywood, CA 90028, (213)462-6252

City Hall Records, 15 Tiburon St., San Rafael, CA 94901, (415)457-9080

City One Stop, P.O. Box 58900, Los Angeles, CA 90058, (213)234-3336

Eastern Pacific, 6325 De Soto Ave., Suite J, Woodland Hills, CA 91367-2681, (818)884-2234

Important Records, 1830 W. 208th St., Torrance, CA 90501, (213)212-0801

Jem Records, 18629 Topham St., Reseda, CA 91355, (818)996-6754

MCA, Inc., 100 Universal City Plaza, Universal City, CA 91608, (818)777-1000

Motown Record Corp., 6255 Sunset Blvd., Los Angeles, CA 90028, (213)468-3500

Pacific Coast, 9535 Cozycroft Ave., Chatsworth, CA 91311, (818)709-3640

Polygram Records, Inc., 810 Seventh Ave., New York, NY 10019, (212)333-8000

Pyramid Distributors, 1577 Barry Ave., Los Angeles, CA 90025, (213)207-2944

The Shelby Singleton Corp., 3106 Belmont Blvd., Nashville, TN 37212, (615)385-1960

Star Song Records, 2223 Strawberry Village, Pasadena, TX 77502, (713)484-5505

Systematic, 1331 Folsom St., San Francisco, CA 94103, (415)431-9377

USS&M, P.O. Box 4372, Panorama City, CA 91412, (818)901-1331

Vanguard Recording Society, 71 West 23rd St., New York, NY 10010, (212)255-7732

Warner Brothers Records, 3300 Warner Blvd., Burbank, CA 91510, (818)846-9090

Macroenvironment Issues

Home Taping Issues

An understanding of the issue of consumer home audio and video taping rights and the concerns of software manufacturers to protect their copyrights is very important to anyone entering into this business. This complex controversy involves economic, legal, philosophical, marketing, and technological issues. On its simplest terms, it is a classic case of consumer rights versus big business profits. The record industry claims it is losing significant revenues each year from unauthorized pirating of copyrighted software materials while the consumer complains that he is being hindered in his legal right to copy for personal use those materials he has already paid for. The CD stores will ultimately lose significant sales if consumers are taping their friends' CDs instead of buying them.

From a historical viewpoint, the introduction of new technology has always resulted in controversy and inevitable changes in the home entertainment marketplace. For example, the arrival of television during the 1950s was cause for consumer celebration while the movie industry complained about declining revenues. The consumer could now stay at home and watch movies for free. In response, the motion picture industry countered with 3-D movies, drive-in theaters, and even initially refused to make TV programming or sell their old movies.[31] In later years, broadcast television, in turn, was placed on the defensive as the coming of age for cable television in the 1970s meant lower profits for the broadcasters. These same patterns have been repeated in recent years with CDs and digital tape recorders as will be shown.

The relatively recent arrival of the videotape recorder and a Supreme Court ruling in favor of its use has had a significant impact on virtually every aspect of the television and, indirectly, the music industries. Television

---

[31] *Forbes* (Nov. 3, 1986), p. 206.

executives, for example, point to declining revenues and blame videotape recorders. The movie industry, however, seized the opportunity to sell their movies in video format to the consumer. In addition, having grown accustomed to this new source of revenue, the industry now fears declining sales from tape pirating and they have introduced a copy guard system called "Macrovision" to prevent it.[32] Further complicating matters is the recent introduction of Super VHS and HI-band 8 tape machines which offer resolution exceeding even broadcast quality.

These same issues are mirrored in the prerecorded music business. In the early 1970s, cassette tape decks first gained widespread popularity. Up until that point record executives and retailers were largely unconcerned with tape recording. The existing reel-to-reel format was expensive, bulky, and did not significantly affect record earnings. The cassette deck, however, was compact and was substantially less costly. The fact that it could be placed in an automobile also contributed to its eventual widespread popularity. Cassette tape initially was developed for Dictaphones but was quickly adapted as a musical storage medium with the invention of Dolby circuits in the late 1960s. The Dolby process largely eliminated annoying tape hiss and allowed the cassette player to be marketed as a high fidelity stereo component. The advent of Dolby c, an enhancement of the original Dolby b circuit, and the introduction of dbx noise reduction has further enhanced the cassette player's image as rivaling the best reel-to-reel decks in sound quality.

The cassette deck greatly worried record executives in the 1970s and 1980s as LP record sales declined in direct relationship to a substantial increase in blank tape sales. It was assumed that consumers were taping record albums from friends rather than buying the albums themselves. The record industry has long advocated a royalty tax on blank tape sales (see discussion in the section "Royalty Tax on Tape Sales") to remedy this situation.[33] Consumers, however, claimed they were only taping off records they had purchased earlier and wanted the tapes for personal use in the car or just to record the particular songs they like off an album. As it turned out, the record companies adapted to the new format and began selling prerecorded cassette tapes and made plenty of money from this former threat.

The introduction of the digitally-encoded compact disc (CD) has just about killed LP record sales, but this has obviously helped rather than hindered overall music industry revenues as consumers bought high-margin CDs rather than records and have even replaced their worn LPs with CDs. CDs are based on digital technology, which is a superior recording medium to the older analog system, and the music industry was grateful for the shot in the arm these CD sales provided.

The record industry is not happy though about the latest digital advance which involves tape recorders and digital audiotape (DAT). The arrival of Japanese DAT recorders has the industry very worried again since these machines are capable of making essentially perfect copies of CDs which in turn are nearly perfect copies of the master tapes themselves. The potential threat of DAT recorders is that anyone could turn out thousands of master tape quality recordings from a single CD. Actually, advanced cassette recorders which are almost as good as the digital recorders have been around for about 10 years, so this "new" threat of digital recorders is not really a new issue.

One solution proposed in the past by the music industry, and likely to be resuscitated again at some point in the future, was an encoding system in the recorders which would prevent copying of specially encoded software. A bill requiring such a system was introduced in Congress in the late 1980s. However, after extensive hearings and publicity on the matter, the idea was rejected by the Congress. A similar bill was also rejected in the California State Assembly.[34]

The introduction of new technology has always proven to be a double-edged sword in both the audio and video industries. On the one hand, it has allowed consumers to acquire high

---

[32] *Video Review* (Dec. 1986), p. 51.
[33] *Business Week* (Nov. 18, 1985), p. 45.

[34] *Los Angeles Times* (Aug. 18, 1987), p. 18.

quality tape recorders which are capable of making perfect copies of copyrighted materials. But, technology has also provided manufacturers with the ability to attempt to protect their copyrights with encoding processes and antitaping chips. Consumers say this is an infringement of their Supreme Court supported right to tape.

The BetaMax Decision

Both the film and music industries have always attempted to stop or control the spread of home taping. In the case of video, the president of the Motion Picture Association of America, Jack Valenti, "portrayed the VCR—and the VCR user as a parasite on the movie business. 'Even as home video becomes an important means of recouping production costs, back-to-back copying displaces sales of videocassettes and discs eroding our revenue base,' Valenti told the Senate, calling VCR copying a 'malevolent threat to the feature film industry.' He suggested Congress require modification of VCRs that would make them incapable of certain types of recording."[35] This plan was very similar to the approach used against DAT recorders. Fortunately for the consumer, the Congress rejected this request. The industry claims that professional piracy around the world costs the studios approximately $1 billion each year, including losses in the United States amounting to more than $200 million. These statistics, however, have nothing to do with consumers taping for their own private use at home.[36]

Within a year of Sony's introduction of the BetaMax VCR, Universal Studio and Disney went to court, charging that home recording was an infringement of their movie copyrights. During this time, both the video and audio industries also pursued legislation in Congress which would levy a special royalty tax on VCRs and blank tapes. If this was successful, of course, the next step would logically be to do the same with audio-related recording tape. This income would be divided up among the copyright holders. Congress, however, never acted upon this proposed legislation. Some years later, in 1984, the landmark BetaMax

decision was handed down by the Supreme Court and home videotaping of any TV programs received over the air was declared legal.[37] It also had the effect of protecting consumers in their practice of taping music.

But the video and music industries have not yet given up. Since they cannot prevent the public from owning tape recorders, they have decided to use encoding devices to discourage their use.

On the video front, for example, Macrovision-encoded videocassette tapes first appeared in early 1985. An ill-fated "CopyGuard" system had been tried earlier and was discarded before it got off the ground because of the adverse effect it had on picture quality. The Macrovision process is supposedly not noticeable until a copy of it is made. The duped copy will typically suffer from brightness variations, a darkened picture, loss of color, loss of vertical hold, and picture breakup. The system is currently used by at least seven studios and costs about 10 cents a tape to process.[38]

In order to combat Macrovision, at least two companies developed add-on stabilizer boxes which they claim will defeat the encoding process. In anticipation of this development, however, Macrovision executives claim they have taken out patents on all the possible defeat processes. Undoubtedly these companies will go to court over these patents.[39] Should a similar type system be adapted to prerecorded music, it should be expected that someone will come up with a similar defeat type box. There is definitely a market for black boxes that defeat encoding efforts.[40]

The Music Industry and DAT Recorders

The music industry has attempted to introduce a bill in Congress to require an antitaping chip to be placed in all DAT recorders imported from Japan into the United States. Unless these recorders had this chip, their importation would be held up for one year. This idea gained further impetus from President Reagan's State of the Union address that year when he came out in favor of this type of legislation. The

---

[35] *Video Review* (Aug. 1987), p. 33.
[36] Ibid.
[37] Ibid.
[38] *Video Review* (Dec. 1986), p. 52.
[39] Ibid., p. 174.
[40] Ibid.

recording industry paraded several well-known entertainers before the Senate and House committees, including Emmylou Harris and Mary Travers, in an attempt to get this bill passed. These women argued that unrestricted DAT recorders would cut record industry revenues, slash royalties, and mean less money for the development of new artists. The music industry feels that with DAT machines anyone can duplicate their software and sell it for less, effectively stealing revenues from the record industry.[41]

The difficulty with these arguments is that high quality cassette decks have been available for the last decade which are also capable of making near perfect copies of musical information. In addition, the music industry itself is responsible for making the master tapes available to the public in the form of CDs which are nearly perfect replicas. And the industry has certainly profited from the sales of these high-margin CDs. If the industry is not going to suffer as they claim from DAT recorder sales, why have they attacked DATs? Some analysts believe the music industry wants to hold up this new technology because the introduction of DATs will cut into profitable CD sales. The upshot is that prerecorded DATs could sell for as low as $8 versus the $15 currently charged for CDs. In addition, since CDs are relatively new in the marketplace, the industry wants to avoid causing consumer confusion by introducing yet another competing format.[42]

"Every time there's a new technology, the instant reaction is that it's a threat to the status quo," says Charles D. Ferris, former head of the FCC, now representing Japanese manufacturers. "What's happened historically is that in the end, it becomes a big new revenue source and a tremendous opportunity for the very people doing the complaining."[43] As small labels begin producing prerecorded DATs, the larger labels will be forced to follow suit in order to maintain market share. GRP Records, a small label, was one of the first to make their products available on DATs.[44]

Another argument against the DAT encoding process proposed is that it seriously degrades the sound quality of the recording it protects. The encoding process works in tandem with a "spoiler" chip installed in the DAT recorder. When this chip senses encoded signals in the source material, it records a blank for 25 seconds. The problem with this approach is that encoding the software involves removing a portion of the music at a certain frequency. While the Recording Industry Association (RIAA) maintains you can't hear the difference, others clearly disagree. Several consumer groups and artists, including Stevie Wonder and Herbie Hancock, are staggered by the prospect of tampering with music to any degree.[45] One reason that audiophiles flocked to CDs to begin with was the dream of a perfect machine playing perfect replicas of master tapes. A retreat from this ideal is not going to win any new converts in the audiophile community.

Yet another argument against encoding is that it may not be necessary as DAT technology has not yet been proven in the marketplace. Is it really a durable product? After all, it is well known that all magnetic tapes wear out eventually. "Some say if you play it a lot, it starts to go," says Doug Sax, the president of the Mastering Lab, in Los Angeles, "There's a lot of information in a small amount of space," he says. "Twenty plays on those tapes, and it might be good night. I don't know a teenager who doesn't play a new song 20 times. The RIAA doesn't want to do anything but present the bleakest picture—the format is perfect, nobody's going to buy anything anymore, they're going to tape it."[46]

Royalty Tax on Tape Sales

The real purpose of all the publicity over taping seems to be directed at gaining public awareness of the music and motion picture industry's purported woes in order to win support for what they really want—a royalty tax. Perhaps they will offer not to encode recordings if Congress will allow these royalties. This would add substantially to the cost of blank tape, which of course the consumer is expected to

[41] *Fortune* (June 9, 1986), p. 89.
[42] *Rolling Stone* (Sept. 10, 1987), p. 72.
[43] *Forbes* (Nov. 3, 1986), p. 206.
[44] *Rolling Stone* (Sept. 1987), p. 70.

[45] *Stereo Review* (Sept. 1987), p. 4.
[46] *Rolling Stone* (Sept. 10, 1987), p. 72.

bear. But why should a person who tapes for home use have to pay an additional royalty on something he has already paid for?

"When faced with a similar situation—widespread photocopying of their works—book and magazine publishers did not ask for a tax on photocopiers or blank paper. Instead they sought and won, a revised copyright law permitting them to charge copying fees . . . from major corporate and university libraries that copy in bulk. Individuals who copy for their own use were ignored."[47]

III. OPPORTUNITY AND ISSUE ANALYSIS

Opportunities

Used CDs

The opportunities for the small CD store include the tremendous growth and acceptance of the CD as a major music medium. Because the CD doesn't wear out and because millions have been sold over the last decade, the potential market of consumers who want to trade in their old CDs is growing all the time. The relatively high price of new CDs ($10–$16 retail) versus the used CDs ($5–$10) automatically creates a market for the used CDs. The 100% markup on the used CD trade-ins guarantees a significant profit for the store. The threat, outlined in detail elsewhere in this plan, is that the large chains will enter the used business, thereby creating more competition.

Mail-Order CD Clubs

An area of indirect competition is the direct mail-order business from the record clubs. The two major clubs are Columbia House and BMG (RCA). Basically, this is how they work; you send in $1 for six or seven CDs up front and agree to buy six or seven more within three years at "regular club prices" (this means the highest possible retail price you would pay in a store). You also pay about $2 to $3 for shipping and handling and taxes. After completing membership requirements you can qualify for a 'two for the price of one'

type of arrangement. On average, after completion of the program, the consumer gets a slightly lower price per CD in comparison to the cost at a retail store.

The downside for retailers is the increased competition these operations cause (they currently have about 20% of the market). However, these programs are actually a mixed blessing for the small retailer because the up-front "free" CDs are often sold by consumers to the CD stores as used thereby creating a steady source of inventory for the retailer. Often they are sold without the protective packaging removed which allows the product to be resold for more money as "new" or at least as "never played." "Record clubs are one of main sources of supply for the used-CD business. Kids buy eight CDs for a penny, and then can trade them into used CD stores for $3 dollars each."[48]

The threat is that instead of buying CDs from the retail outlets, and from the small retailer who sells used CDs in particular, the consumer will mail-order directly from the record companies. The advantage that the CD store has is that the urge to buy a CD and play it now is only satisfied by the store sale. Many consumers don't want to wait two or three weeks for a mail order to arrive.

Also, the very latest CD releases are not offered by mail order until about two months after they hit the CD stores. A large percentage of CD sales are from new releases. Also, in practice, many people tire of having to pay for a stamp and having to fill out a card each month to mail back to the record club. Turnover in these clubs is fairly high. Of the dozen people I personally know who joined these clubs, each one stayed in the club only long enough to fulfill their requirement and then got out. The clubs' selection of CDs is not very extensive, and after the 15 or more CDs are bought, the consumer finds it difficult to locate any additional CDs that he wants.

Import CDs and "Bootlegs"

A novel and interesting niche is the grey market or "bootleg" CDs. While commonly assumed by the general public to be illegal, in

---

[47] *Business Week* (Nov. 18, 1985), p. 45.

[48] *Billboard* (Mar. 20, 1993), p. 84.

most cases they are not.[49] People are often confused by the term "bootleg" and assume it is the same as a "pirate"—these are very different items. A pirate is an illegal copy of a legitimately released CD, which is an attempt to fool the consumer into believing that it is a legitimate product.

Pirates were a big problem for the record companies with LPs. For example, a former buyer at Music Plus told me that it is commonly known in the industry that one of the biggest record sellers in the 1970s, *Saturday Night Fever,* was so heavily pirated that an estimated one out of four copies sold in the country was not legitimate. Even the experts couldn't tell the real from the fake.

Bootlegs are CDs that are not commercially available from the record labels. Sometimes these are alternate studio recordings that are commonly referred to as outtakes. For example, recently many of the Beatles' outtakes have become available in perfect quality on bootlegs.[50] There is a huge market for this material. Perhaps 100,000 copies have been sold in Europe. More often, though, bootlegs are recordings of live material that is not available to the consumer in any other format.

Record companies do not lose revenue from bootleg CDs because even though they usually possess the master tapes, they do not offer them for sale, which is their choice. If they did sell them, the "bootlegs" would then become "pirates" and thus would be subject to legal action.

In Europe, bootleg CDs are perfectly legal and furthermore are openly sold next to "legitimate product." And because they are legal in Europe, if they are imported to this country there is some question as to whether or not they are illegal in this country.[51]

In the United States, it is absolutely not illegal to own bootlegs; however, it is illegal to import any CDs that are already available domestically because of recent record industry lobby efforts. The record companies do not want cheaper foreign subsidiary-produced CDs to compete with higher costing domestic CDs in this country. If that happened, the domestic market would lose some of its profitability. However, once in this country, imports are widely distributed and are legal to own and to sell.[52]

The real reason the average consumer doesn't see much of this product in this country is that the record companies are very much opposed to their existence and will refuse to sell product to any store that openly carries them. There is a small, but thriving business at swap meets and small CD stores for this type of product. A small used CD store that doesn't buy product directly from the record companies doesn't have to worry about pressure from the record companies. Most import CDs are perfectly legal to sell and generally have a high markup—they are bought from import distributors for about $10 to $12 and sold for $25 to $30.

Audiotapes

While the main draw to the store will be the CDs, tapes are a related medium that commands a large share of the prerecorded music market and cannot be ignored. Some consumers buy only tapes; others buy both. While used tapes can also be sold, because they are not as durable as CDs, few consumers are interested in them. As a result most small retailers do not bother to sell used tapes. New tapes, however, could be sold with about the same markup (about 70% on average) as the CDs. In addition, blank audiotape can also be sold at the same markup.

Videotapes

Music videos can be sold along with CDs as a speciality item. Indeed many CD stores (including Tower Records) place music videos directly above the CD bins of the related artists. Video is also a 70% markup item. This is a natural extension of the CD business because of the musical tie-in on cable television shows such as MTV and Video One.

The video rental business, however, is a different business than the prerecorded music sales business. It attracts a somewhat different clientele and requires a major commitment to retail space and volume. A much larger store

[49] *International CD Exchange Newsletter* (Feb. 1990), p. 5.
[50] *International CD Exchange Newsletter* (Nov. 1988), p. 1.
[51] *International CD Exchange Newsletter* (Dec. 1989), p. 4.
[52] *International CD Exchange Newsletter* (Mar. 1990), p. 4.

would be needed to accommodate both the CD and video inventory. Because of the guaranteed walk-in traffic flow from the video rentals, CD sales would be enhanced. However, the drawback is that for the two businesses to be successfully mixed, a much larger retail operation would be required than we are considering here. The combined CD and video stores are really the domain of the large CD store chains such as the Wherehouse and Tower Records. Not many examples of successful independent CD and video combination stores can be found in the marketplace. This is due in part to the additional staff required and the lack of the ability to rotate inventory between various locations (customers want more variety after a few months than a small video store can offer) that the large chain competitors can easily offer. Because of these drawbacks, the smaller CD retailer would do better to focus all of his resources on just one primary business—prerecorded music with some small portion of the business devoted to music videos and blank videotape.

Digital Recording Mediums

In addition to digital audiotape (DAT), which was introduced in the marketplace about five years ago, there are two other new digital mediums. Sony has introduced a MiniDisc and Phillips has introduced a Digital Compact Cassette format.[53] None of these formats is compatible with the others, and they compete with each other for market share. Each has prerecorded tapes offered for sale and each can digitally record music. As of this point in time, none has a clear lock on the market and none has significant market share. The retailer can safely ignore them for now. Should any of these formats gain widespread acceptance, the retailer should begin to sell them in the store.

CD-ROM

CD-ROM is a computer-based system that is connected to a PC. It can store about as much information on a disc as 450 floppy discs. It is estimated that there were about 600,000 to 800,000 CD-ROM drives in American homes by the end of 1992.[54] Multimedia publisher

Compton's NewMedia is attempting to expand its sales of CD-ROM products to CD stores. "In regards to record stores, Compton's VP of marketing and sales, Thomas R. McGrew, says, 'They have the interest [in CD-ROM] but don't know how to position it. I think they can do more than computer stores. They have more space, more traffic, better locations, and there are more of them. And in the consumer's mind, it's just another shiny disc."[55] Three titles were targeted specifically for the CD stores; "Jazz: a Multimedia History" ($99.95), "The Multimedia Grammy Awards: 1992 edition" ($69.95), and "The Billboard History of Rock 'N Roll" (price not set).[56] "Compton's is offering a variety of co-op advertising programs and market development funds" to the participating CD store outlets as well as on-site training programs.[57] Currently the only stores to carry CD-ROM in Los Angeles are Tower Record outlets.

This is an area of opportunity for the small retailer that should not be overlooked. The CD stores could have advanced into the computer software business some years back, for example, and many are now sorry they didn't have more foresight.

Books

Another area that CD stores can get into are music-related books. Like music videos, this is a natural tie-in to the CD business. For the first time, Time Warner recently cross-promoted a new book along with the artist's new CD release. Madonna's new book, *Sex*, was sold in CD stores alongside her *Erotica* CD.[58]

Electronic Delivery Systems

Blockbuster is attempting to launch a new product that will definitely affect the CD marketplace. "Soundsation is simple in concept. Customers would be able to preview their choices and to access a database that would send selections—either a single album or a mix—to the store via a bank of dedicated phone lines. At that point, the data would be

---

[53] *Stero Review* (Oct. 1991), pp. 54–58.
[54] *Billboard* (Sept. 5, 1992), p. 1.
[55] Ibid.
[56] Ibid.
[57] Ibid.
[58] *Billboard* (Oct. 24, 1992), p. 12.

recorded onto a blank CD very rapidly."[59] Blockbuster estimates . . . "that some 43% of shoppers who seek a specific recording leave stores empty-handed, resulting in lost sales worth at least $1 billion a year."[60]

While the potential for such an operation is great, there are some hurdles to overcome. Currently, blank recordable CD discs cost about $40 to $50 each, and licensing and royalties costs also have to be worked out. Also, it is questionable that the record labels are going to do anything overnight that will upset their currently profitable distribution systems to the chains.[61] It is too early to tell if this product is really viable. It may not turn out to be profitable. It is interesting to note that a similar cassette-based operation called Personics recently declared bankruptcy after two years in the marketplace.[62]

Records

Records have been completely eclipsed by CDs as the most important prerecorded music medium. The market for records is now in the hands of a few collector-type niche stores.

Magazines

Magazines that are music related should be carried in the display racks as this will also draw some customers into the store. *Rolling Stone* and *CD Review* are two examples of popular titles.

Issues

Southern California Economy

It is important to analyze whether or not to go into the CD store business at this time. The national economy has moved out of the recession, but Southern California still lags behind. It is widely reported in the press that the California economy is projected to improve in 1994. This may be an excellent opportunity to start a business while long-term leases are historically low and many competitive businesses have departed from the area. Certainly

it is far more prudent to be starting a business just after a recession than to start one going into a recession.

CDs Are a Growth Industry

It should also be noted that the CD retail business is very much a growth industry, "What recession? The recorded music industry has the boomers to thank for a great year [1992]. The sound recording market grew over 15 percent to $9 billion in 1992, based on the shipment of $895.5 million units of records, tapes, CDs, and music videos. According to the Recording Industry Association of America, Inc. (RIAA)."[63]

The Consolidation Threat

What about the long-term issues such as the used CD business and consolidations in the industry? If the courts rule that the Wherehouse can go into the used CD business, then the small retailer must consider that the competition will intensify. The same thing happened with the record business 20 years ago when the Wherehouse first got into the business.

Before that time consumers had two basic choices, buy from a small mom and pop store or go to a department store. The mom and pop store would usually focus on just records and tapes. For these stores, location was the key to success. In the early 1970s, however, some consolidation activity began in earnest. In Southern California, the Wherehouse chain, for example, became very prominent and its success forced a gradual shakeout of many of the mom and pop stores which continues today. The Wherehouse's advantage over the smaller stores is obvious: better locations (often in the malls) larger inventory and selection, earlier receipt of new chart-busting records, major advertising campaigns, and lower pricing often based on volume discounts from the major record companies. The Wherehouse's growth in Southern California was tempered by the growth of other chains such as Tower Records and Music Plus. Some additional consolidation between the chains occurred when Music Plus bought out Liquorish Pizza in the late 1990s.

---

[59] *Los Angeles Times* (Jul. 23, 1993), p. D1.
[60] Ibid.
[61] Ibid.
[62] Ibid.

[63] *Entertainment* (June 15, 1993), p. 6.

The advent of video in the 1980s caused a new type of competition and opportunity for the small record stores. However, the same type of consolidation that had occurred in the record retail industry began to occur with video. Large exclusive tape rental chains such as Blockbuster and record and tape chains like the Wherehouse began to dominate the marketplace. Currently, virtually all small retail operations focus on either the CD or the video businesses, but not both.

Gradually over the last decade, many of the small retailers were shaken out. The video business followed the same pattern. Initially, there were just small retail stores until large chains like Blockbuster gained market share. On the bright side, it should be noted that hundreds of small independent CD stores and video stores in the greater Los Angeles area have survived by establishing a niche such as the used CD market or by focusing on musical preferences for jazz or blues, for example.

Other Long-Term Issues

It is possible that direct delivery systems (i.e., electronic transfer of prerecorded music directly to the home, bypassing the retail outlets) will be developed. "Some observers believe electronic home delivery of music software could be technologically feasible by the end of this decade."[64] However until then, "direct delivery systems are still a thing of the future . . . until the installed base is in place to accept music over the wire—whether it be a coaxial, fiber optic or phone cable—no one will know exactly how record stores will be affected by direct selling."[65]

Another suggestion the industry is discussing is the sale of the top 50 CDs in vending machines.[66] No one really knows how this would work, but it is yet another example of how different ideas are constantly popping up within this dynamic industry. Anyone who enters into this business will have to keep abreast of the latest ideas in order to remain competitive.

---

[64] *Billboard* (Jan. 18, 1992), p. 49.
[65] *Billboard* (Mar. 13, 1993), p. 100.
[66] *Billboard* (Jan. 18, 1992), p. 49.

IV. OBJECTIVES

Financing Objectives

The main financing objective is to earn $48,000 per year and to increase that profit by 3% to 4% per year.

Generally, a rule of thumb is that retail rental space should not exceed 5% to 10% of the business's gross income. This means that based on a 1,200 square foot location renting for $1.35 sq. ft./mo., the retailer should generate at least $97,200 to $194,400 per year. Total gross sales in the first year are $121,819, which results in a net profit after taxes of approximately $48,021. Each year thereafter, the net profit is projected to increase by a minimum of 4.7% to 4.9% (see Section VII for detail).

Net present value of the initial investment in the CD store should at least exceed the value of the same investment in the stock market or other less risky investments. Based on an initial investment of $65,000 to $86,000 and a 5% return, the net present value of this investment after five years is expected to be between $178,000 and $199,000.

Marketing Objectives

The main objective for year one is to sell more than 16,425 used CDs per year or 315 per week. New CD sales are projected at 7,300 per year or 140 per week. Cassettes are expected to sell at 3,650 per year or 70 per week. Please refer to Section VII for the detail of the projected income statement for five years.

It must be emphasized that the estimates presented in this plan on sales levels generated from the CD store are on the conservative side. It is entirely possible that significantly higher profits could be earned should (1) a marketing strategy be found that greatly improves sales and or (2) the economy improves significantly in Southern California.

V. MARKETING STRATEGY

Advertising and promotions should be focused on identifying potential customers and persuading them to buy from the CD store. This could be initially accomplished by a survey distributed during a grand opening sales promotion. Flyers could be printed up that include the survey on the back (see examples on. These handouts could be given in the shopping center outside the high-volume anchor store (supermarket) and also hand-delivered to houses in the local neighborhood.

If the consumer fills out the survey (which only takes a minute to complete), then he or she will receive a credit good for a dollar off up to five CDs in the store. The survey would get the customer's name, address, age, and musical preference by category, also the name of three of their favorite artists. Then, if they buy 10 more CDs in the next two months, they will get credits good for two free used CDs.

The key to this marketing campaign is that the collected surveys will serve as a basis for a customer mailing list (supplemented by an in-store sign-up sheet). The survey will help the owner determine who the potential customers are and what they want to buy. It is believed that the survey will be completed by most people who are interested in CDs because of the savings promised when the survey is brought into the store.

In the store at various locations, CD players are set up so that each plays a different new CD release through consumer-accessible headphones. This way the customers can selectively hear the latest CDs before they buy them. This set up is currently being tried at several of the Wherehouse stores in Long Beach. The CD players are paid for as a promotional item by the record labels. However, the small CD store would probably have to pay for this equipment. About five CD players (about $150 each) would be preferred. In addition, two or more CD players are necessary for consumers who want to listen to used CDs before they buy them.

Place full-page ads in local newspapers (see example) outlining sales campaigns.

Differentiate trade-in as cash or credit—this is a very important concept. Cash is one dollar less than the consumer would get for a credit—obviously the retailer is better off if the consumer chooses this option. If a credit slip is issued, the retailer benefits if the consumer loses it or forgets to redeem a CD with it. If the credit is used to purchase CDs then the retailer is essentially trading for two or even three CDs

versus one CD sold—a cheap way to build up inventory. (See ad on page 9·20.)

Format for Survey

Fill out this survey and get a coupon worth one dollar off each of the next five CDs you buy from the Compact Disc Store. Just one coupon per customer.

Name _____

Address _____

Musical Preference—please check just one or two:

_____ Rock

_____ Pop

_____ Black/Dance

_____ Country

_____ Classical

_____ Gospel

_____ Jazz

How many *new* CDs did you buy last month?_____

How many last year?_____

How many *used* CDs did you buy last month?_____

How many last year?_____

Please name two or three of your favorite artists:

_____

How did you hear about this store?_____

How often do you shop at this shopping center (how many times per month)? _____

Where do you usually buy your CDs? _____

Why?_____

VI. ACTION PROGRAMS

Immediately after the store is leased and stocked with CDs, the preceding marketing strategies should be implemented. The expected costs for the first three months (including the grand opening sales promotion) are as follows (please see the detail of start-up expenses in Section VII);

- Ads in the local newspapers—$500.
- Flyers—5,000 at about $50–$75.
- Distribution of flyers door to door—$400.
- Direct mailings—$1,000.

The Compact Disc Store
Specializing in Used CDs

Beatles CD Sale – The best Rock 'N Roll at the lowest prices

All Beatles single CDs are now $10.99
All Beatles double CDs are now $19.99

All John Lennon single CDs are now $10.99
All John Lennon double CDs are now $19.99

All Paul McCartney single CDs are now $10.99
All Paul McCartney double CDs are now $19.99

All George Harrison single CDs are now $10.99
All George Harrison double CDs are now $19.99

All Ringo Starr single CDs are now $10.99
All Ringo Starr double CDs are now $19.99

Thousands of Used (and new) CDs
We pay cash for used CDs

Bixby Knolls Shopping Center
4400 Atlantic Blvd.
310-426-0000

VII. FINANCIAL STATEMENTS

Compact Disc Store
Income Statement

	1994	1995	1996	1997	1998
Number of items sold:					
Used CDs	16,425	17,000	17,595	18,211	18,848
New CDs	7,300	7,556	7,820	8,094	8,377
Cassettes	3,650	3,778	3,910	4,047	4,188
Books	1,825	1,889	1,955	2,023	2,094
Music Videos	730	756	782	809	838
Blank Tapes	3,650	3,778	3,910	4,047	4,188
CD-ROM & Other	365	378	391	405	419
Net Sales:					
Used CDs	$ 147,825	$ 152,999	$ 158,354	$ 163,896	$ 169,633
New CDs	94,900	98,222	101,659	105,217	108,900
Cassettes	29,200	30,222	31,280	32,375	33,508
Books	27,375	28,333	29,325	30,351	31,413
Music Videos	14,600	15,111	15,640	16,187	16,754
Blank Tapes	10,950	11,333	11,730	12,140	12,565
CD-ROM & Other	14,600	15,111	15,640	16,187	16,754
Total Net Sales	339,450	351,331	363,627	376,354	389,527
Cost of Goods Sold:					
Used CDs	73,913	76,499	79,177	81,948	84,816
New CDs	71,175	73,666	76,244	78,913	81,675
Cassettes	21,900	22,667	23,460	24,281	25,131
Books	20,531	21,250	21,994	22,763	23,560
Music Videos	10,950	11,333	11,730	12,140	12,565
Blank Tapes	8,213	8,500	8,797	9,105	9,424
CD-ROM & Other	10,950	11,333	11,730	12,140	12,565
Total COGS	217,631	225,248	233,132	241,292	249,737
Gross Profit/Revenues:					
Used CDs	73,913	76,499	79,177	81,948	84,816
New CDs	23,725	24,555	25,415	26,304	27,225
Cassettes	7,300	7,556	7,820	8,094	8,377
Books	6,844	7,083	7,331	7,588	7,853
Music Videos	3,650	3,778	3,910	4,047	4,188
Blank Tapes	2,738	2,833	2,932	3,035	3,141
CD-ROM & Other	3,650	3,778	3,910	4,047	4,188
Total Gross Profit/Revenues	121,819	126,082	130,495	135,063	139,790
G%A Expenses:					
Insurance	1,000	1,000	1,000	1,000	1,000
Lease/Rent Expense	21,600	21,600	21,600	21,600	21,600
Advertising	10,184	10,540	10,909	11,291	11,686
Utilities/Phone	100	100	100	100	100
Salaries	7,800	7,800	7,800	7,800	7,800
Supplies	500	500	500	500	500
Depreciation	600	600	600	600	600
Total Operating Expenses	41,784	42,140	42,509	42,891	43,286
Operating Income	80,035	83,942	87,986	92,172	96,504
Taxes	32,014	33,577	35,195	36,869	38,602
Net Profit	$ 48,021	$ 50,365	$ 52,792	$ 55,303	$ 57,902
Yr to Yr Net Profit Change		4.9%	4.8%	4.8%	4.7%

Compact Disc Store

Start-Up Expenses for the First Three Months

Items:		Range	
Insurance	$ 250	to	$ 500
Lease/Rent Expense	5,400	to	6,000
Utilities/Phone	100	to	200
Supplies	300	to	300
Initial Inventory	40,000	to	50,000
Equipment/Fixtures	6,000	to	10,000
Leasehold Improvements	5,000	to	8,000
Licenses/Taxes	50	to	150
Advertising & Grand Opening	2,000	to	3,000
Professional Services	200	to	300
Salaries	1,950	to	1,950
Depreciation	600	to	600
Total Operating Expenses	61,850	to	81,000
Operating Capital	3,000	to	5,000
Total Start-Up Expenses	$ 64,850	to	$ 86,000

VIII. CONTROLS

The main tracking mechanism to control the business would be to track the number of CDs sold per week. Any inventory system that is used should be able to keep track of these figures as well as for cassettes, books, and all other sales. Ideally, a barcode system should be used that would automatically keep track of sales and inventory as well. For promotional activities, this would be an invaluable tool to track how successful a particular advertising campaign was in promoting sales.

Another tracking mechanism would be the gross sales figures each week, which will provide feedback on how successful that week's marketing efforts were.

The store owner should carefully monitor customer traffic. The owner should consider closing the store during regularly observed periods of inactivity, thereby saving labor costs. For example, it may make more sense to close the store during a lull between 2 P.M. and 4 P.M. on the weekdays and instead maintain extended hours until midnight on Fridays and Saturdays.

In the event that sales fall below target for an extended period of time, the owner may want to redesign the survey and try another campaign. The owner should also consider cutting back the hours of the one or two part-time helpers or redeploying them outside the store armed with discount coupons to draw customers into the store. The part-time helpers should only be employed in the store during hours of peak activity when they are absolutely needed.

BIBLIOGRAPHY

"A Music Industry Bill That's Striking the Wrong Cord," *Business Week* (Nov. 18, 1985).

American Entrepreneur Association Business Manual No. X1308 (1987).

"An Open Conversation with Italian Bootlegger," *International CD Exchange Newsletter* (Dec. 1989).

"Beatle Bootlegs Have EMI Execs Puzzled," *International CD Exchange Newsletter* (Nov. 1988).

"Blockbuster May Bust Out Customized-CD Technology," *Billboard* (Jan. 23, 1993).

"Compton's Broadening Exposure Takes New CD-ROM Titles to Variety of Outlets," *Billboard* (Sept. 5, 1992).

"Digital Audio Tape: Issues and Answers," *Stereo Review* (Mar. 1987).

"Digital Audio Tape Recorders Cause New Stir," *Rolling Stone* (Jan. 29, 1987).

"Digital Decision," *Stereo Review* (Oct. 1991).

"Digital Dream, Digital Nightmare," *Forbes* (Nov. 3, 1986).

"Digital Hegemony," *High Fidelity* (Nov. 1986).

"Digital Home Taping Bill Stalls, Put on Rewind" *Los Angeles Times* (Aug. 19, 1987).

"Don't Tax My Tape," *Stereo Review* (Dec. 1985).

"Exec VP Horovitz on Tagging, Configurations & the Changing Environs of Retail," *Billboard* (Mar. 13, 1993).

"Former Foes Now in Musical Harmony," *Los Angeles Times* (July 23, 1993).

"Home Tapers Beware!" *Video Review* (Aug. 1987).

"Looking for the Jolly Roger," *High Fidelity* (May 1987).

"Major Labels Try Direct-Sales Rout—Tap Market via Mail Order," *Billboard* (Jan. 18, 1992).

"Majors Lash Out at Used-CD Biz," *Billboard* (Mar. 20, 1993).

"Marantz Recorder Causes Heavy Static in the Music World," *Los Angeles Times* (Aug. 18, 1987).

"Record Dealers Ask for 'Sex' Too," *Billboard* (Oct. 24, 1992).

"Record Executives Are on Pins and Needles," *Business Week* (Feb. 16, 1987).

"Retailers Have Piece of the Direct-Marketing Action, Too," *Billboard* (Jan. 18, 1992).

"RIAA, Customs Turning Up Heat on Illicit CDs," *International CD Exchange Newsletter* (Feb. 1990).

"Still a Major Market for Music" *Entertainment* (June 15, 1993).

"Swingin' Pig Raided, Busted for Beatles CDs," *International CD Exchange Newsletter* (March 1990).

"Tape Format Face-off," *High Fidelity* (Oct. 1985).

"The DAT Debate," *Stereo Review* (Sept. 1987).

"The Macrovision Mess," *Video Review* (Dec. 1986).

"The New Sound of Music," *U.S. News & World Report* (Jan. 26, 1987).

"The Quest for Perfect Sound," *New Republic* (Dec. 30, 1985).

"Topic No. 1—With a Bullet," *Los Angeles Times* (July 23, 1993).

"Pursuing Perfect Audio," *Science Digest* (May 1986).

"What is DAT, and Why Are the Record Companies Trying to Keep It from You?" *Rolling Stone* (Sept. 10, 1987).

"What's Next in Hi-Fi: Digital Tape Recorders," *Fortune* (June 9, 1986).

APPENDIX A

Sources of Additional Market Research

Following are more than 100 sources based on bibliographies but together by Lloyd M. DeBoer, Dean of the School of Business Administration at George Mason University, Fairfax, Virginia, and the Office of Management and Training of the SBA.

U.S. GOVERNMENT PUBLICATIONS

The publications in this section are books and pamphlets issued by federal agencies and listed under the issuing agency. Where availability of an individual listing is indicated by GPO (Government Printing Office), the publication may be ordered from the Superintendent of Documents, U.S. Government Printing Office, Washington, DC 20402. When ordering a GPO publication, give the title and series number of the publication, and name of agency. You may also order by phone by calling (202) 783-3238. Contact GPO for current prices.

Publications should be requested by the title and any number given from the issuing agency. Most libraries have some listings to identify currently available federal publications. Some keep a number of selected government publications for ready reference through the Federal Depository Library System.

American Statistics Index: A Comprehensive Guide and Index to the Statistical Publications of the United States Government. Washington, DC: Congressional Information Service, 1973–. Monthly, with annual cumulations. This is the most comprehensive index to statistical information generated by the federal agencies, committees of Congress, and special programs of the government. Approximately 7,400 titles of 500 government sources are indexed each year. The two main volumes are arranged by issuing breakdown, technical notes, and time period covered by publication. Separate index volume is arranged by subject and title and also includes the SIC code, the Standard Occupation Classification, and a list of SMSAs (standard metropolitan statistical areas).

Bureau of the Census
Department of Commerce
Washington, DC 20233

Contact the Public Information Office for a more complete listing of publications. The following is a sample:

Catalog of United States Census Publications. Published monthly with quarterly and annual cumulations. A guide to census data and reports. This catalog contains descriptive lists of publications, data files, and special tabulations.

Census of Agriculture. Performed in years ending in 4 and 9. Volumes include information on statistics of county; size of farm; characteristics of farm operations; farm income; farm sales; farm expenses; and agricultural services.

Census of Business. Compiled every five years (in years ending in 2 and 7). Organized in three units: *Census of Construction Industries.* Information from industries based on SIC codes. Included is information about number of construction firms; employees; receipts; payrolls; payments for materials; components; work supplies; payments for machinery and equipment; and depreciable assets.

Census of Governments. Done in years ending in 2 and 7. This is the most detailed source for statistics on government finance. *Census of Housing.* Provides information on plumbing facilities whether a unit is owned or rented, value of home, when built, number of bedrooms, telephones, and more.

Census of Manufacturers. Compiled every five years (in years ending in 2 and 7). Reports on 450 different classes of manufacturing industries. Data for each industry includes: information on capital expenditures, value added, number of establishments, employment data, material costs, assets, rent, and inventories. Updated yearly by the *Annual Survey of Manufacturers.*

Census of Mineral Industries. Covers areas of extraction of minerals. Information on employees; payroll; work hours; cost of materials; capital expenditures; and quantity and value of materials consumed and products shipped.

Census of Population. Compiled every ten years (in years ending in 0). Presents detailed data on population characteristics of states, counties, SMSAs, and census tracts. Demographics data reported include: age, sex, race, marital status, family composition, employment income, level of education, and occupation. Updated annually by the *Current Population Report.*

Census of Retail Trade. This report presents statistics for over one hundred different types of retail establishments by state, SMSAs, counties, and cities with populations over 2,500. It includes data on the number of outlets, total sales, employment, and payroll. Updated each month by *Monthly Retail Trade.*

Census of Selected Services. Provides statistics similar to those reported by the *Census of Retail Trade* for retail service organizations such as auto repair centers and hotels. Does not include information on real estate, insurance, or the professions. Updated monthly by *Monthly Selected Service Receipts.*

Census of Transportation. Information on four major phases of U.S. travel. (1) National Travel Survey, (2) Truck Inventory and Use of Survey, (3) Commodity Transportation Survey, and (4) Survey of Motor Carriers and Public Warehousing.

Census of Wholesale Trade. Statistics for over 150 types of wholesaler categories. The data detail the number of establishments, payroll, warehouse space, expenses, end-of-year inventories, legal form of organization, and payroll. Updated each month by *Monthly Wholesale Trade.*

Statistical Abstract of the United States. Published annually. This is a useful source for finding current and historical statistics about various aspects of American life. Contents include statistics on income, prices, education, population, law enforcement, environmental conditions, local government, labor force, manufacturing, and many other topics.

State and Metropolitan Area Data Book. A Statistical Abstract Supplement. Presents a variety of information on states and metropolitan areas in the U.S. on subjects such as area, population, housing, income, manufacturers, retail trade, and wholesale trade.

County and City Databook. Published every five years, this supplements the *Statistical Abstract.* Contains 144 statistical items for each county and 148 items for cities with a population of 25,000 or more. Data is organized by region, division, states, and SMSAs. Standard demographics are contained in addition to other harder-to-find data.

County Business Patterns. Annual. Contains a summary of data on number and type (by SIC number) of business establishments as well as their employment and taxable payroll. Data are presented by industry and county.

Bureau of Economic Analysis
Department of Commerce
Washington, DC 20230

Business Statistics. This is the biennial supplement to the *Survey of Current Business* and contains data on 2,500 series arranged annually for early years, quarterly for the last decade, and monthly for the most recent five years.

Bureau of Industrial Economics
Department of Commerce
Washington, DC 20230

United States Industrial Outlook. Projections of sales trends for major sectors of the United States economy including business services; consumer services; transportation; consumer goods; and distribution.

Domestic and International Business Administration
Department of Commerce
Washington, DC 20230

County and City Data Book. Published every other year, supplements the *Statistical Abstract.* Using data taken from censuses and other government publications, it provides breakdowns by city and county for income, population, education, employment, housing, banking, manufacturing, capital expenditures, retail and wholesale sales, and other factors.

Measuring Markets: A Guide to the Use of Federal and State Statistical Data. GPO. Provides federal and state government data on population, income, employment, sales, and selected taxes. Explains how to interpret the data to measure markets and evaluate opportunities.

Selected Publications to Aid Business and Industry. Listing of federal statistical sources useful to business and industry.

Statistics of Income. Annual. Published by the Internal Revenue Service of the Treasury Department. This publication consists of data collected from tax returns filed by corporations, sole proprietorships and partnerships, and individuals.

State Statistical Abstract. Every state publishes a statistical abstract, almanac, or economic data book covering statistics for the state, its counties and cities. A complete list of these abstracts is in the back of each volume of the *Statistical Abstract* and *Measuring Markets.*

International Trade Administration
Department of Commerce
Washington, DC 20230

Country Market Survey. These reports describe market sectors and the markets for producer goods, consumer goods, and industrial material.

Global Market Surveys. Provides market research to verify the existence and vitality of foreign markets for specific goods as well as Department of Commerce assistance to United States business to help in market penetration.

Foreign Economic Trends. Prepared by United States embassies abroad. Each volume has a table of "Key Economic Indicators" and other data on the current economic situation and trends for the country under discussion.

Overseas Business Reports. Analyses of trade opportunities, marketing conditions, distribution channels, industry trends, trade regulations, and market prospects are provided.

Trade Opportunity Program (TOP). On a weekly basis indexes trade opportunities by product as well as type of opportunity.

U.S. Small Business Administration
Washington, DC 20416

SBA issues a wide range of management and technical publications designed to help owner-managers and prospective owners of small business. For general information about the SBA office, its policies, and assistance programs, contact your nearest SBA office.

A listing of currently available publications can be obtained free from the Small Business Administration, Office of Public Communications, 409 Third St. SW, Washington, DC 20416 or call 1-800-U-ASK—SBA toll free. The SBA offers 51 publications currently. One particular publication, *Basic Library Reference Sources,* contains a section on marketing information and guides to research. Get the latest *Directory of Publications* by writing or calling the 800 number. You can also obtain a free booklet, *Your Business and the SBA* which gives you an overview of all SBA services and programs.

Management Aids (3- to 24-page pamphlet). This series of pamphlets is organized by a broad range of management principles. Each pamphlet in this series discusses a specific management practice to help the owner-manager of a small firm with management problems and business operations. A section on marketing covers a wide variety of topics from advertising guidelines to marketing research to pricing.

PERIODICALS

United States. International Trade Administration. *Business America: The Magazine of International Trade.* Biweekly. Activities relating to private sector of the Department of Commerce are covered including exports and other international business activities.

United States. Department of Commerce. Bureau of Economic Analysis. *Business Conditions Digest.* Washington, DC: U.S. Government Printing Office. Monthly. Title includes estimates on forecasts for recent months. Very useful for data not yet published elsewhere.

United States. Council of Economic Advisors. *Economic Indicators.* Washington, DC: U.S. Government Printing Office. Monthly. Statistical tables for major economics indicators are included. Section on credit is useful for marketers. Statistics quoted annually for about six years and monthly for the past year.

United States. Board of Governors of the Federal Reserve System. *Federal Reserve Bulletin.* Washington, DC: U.S. Government Printing Office. Monthly. Contains official statistics on national banking, international banking, and business.

United States. Bureau of Labor Statistics. *Monthly Labor Review.* Washington, DC: U.S. Government Printing Office. Monthly. This publication covers all aspects of labor including wages, productivity, collective bargaining, new legislation, and consumer prices.

United States. Department of Commerce. Bureau of Economic Analysis. *Survey of Current Business.* Washington, DC: U.S. Government Printing Office. Monthly, with weekly supplements. The most useful source for current business statistics. Each issue is divided into two sections. The first covers general business topics; the second, "Current Business Statistics," gives current data for 2,500 statistical series or topics. Also, indexed in *Business Periodicals Index.*

United States. Department of the Treasury. *Treasury Bulletin.* Washington, DC: U.S. Government Printing Office. Monthly. Statistical tables are provided on all aspects of fiscal operations of government as well as money-related activities of the private sector. Useful for consumer background or from a monetary view.

DIRECTORIES

The selected national directories are listed under categories of specific business or general marketing areas in an alphabetical subject index.

When the type of directory is not easily found under the alphabetical listing of a general marketing category, such as "jewelry," look for a specific type of industry or outlet, for example, "department stores."

Apparel

Hat Life Year Book (Men's). Annual. Includes renovators, importers, classified list of manufacturers, and wholesalers of men's headwear. Hat Life Year Book, 551 Summit Ave., Jersey City, NJ 07306.

Knitting Times—Buyer's Guide Issue. Annual. Lists manufacturers and suppliers of knitted products, knit goods, materials, supplies, services, etc. National Knitwear and Sportswear Association, 386 Park Ave. South, New York, NY 10016.

Men's & Boys' Wear Buyers, Nation-Wide Directory of (exclusive of New York metropolitan area). Annually in August. More than 20,000 buyers and merchandise managers for 6,100 top department, family clothing, and men's and boys' wear specialty stores. Telephone number, buying office, and postal zip code given for each firm. Also available in individual state editions. The Salesman's Guide, Inc., 1140 Broadway, New York, NY 10001. Also publishes *Metropolitan New York Directory of Men's and Boys' Wear Buyers*. Semiannually in May and November. (Lists same information for the metropolitan New York area as the nationwide directory.)

Women's & Children's Wear & Accessories Buyers, Nationwide Directory of (exclusive of New York metropolitan area). Annually in October. Lists more than 25,000 buyers and divisional merchandise managers for about 6,100 leading department, family clothing, and specialty stores. Telephone number and mail zip code given for each store. Also available in individual state editions. The Salesman's Guide, Inc., 1140 Broadway, New York, NY 10001.

Appliances—Household

Appliance Dealers—Major Household Directory. Annual. Lists manufacturers and distributors in home electronics, appliances, kitchens. Gives complete addresses and phone. Compiled from Yellow Pages. American Business Directories, Inc., 5711 S. 86th Circle, Omaha, NE 68127.

Automatic Merchandising (Vending)

NAMA Directory of Members. Annually in June. Organized by state and by city, lists vending service companies who are NAMA members. Gives mailing address, telephone number, and products vended. Also includes machine manufacturers and suppliers. National Automatic Merchandising Association, 20 N. Wacker Dr., Chicago, IL 60606.

Automotive

Manufacturers' Representatives Division. Irregular. Alphageographical listing of about 300 representatives including name, address, telephone number, territories covered, and lines carried. Automotive Service Industrial Association, 444 N. Michigan Ave., Chicago, IL 60611.

Automotive Warehouse Distributors Association Membership Directory. Annually in April. Includes listing of manufacturers, warehouse distributors, their products, personnel, and territories. Automotive Warehouse Distributors Association, 9140 Ward Parkway, Kansas City, MO 64114.

Automotive Consultants Directory. Annually in November. Lists 380 consultants and consulting firms in automotive engineering specialties, including safety, manufacturing, quality control, engine design, marketing, etc. Society of Automotive Engineers, 400 Commonwealth Dr., Warrendale, PA 15096-0001.

Aviation

World Aviation Directory. Published twice a year in March and September. Gives administrative and operating personnel of airlines, aircraft, and engine manufacturers and component manufacturers and distributors, organizations, and schools. Indexed by companies, activities, products, and individuals. McGraw-Hill, Inc. 1156 15th St. NW, Washington, DC 20005.

Bookstores

Book Trade Directory, American. Annually in July. Lists more than 25,000 retail and wholesale booksellers in the United States and Canada. Entries alphabetized by state (or province), and then by city and business name. Each listing gives address, telephone numbers, key personnel, types of books sold, subject specialties carried, sidelines and services offered, and general characteristics. For wholesale entries gives types of accounts, import-export information, and territory limitations. R. R. Bowker Company, 245 W. 17th St., New York, NY 10011.

Building Supplies

Building Supply News Buyers Guide. Annually in May. Classified directory of manufacturers of lumber, building materials, equipment, and supplies. Cahners Publishing Co., 1350 E. Touhy Ave., Des Plaines, IL 60018.

Business Firms

Dun & Bradstreet Million Dollar Directory—Top 50,000 Companies. Annually. Lists about 50,000 top corporations. Arranged alphabetically. Gives business name, state of incorporation, address, telephone number, SIC numbers, function, sales volume, number of employees, and names of officers and directors, principal bank, accounting firm, and legal counsel. Dun's Marketing Services, Dun & Bradstreet, Inc., 3 Sylvan Way, Parsippany, NJ 07054-3896.

Dun & Bradstreet Million Dollar Directory. Annually in February. Lists about 160,000 businesses with a net worth of $500,000 or more. Arranged alphabetically. Dun's Marketing Services, Dun & Bradstreet, Inc., 3 Sylvan Way, Parsippany, NJ 07054-3896.

Buying Offices

Buying Offices and Accounts, Directory of. Annually in March. Approximately 220 New York, Chicago, Los Angeles, Dallas, and Miami resident buying offices, corporate offices, and merchandise brokers together with 7,700 accounts listed under its own buying office complete with local address and alphabetically by address and buying office. The Salesman's Guide, Inc., 1140 Broadway, New York, NY 10001.

China and Glassware

American Glass Review. Glass Factory Directory Issue. Annually in March. Issued as part of subscription (13th issue) to *American Glass Review:* Lists companies manufacturing flat glass, tableware glass and fiber glass, giving corporate and plant addresses, executives, type of equipment used. Doctorow Communications, Inc., 1115 Clifton Ave., Clifton, NJ 07013.

China Glass & Tableware Red Book Directory Issue. Annually in September. Issued as part of subscription (13th issue) to *China Glass & Tableware.* Lists about 1,000 manufacturers, importers, and national distributors of china, glass, and other table appointments, giving corporate addresses and executives. Doctorow Publications, Inc., 1115 Clifton Ave., Clifton, NJ 07013.

City Directories Catalog

Municipal Year Book. Annual. Contains a review of municipal events of the year, analyses of city operations, and a directory of city officials in all the states. International City Management Association, 777 N. Capitol St. NE, Washington, DC 20002-4201.

College Stores

College Stores, Directory of. Published every two years. Lists about 3,000 college stores, geographically with manager's name, kinds of goods sold, college name, number of students, whether men, women, or both, whether the store is college owned or privately owned. B. Klein Publications, P.O. Box 8503, Coral Springs, FL 33065.

Confectionery

Candy Buyers' Directory. Annually in January. Lists candy manufacturers; importers and United States representatives, and confectionery brokers. The Manufacturing Confectionery Publishing Co., 175 Rock Rd., Glen Rock, NJ 07452

Construction Equipment

Construction Equipment Buyer's Guide. Annually in November. Lists 1,500 construction equipment distributors and manufacturers; includes company names, names of key personnel, addresses, telephone numbers, branch locations, and lines handled or type of equipment produced. Cahners Publishing Co., 1350 E. Touhy Ave., Des Plaines, IL 60018.

Conventions and Trade Shows

Directory of Conventions. Annually in January. Contains over 18,000 cross-indexed listings of annual events, gives dates, locations, names and addresses of executives in charge, scope, expected attendance. Bill Communications, Inc., 633 Third Ave., New York, NY 10017.

Trade Show and Exhibits Schedule. Annually in January with supplement in July. Lists over 10,000 exhibits, trade shows, expositions, and fairs held throughout the world with dates given two years in advance. Listings run according to industrial classification covering all industries and professions; full information on dates, city, sponsoring organization, number of exhibits, attendance; gives title and address of executive in charge. Bill Communications, Inc., 633 Third Ave., New York, NY 10017.

Dental Supply

Dental Supply Houses, Hayes Directory of. Annually in August. Lists wholesalers of dental supplies and equipment with addresses, telephone numbers, financial standing and credit rating. Edward N. Hayes, Publisher, 4229 Birch St., Newport Beach, CA 92660.

Department Stores

Sheldon's Retail. Annual. Lists 1,500 large independent department stores, 600 major department store chains, 150 large independent and chain home-furnishing stores, 700 large independent women's specialty stores, and 450 large women's specialty store chains alphabetically by states. Gives all department buyers with lines bought by each buyer, and addresses and telephone numbers of merchandise executives. Also gives all New York, Chicago, Dallas, Atlanta, and Los Angeles buying offices, the number and locations of branch stores, and an index of all store/chain headquarters. Phelon, Sheldon & Marsar, Inc., 15 Industrial Ave., Fairview, NJ 07022.

Discount Stores

Discount Department Stores, Directory of. Annually. Lists headquarters address, telephone number, location, square footage of each store, lines carried, leased operators, names of executives and buyers (includes Canada). Also special section on leased department operators. Chain Store Guide Publications, 425 Park Ave., New York, NY 10022.

Drug Outlets—Retail and Wholesale

Chain Drug Stores Guide, Hayes. Annually in September. Lists headquarters address, telephone numbers, number and location of units, names of executives and buyers, wholesale drug distributors. Edward N. Hayes, 4229 Birch St., Newport Beach, CA 92660.

Druggist Directory, Hayes. Annually in March. Lists about 52,900 retail and 700 wholesale druggists in the United States, giving addresses, financial standing, and credit rating. Also publishes regional editions for one or more states. Computerized mailing labels available. Edward N. Hayes, 4229 Birch St., Newport Beach, CA 92660.

Drug Topics Red Book. Annually in March. Gives information on wholesale drug companies, chain drug stores headquarters, department stores maintaining toilet goods or drug departments, manufacturers' sales agents, and discount houses operating toilet goods, cosmetic, proprietary medicine or prescription departments. Medical Economics Company, 680 Kinderkamack Rd., Oradell, NJ 07649.

National Wholesale Druggists' Association Membership and Executive Directory. Annually in January. Lists 800 American and foreign wholesalers and manufacturers of drugs and allied products. National Wholesale Druggists' Association, Box 238, Alexandria, VA 22313.

Electrical and Electronics

Electronic Industry Telephone Directory. Annually in August. Contains over 22,890 listings of manufacturers, representatives, distributors, government agencies, contracting agencies, and others. Harris Publishing Co., 2057 Aurora Rd., Twinsburg, OH 44087.

Electrical Wholesale Distributors, Directory of. Detailed information on 3,400 companies with over 7,630 locations in the United States and Canada, including name, address, telephone number, branch and affiliated houses, products handled, etc. McGraw-Hill, Inc., 1221 Avenue of the Americas, New York, NY 10020.

Who's Who in Electronics, Regional/National Source Directory. Annually in January. Detailed information (name, address, telephone number, products handled, territories, etc.) on 12,500 electronics manufacturers, and 4,800 industrial electronic distributors and branch outlets. Purchasing index with 1,600 product breakdowns for buyers and purchasing agents. Harris Publishing Co., 2057 Aurora Rd., Twinsburg, OH 44087.

Electrical Utilities

Electrical Utilities, Electrical World, Directory of. Annually in November. Complete listings of electric utilities (investor-owned, municipal, and government agencies in United States and Canada) giving their addresses and personnel, and selected data on operations. McGraw-Hill, Inc., Directory of Electric Utilities, 1221 Avenue of the Americas, New York, NY 10020.

Embroidery

Embroidery Directory. Annually in November. Alphabetical listing with addresses and telephone numbers of manufacturers, merchandisers, designers, cutters, bleacheries, yarn dealers, machine suppliers, and other suppliers to the Schiffli lace and embroidery industry. Schiffli Lace and Embroidery Manufacturers Association, Inc., 8555 Tonnelle Ave., North Bergen, NJ 07087.

Export and Import

American Export Register. Annually in September. Includes over 30,000 importers and exporters and products handled. Thomas International Publishing Co., Inc., 1 Penn Plaza, 250 West 34th St., New York, NY 10119.

Canadian Trade Directory, Fraser's. Annually in May. Contains more than 42,000 Canadian companies. Also lists over 14,000 foreign companies who have Canadian representatives. Fraser's Trade Directories, Maclean Hunter Ltd., 777 Bay St., Toronto, Ontario, Canada, M5W 1A7.

Flooring

Flooring Directory and Buying Guide Issue. Annually in October. Reference to sources of supply, giving their products and brand names, leading distributors, manufacturers' representatives, and associations. Edgell Communications, 7500 Old Oak Ave., Cleveland, OH 44130.

Food Dealers—Retail and Wholesale

Food Brokers Association, National Directory of Members. Annually in April. Arranged by states and cities, lists member food brokers in the United States and Europe, giving names and addresses, products they handle and services they perform. National Food Brokers Association, 1010 Massachusetts Ave., Washington, DC 20001.

National Frozen Food Association Directory. Annually in January. Lists packers, distributors, supplies, refrigerated warehouses, wholesalers, and brokers; includes names and addresses of each firm and their key officials. Contains statistical marketing data. National Frozen Food Association, 604 W. Derry Rd., Hershey, PA 17033.

Food Industry Register, Thomas'. Annually in May. Volume 1: Lists supermarket chains, wholesalers, brokers, frozen food brokers, exporters, warehouses. Volume 2: Contains information on products and services, manufacturers, sources of supplies, importers. Volume 3: A-Z index of 48,000 companies. Also, a brand name/trademark index. Thomas Publishing Co., One Penn Plaza, New York, NY 10119.

Tea and Coffee Buyers' Guide, Ukers' International. Annual. Includes revised and updated lists of participants in the tea and coffee and allied trades. The Tea and Coffee Trade Journal, Lockwood Trade Journal, Inc., 130 W. 42nd St., 22nd Floor, New York, NY 10036.

Gas Companies

Gas Companies, Brown's Directory of North American and International. Annually in November. Includes information on every known gas utility company and holding company worldwide. Energy Publications Division, Edgell Communications, Inc., 1 East First St., Duluth, MN 55802.

LP/Gas. Annually in March. Lists suppliers, supplies, and distributors. Energy Publications Division, Edgell Communications, Inc., 1 East First St., Duluth, MN 55802.

Gift and Art

Gift and Decorative Accessory Buyers Directory. Annually in September. Included in subscription price of monthly magazine, *Gifts and Decorative Accessories.* Alphabetical listing of manufacturers, importers, jobbers, and representatives in the gift field.

Listing of trade names, trademarks, brand names, and trade associations. Geyer-McAllister Publications, 51 Madison Ave., New York, NY 10010

Gift, Housewares and Home Textile Buyers, Nationwide Directory of. Annually with semiannual supplement. For 7,000 types of retail firms lists store name, address, type of store, number of stores, names of president, merchandise managers, and buyers, etc., for giftwares and housewares. State editions also available. The Salesman's Guide, Inc., 1140 Broadway, New York, NY 10001.

Gift & Stationery Business Directory Issue. Annually in September. Alphabetical listing by category of each (manufacturer, representative, importer, distributor, or jobber) of about 1,900. Includes identification of trade names and trademarks, and statistics for imports, manufacturing, and retail sales. Gralla Publications, 1515 Broadway, Suite 3201, New York, NY 10036.

Gift Shops Directory. 68,490 listings. American Business Directories, Inc., 5711 S. 86th Circle, Omaha, NE 68127.

Hardware

Wholesaler Directory (Hardware). Irregularly issued. Alphabetical listing of hardware wholesalers, and distributors of lumber and building materials. National Retail Hardware Association, 5822 W. 74th St., Indianapolis, IN 46278.

Home Furnishings

The Antique Dealers Directory. Annual. Lists 31,000 dealers with name, address, and phone number as well as size of advertisement and first year advertised in Yellow Pages. American Business Directories, Inc. 5711 S. 86th Circle, Omaha, NE 68127.

Home Fashions—Buyer's Guide Issue. Annually in December. Lists names and addresses of manufacturers, importers, and regional sales representatives. Fairchild Publications, Capital Cities Media, Inc., 7 E. 12th St., New York, NY 10003.

Interior Decorator's Handbook. Semiannually in spring and fall. Published expressly for decorators and designers, interior decorating staff of department and furniture stores. Lists firms handling items used in interior decoration. Columbia Communications, Inc., 370 Lexington Ave., New York, NY 10017.

Hospitals

Hospitals, Directory of. Annually in January. Lists 7,800 hospitals, with selected data. SMG Marketing Group, Inc., 1342 N. LaSalle Dr., Chicago, IL 60610.

Hotels and Motels

Hotels and Motels Directory. Annually. Lists more than 61,040 hotels and motels. American Business Directories, Inc. 5711 S. 86th Circle, Omaha, NE 68127.

OAG Travel Planner and Hotel Red Book. Quarterly. Lists over 26,000 hotels in the United States. Also lists 14,500 destination cities, etc. Official Airline Guide Inc., 2000 Clearwater Dr., Oak Brook, IL 60521.

Hotel Systems, Directory of. Annually in March. Lists over 800 hotel systems in the Western hemisphere. American Hotel Association Directory Corporation, 1201 New York Ave. NW, Washington, DC 20005.

Housewares

NHMA Membership Directory and Buyer's Desk Top Guide to Houseware Manufacturers. Annually in March. Compilation of resources of the housewares trade, includes listing of their products, trade names, and a registry of manufacturers' representatives. National Housewares Manufacturers Association, 1324 Merchandise Mart, Chicago, IL 60654.

Jewelry

Jewelers' Circular/Keystone-Jewelers' Directory Issue. Annual in June. Lists manufacturers, importers, distributors, and retailers of jewelry; diamonds; precious, semi-precious, and imitation stones; watches, silverware; and kindred articles. Includes credit ratings. Chilton Co., Chilton Way, Radnor, PA 19098.

Liquor

Wine and Spirits Wholesalers of America—Member Roster and Industry Directory. Annually in January. Lists names of 700 member companies; includes parent house and branches, addresses, and names of managers. Also, has register of 1,900 suppliers and gives state liquor control administrators, national associations, and trade press directory. Wine and Spirits Wholesalers of America, Inc., 1023 15th St. NW, Fourth Fl., Washington, DC 20005.

Mailing List Houses

Mailing List Houses, Directory of. Lists 1,800 list firms, brokers, compilers, and firms offering their own lists for rent; includes the specialties of each firm. Arranged geographically. Todd Publications, 18 N. Greenbush Rd., West Nyack, NY 10994.

Mail Order Businesses

Mail Order Business Directory. Lists 10,000 names or mail order firms with buyers' names, and lines carried. Arranged geographically. B. Klein Publications, P.O. Box 8503, Coral Springs, FL 33065.

Manufacturers

MacRae's Blue Book. Annually in March. In three volumes: Volume 1—Corporate Index lists company names and addresses alphabetically, with 40,000 branch and/or sales office telephone numbers. Volumes 2 and 3—companies listed by product classifications. MacRae's Blue Book, Business Research Publications, 817 Broadway, New York, NY 10003.

Manufacturers, Thomas' Register of American. Annual. Volume 1–14—products and services; suppliers of each product category grouped by state and city. Vols. 15–16 contain company profiles. Vols. 17–23—manufacturers' catalogs. More than 150,000 firms are listed under 50,000 product headings. Thomas Publishing Co., One Penn Plaza, New York, NY 10119.

Manufacturers' Sales Representatives

Manufacturers & Agents National Association Directory of Members. Annually in May/June. Contains individual listings of manufacturers' agents throughout the United States, Canada, and several foreign countries. Listings cross-referenced by alphabetical, geographical, and product classification. Manufacturers' Agents National Association, Box 3467, Laguna Hills, CA 92654.

Mass Merchandisers

Major Mass Market Merchandisers, Nationwide Directory of (exclusive of New York, metropolitan area). Annual. Lists men's, women's, and children's wear buyers who buy for about 257,000 units—top discount, variety, supermarket and drug chains; factory outlet stores; leased department operators. The Salesman's Guide, Inc., 1140 Broadway, New York, NY 10001.

Metalworking

Metalworking Directory, Dun & Bradstreet. Annually in June. Lists about 65,000 metalworking and metal producing plants with 20 or more production employees. Arranged geographically. Dun's Marketing Services Division, Dun & Bradstreet Corporation, 3 Sylvan Way, Parsippany, NJ 07054-3896.

Military Market

Military Market Magazine—Buyers' Guide Issue. Annually in January. Lists manufacturers and suppliers of products sold in military commissaries. Also lists manufacturers' representatives and distributors. Army Times Publishing Co., Times Journal Co., 6883 Commercial Dr., Springfield, VA 22159.

Paper Products

Sources of Supply Buyers' Guide. Lists 1,700 mills and converters of paper, film, foil, and allied products, and paper merchants in the United States alphabetically with addresses, principal personnel, and products manufactured. Also lists trade associations, brand names, and manufacturers' representatives. Advertisers and Publishers Service, Inc., 300 N. Prospect Ave., Park Ridge, IL 60068.

Physicians and Medical Supply Houses

Medical Directory, American. Volumes 1–4 give complete information about 633,000 physicians in the United States and possessions—alphabetical and geographical listings. American Medical Association, 535 North Dearborn St., Chicago, IL 60610.

Physician and Hospital Supply Houses, Hayes' Directory of. Annually in August. Listings of 1,850 U.S. wholesalers doing business in physician, hospital and surgical supplies and equipment; includes addresses, telephone numbers, financial standing, and credit ratings. Edward N. Hayes, Publisher, 4229 Birch St., Newport Beach, CA 92660.

Plumbing

Manufacturers' Representatives, Directory of. Annually in February. Lists 2,000 representatives of manufacturers selling plumbing, heating and cooling equipment, components, tools and related products to this industry through wholesaler channels, with detailed information on each. Delta Communications, 400 N. Michigan Ave., Chicago, IL 60611.

Premium Sources

Premium Suppliers and Services, Directory of. Annually in February. Lists about 1,800 suppliers with title, telephone number, address. Gralla Publications, 1515 Broadway, Suite 3201, New York, NY 10036.

Incentive Resource Guide Issue. Annually in February. Contains classified directory of suppliers, and list of manufacturers' representatives serving the premium field. Also, lists associations and clubs, and trade shows. Bill Communications, 633 Third Ave., New York, NY 10017.

Purchasing—Government

U.S. Government Purchasing and Sales Directory. Irregularly issued. Booklet designed to help small business receive an equitable share of government contracts. Lists types of purchases for both military and civilian needs, catalogs procurement offices by state. Lists SBA regional and branch offices. Order from Superintendent of Documents, U.S. Government Printing Office, Washington, DC 20402.

Refrigeration and Air Conditioning

Air Conditioning, Heating & Refrigeration News—Directory Issue. Annually in January. Lists 1,900 manufacturers and 3,000 wholesalers and factory outlets in refrigeration, heating, and air-conditioning. Business News Publishing Co., 755 W. Big Beaver Rd., 10th Fl., Troy, MI 48084.

Restaurants

Chain Restaurant Operators, Directory of. Annually in May. Lists headquarters address, telephone number, number and location of units, trade names used, whether unit is company operated or franchised, executives and buyers, annual sales volume for chains of restaurants, cafeterias, drive-ins, hotel and motel food operators, industrial caterers, etc. Chain Store Information Services, 425 Park Ave., New York, NY 10022.

Roofing and Siding

RSI Trade Directory Issue. Annually in April. Has listing guide to products and equipment manufacturers, jobbers and distributors, and associations in the roofing, siding, and home improvement industries. RSI Directory, Edgell Communications, Inc., 7500 Old Oak Blvd., Cleveland, OH 44130.

Selling Direct

Direct Selling Companies, World Directory. Annually in April. About 30 direct selling associations and 750 associated member companies. Includes names of contact persons, company product line, method of distribution, etc. World Federation of Direct Selling Associations, 1776 K St. NW, Suite 600, Washington, DC 20006.

Shoes

National Directory of Footwear Companies/Footwear Buyers' Guide. Biennial. Lists about 400 New York and 300 out-of-town and foreign manufacturers. New York City Footwear Buyers' Guide, 47 W. 34th St., Suite 601, New York, NY 10001

Shopping Centers

Shopping Center Directory. Annual. Alphabetical listing of 30,000 shopping centers, location, owner/developer, manager, physical plant (number of stores, square feet), and leasing agent. National Research Bureau, Division of Information, Product Group, Automated Marketing Systems, Inc., 310 S. Michigan Ave., Chicago, IL 60604.

Specialty Stores

Women's Apparel Stores, Phelon's. Lists over 7,000 women's apparel and accessory shops with store headquarters name and address, number of shops operated, New York City buying headquarters or representatives, lines of merchandise bought and sold, name of principal officers and buyers, store size, and price range. Phelon, Sheldon, & Marsar, Inc., 15 Industrial Ave., Fairview, NJ 07022.

Sporting Goods

Sporting Goods Buyers, Nationwide Directory of. Including semiannual supplements. Lists over 7,500 top retail stores with names of buyers and executives, for all types of sporting goods, athletic apparel and athletic footwear, hunting and fishing, and outdoor equipment. The Salesman's Guide, Inc., 1140 Broadway, New York, NY 10001.

Sporting Goods Business—Directory of Products, Services and Suppliers Issue. Annually in August. 3,000 suppliers of sporting goods merchandise and equipment. Gralla Publications, 1515 Broadway, Suite 3201, New York, NY 10036.

Stationers

Giftware and Stationery Business—Directory Issue. Annually in September. Alphabetical listing by company of over 1,900 manufacturers, importers, distributors, and representatives. Gralla Publications, 1515 Broadway, Suite 3201, New York, NY 10036.

Textiles

Textile Blue Book, Davison's. Annually in February. Contains over 8,400 separate company listings (name, address, etc.) for the United States and Canada. Firms included are cotton, wool, synthetic mills, knitting mills, cordage, twine, and duck manufacturers, dry goods commission merchants, converters, yarn dealers, cordage manufacturers' agents, wool dealers and merchants, cotton merchants, exporters, brokers, and others. Davison Publishing Co., Box 477, Ridgewood, NJ 07451.

Toys and Novelties

Playthings—Who Makes It Issue. Annually in June. Lists manufacturers, products, trade names, suppliers to manufacturers, supplier products, licensors, manufacturers' representatives, toy trade associations, and trade show managements. Geyer-McAllister Publications, Inc., 51 Madison Ave., New York, NY 10010.

Trailer Parks

Campground Directory, Woodall's. Annual. Lists and star-rates public and private campgrounds in North American continent alphabetically by town with location and description of facilities. Also lists more than 800 RV service locations. Regional editions available. Woodall Publishing Company, 28167 North Keith Dr., Lake Forest, IL 60045

Trucking

Trucksource: Sources of Trucking Industry Information. Annually in November. Includes over 700 sources of information on the trucking industry, classified by subject. American Trucking Association, 2200 Mill Road, Alexandria, VA 22314-4677.

Variety Stores

General Merchandise, Variety and Specialty Stores, Directory of. Annually in March. Lists headquarters address, telephone number, number of units and locations, executives and buyers. Chain Store Guide Information Services, 425 Park Ave., New York, NY 10022.

Warehouses

Public Warehousing, Guide to. Annually in July. Lists leading public warehouses in the United States and Canada, as well as major truck lines, airlines, steamship lines, liquid and dry bulk terminals, material handling equipment suppliers, ports of the world and railroad piggyback services and routes. Chilton Co., Chilton Way, Radnor, PA 19089.

Members Associated Warehouses, Directory of. Irregularly. Listing of 90 members. Associated Warehouses, Inc., Box 471, Cedar Knolls, NJ 07927.

Small World—Directory Issue. Annually in December. Lists 200 wholesalers, manufacturers, manufacturers' representatives of toys, games, and hobbies for children and infants. Earnshaw Publications Inc., 225 West 34th St., Suite 1212, New York, NY 10122.

OTHER IMPORTANT DIRECTORIES

The following business directories are helpful to those persons doing marketing research. Most of these directories are available for reference at the larger libraries. For additional listings, consult the *Guide to American Directories* at local libraries.

AUBER Bibliography of Publications of University Bureaus of Business and Economic Research. Lists studies published by Bureaus of Business and Economic Research affiliated with American colleges and universities. Done for the Association for University Bureaus of Business and Economic Research. Issued annually. Previous volumes available. Association for University Business and Economic Research, c/o Indiana Business Research Center, 801 W. Michigan St., BS 4015, Indianapolis, IN 46223.

Bradford's Directory of Marketing Research Agencies and Management Consultants in the United States and the World. Gives names and addresses of over 1,600 marketing research agencies in the United States, Canada, and abroad. Lists service offered by agency, along with other pertinent data, such as date established, names of principal officers, and size of staff. Bradford's Directory of Marketing Research Agencies, P.O. Box 276, Fairfax, VA 22030.

Consultants and Consulting Organizations Directory. Contains 16,000 entries. Guides reader to appropriate organization for a given consulting assignment. Entries include names, addresses, phone numbers, and data on services performed. Gale Research Company, 835 Penobscot Bldg., Detroit, MI 48226-4094.

Research Centers Directory. Lists more than 11,000 nonprofit research organizations. Descriptive information provided for each center, including address, telephone number, name of director, data on staff, funds, publications, and a statement concerning its principal fields of research. Has special indexes. Gale Research Company, 835 Penobscot Bldg., Detroit, MI 48226-4094.

MacRae's Blue Book—Manufacturers. Annual. In three volumes: Vol. 1 is an index by corporations; Vols. 2–3 are a classification by products showing under each classification manufacturers of that item. Business Research Publications, Inc., 817 Broadway, New York, NY 10003.

Thomas' Food Industry Register. Annually in May. Lists wholesale grocers, chain store organizations, voluntary buying groups, food brokers, exporters and importers of food products, frozen food brokers, distributors and related products distributed through grocery chains in two volumes. Thomas Publishing Company, One Penn Plaza, New York, NY 10019.

Thomas' Register of American Manufacturers. Annually in February. In 23 volumes. Vols. 1–14 contain manufacturers arranged geographically under each product, and capitalization or size rating for each manufacturer, under 50,000 product headings. Vols. 15 and 16 contain company profiles and a brand or trade name section with more than 112,000 listings. Vols. 17–23 are catalogs from more than 1,500 firms. Thomas Publishing Co., One Penn Plaza, New York, NY 10019.

SOURCES OF ADDITIONAL INFORMATION

Business Competition Intelligence, by William L. Sammon, Mark A. Kurland, and Robert Spitalnic, published by John Wiley & Sons, Inc., 605 Third Avenue, New York, NY 10158.

Business Research: Concept and Practice, by Robert G. Murdick, published by Richard D. Irwin, Inc., 1818 Ridge Road, Homewood, IL 60430.

Competitor Intelligence, by Leonard M. Fuld, published by John Wiley & Sons, Inc., 605 Third Avenue, New York, NY 10158.

Do-It-Yourself Marketing Research, by George E. Breen, published by McGraw-Hill Book Co., 1221 Avenue of the Americas, New York, NY 10020.

Honomichl on Marketing Research, by Jack J. Honomichl, published by NTC Business Books, 4255 West Touhy Avenue, Lindenwood, IL 60646-1975.

A Manager's Guide to Marketing Research, by Paul E. Green and Donald E. Frank, published by John Wiley & Sons, Inc., 605 Third Avenue, New York, NY 10158.

Market and Sales Forecasting, by F. Keay, published by John Wiley & Sons, Inc., 605 Third Avenue, New York, NY 10158.

Marketing Research: A Management Overview, by Evelyn Konrad and Rod Erickson, published by AMACOM, a division of the American Management Association, 135 West 50th Street, New York, NY 10020.

Research for Marketing Decisions, by Paul E. Green and Donald S. Tull, published by Prentice-Hall, Inc., Englewood Cliffs, NJ 07632.

Forms to Help You Develop the Business Plan

Objectives, Goals, Differential Advantage Statement

Objectives	*Time to Achieve*
1. _____	_____
2. _____	_____
3. _____	_____
4. _____	_____
5. _____	_____

Goals	*Time to Achieve*
1. _____	_____
2. _____	_____
3. _____	_____
4. _____	_____
5. _____	_____

Statement of Differential Advantage:

_____

_____

_____

_____

_____

_____

_____

_____

_____

_____

_____

_____

_____

_____

_____

_____

_____

_____

Copyright © 1985 by Dr. William A. Cohen.

Situational Analysis: Environmental Questions for the Marketing Plan

Target Market

Geographic location _____

Special climate or topography _____

_____

Consumer Buyers

Cultural, ethnic, religious, or racial groups _____

_____

_____

Social class(es) _____

Reference group(s) _____

Basic demographics: Sex _____   Age range _____

Education _____   Income _____

Household size and description _____

_____

Stage of family life cycle _____

Family work status: Husband _____   Wife _____

Occupation (husband and wife) _____

Decision maker _____   Purchase agent _____

Risk perception: Functional _____   Psychological _____

Physical _____   Social _____   Financial _____

Income for each family member _____

Disposable income _____

Additional descriptions, classifications, and traits of target market _____

_____

_____

_____

_____

_____

Target market wants and needs 1. _____

2. _____   3. _____

4. _____   5. _____

Product general description _____

_____

Frequency of usage _____   Traits _____

Situational Analysis: Environmental Questions for the Marketing Plan   (*Continued*)

Marketing factor sensitivity _____

_____

_____

Size of target market _____

Growth trends _____

Media Habits

	Hours/Week	Category
Television	_____	_____
Radio	_____	_____
Magazines	_____	_____
Newspapers	_____	_____

Industrial Buyers

Decision makers _____

_____

_____

_____

Primary motivation of each decision maker _____

_____

_____

_____

_____

_____

Amount of money budgeted for purchase _____

_____

_____

Purchase history _____

_____

_____

_____

_____

Additional descriptions, classifications, and traits of target market _____

_____

_____

Situational Analysis: Environmental Questions for the Marketing Plan   (*Continued*)

Target market wants and needs 1. _____

2. _____   3. _____

4. _____   5. _____

Product general description _____

_____

Frequency of usage _____   Traits _____

Marketing factor sensitivity _____

_____

_____

Size of target market _____

Growth trends _____

Media Habits

	Hours/Week	Category
Television	_____	_____
Radio	_____	_____
Magazines	_____	_____
Newspapers	_____	_____

	Number/Year	Category
Trade shows	_____	_____
Conferences	_____	_____

Competition

Competitor	Products	Market Share	Strategy
	_____	_____	_____
	_____	_____	_____
	_____	_____	_____
_____	_____	_____	_____
	_____	_____	_____
	_____	_____	_____
	_____	_____	_____
_____	_____	_____	_____
	_____	_____	_____
	_____	_____	_____
	_____	_____	_____

Situational Analysis: Environmental Questions for the Marketing Plan   (*Continued*)

Competition   (Continued)

Competitor	Products	Market Share	Strategy

Resources of the Firm

Strengths: 1. _____

2. _____

3. _____

4. _____

5. _____

Weaknesses: 1. _____

2. _____

3. _____

4. _____

5. _____

Technological Environment

_____

_____

_____

Economic Environment

_____

_____

_____

Political Environment

_____

_____

_____

_____

Legal and Regulatory Environment

_____

_____

_____

_____

Situational Analysis: Environmental Questions for the Marketing Plan   (*Continued*)

Social and Cultural Environment

_____

_____

_____

Other Important Environmental Aspects

_____

_____

_____

_____

_____

Problems/Threats

1. _____

2. _____

3. _____

4. _____

5. _____

Opportunities

1. _____

2. _____

3. _____

4. _____

5. _____

Copyright © 1985 by Dr. William A. Cohen. *Note:* This form is based on an earlier form designed by Dr. Benny Barak, then of Baruch College.

Competitive Profiles

Date _____	Attributes/Performance Characteristics						
Products							

Copyright © 1983 by Dr. William A. Cohen.

Percentages of Sales in Your Business Area

Product _____ Date _____		Introduction	Growth	Maturity	Decline
Current	Sales %				
	Profits				
Target	Sales %				
	Profits				

Copyright © 1983 by Dr. William A. Cohen.

Recent Trends of Competitor's Products, Share, and Strength

Your Product _____   Date _____

Strength code: VW = very weak   W = weak   M = medium   S = strong   VS = very strong

Competitor	Market Share	Strength	Products

Copyright © 1983 by Dr. William A. Cohen.

Historical Trend Analysis Matrix

Product _____ Date _____					
	Period 1	**Period 2**	**Period 3**	**Period 4**	**Trend**
Sales					
Profits					
Margins					
Market share					
Prices					

Complete matrix with following information:

Very low or very small

Low or small

Average

High or large

Very high or very large

Characterize trends as:

Declining steeply

Declining

Plateau

Ascending

Ascending steeply

Copyright © 1983 by Dr. William A. Cohen.

Cash-Flow Projections

	Start-Up or Prior to Loan	Month 1	Month 2	Month 3	Month 4	Month 5	Month 6	Month 7	Month 8	Month 9	Month 10	Month 11	Month 12	Total
Cash (beginning of month)														
Cash on hand														
Cash in bank														
Cash in investments														
Total Cash														
Income (during month)														
Cash sales														
Credit sales payments														
Investment income														
Loans														
Other cash income														
Total Income														
Total Cash and Income														
Expenses (during month)														
Inventory or new material														
Wages (including owner's)														
Taxes														
Equipment expense														
Overhead														
Selling expense														
Transportation														
Loan repayment														
Other cash expenses														
Total Expenses														
Cash Flow Excess (end of month)														
Cash Flow Cumulative (monthly)														

Product/Project Development Schedule

Task	1	2	3	4	5	6	7	8	9	10	11	12

Strategy Development Actions

SPU # _____												
List of Strategic Actions	Months after Strategy Initiation/$ Allocated											
	1	2	3	4	5	6	7	8	9	10	11	Total $
Total $ Allocated												

Copyright © 1983 by Dr. William A. Cohen.

Balance Sheet

	Year 1	Year 2
Current Assets		
Cash		
Accounts receivable		
Inventory		
Fixed Assets		
Real estate		
Fixtures and equipment		
Vehicles		
Other Assets		
Licenses		
Goodwill		
Total Assets		
Current Liabilities		
Notes payable (due within 1 year)		
Accounts payable		
Accrued expenses		
Taxes owed		
Long-Term Liabilities		
Notes payable (due after 1 year)		
Other		
Total Liabilities		
Net Worth (assets minus liabilities)		

Note: Total liabilities plus net worth should equal assets.

SWOTS Analysis Sheet

Product _____   Date _____

Strengths _____

_____

_____

_____

_____

Weaknesses _____

_____

_____

_____

_____

Opportunities _____

_____

_____

_____

_____

Threats _____

_____

_____

_____

_____

Sales _____

_____

_____

_____

_____

Copyright © 1983 by Dr. William A. Cohen.

Analysis of Competitor Short-Term Tactics

Your Product _____ Date _____			
Competitor	Actions	Probable Meaning of Action	Check Most Likely

Copyright © 1983 by Dr. William A. Cohen.

Recent Trends in Competitive Products

Your Product _____ Date _____				
Company	Product	Quality and Performance Characteristics	Shifts in Distribution Channels	Relative Advantage of Each Competitive Product

Products versus Potential Market Segments

Date _____

Products	Potential Market Segments																	

Numerical code:

1 = Currently meets needs fully.

2 = Minor changes in product needed.

3 = Significant changes in product needed.

4 = Major changes in product needed.

5 = Totally new product required.

Copyright © 1983 by Dr. William A. Cohen.

Index

American Statistics Index, A·1

Books, government, xvi
Break-even, xxi–xxiii
    American Baby Food Company, 4·20
    Baby's Cornucopia, 2·17
    Mischa's Silverlake Cookies, 7·14
    Onyx Marketing Group, 6·17–18
    ORCA Computer Systems, 1·1–39
    Sneak Peek: A Student's Guide to University
        Courses, 3·28
    Venchertech Industries, Inc., 8·15–16
Business plan:
  American Baby Food Company, 4·1–24
    appendix, 4·22–24
    bibliography, 4·21
    competitive advantage, differential, 4·10–11
    endnotes, 4·21
    executive summary, 4·2–3
    implementation and control, 4·12–20
    introduction, 4·5–8
    marketing strategy and tactics, 4·11–12
    objective and goals, business, 4·11
    problems and opportunities, 4·9–11
    summary, 4·21
    table of contents, 4·4
    target markets, 4·8–9
  Baby's Cornucopia, 2·1–37
    appendix, 2·15–37
    company profile, 2·5
    environ, business, 2·7–9
    executive summary, 2·2
    implementation and control, 2·13–14
    marketing tactics, 2·10–12
    promotion mix, 2·12–13

    research, marketing, 2·9–10
    situation analysis, 2·5–7
    summary, 2·14
    table of contents, 2·3–4
    target market, 2·7
  Compact Disc Store Specializing in Used CDs,
    9·1–23
    action programs, 9·19
    bibliography, 9·22–23
    controls, 9·22
    executive summary, 9·3
    financial statements, 9·21–22
    marketing strategy, 9·18–19
    objectives, 9·18
    opportunity and issue analysis, 9·14–18
    situation, current marketing, 9·3–14
    table of contents, 9·2
  Mischa's Silverlake Cookies, 7·1–25
    control and implementation, 7·19–23
    endnotes, 7·23–24
    executive summary, 7·2
    figures, list of, 7·5
    introduction, 7·6
    marketing strategy, 7·15–19
    problems and opportunities, 7·14–15
    references, 7·24–25
    situational analysis, 7·6–12
    table of contents, 7·3
    tables, list of, 7·4
    target market, 7·12–14
  Mudville Greeting Cards, 5·1–25
    bibliography, 5·25
    competition, 5·8–11
    concept, 5·4
    contingency plan, 5·23–24

Business plan *(Continued)*
  Mudville Greeting Cards *(Continued)*
    deal, 5·24–25
    executive summary, 5·2
    financial plan, 5·17–21
    growth plan, 5·22–23
    management and organization, 5·4–5
    marketing plan, 5·13–17
    operating and control system, 5·21
    pricing, 5·11–12
    product, 5·5–7
    production plan, 5·7–8
    schedule, 5·21–22
    table of contents, 5·3
  Onyx Marketing Group, 6·1–22
    background, 6·4
    company mission, scope, and goals, 6·4–5
    conclusion, 6·17
    control and continuity, 6·15
    executive digest, 6·4
    introduction, 6·4
    marketing strategy, 6·11–15
    objectives, market, 6·10
    profit analysis, 6·10
    references, 6·17
    situation analysis, 6·5–10
    table of contents, 6·3
    tasks, 6·15
  ORCA Computer Systems, 1·1–40
    appendix, 1·38–40
    executive summary, 1·5
    implementation and control, 1·20–22
    introduction, 1·6
    list of exhibits, 1·4
    marketing strategy, 1·18–19
    marketing tactics, 1·19–20
    objectives and goals, 1·18
    problems and opportunities, 1·16–17
    references, 1·22
    situation analysis, 1·6
    table of contents, 1·2–3
    target market, 1·14–16
  Sneak Peek: A Student's Guide to University
      Courses, 3·1–33
    appendix, 3·14–33
    bibliography, 3·13
    conclusion, 3·13
    executive summary, 3·2
    financial analysis, 3·8
    financial data, 3·12–13
    implementation schedule, 3·12
    introduction, 3·4
    marketing strategy, 3·9–12
    operational aspects, 3·8–9
    problems and opportunities, 3·7–8
    references, 3·13
    situational analysis, 3·4–7
    table of contents, 3·3
  Venchertech Industries, Inc., 8·1–16
    control and implementation, 8·15–16
    differential advantage, 8·12–13
    endnotes, 8·16
    executive summary, 8·2
    introduction, 8·5
    marketing strategy, 8·13
    marketing tactics, 8·13–15
    objective and goal, business, 8·12
    situation analysis, 8·5–10
    summary, 8·16
    SWOT analysis, 8·11–12
    table of contents, 8·3
    tables, list of, 8·4
    target market, 8·10–11
Business plan structure, xi–xii
Business Statistics, A·3

Catalog of United States Census Publications, A·2
Census of Agriculture, A·2
Census of Business, A·2
Census of Governments, A·2
Census of Manufacturers, A·2
Census of Mineral Industries, A·2
Census of Population, A·2
Census of Retail Trade, A·2
Census of Selected Services, A·2
Census of Transportation, A·2
Census of Wholesale Trade, A·3
Chambers of Commerce, xvi
Competitive advantage, xviii
  American Baby Food Company, 4·2, 4·10
  Venchertech Industries, Inc., 8·12–13
Country Market Survey, A·4
County and City Databook, A·3
County Business Patterns, A·3

Data bases, xv
Department of Commerce, xv–xvi
Directories, A·5–19
  apparel, A·6
  appliances, household, A·6
  automatic merchandising (vending), A·6
  automotive, A·6–7
  aviation, A·7
  bookstores, A·7
  building supplies, A·7
  business firms, A·7
  buying offices, A·7–8
  china and glassware, A·8
  cities directories catalog, A·8
  college stores, A·8
  confectionery, A·8
  construction equipment, A·8
  conventions and trade shows, A·8–9
  dental supply, A·9
  department stores, A·9
  discount stores, A·9
  drug outlets, retail and wholesale, A·9–10
  electrical and electronics, A·10
  electrical utilities, A·10
  embroidery, A·10
  export and import, A·10–11
  flooring, A·11
  food dealers, retail and wholesale, A·11
  gas companies, A·11
  gift and art, A·11–12
  hardware, A·12
  home furnishings, A·12
  hospitals, A·12
  hotels and motels, A·12–13
  housewares, A·13
  jewelry, A·13
  liquor, A·13
  mailing list houses, A·13
  mail order businesses, A·13
  manufacturers, A·13–14
  manufacturers' sales representatives, A·14
  mass merchandisers, A·14
  metalworking, A·14
  military market, A·14
  other important, A·18–19
  paper products, A·14
  physicians and medical supply houses, A·14–15
  plumbing, A·15
  premium sources, A·15
  purchasing, government, A·15
  refrigeration and air conditioning, A·15
  restaurants, A·15
  roofing and siding, A·16
  selling direct, A·16
  shoes, A·16
  shopping centers, A·16
  specialty stores, A·16
  sporting goods, A·16
  stationers, A·16–17
  textiles, A·17
  toys and novelties, A·17
  trailer parks, A·17
  trucking, A·17
  variety stores, A·17
  warehouses, A·17–18

Embassies and consulates, xvi
Executive summary, xiii
  American Baby Food Company, 4·2
  Baby's Cornucopia, 2·2
  Compact Disc Store Specializing in Used CDs, 9·3
  Mischa's Silverlake Cookies, 7·2
  Mudville Greeting Cards, 5·2
  ORCA Computer Systems, 1·5
  Sneak Peek: A Student's Guide to University Courses, 3·2
  Venchertech Industries, Inc., 8·2

Foreign Economic Trends, A·4
Forms (for help in business plan preparation), B·1–19
  balance sheet, B·15
  cash flow projections, B·12
  competitive products, recent trends in, B·18
  competitive profiles, B·8
  competitor short term tactics, analysis, B·17
  competitor's products, share, and strength, recent trends, B·10
  historical trend analysis matrix, B·11
  objectives, goals, differential advantage statement, B·2
  percents of sales in your business areas, B·9
  product/product development schedule, B·13

Forms (for help in business plan preparation)
    (Continued)
    products versus potential market segments, B·19
    situational analysis: environmental questions,
        B·3–7
    strategy development actions, B·14
    SWOTS analysis sheet, B·16

Global Market Survey, A·4

Implementation and control, xix, xxi
    American Baby Food Company, 4·12–20
    Baby's Cornucopia, 2·13–14
    Compact Disc Store Specializing in Used CDs,
        9·22
    Mischa's Silverlake Cookies, 7·19–23
    Onyx Marketing Group, 6·15
    ORCA Computer Systems, 1·21–22
    Sneak Peek: A Student's Guide to University
        Courses, 3·12
    Venchertech Industries, Inc., 8·15–16
Introduction:
    American Baby Food Company, 4·5–7
    Mischa's Silverlake Cookies, 7·6
    Onyx Marketing Group, 6·4
    ORCA Computer Systems, 1·6
    Sneak Peek: A Student's Guide to University
        Courses, 3·12
    Venchertech Industries, Inc., 8·5

Magazine and newspaper articles, xv
Management Aids, A·5
Marketing research, primary, xvi–xvii
Marketing strategy, xviii–xix
    American Baby Food Company, 4·11–12
    Compact Disc Store Specializing in Used CDs,
        9·18–19
    Mischa's Silverlake Cookies, 7·15–19
    Onyx Marketing Group, 6·11–12
    ORCA Computer Systems, 1·18–19
    Sneak Peek: A Student's Guide to University
        Courses, 3·9–12
    Venchertech Industries, Inc., 8·13
Marketing tactics, xix
    American Baby Food Company, 4·11–12
    Baby's Cornucopia, 2·10–12
    ORCA Computer Systems, 1·19–20
    Venchertech Industries, Inc., 8·13–15

Measuring Markets: A Guide to the Use of Federal
    and State Statistical Data, A·4

Objective and goals, xvii–xviii
    American Baby Food Company, 4·11
    Compact Disc Store Specializing in Used CDs,
        9·18
    Mischa's Silverlake Cookies, 7·12
    Onyx Marketing Group, 6·10
    ORCA Computer Systems, 1·18
    Venchertech Industries, Inc., 8·12
Overseas Business Reports, A·4

Periodicals, A·5
    United States Bureau of Labor Statistics, A·5
    United States Council of Economic Advisors, A·5
    United States Department of Commerce, A·5
    United States Department of the Treasury, A·5
    United States International Trade Association,
        A·5
Problems, threats, and opportunities, xvii
    American Baby Food Company, 4·9–11
    Mischa's Silverlake Cookies, 7·14–15
    Onyx Marketing Group, 6·9–10
    ORCA Computer Systems, 1·16–17
    Sneak Peek: A Student's Guide to University
        Courses, 3·7–8
Professional and trade associations, xv
Publications, U.S. Government, A·1–5
Publications, U.S. Business Administration, A·4–5

Schedules, budget, and marketing actions, xix
Selected Publications to Aid Business and Industry,
    A·4
Situation analysis, xiv
    American Baby Food Company, 4·7–9
    Baby's Cornucopia, 2·5–7
    Compact Disc Store Specializing in Used CDs,
        9·3–14
    Mischa's Silverlake Cookies, 7·6–12
    Onyx Marketing Group, 6·5–10
    ORCA Computer Systems, 1·6–14
    Sneak Peek: A Student's Guide to University
        Courses, 3·4–7
    Venchertech Industries, Inc., 8·5–10
Sources of additional market research, A·1–19
Specialized books about your business, xv
State and Metropolitan Area Data Book, A·3

State Statistical Abstract, A·4
Statistical Abstract of the United States, A·3
Statistics of Income, A·4

Target market:
American Baby Food Company, 4·8–9
Baby's Cornucopia, 2·7
Mischa's Silverlake Cookies, 7·12–13
Onyx Marketing Group, 6·5
ORCA Computer Systems, 1·14–16
Venchertech Industries, Inc., 8·10
Table of Contents, xiii–xiv
American Baby Food Company, 4·4
Baby's Cornucopia, 2·3–4

Compact Disc Store Specializing in Used CDs,
9·2
Mischa's Silverlake Cookies, 7·3–5
Mudville Greeting Cards, 5·3
Onyx Marketing Group, 6·3
ORCA Computer Systems, 1·2–3
Sneak Peek: A Student's Guide to University
Courses, 3·3
Venchertech Industries, Inc., 8·3–4
Trade Opportunity Program, A·4

United States Industrial Outlook, A·3
United States Small Business Administration,
A·4–5